Social Psychology

HARPERCOLLINS COLLEGE OUTLINE
Social Psychology

Ann L. Weber, Ph.D.
University of North Carolina at Asheville

HarperPerennial
A Division of HarperCollins*Publishers*

With affection and appreciation, this book is dedicated to my students, and to the memory of three I will never forget: Ginger Johnson, Jean Macknew, and Denise Poupore.

An American BookWorks Corporation Production

Project Manager: Judith A.V. Harlan
Editor: Thomas H. Quinn

LIBRARY OF CONGRESS CATALOG NUMBER 91-58279
ISBN: 0-06-467157-7

92 93 94 95 96   ABW/RRD   10 9 8 7 6 5 4 3 2 1

Contents

Preface

I took my first class in social psychology when I was a college freshman at Catholic University in 1970. The professor, James Statman, was an enthusiastic and innovative instructor, a terrific teacher. The issues we studied were vital and timely: person perception, attraction, altruism, cognitive dissonance, achievement, social interaction, obedience and conformity, group conflict and peacemaking. The class was large enough to be innovative, and our simulations and discussions were involving and enlightening. I remember that, above all, the subject matter was positively riveting. This view of human behavior in social context was fascinating, but also practical. I was always interested, and everything made so much sense. I imagined how wonderful it would be to keep studying social psychology. I hoped someday to be as good a teacher as my professor had been.

Time has flown; today I am a professor and I teach social psychology. It is still my favorite course—to take or teach—although the subject matter today reflects a different history. Some topics considered standard then are barely mentioned in most social psychology texts today. Other topics are new to social psychology in recent decades: environmental psychology, health, law and politics. I have learned much by reviewing the excellent texts available to today's social psychology student. I have tried to reflect these authors' contemporary sense of issues, organization, and style. I have also tried to convey a sense of how the earlier texts in social psychology have guided and inspired me and my colleagues. I hope I have been able to balance the freshness and relevance of current works with the power and timeless meaning of the classics.

This is an outline text. It reviews in spare form the key themes and common points of the major social psychology texts. While it could "stand alone" for the casual newcomer to social psychology, it must be paired with a full-length text for students' best experience. Reducing rich history, lab lore, and practical implications to key points in twenty chapters has been a sometimes painful labor of love for me. My only consolation in trimming the fascinating detail from this presentation lies in the belief that students will, on reading something here, be then more likely to consult a full-length text or an original source.

I welcome scrutiny, constructive criticism, and feedback. I fully expect to make changes in this material. Social psychology does not sit still; it is a dynamic and demanding discipline. Among the social sciences, it can also be a passion. I welcome the compassion of readers who find this is true for them, as well.

ACKNOWLEDGMENTS

It goes without saying that the strength of an outline text like this one is in its original sources. I thank first and foremost the authors of the texts that most influenced me in this project, listed here in alphabetical order: Elliot Aronson; Reuben M. Baron and William G. Graziano; Robert A. Baron and Donn Byrne; Sharon S. Brehm and Saul M. Kassin; John C. Brigham; Roger Brown; Kenneth J. Gergen and Mary M. Gergen; John H. Harvey and William P. Smith; Richard A. Lippa; David G. Myers; Louis A. Penner; David O. Sears, L. Anne Peplau, and Shelley E. Taylor; Stephen Worchel, Joel Cooper, and George R. Goethals; and Kay Deaux, Lawrence S. Wrightsman, and Francis C. Dane. I consulted many references, but these are the books left with dog-eared pages and cracked binding. They are outstanding texts and I enjoyed the view from their shoulders.

John Lazo of the American Psychological Association's Directory Office was a gold mine of information, thoughtfully dropping everything whenever I called him to help me track down biographical information about theorists and researchers.

Writing a book involves having congenial colleagues who support and cover for the writer's preoccupation, tardiness, and office clutter. I appreciate the altruism and good humor of my colleagues in the Psychology Department at UNCA, especially my ever-supportive chair, Theodore L. Seitz, and our Vice Chancellor for Academic Affairs, Lauren Wilson.

I offer sincere thanks to my nurturing, perspicacious, and professional editors and handlers: Judith A. V. Harlan, my managing editor, kindred spirit, and pen pal; Tom Quinn, my hawkeyed, honey-worded copy editor; and Fred Grayson, the congenial President of American BookWorks Corporation, who believed I could do this in the first place.

I want to express loving gratitude to my friends and family for supporting me and being understanding about not hearing from me. I have benefitted greatly from the humor and wisdom of my dear friend and mentor, John Harvey. I owe a lifetime debt to my lifetime partner, John Quigley, for patience, encouragement, laughter, and hot tea.

Thanks to all of you. If this book is good, you are the reasons.

Ann L. Weber, Ph. D.
Asheville, North Carolina
August 1991

1

Introduction to Social Psychology

*P*sychology, *the scientific study of behavior and mental processes, addresses a broad scope of phenomena. Psychologists may study nonhuman as well as human behavior. They may examine observable behaviors, or draw inferences from such behaviors about less obvious processes like thoughts and emotions. Like other scientists, psychologists employ systematic methods in order to understand, predict, and control the effects of their subject matter.*

Within the discipline, psychologists' work is further distinguished among different fields—particular sets of phenomena and applications that psychologists "specialize" in—and by different levels of analysis. Some fields of psychology adopt an intraindividual approach, examining the processes and factors within the individual under study. These include physiological, experimental, and cognitive psychology. Other fields of psychology—including developmental, personality, clinical and counseling specialties—adopt a directly individual level of analysis, examining the lifespan and behavior patterns of the individual as a whole, rather than examining the individual's interior workings. Finally, one field of psychology takes a distinctively inter-individual approach, studying how the individual functions among others; this field is social psychology.

The subject matter of social psychology will be defined as individual processes within the social context. Social psychology's focus distinguishes it from other fields of psychology as well as from separate but related disciplines like sociology and communication studies. The subject matter of social psychology, somewhat restricted by this definition, still encompasses a very broad range of phenomena. These diverse topics can be grouped under three collective headings: individual processes; interpersonal processes; and group processes. In chapters to come, examples and explanations of these processes will be reviewed in detail.

Because the subject matter of social psychology—the individual within her or his social world—is so close at hand, its findings are of great interest to amateurs as well as to professional scientists. Some findings are so well documented or easily observable that social psychology might be erroneously dismissed as being "mere common sense." In chapters to come the reader is encouraged to develop an appreciation of the challenge of applying the scientific method to the intensely personal subject of how we live in our social world.

DEFINING SOCIAL PSYCHOLOGY

Social psychology can be more easily described than defined, as its historical development (below) will make clear. To define social psychology, it is helpful to contrast it with other fields of psychology, to chart its relationship with other disciplines, and to identify its characteristic point of view or perspective.

Fields of Psychology

As the science of behavior and mental processes, psychology examines an incredibly broad range of processes, from subtle or invisible processes like emotional arousal or insight learning to more overt and observable processes like trial-and-error learning and aggressive action.

INTERNAL VERSUS EXTERNAL PROCESSES

The different fields of psychology could be arranged on a continuum, with interior or hard-to-observe processes at one end and obvious, beyond-the-individual processes at the other extreme. Along this "internal-external" focus continuum, we would place experimental, physiological, and cognitive psychology closer to the "internal" end. Closer to the middle, between the two extremes, we would locate personality psychology and developmental psychology. As we approach the "external" extreme, however, we find only one field of psychology, social psychology.

PERSONAL VERSUS SITUATIONAL FACTORS

Phrased another way, social psychology examines and tries to explain individual behavior and thought processes in terms of the individual's social context. Social psychology can examine the same questions about individual behavior or cognitive processes that are undertaken by other fields of psychology, but it will focus on factors that have to do with situations surrounding the individual rather than personal or internal conditions.

For example, psychologists are interested in finding ways to improve children's learning. A physiological psychologist might study whether nutrition and mealtimes could be scheduled to improve young students' abilities to pay attention or concentrate in the classroom. A developmental psychologist would consider the different abilities and concerns children have at different ages, and how such knowledge can help design a more successful grade school curriculum. A social psychologist would ask questions about the social context of children's learning: how large are the classes; do children work in study groups or alone; do parents and role models encourage schoolwork and achievement; is the physical environment of the classroom a source of support or distraction?

In the above example, the reader can see that the more "internally" focused fields of psychology look for personal factors—biological, developmental and cognitive processes—to explain the phenomenon of interest. In contrast, social psychologists examine the many different features of the situation that might influence individual function.

Despite differences in level of analysis and methodology, all fields of psychology share common interests. Therefore, social psychology is best understood as complementing rather than challenging other fields of psychology.

SOCIAL AND PERSONALITY PSYCHOLOGY

Within psychology, the field most sympathetic to social psychology is personality psychology, or the study of individual differences. Personality is defined as an individual's pattern of behavior and cognitive processes over time and in varied situations. Personality psychologists focus not on the circumstances that influence behavior but on the ways people's actions and tendencies are similar to or different from each other.

Social psychology is naturally complementary to personality psychology. For example, the study of aggression would include both an understanding of how and why some individuals are more aggressive than others (personality psychology, or individual differences) and of the situational influences that might prompt any individual to express or inhibit aggressive tendencies.

Other Disciplines

Social psychological research, theory, and applications are often integrated with the work of disciplines outside psychology.

SOCIOLOGY

Because social psychology is at the "social end" of the psychological continuum, it has much in common with sociology, the scientific study of groups and organizations. Unlike sociology, social psychology focuses on the individual within the context of these groups and institutions, not on the groups themselves.

For example, both social psychologists and sociologists are interested in the influence of different social classes. A sociologist might examine how class membership is affected by education. As women from working class families acquire more formal education or training than their parents, do they evaluate themselves and their goals in terms more typical of the middle class? Is this change in class membership a characteristic function of formal education?

In contrast, a social psychologist might focus on the class-education relationship by looking at the individual within this context. If a woman from a working class family completes college, does she reject the values and norms of her parents, who never finished high school, in favor of those of her classmates? By using the language and skills she has learned, does she alienate her family, who might be uncomfortable with her vocabulary and political opinions? While the sociologist might ask a question about collective influences and outcomes, the social psychologist focuses more particularly on the dynamics of individual thought, feeling, and behavior within the social context.

ANTHROPOLOGY

Social psychology examines such cultural influences as the formation and transmission of norms, which are accepted and expected rules for behavior. In this regard it shares common interests with anthropology, the study of human culture. Some social psychological topics with an anthropological "flavor" include norms and roles, gender roles and how they are socialized, status and power, and group leadership.

Like anthropologists, social psychologists usually study humans in order to learn about social behavior and cognition. However, sometimes social psychologists will study the behavior of other species in order better to understand humans. For example, in studying the phenomenon of social facilitation (see chapter 11), some psychologists studied how the behavior of chickens and cockroaches was influenced by the presence of other members of their own species. These observations helped in refining a social psychological theory of human performance in the presence of others.

CRIMINOLOGY

Most criminologists—scientists who study criminal behavior—use social psychology and its situational perspective at some time in their work. Criminologists are also likely to use the tools and viewpoints of medicine, sociology, economics, and the legal system. Most of criminology emphasizes an applied orientation, with a view to finding results that are relevant in solving real-world problems of crime and justice. Social psychology is equally likely to emphasize both basic and applied research.

OTHER SOCIAL SCIENCES

Disciplines like economics, political science, and education all involve and apply principles of social psychology. Within these fields, specific rules may involve applying a general theory of social psychology within a particular context, like financial exchange or political influence. Moreover, some theories originally developed in other fields have provided clues to social psychologists for explaining general trends in social behavior. For example, some aspects of social exchange theory (see chapter 16) were originally developed by economic theorists.

In sum, the relationships among these fields and social psychology tend to be mutually supportive and informative rather than competitive. No one discipline presumes to offer the "only" perspective, just as no one field of psychology can give the "best" view of human behavior and cognition.

The Situational Perspective

Gordon Allport, an important early theorist in social psychology (see discussion below), defined social psychology as examining the ways in which the actual, implied, or imagined presence of others affects the thoughts, feelings, and behaviors of an individual. Thus, social psychology looks at the behavior of a person from a particular point of view or perspective.

SITUATIONAL EFFECTS ON BEHAVIOR

The field of social psychology is distinguished not so much by *what* it studies as by *how* it studies what it studies. In brief, social psychology adopts a situational perspective in studying individual behaviors and cognitive processes. This means that whatever an individual does, says, thinks, or feels is examined and perhaps explained in terms of the surrounding situation.

For example, imagine that you meet a good friend of yours as you leave class one day. If your friend seemed unusually distant or preoccupied, and failed to greet you or act in the way you would normally expect, how would you explain this surprise to yourself? You could adopt a situational perspective by asking whether the situation might explain this unusual pattern. For example, was the weather gloomier than usual? Were there too many people around for your friend to confide in you about something at that moment? Was anyone else present who could have had this effect on your friend?

In contrast, a more personal analysis would involve questioning your friend's moods, motivations, eating behavior, and other habits. All of these might explain why a friend fails to act friendly. The situational perspective completes the investigation by taking into account factors and circumstance outside or surrounding the individual, which can also be quite influential.

LEVELS OF ANALYSIS

Another way to characterize the situational perspective is to consider the different levels of analysis a scientist can view. If your subject is a person and her behavior, you can adopt three different levels of analysis: intraindividual, individual, or interindividual.

What makes her tick? On an intraindividual (within-individual) level, a scientist could consider what goes on inside the person: biological functions, health, conscious and unconscious thought processes, the effects of different nutrients and drugs.

On an individual level, an investigator might examine this individual's life history, her personality characteristics, and her relative adjustment and effectiveness compared to others who are similar to her.

Finally, on an interindividual (between-individuals) level, the scientist looks at the context—including people, places, pressures, and other conditions—that surrounds the person. Who is with her? Whom has she just finished meeting? Where is she now, and how crowded, hot, noisy, or uncomfortable is her setting? How are others treating her, and how does she react to this treatment? How does her behavior change when she is in different company and different settings?

This interindividual level of analysis distinguishes the situational perspective of the social psychologist. It does not discount the value of other perspectives or disciplines. Ideally the findings of social psychology enhance and complete what is discovered by other fields and disciplines with different levels of analyses.

A WORKING DEFINITION

Social psychology is the field of psychology that studies the individual in social context. Like all psychology, social psychology employs the scientific method. Like other fields of psychology, it focuses on individual behavior and cognitive processes. Distinct among other fields of psychology, it employs a situational perspective in studying and understanding these phenomena.

HISTORY OF SOCIAL PSYCHOLOGY

Social psychology is one of the newest fields of psychology, itself a young discipline. Scientific psychology in general is often attributed a birthdate of 1879, the year in which the first psychological laboratory was established in Leipzig, Germany, by the experimentalist Wilhelm Wundt. While the roots of social psychology are as deep historically as those of psychology in general, their fruition as a distinguishably separate field only came some decades later.

*Philosophical
Roots of Social
Psychology*

The discipline of psychology is said to have a short history but a long past, because its roots are as old as human awareness although its establishment as a science is fairly recent. Similarly the field of social psychology traces its roots through centuries of philosophical inquiry, as well as more recent decades of research and theory.

PLATO

An interest in social psychological concerns can be traced as far back as the writings of the ancient Greek philosopher Plato (427–347 B.C.). Among his writings, Plato speculated on how group organization could band people together toward reaching common goals, and how individuals might best find their life callings or social roles. Plato's conclusions are influenced by his own times and worldview, as is evident in his assumptions that only men might be rulers, and that rulers are inherently superior to the unruly masses they must govern and discipline.

PRE-ENLIGHTENMENT IDEAS

Ancient and medieval "theories" of behavior tended to be either spiritual (offering divine explanations for unusual behavior) or constitutional (attributing one's actions to bodily conditions and forces). No systematic use of a situational perspective is identified in Western cultures until the Enlightenment, the 17th and 18th century intellectual culture in Europe and the United States. Enlightenment philosophers urged an abandonment of mystical or superstitious explanations for natural events, and emphasized reason as the proper basis of belief and human conduct.

THOMAS HOBBES

Early in this tradition, an important social theorist was Thomas Hobbes (1588–1679), a British philosopher who asserted that all people are motivated by the quest for power. This explains interpersonal and international conflict, competition, and alliances with stronger entities. While power motivation does not explain all social behavior, the concept has proven useful and has been supported by some scientific research.

JEREMY BENTHAM

Within Enlightenment thought, British philosopher Jeremy Bentham (1748–1832) argued that all human behavior is motivated by the quest for pleasure, a principle known as hedonism. By extension, therefore, all social behavior is hedonistic: in their interactions, people seek to maximize their benefits and minimize their costs. Simple as it is, variants of hedonism surface as explanations of interpersonal attraction, long-term relationships, and helping behavior, as will be seen in later chapters.

HERBERT SPENCER

Bentham's ideas were extended by compatriot philosopher Herbert Spencer (1820–1903). Spencer linked hedonism to the concept of natural selection that had been promoted by evolutionary theorist Charles Darwin (1809–1882). In the survival of the fittest, Spencer reasoned, those behaviors which brought one pleasure would be repeated. Thus actions that would promote survival should be associated with pleasure (e.g., eating, sex) while those that threaten survival should bring pain (e.g., fasting, bodily injury). While hedonism alone cannot explain many social behaviors, these ideas have clear ties to modern psychological concepts of reinforcement and punishment.

AUGUST COMTE

A theorist with a broader view was French philosopher August Comte (1798–1857). Comte identified a pattern among developing fields of inquiry, and distinguished between pure sciences (basic sciences that acquire knowledge for its own sake) and applied sciences (practices that apply existing knowledge in particular settings). For example, biology is a pure science; a related applied science is medicine.

Comte also argued that pure sciences develop over time as they free themselves of religious explanations for phenomena.   In Comte's hierarchical arrangement, mathematics and astronomy were among the first pure sciences to divest themselves of religious interpretations. The last pure sciences to do so were the "psychic" sciences, including sociology and a psychological science Comte called "la morale."

For Comte, social psychology might reside at this psychic level, most recently steeped in religious and superstitious interpretation, between sociology and "la morale."

KARL MARX

One of the best known modern social theorists is Karl Marx (1818–1883), an exiled German intellectual whose literary research and writing focused on large social institutions. Social behavior, according to Marx, is determined by its surrounding economic conditions. For example, a feudal economy would foster one pattern of thought and action among its citizens, while a communal (or communist) structure would develop a very different way of thinking and behaving. To change the way a person thinks, feels, and acts, according to Marx, it is essential first to change those engulfing economic institutions.

While it is hard to argue with Marx's analysis as simplistically presented here, it is also obvious that it does not tell the whole story. Modern social psychological research indicates that individuals and institutions are mutually influential; people are not merely passive recipients of the lessons of their classes or economies.

Theoretical Roots of Social Psychology

These many strands of philosophical inquiry had been interwoven by the late 19th century and formed the first social sciences. Psychology and sociology both shifted, at different rates and in different ways, to favor a scientific basis for the study of social behaviors and phenomena. The scientific method (see chapter 2) advocates basing conclusions about the nature of reality on empirical or experience-based observations. Patterns among data are explained by educated guesses known as hypotheses. Hypotheses are tested, and the results of these tests pooled to develop broader theories or explanations.

By the late 19th century, therefore, curiosity about the causes and interrelationships of social behaviors was increasingly transformed into hypothesis-testing. This seminal research developed into a body of work that marked the new field of social psychology as distinct among the social sciences.

GUSTAVE LEBON

The French physician and sociologist Gustave LeBon (1841–1931) had a particular interest in crowd psychology. He formulated several explanations for the transformation of orderly assemblies into unruly and even bloodthirsty mobs. He made some observations while traveling abroad, adding these to his reading of history (especially of the French Revolution of the late 18th century). He published his conclusions in his best known work, *The Psychology of Crowds* (1895).

Many of his ideas—including those about national character and racial superiority—were justly and thoroughly discredited. Others proved useful and have survived in modern theories. For example, LeBon argued that, once immersed in a crowd, individuals would "catch" the sentiment and motives of the group through a process of social contagion. In recent decades, scientific research has identified such processes as suggestibility and deindividuation to account for the conformity and disinhibition of people's behavior in crowds.

NORMAN TRIPLETT

If LeBon's "research" was really a combination of prejudiced observation and historical interpretation, Norman Triplett's contribution to social psychology was elegant in its practical simplicity. Triplett was a bicycling enthusiast who was curious about the effect on cyclists' speed of the presence of other cyclists. He conducted experiments to identify the social facilitation effect: in the presence of competing or coacting others, individuals perform simple tasks (like bicycling or reeling in fishing line) significantly faster and better. Triplett's study was published in 1898 and is credited as the first social psychological experiment.

Triplett's was an isolated experiment, and this work did not directly lead to the development of experimental social psychology. In fact, more recent research on social facilitation has shown that the presence of others can paradoxically hinder performance on difficult or novel tasks (see chapter 11). However, Triplett's distinction was that he employed the scientific method—experimentation to test a hypothesis—in investigating factors affecting social behavior.

EDWARD A. ROSS

The first social psychology text was Edward A. Ross's *Social Psychology,* published in 1908. Its topics indicate Ross's sociological orientation: the collective mind and mob behavior, social customs, fads and fashions, social opinions and conflicts. According to Ross (1866–1951), the processes of imitation and suggestion accounted for such phenomena. Like LeBon, Ross was particularly interested in the crowd behavior and the "group mind."

WILLIAM MCDOUGALL

Also in 1908, the instinct theorist William McDougall (1871–1938) published a text, *An Introduction to Social Psychology*. In contrast with Ross's sociological perspective, McDougall favored biological and psychological instincts as the underlying motivations for most social behavior. In some critics' view, McDougall underestimated the role of the physical and social environment in influencing thought and behavior.

FLOYD H. ALLPORT

A more recognizably modern text, *Social Psychology*, was produced in 1924 by Floyd H. Allport (1890–1978). Allport's book accommodated appealing new ideas about behaviorism, the school of American psychology that favored the study of overt behaviors rather than speculation about hidden processes like consciousness or instinctive motivation. In line with early learning theorists, Allport maintained that social behavior consisted of the actions individuals learned within a social context.

Allport's text made social psychology an acceptable standard course in university psychology departments. It also marked an early formal separation of the psychological from the sociological tradition in social psychology.

GORDON W. ALLPORT

Distinguished more for his work in personality psychology, Floyd Allport's younger brother Gordon W. Allport (1897–1967) nonetheless made significant contributions to the burgeoning field of social psychology. Allport's interests in traits and attitudes reflected his concern with the subjects in which social and personality psychology come together: the processes and contexts that reveal and shape individual differences.

Gordon Allport was also influential as a commentator on the state of social psychology, identifying important emphases in research (e.g., attitudes), and observing social psychology's progress as a behavioral science with a social conscience.

KURT LEWIN

Modern social psychology is eclectic in its working concepts, borrowing ideas and even terminology from various schools of thought and different disciplines. An obviously influential theme, however, is Gestalt psychology's emphasis on the power of context or overall meaning. *Gestalt* is a German word loosely translated as "pattern" or "configuration." Since the early 20th century, Gestalt psychologists have emphasized the importance in human perception and thought of the search for meaningful patterns. (For example, your ability to read a smudged word on a page of text depends on your ability to find clues in the more legible words around it). The Gestalt influence in social psychology is evident today in theories of social cognition, social influence, and interpersonal relationships.

An important agent of the value of Gestalt theory to social psychology was Kurt Lewin (1890–1947), who fled Nazi Germany in the early 1930s to work in the United States. Lewin argued passionately for a wedding of basic and applied research in social psychology, noting that good theories would inevitably have important relevance in solving real-world problems.

During and after World War II, questions about social behavior extended to an international scope. Work on group processes led to research on the dynamics of culture, nations, war, and peace. Telecommunications and modern technology made the world a smaller neighborhood of people trying to understand and get along with each other. The role of social psychology became recognizably practical as well as scientifically engaging.

Psychological versus Sociological Social Psychology

Although most social psychologists today would qualify themselves as psychologists first, throughout its history the field has blended the interests and techniques of both psychology and sociology. The term "social psychology," depending on the time and place it is used, may still represent either tradition. It is helpful to understand some important distinctions between the two.

SOCIOLOGICAL SOCIAL PSYCHOLOGY

Sociology is an older discipline than psychology, and its influence is apparent in the earliest designations of social psychology.

A Broader View. Sociological social psychology investigates larger groupings than its psychological counterpart, such as social classes or the church rather than clusters of coworkers or groups of friends.

Social Problems. Sociological social psychology likewise focuses on broader social questions and problems than does psychological social psychology. For example, the former might examine issues of poverty or delinquency, while the latter focuses on how an individual might be influenced to commit aggressive or criminal acts.

Sociological Concepts. Sociological social psychology employs sociological (group-based) theoretical constructs to explain social behavior and meanings. An instance of such a construct is symbolic interactionism. According to this concept, an individual's experiences and actions become meaningful because of the social evaluations that are attached to them.

For example, when a woman is promoted in her corporation, she may be given a key to the "executive women's washroom" as a reward or perquisite of her new status. The key itself is intrinsically almost worthless, of course, but it symbolizes a new social class, a new set of social contacts, physical surroundings, comfort, and style. Thus the meaning of the key is determined by the experiences and ideas the woman has acquired from her interactions before her promotion. This is the process and product of symbolic interaction.

PSYCHOLOGICAL SOCIAL PSYCHOLOGY

In contrast, psychological social psychology embraces individual processes and interpersonal relationships, as well as group processes. Most social psychologists are psychological social psychologists, and theirs is the orientation of this text.

Individual Processes. Individual processes include such topics as how an individual perceives and thinks about other people; the ways an individual becomes socialized, or trained in the norms and roles of the culture; and attitudes, the value-laden reactions individuals form toward people and things in their social world.

Interpersonal Relationships. Examples of topics in interpersonal relationships include impression formation, interpersonal attraction, conformity and obedience, helping, aggression, cooperation and competition. It can be seen that these are really extensions of individual processes rather than distinct categories of behavior.

Group Processes. For the psychological social psychologist, group processes are also extensions of individual and interpersonal processes. Group processes include social norms and roles, forms and uses of social power, group dynamics, leadership, collective action, and intergroup relations.

Psychological social psychology makes liberal use of psychological concepts and theories, as well as the sociological ideas of its counterpart.

RECONCILING TWO ORIENTATIONS

For practical purposes, the reader may conclude that the differences between sociological and psychological social psychology are subtle matters of scope and orientation. In the pragmatic spirit of Lewin's arguments (above), what matters to the social psychologist is less where an idea comes from than how well it works in explaining social thinking and behavior.

Trends in Social Psychological Research

Social psychologists, interested in the influences of social context, are creatures of that context themselves. In its brief history social psychology has examined, in their turn, various issues made relevant by the times.

Historical events and social issues have contributed to the *zeitgeist* (German for "spirit of the times") that influenced each major trend or shift in social psychological research since the early 20th century.

THE 1920s AND 1930s

Social psychology's infancy was set in a time of social upheaval and cultural reevaluation in Europe and the United States. During this time central research topics accordingly included attitudes, norms, measuring public opinion, and addressing social issues.

THE 1940s AND 1950s

The decade of the 1940s was dominated by World War II and its aftermath in social, economic, and technological change. Dominant social psychological topics in these years included attitude change (persuasion and propaganda), leadership, prejudice, and authoritarianism (an obedient, punitive behavior pattern).

Post-war social psychology shifted its focus to problems "at home" rather than abroad. Personal and cognitive processes that were researched at this time included cognitive dissonance (see chapter 8) and balance (agreement among one's various attitudes and actions). Interpersonal processes research included further work on attitude change (e.g., as applied to communication and advertising), group and norm formation, and conformity.

THE 1960s

The social concerns that had nurtured social psychology thus far blossomed into a profusion of distinctive work in the 1960s. Lingering concerns about war and militarism led to landmark studies of obedience to authority, conflict, and decision making. Work on attribution (explaining behavior) advanced understanding of how social events are perceived.

In America, the civil rights movement encouraged important research on the sources and consequences of racial prejudice and discrimination. Urbanization and its attendant crowding and alienation led to a new social consciousness about environmental and social stressors. This in turn spawned important work in, on the one hand, aggression, and on the other, helping behavior.

THE 1970s AND 1980s

Political assassinations, the war in Vietnam, and the Watergate scandal all contributed to American social psychology's renewed focus on aggression, violence, and social compliance in the 1970s. The second feminist movement of the 20th century had begun quietly in the 1960s, and its political visibility created widespread research interest in gender roles and sexism a decade later.

Energy crises and threats of mishandled nuclear energy in the mid– and late 1970s renewed interest in changing attitudes and behavior. The juxtaposition of the peace movement, the continued Cold War, and terrorizing tensions in the Middle East also contributed to more vigorous efforts to understand and promote conflict resolution techniques (e.g., bargaining and negotiation).

By the early 1980s, the information revolution fostered by telecommunications and computer technology drew social psychologists to examine social cognition, its limitations as well as its possibilities. The mobility and freedom enjoyed by people of many industrial nations led to such varied effects as rising divorce rates and renewed concern with the qualities of satisfying relationships. Social psychology reflected these concerns in new research on intimacy processes and happiness.

Perhaps ironically, the 1980s also saw the emergence of numerous social psychological processes of the self: self-awareness, self-perception, self-justification, self-presentation, self-monitoring, self-handicapping, and self-disclosure—among others.

THE 1990s AND BEYOND

In recent years, as the Baby Boomers (the disproportionately large population group born in the 1946–1964 post-war "boom") enter middle age, social psychologists are focusing on related experiences. The elderly are becoming a larger and more vocal force to be reckoned with, and ageist attitudes are scrutinized along with racism and sexism. Proactive efforts to combat illness and ageing have drawn an application of social psychology to issues of health and health-care.

Social science is increasingly accepted as offering practical solutions to problems of organizations, the law, and the workplace. Social psychological research consequently has focused more and more on, respectively, management, justice, and jobs.

People continued to be fascinated by other people. Coming of age at the turn of the millennium means taking for granted such social phenomena as mass media that mix news, advertising, and entertainment; "high tech" warfare; Acquired Immune Deficiency Syndrome (AIDS); personal computers; and blended families. These and other challenges guarantee that the subject matter of social psychology will be both useful and interesting well into the next millennium.

Social psychology is the scientific study of the functioning of the individual within a social context. Social psychologists adopt a situational perspective in studying the thoughts, feelings, and actions of persons in terms of their social and environmental surroundings.

Among other fields of psychology, social psychology adopts a more external focus, emphasizing situational rather than personal factors. Strongly influenced by sociology, social psychology also has much in common with other social sciences like anthropology, criminology, economics, and political science. Like other fields of psychology, its focus is the individual rather than the group or institution. In explaining the social cognition and behavior of the individual, a social psychologist adopts an interindividual level of analysis.

Like psychology itself, social psychology has its roots in centuries of philosophical inquiry. Ideas about the individual within the social context have been contributed by the ancient Greek philosopher Plato; Enlightenment writers like Hobbes, Bentham, Spencer, and Comte; and modern social theorists like Marx.

The modern theoretical roots of social psychology include the prejudiced but intriguing claims of LeBon's "crowd psychology," the sociological orientation of Ross, and the instinct theories of McDougall. Both Ross and McDougall produced early texts on aspects of social psychology.

The first experiment in social psychology was conducted by Triplett, who was interested in the phenomenon known today as social facilitation. Increasing interest in empirical work led to the modernization of social psychology, evident in the influential work of Floyd Allport and Gordon Allport. With the work of Kurt Lewin, from the German Gestalt tradition, social psychology developed a wedding of basic research with practical, real-world problem solving.

To some extent modern social psychology still reflects its earlier sociological origins. Sociological social psychology investigates larger groups, is more concerned with social problems, and employs some distinctively different concepts in comparison with its counterpart, psychological social psychology. The latter includes individual processes, interpersonal relationships, and group processes. While most social psychologists are more psychological than sociological in orientation, the two traditions harmoniously blend to examine interests that are more similar than different.

Social psychological research has been strongly influenced by its life and times. The zeitgeist of each decade of 20th century history in American and elsewhere has been reflected in the particular concerns of social psychological inquiry.

Selected Readings

Allport, G. W. (1985). The Historical Background of Modern Social Psychology. In G. Lindzey and E. Aronson (Eds.), *The Handbook of Social Psychology,* (Vol. 1), 2nd edition. New York: Random House.

Aron, A. and Aron, E. (1990). *The Heart of Social Psychology,* 2nd edition. Lexington, MA: D. C. Heath.

Bandura, A. (1977). *Social Learning Theory.* Englewood Cliffs, NJ: Prentice-Hall.

Baron, R. A. and Greenberg, J. (1990). *Behavior in Organizations: Understanding and Managing the Human Side of Work,* 3rd edition. Boston: Allyn and Bacon.

Dane, F. C. (1988). *The Common and Uncommon Sense of Social Behavior.* Belmont, CA: Brooks/Cole.

Deutsch, M. and Krauss, R. M. (1965). *Theories of Social Psychology.* New York: Basic Books.

Festinger, L. (Ed.). (1980). *Retrospections on Social Psychology.* New York: Oxford University Press.

Hilgard, E. R. (1987). *Psychology in America: A Historical Survey.* New York: Harcourt Brace Jovanovich.

Marrow, A. J. (1969). *The Practical Theorist.* New York: Basic Books.

Parker, I. (1989). *The Crisis in Modern Social Psychology—And How It Ended.* London: Routledge and Kegan Paul.

Rosnow, R. L. and Rosenthal, R. (1984). *Understanding Behavioral Science.* New York: McGraw-Hill.

Ross, L. and Nisbett, R. E. (1991). *The Person and the Situation: Perspectives on Social Psychology.* New York: McGraw-Hill.

Sampson, E. E. (1991). *Social Worlds, Personal Lives: An Introduction to Social Psychology.* New York: Harcourt Brace Jovanovich.

West, S. G. and Wicklund, R. A. (1980). *A Primer of Social Psychological Theories.* Monterey, CA: Brooks/Cole.

2

Social Psychological Research

*P*sychology is a science; this means that the knowledge of the discipline is acquired by means of the scientific method. The scientific method is distinct among traditional approaches to knowledge in that it emphasizes the importance of collecting evidence about natural phenomena through sensory experience. In other words, if a scientist wants to understand how people behave, rather than speculating about it privately or relying on secondhand or fictitious accounts, he or she examines direct evidence of people's behavior.

The scientific method was originally developed to promote the study of such "natural" phenomena as the subject matter of chemistry and physics. The study of inanimate objects is deceptively simplified since there are few questions about moods, predictability, or ethics. The application of science to the study of people—and particularly of people's social behavior—is much more complex.

To understand social psychological research, it is necessary to review the essential components and steps in the scientific method. Methods of social research vary by both design and setting. Social researchers must also be concerned about achieving validity, abiding by ethical standards, and striking the right balance between objective study and human values.

SCIENTIFIC RESEARCH

Science is a method rather than a specific body of knowledge. The word "science" can be traced to a Latin root (*sciens*) meaning "knowing" rather than "knowledge." Thus science is a matter of process more than product.

Once a researcher has a question to investigate, the scientific method proceeds in a sequence of three broad steps: conducting empirical (experience-based) observations (data collection); formulating and testing hypotheses (reasonable guesses or explanations about the data); and developing theory (a broad explanation for sets of similar events and observations).

Research Questions

All research begins with a question. It may be motivated by simple curiosity: "I wonder why people sometimes hit inanimate objects when they are angry." It may rather be motivated by a program of preexisting research: "Research already shows that frustration often causes aggression. I wonder whether certain kinds of frustration are more or less likely to erupt into aggressive behavior." Finally, a research question can have an applied orientation, motivated by a desire to solve a real-world problem: "I wonder what would be the most effective ways to reduce aggressive behavior among a particular population."

VARIABLES

Most research questions involve relationships between specified variables. A variable is anything that can change in value or quantity; age, temperature, body weight, self-esteem, interpersonal distance, and attitude change are all variables, because they can change in the course of study.

PHRASING

An effective research question is phrased in terms of the relationship between variables. For example: "Does an increase in frustration cause an increase in aggression?" If the relationship in question is not clearly causal, the question may be phrased in terms of correlation (relationship among the variables): "Are levels of frustration related to levels of aggressive behavior?"

OPERATIONAL DEFINITIONS

Once a research question is articulated, its terms must be operationally defined. This means that the variables being studied must be redefined in terms of the exact operations or procedures the researcher will undertake to measure and apply them. For example, a researcher cannot study all forms of frustration or all manifestations of aggression. For practical reasons, in a given research study, "frustration" may be defined as "having missed at least one meal," and "aggression" might be defined as "symbolically attacking an opponent in a competitive board game." (Note that "frustration" could also be defined as "starving" and "aggression" could be defined as "physically striking an innocent victim," but these involve treatments and conditions that violate ethical standard—and common sense).

Empirical Observations

Data collection should be systematic; this means it should proceed in a logical manner from the research question. The research question and the operational definitions of its terms must be specified so that the researcher can collect empirical evidence.

Empirical observations of people in the natural social world are complicated by the fact that people are highly reactive. This means that the subjects of social research may behave differently if they are aware they are being studied.

Another complication arises from the fact that people-watchers are easily biased or distracted. A poll-taker conducting a survey might prefer to ask for help from a smiling woman rather than from a scowling man, approaching the former but not the latter. Such selective observations yield biased data that do not describe the social world accurately.

Finally, if a researcher tries to reduce reactivity and bias by watching people secretly and recording their actions, there are ethical concerns. Are such studies an invasion of privacy? Should subjects provide their consent before researchers are permitted to conduct their observations?

In sum, empirical observations of human social behavior are challenged by issues of subject response, researcher bias, and ethical conduct. Such considerations require considerable creativity and flexibility in designing research that will be comprehensive and informative.

Hypotheses

A hypothesis is a possible explanation for a relationship among the variables being studied. The research question—"Does an increase in frustration cause an increase in aggression?"—can be developed through operational definitions into the following hypothesis: "The more meals a subject has missed, the more often she will attack an opponent while playing a competitive board game."

HYPOTHESIS-TESTING

Research itself is conducted to test the hypothesis. Continuing with the above example, subjects may be recruited who are deprived of one, two, or three meals in a 12-hour period, or who miss no meals (for comparison purposes). Subjects in each meal group are set to play a competitive board game, and their behavior is observed and recorded. When their behavior is compared across the different meal conditions, the researcher will be able to determine whether the earlier hypothesis was accurate in predicting subjects' action tendencies.

Theories

The goal of all hypothesis testing is theory development. A theory is a broad explanation, a set of principles that explain and predict natural events. A good theory summarizes many observations, predicts natural events, and can be tested.

TESTABILITY

In its simplest form, a theory summarizes many observations and helps to anticipate what will happen in novel circumstances. A scientific theory, however, must be subject to the scientific method: it must be testable. If a theory cannot be tested—proven or discarded, one way or the other—then technically it is not a theory.

For example, one may have a theory that "experiencing any form of threat will increase one's readiness to behave aggressively." This is a testable theory: threat can be induced and the effect on aggression observed; aggression can be studied to identify whether threatening conditions preceded it.

However, if one has an idea that "murderers are possessed by an invisible evil spirit who commands them to kill," this will not qualify as a scientific theory. The existence of the "evil spirit" cannot be proven—or disproven. Murderers cannot be "dissected" in order to show the existence of such spirits. This idea may be a strongly held belief, but because it is untestable one way or the other, it does not qualify as a theory.

THEORIES AND COMMON SENSE

This distinction between testable and untestable is important in distinguishing between "common sense" and practical scientific information. Many common-sense beliefs seem useful but cannot be practically or realistically tested, and so they cannot be considered "theories."

Alternatively, many scientific discoveries do not "make sense" at first, but as long as they contribute to testable theories, our understanding of them can be refined with further research and improved.

METHODS OF SOCIAL RESEARCH

People are challenging subject matter for scientific study. They refuse to hold still; they move around, change their minds, say one thing and do another. Each human action is made up of a multitude of seen and unseen activities, from emotional reactions to biological processes to chemical reactions. By definition, no explanation for any human behavior can be considered "simple."

The challenge to the scientist is substantial, but the scientific method offers systematic choices to the researcher seeking answers. Generally there are two approaches a social psychologist can adopt in conducting research: correlational methods and experimental methods.

Correlational Methods

A correlation is a relationship among variables such that trends in one are accompanied by trends in the other. Correlation is broader than causation; the relationship between the variables *may* be causal, but the correlation does not *specify* causality.

For example, church attendance may be correlated with racial prejudice: those who attend church more frequently may be found to have stronger racist attitudes than nonchurchgoers. This correlational relationship does not specify causality. Perhaps attending church *causes* people to become more racist. Or perhaps being prejudiced *causes* people to attend church more regularly. But alternative explanations are also possible: both church attendance and racial attitudes may be related to a third set of conditions, such as geographic region and the norms that prevail there.

Much social research begins with correlational methods. In this way a researcher can narrow down plausible hypotheses by beginning with broad relationships and confirming whether variables are connected in certain ways. The most common correlational methods in social research are archival studies, survey techniques, and observations.

ARCHIVAL RESEARCH

Archives are storage facilities for records of past events, such as document libraries and statistical records. Some research questions can be answered by consulting archival records for particular populations and time periods.

For example, if a researcher noted that a power outage caused an extensive "blackout" in a major city on a particular date, and then found that vital statistics showed an unusual peak in the city's birth rate nine months later, she might have a fair basis for speculating about how people passed the time while they were stuck in the dark.

One problem with archival research is that the records available may be incomplete, or insufficiently detailed. The archival researcher has no witnesses or subjects to interview or observe. Therefore missing data or confounding variables—unrecorded influences that might explain observable trends—cannot be supplied or confirmed.

SURVEY RESEARCH

Surveys—questionnaires distributed to large numbers of respondents—are popular because they are easy to conduct and collect. An opinion poll—conducted by telephone or with paper-and-pencil forms—is an example of a survey.

With the survey method, a researcher can ask specific questions of respondents—e.g., lifestyle habits, or preferences for television programs, consumer products, or political candidates. The survey can also request other information about demographics—e.g., a respondent's age, gender, occupation, geographic region, and the like. Compilation of many survey responses may then yield a correlation between certain demographic variables and certain response patterns.

For example, a surveyor may discover that women in one geographic region prefer to listen to soft, melodic music, while men prefer jazz or a stronger bass rhythm. Advertisers could then choose to compose product theme songs accordingly, using a lyrical song to promote products to women as opposed to a rock-and-roll hit to sell to men.

Although surveys are relatively easy to conduct, they can be deceptively superficial. A survey is, like other self-report techniques, subject to a variety of errors and distortions. Investigators must consider several criteria in designing effective surveys: the importance of random sampling; the size of the sample; and the dangers of respondent bias.

Random Sampling. The group of people about whom the researcher wants to know is called the population. Most populations—e.g., "adults eligible to vote in the United States"—are too large for surveyors to study in an inexpensive and timely fashion. Thus a survey is usually administered to a sample, which is a subset of the population.

The easiest way of obtaining respondents is not necessarily the fairest way. For example, a college student might print a survey of student opinion in the campus newspaper, asking readers to complete the questionnaire and send her their responses. She may receive a large number of replies; but do her respondents fairly represent the campus student population? It is highly likely that only the most curious or opinionated students took the time to complete and send in the survey, and possible that their opinions are very different from the majority.

To yield valid information, a survey sample should be as representative of the entire population as possible. One way to ensure fairness and objectivity in selecting the sample is to choose its members randomly. A sample is randomly selected when every member of the population has an equal chance of ending up in the sample. Choosing names out of a hat or by chance out of an alphabetical listing are ways of random sampling.

For example, if a college student wants to survey opinion about grading policies at his school, he might decide to distribute a questionnaire to 100 students of the 10,000 student population. Which 100 students will he survey? If he selects them randomly—by chance—from a complete student directory, he will get a better representation of the entire 10,000-student population's opinions than if he merely surveys the 100 students who live conveniently in his residence hall, or the 100 students in his social psychology class.

Sample Size. The size of the sample is another important consideration. If a sample is randomly selected, it need not be large or unwieldy in order to be useful. However, the larger the sample, the more reflective of the population its responses will be.

For example, if you are interested in knowing about the political preferences of the 10,000 voters in your home town, you will get a better prediction by surveying 100 randomly-selected people than ten people, and an even better prediction by surveying 1,000 randomly-selected people than 100 people. The greater the number of randomly-selected respondents, the greater the confidence in the accuracy of the response.

Statistical analyses have confirmed that, however large the population of interest, a researcher can be 95% confident of survey results if there are at least 1,200 respondents in the sample, with only a 3% margin of error.

For example, if a survey of 1,200 Americans indicated that 60% of the sample said they liked Candidate A while the other 40% preferred Candidate B, the researcher is 95% confident that, in the larger population the sample comes from, 57–63% prefer A (3% on either side of 60%) and 37–43% prefer B (3% on either side of 40%). Obviously, the larger the random sample, the greater the researcher's confidence and the narrower the margin of error in generalizing to the population.

Biases in Survey Research. As mentioned above, the easy path of survey research is paved with pitfalls: respondents may not be accurate or truthful; their answers may be affected by the wording of the survey items, or the ordering of the items within the survey.

Another source of bias in survey research is social desirability: respondents may give not the accurate reply but one which (they think) makes them "look good," to themselves or to the researcher. A researcher can anticipate some social desirability bias, and endeavor to word survey items as neutrally as possible. For example, saying "Please rate your opinion of Brand X on a scale from 1 to 10" is more neutral than "Do you agree with the statement that Brand X is a superior product?"

Additionally, written surveys are more desirability-proof than spoken surveys, since the surveyor's voice or facial expression cannot be consulted for clues about what he or she "wants" the respondent to say.

However, the wording of items and the form of the survey cannot account for all social desirability effects. In general it is best not to rely too heavily on surveys as the source of specific behavioral predictions about populations. Surveys are best utilized when recognized for what they are: depictions of current opinion of the sample—and perhaps the population—under study.

OBSERVATIONAL STUDIES

Given the possible inadequacies of archival methods and the biases possible with surveys, many social psychologists undertake correlational studies by conducting direct observations of social behavior.

The value and accuracy of observations can be limited by the phenomena under study. For example, if a researcher wants to know which are the most popular stores or restaurants in a crowded shopping mall, she can simply go to the locations in question and make a headcount of customers. However, if a researcher wants to know *why* a particular place of business is popular, mere observation of waiting lines will not answer her question. Thus observations of behavior will be most effective in answering questions about overt, observable behavior, and less so for hidden factors and subtle motives.

Participant Observation. In an effort to get closer to those they are observing, researchers may opt to join the activity as participants or as pseudo-participants (pretending to participate). For example, a social psychologist interested in the behavior and motivation of new recruits may join a club or cult and pose as one of them. This may necessitate deception if real members are expected to be uncomfortable or suspicious about being "under observation." Conversely, even if club members insist they do not mind being studied, their behavior may alter subtly as a result of knowing they are "guinea pigs."

Another concern with participant observation is that the participant-observer may alter the natural social phenomenon under study by his or her very presence. For example, a social psychologist might join a small religious group to learn how they deal with crises of faith. When attendance has been low, the mere presence of this "new member" may artificially sustain a group that would otherwise have naturally become demoralized and disbanded.

Unobtrusive Observation. Much interesting social behavior occurs in public places like streetfronts, malls, plazas, and lobbies. Such phenomena as interpersonal distancing, patterns of greeting and leavetaking, nonverbal communication, and gender differences in social behavior can be studied through observation of public behavior. However, the mere presence of an obvious observer—whether uniformed in a laboratory coat and equipped with a clipboard or not—can drastically alter the self-consciousness and behavior of the persons being watched.

Creative observers will develop unobtrusive means of collecting information about social behavior. Unobtrusive measures are data-collection techniques that do not obtrude or intrude on the naturally occurring behavior being studied. One way of being unobtrusive, of course, is to disguise oneself as a member of the scene. For example, a social psychologist studying patterns of greeting and leave-taking at an airport could dress like a traveler, sit in a gate lounge with luggage nearby, and pretend to work on a crossword puzzle while really recording notations about real travelers' words and behavior.

Other unobtrusive measures involve examining not the social behavior itself but its aftereffects or consequences. For example, an unobtrusive way to discover restaurant popularity is to count the cars in different eateries' parking lots. This would not catch walk-in customers but over time could be an accurate reflection of patronage.

Measures of accretion examine evidence that "piles up" as a result of certain social behaviors. For example, finding more cigarette butts on the ground outside one bar would suggest there are more smokers in its clientele compared to a site that is relatively buttless.

Measures of erosion examine social behavior that "wears down" or uses up some resource. For example, the best way to identify favorite student short-cuts in a campus with few sidewalks is to find the dirt paths that many feet have pounded through the grass and foliage.

Unobtrusive measures have the advantage of protecting the behavior under observation from distortion because of observers' presence or subjects' self-consciousness. They have the disadvantage of being incomplete and open to interpretation. Thus unobtrusive measures are best used in combination with other sources of information.

Experimental Methods

Correlational methods may indicate the existence of *some* relationship among variables under study. When a researcher wants to specify this relation more precisely, or identify exactly what is causing what, it is necessary to use experimental methods.

The systematic procedure of the scientific method dictates that an experimenter must choose a specific experimental design and setting. Complicating this process for social psychologists is the fact that an experiment is a specially structured social situation in itself, creating its own world of influences on individual thought, feelings, and behavior. Such effects must be anticipated if they are to be controlled and useful results obtained.

EXPERIMENTAL DESIGNS

In general, experimental studies can be either truly randomized—arranged so that subjects are randomly assigned to treatment conditions—or quasi-experimental when such random assignment is not possible.

Randomized Experimental Designs. In a true experiment, the research question specifies a causal connection between two sets of variables. The variable assumed to cause the effect is called the independent variable; its assignment is independently controlled by the experimenter. The variable that reflects the effect is called the dependent variable; it depends on the changes created by the independent variable.

In symbolic notation, experimenters usually represent the independent variable as X and the dependent variable as Y. Thus an experimental design is composed to test whether $X \rightarrow Y$, where the causal relationship is symbolized by the arrow.

For example, if the research question is whether or not frustration causes aggression, frustration is the independent variable and aggression is the dependent variable. An experimenter constructs a situation in which subjects are treated to experience different levels of frustration; these are the different levels of the independent variable. Subjects are then tested or observed to see if they exhibit different levels of the dependent variable, aggressiveness.

For purposes of the experiment, of course, the variables have been operationally defined as useful examples. If frustration is defined as number of meals missed, some subjects will be asked to miss one meal, some will miss two, and others will miss three. Subjects in a control group—to which other subjects will be compared—will miss no meals.

If aggression is defined as number of attacks on an opponent in a competitive board game, each subject will be watched as she plays the game, and the number of attacks she initiates will be recorded. If frustration causes aggression, then the hungrier subjects (those who missed more meals) should initiate more attacks than those who missed no or fewer meals.

The two most important characteristics of true experimental designs are *random assignment* to levels of the independent variable and *control* of variables not being directly studied.

Random assignment is especially important in true experiments since all subjects are volunteers. They have been recruited for research participation, and they know they are subjects. To be sure their behavior is distorted as little as possible by the experiment itself, they should be assigned to different levels of the independent variable purely by chance. Thus the experimenter should not put the thinnest women in any particular condition, or the hungriest, or the least hungry. Each subject should have an equal chance of being in any of the meal conditions. In this way the experimenter is assured that any differences between the meal groups are due to the meals they missed, not who they were before they participated in the study.

Control is important in order to be sure that other factors have not influenced the results. For example, if some women are tested in a room with a kitchen nearby, and they can smell the aromas of food, they may behave differently from women who are tested in a classroom without such distracting reminders of their hunger. An obvious control strategy would be to arrange to test all subjects in the same environment, with the same background stimuli.

Quasi-Experimental Designs. For some research questions, random assignment to experimental conditions is not possible. For example, if a teacher wishes to discover which of two lecturing styles (independent variable) leads to more class discussion (dependent variable) in a particular course, he might plan to employ one style in his 10 o'clock class and the other in his 11 o'clock class. For a true experiment, he would randomly assign students to take the class at either time; however, this is not possible, because the students are already enrolled in one section or the other for various other reasons.

The students in the two class sections are already different from each other. It is not known whether they are different from each other in important ways, or ways that would make a difference to their involvement in class discussion. In order to test his hypothesis about the causal relationship between lecturing style and class discussion, the teacher-experimenter must employ not a true randomized experimental design but a quasi-experimental design.

Quasi means "almost," and the difference is a subtle change in expectations. Basically, since the two groups are already different and cannot be made "equivalent" by random reassignment to one class or the other, the researcher should *expect* differences in the outcome of the experiment. Before concluding that differences in class discussion were due merely to the differences in lecturing style, the data must be examined for the quality and size of the difference. Quasi-experimental designs thus involve different assumptions and statistical analysis. The validity or strength of the results will also be lower because of the absence of random assignment.

EXPERIMENTAL SETTINGS

In general every experimenter can choose between two kinds of research setting: the controlled environment of the laboratory, or the less controlled but more natural environment of the field.

The Field. The setting in which the social behavior occurs naturally is referred to as the field. This is usually the source of researchers' initial curiosity and observations, and it offers an inspiring range of options. However, field experiments are not true experiments since participants do not volunteer to be subjects and cannot be randomly assigned to experimental conditions.

For example, a researcher wants to know whether the appearance of a stalled vehicle will affect delayed drivers' tendency to honk their horns in protest or anger. For one period, the researcher pretends to stall an old, battered-looking automobile at designated intersections, and records the sounds of subsequent horn-honking from vehicles stuck behind. For another period, he conducts the same sequence with a late-model luxury sedan. After several days of repeating this procedure, the horn sounds on the two sets of tapes are coded and the results compared for the two styles of "stalled" automobile.

One problem with the conclusions of this study is that so many factors in field research cannot be controlled. Time of day might be an important factor in horn-honking, or day of the week, and even specific intersections. Weather conditions like precipitation and temperature could also have been an important determinant of people's tolerance for delay. Finally, some variables could have been important that the experimenter could not anticipate or identify. Field experiments are open to wider interpretation because they afford so little control and no direct random assignment.

The Laboratory. Because field research is so hard to control and can be inconclusive, the experimental setting of choice is usually the laboratory. A laboratory is any controlled environment, like a classroom specially scheduled for testing subjects, or a waiting room that has been specially equipped to expose all subjects to the same features and stimuli.

For example, a subject who has volunteered to participate in a laboratory experiment appears at the appointed time at a small research room in the psychology building. After hearing a description of his role, he examines and rates a series of photographs for their visual appeal. After 30 minutes, he is told the study is complete, and he is free to go.

With such a scenario, an experimenter is free to control many aspects of the subject's experience. For example, a researcher could show all subjects the same set of photographs, but for some subjects preset the thermostat of the room so that it is uncomfortably warm, while for the others it is moderate and comfortable. If the warm-room subjects rate the pictures as less attractive, the researcher can conclude that warm rooms make subjects judge appearance more harshly.

One problem with laboratory studies is that the subjects, who know they are subjects, may speculate privately about the purposes and hypotheses of the experiment. They may guess that the room is unusually warm "on purpose," and attempt to correct their ratings to keep from being manipulated by the experimental condition. Or they could guess wrongly and interpret another condition as important, reacting unusually to that. In other words, there is no way absolutely to control what a subject thinks or the basis for his or her actions.

Another problem with laboratory research is that it achieves relative control at the cost of realism. Subjects may be able to follow instructions to rate the visual appeal of stimuli in a small room, but that is not the way people normally judge the attractiveness of the things they encounter. How much do the results of such a laboratory study reveal about "real world" social behavior?

Realism. The choice of setting for experimental research, therefore, has consequences for realism. There are two kinds of realism experimenters must consider, with different implications: mundane realism, and experimental realism.

If a setting provides *mundane realism,* it resembles the natural setting of the behavior. Mundane means "worldly," so the greater the mundane realism of a research setting, the more a subject therein will feel as though he or she is in the real world.

The greater the mundane realism of a research setting, the greater the researcher's ability to generalize from subjects' behavior to the behavior of other people. This greater generalizability must be tempered, however, by the realization that the lack of control in such settings makes research findings less precise.

Some social psychologists have argued that, given subjects' knowledge of modern scientific techniques, it is not important that a setting resemble the real world. What is important, they argue, is that the setting and structure of the experiment be involving and compelling to the subject, so that his or her behavior is spontaneous and reflective of the experimental conditions. This involving, absorbing quality is known as *experimental realism*.

Experimental realism cannot promise a high level of generalizability— since the experimental versions of the variables being studied are likely to be different from their real-world counterparts—but it provides control which assures precision and clarity of results.

THE SOCIAL PSYCHOLOGY OF THE PSYCHOLOGY EXPERIMENT

As mentioned above, the psychology experiment itself is a social situation. The experimenter's role conveys expertise and authority, which have meaning for how the experimenter and subject will interact. The subject also has a role that usually involves the intention to be a "good" subject. These roles and interactions may become in themselves sources of bias and distortion which must be anticipated and controlled if the experiment is to have value.

Expectancy Effects. The experimenter's greatest challenge is to observe the subject's behavior objectively. This may be difficult if the experimenter has formulated the hypothesis being tested. By this point the experimenter may have formed expectations that the hypothesis will be confirmed. Such expectations have been found to bias experimenters' perceptions of events. The experimenter's tendency to perceive events and behaviors as confirming the expected hypothesis is a particular kind of expectancy effect known as *experimenter bias*.

Experimenter bias can be reduced or controlled by having a naive colleague conduct the experiment instead of the researcher who formulated the original research question. This is known as "blinding" the experimenter to the hypothesis. When both the experimenter and the subjects are naive about the true purpose and hypothesis of the experiment, this control is known as a "double-blind" procedure.

Demand Characteristics. The role of experimental subject can be compelling because of the voluntary commitment the subject has made to participate, and the connotations of authority and expertise associated with the experimenter's role. Volunteers may already be different enough from other people that their behavior does not represent that of the general population. Once in the experimental situation, subjects may deliberately or unintentionally try to guess the experimental hypothesis, and may further try to "help" by providing behaviors they believe will confirm the assumed hypothesis. Rarely, subjects may deliberately try to sabotage the experiment by behaving perversely, doing the opposite of what they think is expected of them.

Clues in the experimental arrangement that suggest what is being studied or expected are known as *demand characteristics*. These can be either obvious or subtle, such as the experimenter's tone of voice while reading standardized instructions. One way to reduce demand characteristics is to remind subjects that they are free to leave or cease participating, so they do not become

artificially compliant. Another way is to have subjects read instructions rather than listen to them being read by the experimenter. Finally, keeping the experimenter blind to the researcher's hypothesis reduces demand characteristics as well as expectancy effects, as noted above.

Convergent Measures

Which method of social research should an investigator employ? Few social psychologists feel they must choose just one approach. Most research questions begin with observation, so that a natural extension might first be correlational research. Once a relationship among variables has been established, experiments may be designed to specify the direction and power of causation.

A pattern of research results is most convincing if a research program has employed convergent measures. These are methods that rely on correlation as well as experimentation, and employ various settings and designs. If most or all of these techniques of study point to the same conclusions, these conclusions can be adopted with greater confidence. No one study or approach has been relied on exclusively, but each supports the others in identifying genuine patterns among observations.

EVALUATING SOCIAL RESEARCH

What is the role of social research in modern science? And how good is social research, given the slippery nature of social behavior and the many challenges to conducting informative research?

Social research can be evaluated in terms of researchers' efforts to abide by values of conduct, and in terms of the values that motivate research in the first place.

Ethical Concerns

Social psychological research typically involves the participation of human respondents or subjects. Survey research, employing respondents rather than subjects, is inherently optional; people can easily refuse to be respondents by bypassing surveyors or failing to return mailed questionnaires.

INFORMED CONSENT

Experimental research depends on the voluntary participation of subjects. Such work has been qualified by a system of ethical safeguards. Experimental subjects must provide their informed consent to participate. This typically involves signing a statement attesting to a general understanding of the research procedure, and an acknowledgement that they are free to terminate participation at any time without penalty.

DECEPTION

Many social psychological experiments study behaviors which could be distorted or altered if subjects knew of the true focus of the research. For such cases deception may be employed.

Deception may be as simple as a false cover story for the experimental arrangement, so that subjects misperceive the reason behind the tasks they are asked to perform. Or deception may be as complex as creating staged events and roles in order to see what subjects would do if they encountered certain unexpected events.

In one of the most famous social psychology experiments involving deception, subjects were recruited for a study of the effects of punishment on learning, and were individually asked to teach another person a word list. Each time the learner made an error, the teacher was required to punish him with an electric shock. In reality, the researchers were interested in knowing whether the teacher-subjects would obey the experimenter's orders to administer those shocks, not in whether the shocks affected the learner's memory. (The learner was, in fact, a confederate of the experimenter and merely acted as if he received shocks. No actual electric shocks were ever delivered, although the teacher-subjects believed they were).

Would the subjects have obeyed the experimenter if they had been told this was an experiment on obedience to authority? Probably not; hence the deception was employed to get the subjects' "real" behavior rather than responses that might have been deemed more socially desirable.

The use of deception has declined since the earlier decades of social psychological research. However, the very nature of social behavior makes it difficult to be sure subjects are naive about the researchers' hypotheses, and deception can be a useful tool.

DEBRIEFING

The ethical constraints on deception usually involve requiring strong reasons for deceiving subjects in the first place, and following any deception with a debriefing. In debriefing, the experimenter explains the true nature of the research to the subject and answers any questions. In this way any surprise or resentment about deception may be reduced, and the subject's participation can be made more instructive and valuable to the subject.

WHEN IS A SUBJECT NOT A SUBJECT?

One gray area left by many ethical guidelines is whether or not a person being observed is a research "subject." For example, if a researcher is watching people at an airport, is the researcher obligated to obtain their informed consent before videotaping or audiotaping their behavior—which is after all in a public place? Since informed consent would certainly alter "natural" behavior in the field, is the researcher obliged to conduct a debriefing after making these observations? Most social psychologists would argue that obviously public locations do not promise privacy, and such ethical guidelines do not apply.

However, some locations are not clearly public. For example, is a public restroom public—or private? You are certainly free to enter the public restroom of your gender and notice how people behave there. But you are also expected by most social norms not to stare. Therefore people using the restrooms might justly feel their privacy had been invaded if you were to make careful observations of strangers' bathroom behavior.

There are no easy answers to fuzzy questions about the ethics of privacy and observation. These continue to be challenging decisions to researchers who are curious about social behavior.

Social Research and Human Values

A more basic challenge to social researchers is maintaining objectivity in the study of social behavior.

OBJECTIVITY VERSUS SUBJECTIVITY

Subjective values—personal goals and opinions—often motivate researchers to ask questions in the first place. Thus values influence research at the very beginning. Feminists become interested in gender roles, peace activists are curious about conflict resolution techniques, and victims of crime want to know how to keep others from blaming them for their fate. While it may not be possible to be objective in the early questioning processes of scientific research, it is essential to the scientific method that researchers be as objective as possible in conducting their observations and analyzing patterns in their data.

HIDDEN VALUES

Some values—and biases—can be hidden in psychological terminology. For example, asking why women are "not as assertive" as men may involve a hidden assumption that assertiveness is good and that women are therefore deficient in some healthy quality. Specific labels may also contain value judgments, as when a subject's behavior is termed "conformist"—a term considered somewhat negative, mindless, sheep-like—rather than "cooperative," which seems a more positive version of the same quality.

Some biases are as subtle as language. Simple sayings like "To each his own" or "No man is an island" may consistently conjure male images to match the male nouns or pronouns. This may have a long term effect of making it difficult for the speaker to imagine women as being more like men than they are different. Language itself retains values and traditions that can have social effects.

THE NATURALISTIC FALLACY

Social scientists live and work within a culture, making it difficult for them to examine that culture itself. Things that have always been done a certain way "make sense," and it may be difficult for social researchers to question tradition. The reverence for tradition may be based on the naturalistic fallacy, the belief that things as they *are* is the way they *ought* to be. For example, arguing that women should not be priests because the church has never had women priests—and there must be a good reason for that—illustrates the naturalistic fallacy.

Social researchers may be particularly challenged to observe their own cultures and social contexts with open eyes and minds. It is all the more important, therefore, to consider cross-cultural and alternative viewpoints before coming to final conclusions about social phenomena.

Social psychology relies on the scientific method as a means of inquiry and acquiring knowledge. Scientific research proceeds in a sequence of formulating research questions, conducting empirical observations, developing and testing hypotheses, and developing theories.

Social researchers can choose to employ either correlational or experimental methods. Correlational methods identify preexisting relationships among variables, while experimental methods specify the direction and power of causality.

Popular correlational methods include archival research, surveys, and behavioral observation. Survey research is fairly easy but requires careful design if it is to be informative. Survey samples must be randomly selected from the population of interest. The larger the sample, the more accurately and confidently the survey results represent those of the population. Surveys should be worded so as to reduce respondent biases like social desirability.

Direct observations are useful if the social behaviors under study are obvious and public. Participant observation balances the role of group member with that of objective researcher. Unobtrusive measures reduce the presence of the observer, or collect indirect accretion or erosion evidence after the fact.

Experimental methods involve selecting designs and settings, as well as decisions about realism and the effects of experimentation itself. A true experiment is only possible if subjects' assignments to experimental conditions can be randomized. The essential qualities of an experiment are randomized assignment and control of variables not under study. Alternatively, a quasi-experimental design permits qualified conclusions about experimental outcomes and internal validity.

Experimental settings can be arranged in the field or the laboratory. Field research is more easily generalizable but affords little control. Laboratory research is more controlled and precise but can be artificial. While mundane realism is attractive it may not be as critical as experimental realism that involves subjects in the procedure.

Experimentation creates a social context for both experimenter's and subjects' behavior. Expectancy effects can be reduced by employing single or double-blind (naive) procedures. Demand characteristics that give subjects "clues" about their expected roles can also be reduced with standardized instructions and blinds.

Researchers develop programs of convergent measures, so that results from various settings and designs indicate genuine tendencies among data.

Social research can be evaluated in terms of how ethical values are applied in conducting research and included in its application. Subjects must give their informed consent for experimental participation, and when deception is used they must be debriefed.

From the beginning, social research involves researchers' values. Values may also be hidden in terminology, labels, and language. Because social psychologists are subject to their own cultural contexts, it may be difficult to avoid committing the naturalistic fallacy of assuming that the way things are is the way they ought to be.

Selected Readings

Campbell, D. T. and J. C. Stanley. (1963). *Experimental and Quasi-Experimental Designs for Research*. Chicago: Rand McNally.

Cook, T. D. and D. T. Campbell. (1979). *Quasi-Experimentation: Design and Analysis Issues for Field Settings*. Chicago: Rand McNally.

Deutsch, M. and R. M. Krauss. (1965). *Theories in Social Psychology*. New York: Basic Books.

Hunt, M. (1985). *Profiles of Social Research: The Scientific Study of Human Interactions*. New York: Russell Sage.

Judd, C. M., E. Smith, and L. H. Kidder. (1991). *Research Methods in Social Relations,* 6th edition. Fort Worth, TX: Holt, Rinehart and Winston.

Lindzey, G. and E. Aronson. (Eds.). (1985). *The Handbook of Social Psychology,* 3rd edition, 2 vols. New York: Random House.

Pyke, S. W. and N. McK. Agnew. (1991). *The Science Game: An Introduction to Research in the Social Sciences*. Englewood Cliffs, NJ: Prentice Hall.

Reich, J. W. (Ed.). (1982). *Experimenting in Society: Issues and Examples in Applied Social Psychology*. Glenview, IL: Scott, Foresman.

Sanders, W. P. and T. K. Pinhey. (1983). *The Conduct of Social Research*. New York: Holt, Rinehart and Winston.

Selltiz, C., L. S. Wrightsman, and S. W. Cook. (1976). *Research Methods in Social Relations*. New York: Holt, Rinehart and Winston.

Webb, E. J., D. T. Campbell, R. D. Schwartz, and L. Sechrest. (1966). *Unobtrusive Measures: Nonreactive Research in the Social Sciences*. Chicago: Rand McNally.

3

Social Cognition

Social behavior usually—but not always—begins with social cognition. While some behavior is so well-learned as to seem almost automatic or mindless, most is the result of deliberation, judgment, beliefs, and/or expectations. This process of forming inferences from social information before taking action is known as social cognition, or more simply, social thinking.

Patterns of social cognition explain specific phenomena of self concepts (chapter 4), social perception and impression formation (chapter 5), attribution (chapter 6), and attitude formation and maintenance (chapter 8). Before applying social cognition to those processes, however, this chapter will review the basic terms and patterns of social cognition.

Most patterns in social cognition are fairly effective and successful. However, much research has identified effective strategies by first pinpointing common errors in social thinking. While errors are overall rarer than successes, they are often the result of extending or overusing processes that are normally effective. A balanced understanding of social cognition depends on an awareness of both effective and erroneous patterns in social cognition.

SOCIAL THINKING PROCESSES

Early work on social cognition assumed a rational model underlying human thought and decision-making. In rational thinking, correct conclusions are derived from a logical assembly of information.

Contrary to the rational model, much everyday social thinking appears to be illogically organized and incompletely collected. Research has therefore concentrated on identifying the strategies and patterns people actually use, rather than seeking to confirm a rational system at work.

Several processes that have been identified in everyday social thinking are social inference, reliance on schemata, and use of mental shortcuts known as heuristics.

Social Inference

An inference is an interpretation or new understanding based on reviewing information. A social inference consists of three steps: collecting social data (information), selecting the data relevant to making a judgment, and pulling these data together to make the judgment or decision.

COLLECTING SOCIAL DATA

People seldom collect social data with truly open minds. Most of us have life experiences that have led us to form expectations. These prior expectations can help us to sift through vast quantities of new information, but they can also cause problems by biasing our interpretations. Prior expectations are most likely to cause problems if they are based on few or single instances of past experience; if we fail to realize we are relying on prior expectations; or if we reject the opportunity to collect new information because of negative expectations.

For example, a woman's friends encourage her to meet and go out with a newly-divorced man they know. Before agreeing, the woman considers what she already "knows" about him, such as his newly-divorced marital status and a description of his work as a botanist. Her decision about whether to meet him can be unfairly biased by her preconceptions if she considers that she once had a bad relationship with a newly-divorced man; if she fails to realize that she is basing her judgment of this new person on inadequate and perhaps irrelevant impressions; and if she concludes that she would have "nothing in common" with a botanist, so a meeting would be pointless.

A more effective data-collection process would take into account the source of the recommendation (the woman's friends). She could also engage in further data-collection: what are this person's hobbies; why does he feel he is ready to date again; what kind of date would he like to arrange with her?

While experience and education can improve the data-collection process, most people are poor gatherers of information. In part this is due to the fact that we seldom encounter proof of erroneous data-collection in our past. The woman who decides not to date the man her friends like will not find out she made a mistake in rejecting him too early. A personnel director who decides not to hire a job applicant will not subsequently see that person on the job, and so will not discover that he let a good employee get away.

INTEGRATING SOCIAL INFORMATION

Once answers to social data-collection questions have been collected, how are they assembled into a meaningful conclusion? Gestalt psychologists suggest that the many separate data are viewed as a whole, which is examined for patterns. This process of fitting pieces of information together with each other is known as information integration.

Information integration is central to much person perception (see chapter 5). It is also employed in problemsolving and decision making. It requires picking and choosing among the data one has collected and judging which information is or is not relevant and useful.

JUDGING COVARIATION

One general rule that helps in social inference is that data which covary are related. When two qualities or events covary, they go together, changing in the same way or at the same time. For example, among children, age and height tend to covary: older children are taller, younger children are shorter. Given your knowledge of this age-height covariance, when you meet two children of different heights, you will most likely judge the taller one to be the older one. Naturally this covariance rule is not infallible, but it works for most practical purposes.

The woman who worries that a newly-divorced man will be a poor dating partner is relying on another perception of covariance. She believes that being newly divorced covaries—goes together—with being distracted, fickle, or selfish. Whether she is correct or not in this particular instance, she bases her social judgment on one lesson of her past experience or conviction.

Schemata

The prior expectations and past experiences that influence our social judgments are generally examples of schemata (the plural form of *schema*). A schema is a set of thoughts, a category that pulls together ideas and information about a particular stimulus. For example, a schema of "being divorced" might include knowledge of personal friends who have been divorced, impressions of media portrayals of divorce and divorced persons, and ideas about accompanying emotions of loss, depression, euphoria, mid-life crisis, and sexual experimentation.

Once a schema is established in a person's mind, he or she will use it to interpret the social environment. New experiences or social encounters will be compared to our schemata. We will rely on schemata in identifying important clues to look for or questions to ask in the new situation. Because schemata affect data selection, they can bias and distort social inferences as well as facilitate them.

ORGANIZATION

Schemata are usually organized hierarchically in one's mind. That is, they begin with general information, and include finer and finer levels of detail and past experiences. For example, if a friend invites you to attend a reception for a new exhibit at a local art museum, you will consult your schema for "art exhibits" before accepting. Your first consideration will be a general impression of what art museums look like, how an exhibit will be arranged, how busy or crowded the reception will be, and what people will be talking about. Your next level of considerations will be more detailed, including your personal feelings about art and art exhibits, and your anticipation of what *this* experience will probably (based on your schema) feel like to *you*. Your social judgment about whether to accept will depend on your decision, at each level of your schema, about the pleasure you associate with these images and experiences.

VARIATIONS

If your friend is an artist and you are not, you will probably have very different schemata about the art exhibit reception. Your friend may conclude that this will be an enjoyable experience and an important career move, while you judge that it will be an unusual experience, irrelevant to your work, and possible not very enjoyable. Thus your different past experiences and preferences may be self-perpetuating as they build schemata which produce exaggerated social judgments. Art students go to art exhibits, while non-art students generally do not.

Other schema differences may be more subtle than general orientations. A man whose last relationship failed because his partner deceived him will value honesty in future partners more than someone who has not had such an experience. He may judge all new acquaintances according to his impression of how honest or sincere they seem to be.

Finally, while schemata can be individually different, they can also share important common elements from one person to another within a culture. Most students will have similar experiences and thus similar schemata about teachers—just as teachers will about students. Travelers will have similar schemata about airports, interstate highways, and luggage. Schemata can thus be like other personality factors in that they explain both similarities and differences among people.

EFFECTIVENESS

How effective are schemata? If they are developed from distinct prior experiences, social judgments may be inevitably biased. However, without schemata our processing of social information might be too time-consuming and inefficient to be successful. If, before you can safely agree to meet a new friend for coffee, you must review all known and unknown information about her without any assumptions from past experience, you may have to postpone the data until later in your life.

Advantages. Schemata provide the advantage of summarizing the lessons of past experience and belief. Thus they aid memory, interpretation, social judgment, and expectations.

When new information is consistent with a schema, the schema helps us to remember it. If you meet someone who says she is majoring in mathematics, and she looks like your schema of a mathematician, you will later more easily recall her face and her major. Conversely, if she "really" looks more like a drama major, violating your math major schema, you may have a poorer memory for her face or her real major. This may explain why we sometimes insist on calling new acquaintances by the same wrong names: they don't "look like" their names to us—in other words, they don't fit our schemata for those names.

Schemata can also make social thinking operate more quickly. If we learn new information about someone that is consistent with our schema about him, we can more easily add it to our thinking and come to new conclusions.

Schemata help us make new interpretations. If you have some of the symptoms of a cold, your schema for "cold" can help you decide which medications are right for you (e.g., a decongestant) and which are wrong (e.g., an antacid).

Finally, schemata include expectations for future events. If one is promoted in her job, her schema for promotion may include a raise in pay. If her salary is not raised, her expectations will be violated and she will react with anger and a sense of betrayal. This also shows the incorporation of emotion (affect) into cognitive schemata.

Disadvantages. Schemata are categories of ideas, information, and feelings—and as such they are simplifications. For given judgments, they may be oversimplifications, overlooking important considerations and omitting useful details.

Besides oversimplification, another disadvantage of schemata is the logical error. The logical error involves assuming that, since some characteristics or events covary—go along with each other—then where one is found the other will always occur. For example, one's schema for athletes may include the assumption that physically strong persons are intellectually inferior. Within such schema, one may unfairly assume that a particular athlete must be unintelligent, a judgment based on the logical error.

Heuristics

Most social judgments involve familiar situations and elements. Consequently people rely on past habits and discoveries when they encounter similar events, rather than reinventing or innovating responses every time.

MENTAL SHORTCUTS

A rule about how to judge or respond, based on past experience or belief, is called a heuristic. A heuristic is a "rule of thumb," a guideline (e.g., when measuring small items without a ruler handy, use the first joint of your thumb to represent about an inch), but not a proven standard. It is handy when decisions need to be made quickly and there is some allowable margin of error.

In social cognition, heuristics allow people to take "mental shortcuts" in integrating information and reaching conclusions. Like geographic shortcuts, they economize on time and effort at the expense of unvarying accuracy. Some social psychologists have likened social cognition to a "cognitive miser," a process that is very stingy about effort and detail. If relying on a heuristic will "save" the miser some investment, this will be done rather than a more painstaking, repetitious, thoughtful process of analysis and reasoning.

When employed occasionally and appropriately, heuristics can be handy tools for reasonable social judgments. When overused or misapplied, however, they are a frequent source of cognitive error and misjudgment.

COMMON HEURISTICS

Many heuristics are idiosyncratic: they are developed uniquely by each person for specific circumstances. A person who rushes to answer a telephone only to find the caller has just hung up may reassure herself by thinking, "It only rang four times, so it must not have been important." This is an example of a personal heuristic; for another person and other conditions, this "rule" may not apply at all.

Because there are common social experiences among human beings, however, we have developed common heuristics to expedite our social thinking. Two common heuristics rely on representativeness and availability.

Representativeness. Suppose you are assigned a new professor, a "Dr. Jones" you have never heard of, as an advisor. One day you seek out your new advisor's office, and find a young woman just inside the door, busily filing papers. "When will the professor be back?" you ask, only to be told to your surprise, "I'm the professor. How can I help you?"

The assumption that a person does (or does not) belong to a group based on his or her resemblance to the "typical" group member is the representativeness heuristic. Although you may know, logically, that a professor can be either male or female, you may also have the accurate impression that most professors are male, and most are not obviously young.

In deciding whether a particular person probably belongs to a category, we tend to consult our impressions of whether he or she seems representative of that category. If our experiences are broad enough, reliance on the representativeness heuristic will usually work. But as in the above example, the assumption that all members of a group are "typical" can ignore exceptions and result in erroneous guesses.

Availability. Is it statistically more risky to travel by automobile or by airplane? Although you may "know" that car accidents are more frequent, the tragedy of air crashes is more likely to draw media attention and to come more readily to mind. If your answers and decisions are influenced by what comes to mind first, you are relying on the availability heuristic.

Generally images and ideas are more available if they are more vivid. Certainly air crashes are more horrible—in the sense that they cause the loss of more lives per accident—than automobile accidents. The vividness of this horror and its replaying in the media may make such images artificially more available than they should be.

One consequence of the availability heuristic is the influence of priming. When current experiences make certain stimuli salient or noticeable, they can "prime" our recall of usually forgotten memories. For example, a psychology student learning about phobias (irrational fears) may find herself wondering if her own discomfort at great heights is "proof" that she is abnormally acrophobic (afraid of heights). In this case, the psychology lesson has primed or activated her sensitivity about her own fearful behavior. But the availability of this self-awareness does not constitute proof that she is actually phobic.

The availability heuristic uses ease or frequency of recall in support of social judgments. To the extent our experiences reflect real occurrences, and we recall events realistically, use of this heuristic will help us to make good decisions. But as in the above example, distortions of experience or information (e.g., media, propaganda) can mean that "available" ideas are not necessarily accurate.

Reliance on the availability heuristic can involve denial of accurate information about event frequency, known as the base-rate. The number of actual plane crashes that occur for all flights in a certain time period is the baserate for that event. To ignore the base-rate and conclude that plane crashes are more likely to occur than car crashes is to commit the base-rate fallacy. The base-rate fallacy can result from overreliance on the availability heuristic.

ERRORS IN SOCIAL THINKING

For every social thinking process reviewed above—social data collection and inference, use of schemata, and reliance on heuristics—the dangers or errors of overuse of the process have also been noted. In reading thus far you will have detected that much of what is known about social cognition has been learned through the study of errors in social thinking.

While most of the above strategies do facilitate accurate and effective social thinking, overreliance or abuse of strategies and shortcuts can lead to errors and biases. These in turn can sabotage the effectiveness of our judgments and decisions. An examination of common errors in social thinking is important to keeping a balanced view of social behavior. Such erroneous patterns include biased perception and memory, framing and anchoring effects, misusing social information, illusory correlation, and expectancy effects.

Biased Perception and Memory

Powerful preconceptions can distort the way we perceive new information as well as the ways we recall previously learned material.

BIASED PERCEPTION

Expectations. One example of biased perception is seeing what one expects to see—although the reality may be different from the expectation. For example, if you strongly expect a friend to compliment you, you may interpret anything she says as a compliment, even though the truth may have been more lukewarm.

Attitudes. Another example of biased perception involves the way attitudes—evaluative reactions to things—can affect our interpretations. For example, if fans on both sides watch a rival match between two schools' basketball teams, each side may perceive the same events in the very differently. What one side calls a "deliberate foul" may be seen by the other as an "accident taken too seriously." Their perceptions of events are biased by their prejudgments, their attitudes in support of their own and against each other's team.

Information. Information can bias sensory perceptions. If you are shown an attractive smiling male face, you will probably interpret the facial expression one way if you are told this man is a serial killer and another way if told he is a fashion model.

Belief Perseverance. When perception is so biased by one's beliefs, events may be perceived only in ways that support and do not disconfirm those beliefs. This is known as belief perseverance.

For example, being rejected by a lover might cause someone to conclude that he is unattractive and unlovable in general. If a later partner is attentive and loving, he may interpret it as a sign of "pity" rather than love—clinging to the old belief rather than reevaluating it in light of this new evidence.

BIASED RECALL

Context Effects. Memory for specific events may be biased by the context in which original events occurred. When you normally leave your home, for example, you may usually—but not always—grab your keys and secure them in your pocket. This habit is the usual context for this particular action. When later trying to remember where you might have misplaced your keys, you may recall leaving home "as usual," and misremember, "I *must* have had my keys with me, since I *always* put them in my pocket after I close the door." This is a context effect on memory, a "recollection" of what should have happened rather than what did happen.

Reconstructive Memory. Many events are not stored in detail at memory input, but rather interpreted later during retrieval (e.g., recall). Biases during retrieval can distort what is remembered. For example, suppose you once disliked someone, but have gotten to know her better and now have a good impression of her. You may now recall—incorrectly—that your first conversation with her was very enjoyable. Your new positive opinion distorts your recall of the earlier, less pleasant events. This makes it hard to recall experiences accurately if they contradict your current opinion.

Reconstructive memory effects have helped to understand the reliability of eyewitness testimony in legal proceedings. Research shows that the wording of questions can affect the ways eyewitnesses describe recalled events (see chapter 20).

Framing and Anchoring

In a different way, context influences decision making. A person ties together information about situations and people to form a pattern. Similarly, social judgments and decisions take context into account along with the terms of choice or problem. For example, when you consider whether to lend money to a friend, you consider *who* the friend is and *why* the friend has requested the loan. Those are contextual aspects of the decision that are very important to its conclusion.

In understanding errors in social cognition, two important forms of context are framing and anchoring.

FRAMING

When a choice is presented to a person, the information provided often includes the consequences of the alternatives. For example, a student deciding whether to buy a used versus a new car may consider that a used car is cheaper but less reliable, while a new car is more reliable but also much more expensive. Such consequences and other contextual information make up the way the choice is "framed" or presented.

The way a choice or decision is framed can influence the way it is interpreted and judged. For example, if an alternative is framed in a negative way—including warnings about what could go wrong if it is chosen—the perceived may judge against it. But if an alternative is presented with a positive frame—for example, selectively quoting the praise of "satisfied customers"—the perceiver may be persuaded to agree.

Research confirms that framing is very influential, and indirect strategies to reduce it may not be effective. For example, increasing a chooser's involvement in a decision does not appear to cancel out framing effects. Even though more involved judges should be more cautious or "know better," they seem to rely heavily on the influence of framing.

ANCHORING

Closely related to framing are anchoring effects. An anchor is a reference point against which other choices are compared. For example, a woman who was laid off from her last job is invited to apply for a position where a friend works. When she asks what it pays, she is told the figure, and assured that the salary is "above average" for the position in this region. However, if instead she compares the salary figure with that of her old job, which was higher, she may be influenced to refuse to apply, thinking she should be able to command at least that much. In this example, she has chosen her old salary as her reference point or anchor, instead of the statistically fairer salary average.

Anchors have been found to be influential in decisionmaking, despite obvious problems with choosing unrealistic or unfair reference points. For example, most people use the asking price of an item as a guide to its value—the more something costs, the more valuable a consumer estimates it to be. In such cases the consumer is allowing the asking price to "anchor" her estimate of the item's value, rather than considering an objective or independent assessment.

Information Misuse

As devoted as social cognition is to collecting information, research shows that people do not process information fairly or well. As indicated above, we are more affected by available or vivid ideas than by base-rates; we seek information to verify rather than challenge cherished beliefs; and we retain faulty beliefs despite the existence of contradictions.

Three specific forms of information misuse are the hindsight bias, ignoring useful information, and using useless information.

THE HINDSIGHT BIAS

An important goal of social thinking is prediction of future events. Our need to be able to predict may at times exceed our ability to do so. One consequence of this need is the hindsight bias, a tendency, once outcomes are known, to believe we could have predicted those outcomes earlier.

The hindsight bias can be simple and insincere, as when a student reacting to a test score exclaims, "I knew it!" Research shows that knowing a decisive outcome can distort one's memory of an earlier prediction. For example, before an election, a survey respondent may feel the race between two candidates is very close. But after the election, when the winner is known, the same respondent may feel "I could have predicted this outcome." This confidence in one's predictive ability is exaggerated in hindsight.

The hindsight bias is also referred to as the I-Knew-It-All-Along bias. It can cause us to misperceive surprising outcomes as "obvious" or "just common sense"—but only after the fact. Information about an outcome is being misused by being misplaced—erroneously included in one's pre-outcome prediction ability. This causes problems because we cannot learn from errors if we refuse to recognize them. By mistakenly believing we "could have predicted" an outcome, we fail to acknowledge and learn from prior misperceptions. If we refuse to admit being surprised by how events have transpired, we will not modify our understanding of the social world—and will, ironically, only become poorer predictors in the future.

IGNORING USEFUL INFORMATION

As described earlier, committing the base-rate fallacy—favoring anecdotal or available ideas rather than statistical frequencies—is an example of ignoring useful information. Why do we disregard important and accurate sources in favor of unreliable influences? One factor may be the compelling nature of a vivid example: it may be difficult to ignore an idea if it has been colorfully presented or seems personally relevant. For example, if a person you find attractive is the subject of a particularly nasty rumor, you may find it hard to ignore the rumor because, if true, it could be important for you to consider.

USING USELESS INFORMATION

Other research suggests that some social judgments are influenced by information that is actually irrelevant. For example, you may know that more people work as truck drivers than as college professors. Someone is described to you as a person who likes to read poetry; is he a truck driver or a college professor? Although statistically the poetry fan is more likely to be a truck driver, you may be influenced by the useless "hint" about liking to read poetry into guessing that he is a college professor. In this case, the useless information was influential because it favored the stereotype (simplistic image) of a college professor but not that of a truck driver.

Other useless information may be influential because of its form rather than its content. For example, people are more likely to grant a request if given a justification than if no justification or reason is offered. Thus if someone asks to get ahead of you in a line, you should be more likely to agree if the requester gives you a convincing reason. One study, however, found that people in a line agreed to let strangers in even when the excuse was useless and provided no information. This suggests that the agreement was given quickly, before the "information" had been analyzed or found wanting.

Apparently, the person who must decide whether to grant the request has a sense of the proper "script" (interactional form) for a request. Part of the script involves the requester offering a reason for the request, in order to be persuasive. Because the requester offered a reason—even an empty one—the statement was treated like information, although it contained no useful data.

Illusory Correlation

Illusory correlation involves seeing events or features as related when they are not. Random events are seen to have a pattern—as when one believes thinking of an old friend "somehow" is connected to a later phone call from that old friend.

Another example of illusory correlation can be traced to mass media. If a headline proclaims that a "Murder Suspect Was Psychiatric Patient," those two labels—Murder Suspect and Psychiatric Patient—seem related, as though one may have caused the other. In actuality most murder suspects are not found to have been psychiatric patients, since most *people* have not been psychiatric patients for any reason. But headlines seldom proclaim "Mentally Healthy Person Charged in Murder." The artificial media connection between two newsworthy labels creates the illusory impression that they are correlated.

Illusory correlation can have other biasing consequences in social cognition. Among these are overconfidence and illusions of control.

OVERCONFIDENCE

People have a tendency to be more confident than correct in social judgments and beliefs. This overconfidence phenomenon can be explained by the confirmation bias, a tendency to verify our beliefs by seeking out information that supports it and ignoring information that might contradict it.

Another factor in overconfidence is event salience, or the degree to which events catch our attention. If you believe you can "make it rain" just by washing your car, it may be because you more readily notice rainy days than nonrainy days, and more easily remember having just washed your car than not washing your car. But putting together the things that happened (raining with car washing) but not the non-events (not raining and not car washing) you conclude that the salient events are connected somehow, with consequences for how lucky or in-control you feel.

ILLUSIONS OF CONTROL

If coincidental or random events appear to be connected, we may falsely conclude that we have control over chance events. For example, if you always wear a yellow scarf while playing cards, and you usually win at cards, you may conclude you can guarantee winning by wearing your "lucky scarf." Another example of an illusion of control is believing chosen numbers have a "greater chance of winning" than randomly assigned lottery numbers.

Expectancy Effects

As discussed above, experiences are frequently summarized into expectations about new events. When expectations are strong, we may perceive outcomes in a distorted fashion. If we apply these expectations to other people, our targets may actually try to live up (or down) to these expectations. Two examples of such social expectancy effects are experimenter bias and self-fulfilling prophecy.

EXPERIMENTER BIAS

As discussed in chapter 2, researchers may formulate hypotheses about experimental outcomes. A strongly-cherished hypothesis may cause an experimenter to perceive results in a biased fashion. For example, an experimenter who expects to get a particular reading on a stopwatch may misread the actual readout.

With human subjects, experimenter expectations may be communicated to the persons trying to be "good" subjects. Subjects may already be looking for *demand characteristics*, clues that suggest what the experimenter is looking for (see chapter 2). If an experimenter is strongly expectant, he or she may contaminate the procedure by reading instructions or asking questions in a biased manner, or by dropping hints (e.g., showing surprise, smiling) about what is "supposed" to happen.

SELF-FULFILLING PROPHECY

When one person has a strong belief and set of expectations about another, his or her treatment of the other person may bring about the expected results. When this occurs, the biased observer may feel as if he or she had prophesied this outcome. In reality, he or she may have caused it rather than predicted it.

For example, classic research involved giving grade school teachers expectations that specific students would show improved performance in coming months. In fact these were false expectations, and the students targeted had been chosen at random, not on the basis of high test scores. Follow-up testing confirmed that the targeted students did show significant improvement later—but this could only have been due to the teachers' expectations, not to any real difference in ability. Thus strongly predicting or prophesying an expected event may cause us to bring about those very events in an act of self-fulfillment.

*S*ocial behavior begins with social cognition. An understanding of social cognition and its effectiveness must be balanced with an appreciation of the limitations of social thinking. Much social cognition research has focused on errors and biases in identifying strategies that usually work well.

Social thinking involves social inference, the use of schemata, and reliance on heuristics. Social inference is a systematic process of basing social judgments on the information that has been gathered. Its three steps are data collection, information integration, and social judgment, especially judgment of covariation.

Schemata are cognitive structures or categories that organize one's ideas and information about a person or event. Most schemata are organized hierarchically, from broader impressions to greater detail. Schemata vary with experience and reveal idiosyncratic differences, despite some cultural commonalities. Schemata are relatively effective in the sense that they expedite social judgments, but can be oversimplified and create distorted impressions and erroneous conclusions.

Heuristics are rules of thumb or mental shortcuts. The representativeness heuristic considers whether a specific case represents what is considered typical for a larger group. The availability heuristic consults recent or available memory for examples in answering questions. Availability can be artificially influenced by vividness, anecdotal and media portrayals of information.

Inappropriate applications and exaggerations of normally useful social thinking strategies can result in erroneous thinking. Common patterns of such errors in social cognition include biased perception and memory, framing and anchoring effects, misuse of information, illusory correlation, and expectancy effects.

Perception can be biased by expectations, strongly-held attitudes, new or salient information, and the belief perseverance phenomenon. Recall can be biased by context effects and reconstruction of memory for events.

Framing and anchoring are context effects on decision making. Framing involves a presentation of information that depicts the consequences of decision alternatives. Anchoring involves using a particular value or experience as a reference point for comparisons. Research indicates that, despite their distortion and error, both framing and anchoring are strong influences whose power is not easily reduced.

As essential as information is in social judgment, people do not collect or handle information in uniformly effective ways. In the hindsight bias, knowledge of an event's outcome can distort one's recall of how accurately one would have predicted that outcome. Once an outcome is known, one is more likely to conclude "I knew it all along." Other misuses of information involve ignoring useful information, such as disregarding the base rate in *favor of vivid examples, and using useless information like stereotypes or empty excuses in making social judgments.*

An important source of error in social thinking is illusory correlation, the illusion that unrelated events are actually related in a meaningful way. Perceiving and falsely linking salient events can lead to a sense of overconfidence, whereby one is more confident than accurate in social judgments. Mistaking coincidence for correlation can also lead to illusions of control over random events.

Expectations can so strongly influence perception that they affect actions and outcomes. Such expectancy effects include experimenter bias and self-fulfilling prophecies. Experimenter bias can contaminate social research when an experimenter allows a cherished hypothesis to distort perception of experimental outcomes. In self-fulfilling prophecy, a person's expectation of another's behavior is so influential that the other acts to meet the expectation, a "prophecy" that has actually been brought about by the expectations of the observer.

Selected Readings

Eiser, J. R. (1980). *Cognitive Social Psychology*. London: McGraw-Hill.

Fiedler, K. and J. P. Forgas. (Eds.). (1988). *Affect, Cognition, and Social Behavior*. Toronto: Hogrefe.

Fiske, S. T. and S. E. Taylor. (1991). *Social Cognition,* 2nd edition. New York: McGraw-Hill.

Gergen, K. J. and K. E. Davis. (1985). *The Social Construction of the Person*. New York: Springer Verlag.

Goleman, D. (1985). *Vital Lies, Simple Truths: The Psychology of Self-Deception and Shared Illusions*. New York: Simon and Schuster.

Hastorf, A. and A. M. Isen. (1982). *Cognitive Social Psychology*. New York: Elsevier-North Holland.

Heider, F. (1958). *The Psychology of Interpersonal Relations*. New York: Wiley.

Higgins, E. T., D. N. Ruble, and W. W. Hartup. (1983). *Social Cognition and Social Development*. Cambridge, England: Cambridge University Press.

Kahneman, D., P. Slovic, and A. Tversky. (Eds.). (1982). *Judgment Under Uncertainty: Heuristics and Biases*. New York: Cambridge University Press.

Langer, E. J. (1989). *Mindfulness*. Reading, MA: Addison-Wesley.

Maital, S. (1982). *Minds, Markets, and Money: Psychological Foundations of Economic Behavior*. New York: Basic Books.

Nisbett, R. and L. Ross. (1980). *Human Inference: Strategies and Shortcomings*. Englewood Cliffs, NJ: Prentice Hall.

Sabini, J. and M. Silver. (1982). *The Moralities of Everyday Life*. New York: Oxford University Press.

Schneider, D. J., A. H. Hastorf, and P. C. Ellsworth. (1979). *Person Perception,* 2nd edition. Reading, MA: Addison-Wesley.

Srull, T. K. and R. S. Wyer. (1988). *Advances in Social Cognition: A Dual Model of Impression Formation*. Hillsdale, NJ: Erlbaum.

4

The Social Self

In the last two decades, one of the most frequently cited phenomena in social psychology is the self: how others create and respond to the self, how self-motivations influence interpersonal relationships and group efforts, and the role of the self in behavior change. If this seems ironic, recall that social psychology focuses on the individual within the social context. Groups and institutions may contribute to a sense of self, but only individuals have *selves. In this regard, the social self is the natural domain of the social psychologist.*

One of the founders of modern psychology, William James (1842–1910), described the self as a process of knowing and thinking, with a subject (the I, *the active self) and an object (the* me, *the self one is aware of). According to James, there are three aspects of* me: *the material self (one's body and possessions), the social self (awareness of how one is seen by others), and the spiritual self (one's personality and psychological aspirations).*

This chapter focuses particularly on the second me, *the social self. The topics of later chapters—person perception, social roles, attitudes and behavior, various forms of social influence and relationships, and the like—all depend more or less on an understanding of the social self. In this chapter, relevant research can be generally reviewed in three broad directions: the self-concept, the social cognition of the self, and self-motivation processes.*

THE SELF CONCEPT

One's thoughts and beliefs about who one is comprise the self-concept. This can be as simple and variable as a child's self-description, "I am eight years old" or "I am the second-best dancer in my class." It can be as multifaceted and detailed as the lines of a resumé. No one is born with a self-concept; it develops through one's lifetime, and varies across individuals. Research has indicated major sources of self-concept, and theories have explained how self-concept functions and changes.

Sources of Self-Concept

In general, self-concept emerges from forces within oneself and influences outside the self.

SELF-ESTEEM

Self-esteem refers to one's evaluation (positive or negative) of oneself. High self-esteem really refers to a high estimation of one's own value, abilities, and promise. Low self-esteem can involve harsh self-judgment for past experiences and low expectations for future achievements.

SOCIAL EVALUATION

Most of our information about ourselves comes from others, not initially from contemplation or self-reflection. Your beliefs about others' opinions of you—whether you are right or wrong, you cannot know—will nonetheless strongly influence your behavior, your willingness to change or not. Social evaluation processes can include reflected appraisal or direct feedback.

Reflected Appraisal. How do others view you? You may get a sense of how you appear to others by considering their actions and words toward you. By inferring another's opinion of you from his or her behavior toward you, and adopting that opinion as your own self-opinion, you are reflecting that other's appraisal. Your reflected appraisals are incorporated into your own self-concept.

In many ways our self-opinions are mirrors (reflections) of others' apparent appraisals of us. It is an easy transition from "Others tell me I'm not a good listener" to "I'm not a good listener."

Direct Feedback. When others—especially significant others like parents and close friends—acknowledge their evaluations of us, we are receiving direct feedback about our qualities and skills. Direct feedback is rarer than reflected appraisals, but is an obviously important source of one's self-concept.

Different personality theories address the importance of direct feedback for personal adjustment and self-actualization (development to the fullest extent of one's abilities). For example, if as a child you were repeatedly told by your parents that, "We'd be so proud of you if you would only do better in school," you develop a poor self-concept, and the sense that others' love and pride is conditional on your performance. In contrast, according to humanistic personality theorists, you are more likely to become a happy, healthy adult if you are given unconditional positive regard from others, direct feedback that love for you is not conditional on your specific behaviors.

Theories of Self-Concept

One's self-concept includes not only ideas about oneself but also cherished beliefs and attitudes. One theory about the self-concept—social comparison theory—focuses on how comparison with others influences our beliefs. Another—self-presentation theory—examines the relationship between our actions and our understanding of our attitudes and goals.

SOCIAL COMPARISON

One of the modern social psychology's most influential theorists was Leon Festinger (1919–1989), whose social comparison theory helps to explain a broad variety of phenomena, including social beliefs, attitude change, and group communication.

Basic Tenets. In its simplest form, social comparison theory has four tenets:

1. Everyone has certain beliefs.

2. It is important for our beliefs to be correct.

3. Some beliefs are harder to verify than others. Those which cannot be objectively verified may be subjectively verified through consensual validation (getting others to agree).

4. When members of a reference group disagree with each other about beliefs, they will communicate until the conflict is resolved.

A key tenet to self-concept is the third point, that subjective beliefs, which cannot be proven objectively, can only be verified when we consult others' opinions. This process of evaluating our own beliefs in terms of others' is social comparison.

A simple example of social comparison involves deciding what to wear to an upcoming social event like a party. You could bring one or two wardrobe changes to the party, look to see how others are dressed, and change to match them if necessary. More simply, you can ask others what they plan to wear, and use their answers to guide your own attire.

Similarity Hypothesis. We usually choose to compare ourselves only with others who are similar to us. This similarity hypothesis is especially true in evaluations of performance. An exception can occur in evaluations of opinions. We may feel our opinions confirmed by others' agreement, even if those others are in most ways dissimilar to us.

Related Attributes Hypothesis. We compare our performance not only to those who are similar, but to those we think should be similar to ourselves. For example, a woman who is a mother and works outside the home may wonder how good she is at both roles. If she compares herself to mothers who do not have outside jobs, she may conclude she is an inferior mother. Likewise if she compares herself with working non-mothers, she will conclude that, compared to them, she is not the most dedicated worker. Both are inappropriate comparison standards. By comparing herself with persons with related attributes—other mothers, approximately her age, with similar outside careers—she will arrive at the fairest self-evaluation.

Downward Comparisons. We usually conduct social comparisons with others who are similar to us or should be. In special cases we may compare ourselves to people we think inferior in some way; these are downward comparisons. They are most likely to occur when we feel personally disappointed or as if we have failed. Research shows that completing sentences like "I'm glad I'm not a..." lead people to feel better about themselves and their circumstances. Thus downward comparisons can lead to mood- or self-improvement at the cost of denigrating others.

Consequences of Social Comparison. In some forms, social comparison may be deliberately biased for purposes of self-enhancement, as in false comparison effects (see Self-Serving Biases, below).

In most cases social comparison is an almost automatic process, however. Social comparison is usually restricted to relevant others. If you wanted to know how well you were doing in your psychology class, you would compare yourself to other students in that class, not students in your history class. Comparing ourselves with relevant others—people with common backgrounds or goals—affects the ways we evaluate ourselves. For example, if you are a new student of the violin, comparing yourself to a famous violinist might lead you to evaluate yourself negatively, and lead to discouragement. If your teacher encourages you to compare your performance to other students your age—or to yourself just a few months ago—you are more likely to develop a positive self-evaluation and to feel encouraged in your efforts.

SELF-PERCEPTION

Socrates's admonition to "know thyself" is easier said than done. Research suggests that we are no more experts about our own actions and intentions than we are about others'. According to theorist Daryl Bem, when assessing our own opinions, we review our obvious behaviors for clues, rather than engaging in deep self-analysis. For example, if you are asked what your favorite color of clothing is, you might mentally review your wardrobe to discover that you own and wear one color more than others—although that might not have been your own guess about yourself. This process of self-perception involves learning about ourselves, and figuring ourselves out, in the same way that we try to understand others.

Self-Attribution. As will be examined further in chapter 6, it is important to explain behavior, or make attributions, for ourselves as well as others. Self-perception theory suggests that in making self-attributions we consult our present and remembered actions and try to perceive an explanation in their pattern.

Research on experiencing and expressing emotions confirms this explanation for self-attribution. By "faking" an emotion—posing one's face to express an extreme feeling, like happiness or anger—one can apparently "make" it real—begin to experience it genuinely. Self-perception theory explains that, when trying to understand how we feel, we believe the evidence of our faces: "I was smiling, so I guess I was enjoying myself."

Overjustification. A similar self-perception process works with inferring our own intentions and goals. For example, knowing that someone is paid well to do a difficult job leads us to conclude that money—an extrinsic goal—is his prime motivation. In contrast, if someone is working very hard on a task for free, we infer that she must enjoy it—that is, she has strong intrinsic motivation.

Conversely, what happens if you are paid for something you have usually enjoyed doing? According to self-perception theory, you may feel overjustified for your behavior, and enjoy it less (lessen your intrinsic motivation) as a result. For example, if a child who likes to do her mathematics homework is given a one-dollar reward for completing it by her well-intentioned parents, she may reconsider her own motives. Feeling overjustified (having enjoyed work on a challenging assignment, plus receiving one dollar), she may perceive herself to be less fond of math. Eventually, the reward tactic may backfire, when she decides that she will only do homework if she is promised a bonus.

Another example of overjustification is made by consumer products that are promoted with promises of extra bonuses or rebates. If you go to the store to buy a box of your favorite cereal, and the package boasts a free toy inside, you may feel overjustified ("cereal I like, plus a free toy"). In a later shopping expedition, when you can only find toy-less boxes, you may feel you lack justification for buying "just the cereal." Thus if a bonus or external reward leads to overjustification, self-perception theory predicts that we reduce our preference for the original behavior or item. This occurs because, in our efforts to understand ourselves, we may reevaluate habits and preferences in terms that make more sense.

SOCIAL COGNITION OF THE SELF

As suggested by William James (above), oneself can be an object of one's own thought processes. Thus an understanding of social cognition (see chapter 3) will help in comprehending much about the social self. In fact one's thinking about oneself is very much a function of one's consideration of the social world. Self-cognition is revealed in research on self-awareness, self-schemata, and the self among others.

Self-Awareness

Self-awareness is a state in which one's attention is focused on oneself, on one's feelings, state of mind, values, intentions, and/or evaluation by others. The context and consequences determine which aspect of self-awareness is most important in one's social behavior.

DEFINING SELF-AWARENESS

A distinction can be made between self-awareness and self-consciousness.

Objective Self-Awareness. One achieves objective self-awareness when one focuses attention on specific aspects of oneself. Some natural experiences can heighten objective self-awareness, such as hearing the sound of one's name or seeing oneself reflected in a mirror. Social experiences like being the only male in a group or making a public presentation can also heighten self-awareness. Research suggests that, when people are made self-aware, they are more likely to act in accordance with their standards. For example, an honest child who is tempted to steal candy may resist the urge if she sees her reflection in a store mirror.

Self-Consciousness. Concern with oneself, of self-consciousness, can be either privately or publicly induced. Private self-consciousness refers to internal concern with oneself, including one's physical sensations and emotional state. Public self-consciousness refers to a concern about how one is being evaluated by others.

REDUCED SELF-AWARENESS

Just as situational factors like hearing your name or seeing your reflection in a mirror can increase your momentary self-awareness, other circumstances appear capable of reducing it. When self-awareness is reduced, we are less likely to act in accord with our values. We may be disinhibited—feeling free to act in ways of which others would normally disapprove.

The state of reduced self-awareness is known as deindividuation. Research on deindividuation indicates that it can be created by stimulus conditions including immersion in a group, physical or social anonymity, and arousing or distracting activities. For example, if you are caught up in the noise and excitement of a crowded concert or sports event, you may find yourself jumping from your seat or screaming—behaviors you would not engage in if you were alone, identifiable, or in calm, quiet surroundings. Deindividuation explains some aspects of crowd behavior and criminal activity as a consequence of social and environmental conditions (see chapter 11).

Self-Schemata

Recall from chapter 3 that schemata are mental categorizations of ideas about stimuli. Applying that meaning, self-schemata are one's own sets of self-generalizations, derived from both personal and other evaluations of self. Schemata guide the way information is processed. Thus your self-schemata affect the way you consider and recall new information and opportunities about yourself.

For example, if your self-schemata includes the idea of being "physically uncoordinated," then you will consult this unathletic schema before agreeing to join a softball game or try out for a school team. Self-schemata might be limiting but for the fact that they are dynamic: they change in the wake of new experiences and information.

SCHEMATICITY

Specific personality traits—stable behavioral tendencies—may be either schematic or aschematic for a person's self-concept.

Schematic Traits. A schematic trait or dimension is one that is relevant, one that is important in the way a person thinks about himself or herself.

For example, a student who prides herself on her school performance may consider "intelligence" a schematic trait. Another student whose family is happy if he makes C's might have more concern with other traits, like honesty or popularity.

Aschematic Traits. Personality traits which are not important to a person's self-concept are termed aschematic for him or her. In the above example, "intelligence" is aschematic for the C-student, although other characteristics and qualities might be highly schematic.

SELF-REFERENCE

Just as some traits are schematic—relevant to one's self-description—so also is some information self-relevant. Such information is considered self-referent. Information that is relevant to oneself is usually better attended and more accurately recalled, a tendency called the self-reference effect.

For example, a woman is planning a career as a music teacher. Music and teaching are thus important to her self-schema—part of the way she thinks about and organizes information in memory. She is more likely, therefore, to notice when news media mention stories about upcoming concert series or legislation that affects teachers' salaries. She is also more likely to remember correctly any details of previously learned information, especially in comparison with information that is not self-referent.

NEGATIVE AFFECT

Self-schemata comprise standards for oneself. In some cases these may perpetuate low self-esteem. In other cases, when one's behavior violates those standards, one experiences disappointment and other negative emotions.

Depression. Are self-schemata always developed in one's best interests? Research indicates that the self-schemata of depressive persons, for example, have a large amount of negative information. Such negative sets can prejudice new experiences by causing one to interpret new information as "proof" of one's lack of worth. Thus negative self-schemata are self-perpetuating in the mind of the depressed person.

Self-Discrepancies. How does one handle experiences and information that contradict one's self-schemata? For example, a man aspires to be a good father to his children, but wishes to advance in a job that demands he work evenings and weekends. He finds that in being a good worker he spends less time with his children; to be a good worker he must compromise his aspirations to be a good father.

Research indicates that different self-discrepancy conflicts result from conflicts among different aspects of oneself. Disparity between one's actual self and one's ideal self (the self one personally aspires to be) results in depression and dejection experiences like disappointment and sadness. Alternatively, conflict between one's actual self and one's "ought" self (the self one feels responsible or duty-bound to be) results in anxiety, and agitations like guilt or discomfort.

POSSIBLE SELVES

Most people are aware that they change in many ways across time and situations. We may also consider that we might be very different today if we had chosen the "road not taken" or selected a different partner, college, or place to live.

Ideal Selves and Ought Selves. It may be that one's "possible selves" are really extensions of parts of one's working self-concept. For example, one of your "ideal selves" might be thinner or fitter than your actual self, another "ideal self" might be a better scholar, and so on. Further, you may possess several "ought selves," one that lives up to your parents' expectations, another that meets the needs of your friends, and so on.

Effects of Possible Selves. Possible selves influence motivation by providing incentive for self-improvement or self-change programs. For example, an overweight woman who imagines a thinner self may work harder to achieve fitness than one who cannot imagine such a possible self.

Possible selves affect discrepancies between one's own self-estimations and others' appraisals. For example, if a young man's parents do not understand his dream of becoming a musician, they may not respect or encourage the work he tries to do to realize his goal. This conflict may develop because he is able to imagine himself as a successful musician, making this a worthwhile goal, while his parents cannot see him in that way, judging his aspirations to be foolish and unrealistic.

Finally, possible selves influence our emotions. As noted earlier, discrepancies between aspects of our self-concept can lead to experiences like anxiety or depression. Conflicts between possible selves may lead to extensions of such mood states that affect immediate and future behaviors.

SELF-MOTIVATION

Much social psychological research has focused on the ways the self is motivated to collect information, remember and process it, and act in the social world. The daunting list of self-motivations can be summarized in the three broad categories of self-consistency, self-enhancement, and self-control.

Self-Consistency

Our conceptions of ourselves are resistant to change. This is equally true of negative and positive self-concepts. An explanation for this is that we are motivated to maintain consistency among our past and present self-evaluations, as well as among various cognitive elements (e.g., attitudes, behavioral intentions; see chapter 8).

THE IMPORTANCE OF CONSISTENCY

Research indicates that, when aspects of self-concept are challenged, people usually respond by reaffirming their original self-appraisals, rather than reconsidering them in light of contradiction. For example, if a normally competitive person is given direct feedback arguing that she does not seem very competitive, she will subsequently behave in a more competitive way (asserting her consistency with her own self-concept), rather than a less competitive way (conforming with the other's opinion).

BALANCE THEORIES

Classic theory in social psychology, developed by Fritz Heider (1896–1988) and others, has posited an individual preference for cognitive balance.

Balance and Imbalance. Cognitive elements like attitudes and intentions are in balance when they agree and are compatible. For example, if you like your psychology professor, you like your best friend, and your best friend also likes your psychology professor, these three sentiments are balanced for you.

In this example, if one of the relationships were negative, the triad would be imbalanced: If your best friend claimed to dislike your psychology professor, you might reconsider all three relationships. Perhaps your best friend is wrong, or perhaps you are wrong about liking your professor. Another possibility might be that you and your best friend are not very much alike after all.

Attitude Change. As can be seen, the need for balance can sometimes motivate us to change our minds. For example, suppose you see a celebrity whom you like recommending a product you have never heard of. Your need to keep your ideas and opinions in balance will predispose you to like this new product, on the strength of this celebrity's recommendation.

Balance can also backfire, as when someone you dislike advocates a position you were neutral about. To keep yourself distant from the disliked person, you might decide against the issue she advocates as well.

The need for elements within oneself to be in balance has important implications for attitude formation and change. Although it will be discussed further in that context (see chapters 8 and 9), it is important to remember that balance is one form of self-consistency.

SELF-JUSTIFICATION

An important form of self-motivation involves our rationalizations for our behavior. While humans are capable of reasoning, it is not evident that all human behavior is well-reasoned before it is enacted. Once committed, however, behavior can be rationalized. Supporting a behavior after it has been committed involves the process of self-justification.

Self-justification is a strong motivator for attitude change. This has been found to be true in cases of *cognitive dissonance,* an experience of tension when cognitive elements are in conflict. For example, a woman who believes that smoking causes cancer but still refuses to quit smoking will experience some cognitive dissonance: her beliefs and her habits are in conflict, so her behavior does not make sense. (See chapters 8 and 9 for further discussion of the role of cognitive dissonance in attitude formation and change).

Leon Festinger, who developed social comparison theory (above), has identified two circumstances that arouse the need to self-justify: insufficient justification and close decisions.

Insufficient Justification. When a person has done something that was unjustified, he may manufacture rationalizations—self-justification—to restore a sense of self-consistency. For example, if a man has spent too much money on a car that looks attractive but has received poor customer ratings, he may argue—to himself and others—that the car has great investment and resale value. He may sincerely believe this, but it is likely that his argument is an effort to justify imprudent spending.

Decision-Making. Self-justification is also prompted after one has made a close or difficult decision. For example, a woman must decide which of two colleges to attend. They are comparable in all the areas she considers important, but still she must decide. After choosing one over the other, she may find herself looking for flaws and problems in the non-chosen college, and identifying "obvious" advantages to having made the choice she did. Such post-decisional arguments are justifications of having made a choice that was, at the time, close and difficult.

Self-Enhancement

A major self-motivation is protection and maintenance of self-esteem. Some critics argue that many people suffer from low self-esteem, and humanistic personality theories cite the dangers of negative evaluations of self. However, social psychological research has largely concluded the resilience of many forms of self-enhancement, challenging others' negative appraisals and sometimes one's own experiences.

Some self-enhancement tendencies are accomplished through other self processes mentioned above: downward social comparisons, reassuring oneself of superiority compared with others; self-justification to rationalize seemingly self-contradictory behavior; and other applications of self-concept.

Beyond those already mentioned, three broad forms of self-enhancement have been studied: self-serving processes, related self-disparagement processes, and patterns of self-presentation processes.

SELF-SERVING PROCESSES

Self-serving processes generally involve forms of social cognition applied to protecting self-esteem. Three forms of self-serving processes are egocentric bias, false comparison effects, and beneffectance.

Egocentric Bias. Egocentricity—self-centeredness—can bias the way information is processed and recalled. When affected by the egocentric bias, one recalls self-relevant information better. One form of egocentric bias in relationships is to take credit for more than one's share of contribution to a combined effort. For example, researchers have found that, in couples describing how household chores are assigned, each partner exaggerates his or her own contribution. This may result from an attentional prejudice: you remember what you have done for your partner, but may not notice what your partner has done for you lately.

False Comparison Effects. As discussed above, social comparison is important in the development of self-concept. A self-enhancing bias in such social comparison involves false or erroneous comparison effects in the evaluation of one's positive or negative behaviors.

For example, if you have done something good and worthy of praise, you may reinforce your good self-opinion by concluding that few others would have reacted as you did. This self-serving process is called the *false-uniqueness effect*.

Another self-serving bias works in converse conditions. If you have done something wrong and worthy of blame, you might reassure yourself that others would surely have done as you did in the same circumstances. This variation is called the *false-consensus effect*.

Both illusory uniqueness and illusory consensus are egocentric biases, motivated by self-enhancement.

Beneffectance. Another self-serving process operates when we draw conclusions about ourselves from our own actions. The tendency to take credit for our successes while blaming away our failures is known as beneffectance. Beneffectance is a bias in attribution, the process of explaining behavior, when applied to oneself (see chapter 6).

Beneffectance is so natural that it is difficult to notice unless observers' contradict the actor's explanation. For example, if you are disappointed to watch your favorite team lose a game through sloppy playing, you will be surprised to hear the players blame their poor showing on bad weather conditions. In this example, your observer's perspective was somewhat more objective, while the actors' eyes were colored by beneffectance.

SELF-DISPARAGEMENT

If most people employ self-serving biases to protect their self-esteem, why would anyone criticize himself or herself? For example, when you compliment a friend for her attire, why would she say, "This dress? It's really old and out-of-fashion, and it doesn't really fit me very well." Research suggests that, rather than merely fishing for compliments, people may be using self-disparagement to meet self-serving ends.

For example, if you expect to do poorly in an important evaluation—like a test or an interview—you will want to reduce the blow to your self-esteem such failure can mean. One way to reduce the impact of failure is to attribute it to a "safer" flaw. If you sleep late the morning of the evaluation, you can later blame your poor showing on your late start. You will still have failed, but it is because you overslept one morning, not because you are inherently a failure.

Such a strategy—guaranteeing failure to provide a preferable excuse for it—is known as *self-handicapping*. It can be seen that self-handicapping is really undertaken to protect onself from an unacceptable failure. The problem with self-handicapping is that choosing a handy excuse guarantees a failure that was only guessed at beforehand.

SELF-PRESENTATION

Ironic processes like self-handicapping highlight the importance of how the self appears to others. Many self-cognitions are motivated by concerns for self-presentation. Three self-presentational processes are dramaturgical self-presentation; social accounting strategies; and self-monitoring.

Dramaturgical Self-Presentation. In his 1959 work *The Presentation of Self in Everyday Life,* sociologist Erving Goffman (1922-1983) introduces the notion that one "performs" for others to achieve desired effects. Popular concepts in this dramaturgical or theatrical approach include "lines" spoken or conveyed to others, arranging a "setting" so that one's home or office affects others evaluations, and relying on a "script" or constructed set of responses. Goffman's ideas may explain why someone behaves one way for one "audience" and differently for another.

Social Accounting. Even when we are with strangers, we feel some pressure to stick to a script. Because strangers do not know us, and cannot know how normal and reasonable we are, we engage in some social accounting to reassure them. One form of social accounting is *facework,* including looking embarrassed when we have committed a social blunder, or smiling briefly when a waiter or cashier makes eye contact.

Another form of social accounting is making *excuses.* These include both genuine excuses ("I'm sorry, please repeat that, I wasn't listening") and manufactured ones. For example, if you are late for a party because you overlooked the invitation, telling the truth might hurt the hostess's feelings (suggesting that it was too unimportant for you to remember). Thus you might instead say, "I apologize for arriving late, but I made a few wrong turns on my way here."

Self-Monitoring. Social psychologists have identified a self-presentational dimension or personality factor in which individuals seem to differ. At one extreme of this dimension are individuals who strongly monitor their social circumstances and produce behaviors that are most appropriate. At the other extreme are persons who present themselves essentially the same way in widely varying situations. These individuals are said to be respectively high or low on the trait of *self-monitoring*.

High self-monitors pay close attention to other people, seeking (and usually succeeding) in tailoring their own responses to best please others. They may say things they think others want to hear, and in extreme cases may distort their real opinions to please their audiences. In contrast, low self-monitors behave consistently across situations, keeping their values close to their actions and guiding their behavior according to principle, not by what is pragmatic.

Self-Control

An important motive identified by work in developmental and clinical psychology is self-control. People seem to need order and predictability in their experiences, at least in moderate levels. Work on social expressions of the self-control motive has identified two patterns: *learned helplessness*, behavior that is characterized by defeat and loss of control; and *self-efficacy*, behavioral strategies for restoring and maximizing self-control once more.

LEARNED HELPLESSNESS

Animals in some learning studies learned that none of their operant (voluntary) responses were effective in preventing painful shocks. Later the same animals in different surroundings did not attempt even simple strategies like escape or avoidance. Their earlier experiences had left them defeated and seemingly unmotivated, a condition termed *learned helplessness*.

Later studies showed not only that humans could also be trained to be helpless, but that helplessness could be learned after only a few defeats. Humans who had learned to be helpless did not attempt to solve problems or shut out unwanted stimuli. Helpless humans behave like victims, passive and unenergized. Learned helplessness has been identified as a danger of institutional care such as nursing homes for the elderly, hospitalization for the sick, and prisons for convicted offenders. With authority figures or skilled professionals taking over so many of one's responsibilities for oneself, a person seems to lose both the ability and the will to take care and make personal efforts.

SELF-EFFICACY

What learned helplessness destroys is a sense of efficacy, the effectiveness or sense of control that comes from having success and power at doing things for oneself.

Self-efficacy is affected by cognitive biases. In other words, thinking negatively—"I can't do this, my efforts will surely fail!"—can cause one to withhold effort. The children's story of "The Little Engine that Could" is a moral lesson in the value of thinking positively. Research shows that people high in self-efficacy are likely to think creatively about solving problems, looking for new approaches rather than giving up too soon.

Self-efficacy can also be enhanced with the experience of success. Therapists treating those with depression—often marked by the resignation and lethargy of learned helplessness—often recommend a program of challenging yet simple (almost guaranteeing success) tasks for behavior change. Each experience of success reverses the helpless or negative thinking pattern. Eventually, a series of successes serve to reassure one that, with skill and practice, one gains a sense of self-control and power.

Social processes begin with the structure and function of the social self. Research on the social self generally has focused on three broad aspects: the self-concept; the social cognition of the self; and self-motivation.

The self-concept consists of one's impressions and evaluations of one's qualities, abilities, and intentions. Two important sources of self-concept are self-esteem and social evaluation. Social evaluation involves interactions between self and others, such as reflected appraisal and direct feedback.

Two broad theories of how self-concept affects social behavior are social comparison and self-perception. Leon Festinger's social comparison theory addresses the way we rely on others to validate our subjective beliefs, and consult them for information about how we ought to behave. We usually rely only on similar others as a basis for comparison, or on people with similar roles or goals. Downward comparisons with those we consider inferior may be undertaken to reassure ourselves. Social comparison may be a relatively unthinking process, or deliberately undertaken for various social motives.

Self-perception theory characterizes people as relatively unknown to themselves until they review their own behavior. After reviewing our own behavior, we are able to make self-attributions of qualities and motives. Self-perception theory also proposes that when intrinsically attractive tasks are overjustified, their intrinsic value will be lessened to accommodate the excess external incentive.

Two broad emphases of research on social self-cognition are self-awareness and self-schemata. Self-awareness involves a focusing of attention on oneself, including processes like objective self-awareness, and both private and public self-consciousness. When self-awareness is reduced, social inhibitions on some behaviors are removed. Such deindividuated persons become caught up in the activities around them, taking less responsibility for their actions.

Social cognitions focused on understanding oneself involve the use of self-schemata, mental categorizations about oneself. Schematic traits are specific qualities seen to be part of one's self-schemata. Qualities considered irrelevant to oneself are termed aschematic traits. Information that is considered self-referent appears to be better processed and remembered than other data. Self-cognitions can powerfully affect individuals' emotions, like depression. Different self-schemata may take the form of different possible selves. Possible selves can motivate goal-directed behavior, but discrepancies among these possible selves have different consequences for behavior and mood.

Three important self-motivations include self-consistency, self-enhancement, and self-control. Self-consistency processes like balance and self-justification involve maintaining harmony among cognitive elements like *attitudes and social relationships. Both self-serving processes and self-presentation strategies are forms of self-motivation. Self-serving tendencies like beneffectance and false comparison effects enhance self-esteem by promoting the best interpretations of one's motives and actions. An important variation is a pattern of self-disparagement, in which one criticizes or undervalues oneself, such as in self-handicapping.*

Self-presentation is also motivated by self-enhancement. Goffman's dramaturgical approach to self-presentation characterizes behavior in theatrical terms. Social accounting behaviors like facework and excuses are undertaken to reassure others of our normality. People vary in self-monitoring tendencies; high self-monitors modify their own behavior to fit the social circumstances, while low self-monitors behave consistently across situations.

A final self-motivation is self-control. Self-efficacy is essential to motivated behavior. Those who have learned to be helpless may defeat their own efforts or refuse to escape aversive conditions. Positive self-cognitions and success experiences have been found to reduce learned helplessness and promote a sense of self-efficacy.

Selected Readings

Bales, R. F. (1970). *Personality and Interpersonal Behavior*. New York: Holt, Rinehart and Winston.

Bandura, A. (1986). *Social Foundations of Thought and Action: A Social-Cognitive Theory*. Englewood Cliffs, NJ: Prentice Hall.

Chaikin, A. L. and V. L. Derlega. (1974). *Self-Disclosure*. Morristown, NJ: General Learning Press.

Duval, S. and R. A. Wicklund. (1972). *A Theory of Objective Self-Awareness*. New York: Academic Press.

Gergen, K. J. (1971). *The Concept of Self*. New York: Holt, Rinehart and Winston.

Goffman, E. (1959). *The Presentation of Self in Everyday Life*. Garden City, NY: Doubleday.

Hewitt, J. P. (1984). *Self and Society: A Symbolic Interactionist Social Psychology*, 3rd edition. Boston: Allyn and Bacon.

Rosenberg, M. (1979). *Conceiving the Self*. New York: Basic Books.

Schlenker, B. R. (1980). *Impression Management*. Monterey, CA: Brooks/Cole.

Schlenker, B. R. (1985). *The Self and Social Life*. New York: McGraw-Hill.

Snyder, C. R., R. L. Higgins, and R. J. Stucky. (1983). *Excuses: Masquerades in Search of Grace*. New York: Wiley.

Snyder, M. (1987). *Public Appearances/Private Realities: The Psychology of Self-Monitoring*. New York: Freeman.

Suls, J. (1982). *Psychological Perspectives on the Self*, Volume 1. Hillsdale, NJ: Erlbaum.

Suls, J. and A. G. Greenwald. (1983). *Psychological Perspectives on the Self*, Volume 2. Hillsdale, NJ: Erlbaum.

Suls, J. and R. J. Miller. (Eds.). (1977). *Social Comparison Processes: Theoretical Empirical Perspectives*. Washington, DC: Hemisphere/Halsted.

Tedeschi, J. T. (Ed.). (1981). *Impression Management Theory and Social Psychological Research.* New York: Academic Press.

Wegner, D. M. and R. R. Vallacher. (1980). *The Self in Social Psychology.* New York: Oxford University Press.

5

Person Perception

*H*umans are social animals. As important as a sense of self is to all aspects of human thought and behavior, other people seem to be consistently more interesting to us than ourselves. As other chapters in this text review, we consult others' opinions in forming our self-concepts (chapter 4), we alter our opinions and actions under persuasion or pressure from others (chapters 9, 10, and 11), and rearrange our physical environments to get a better view of other people (chapter 18).

Social thinking—with both its skills and its flaws—is applied in every contact we have with others. It is important for us to understand others, so that we can predict how they will behave, and thus control how they will affect us in turn.

Strong motivation is no guarantee of accurate person perception. The strategies we rely on can sometimes lead us to incorrect conclusions and mistaken judgments of others. As discussed in chapter 3, such errors and biases result from misuse of processes that usually serve us well. This chapter examines the sequence of social information processing, and reviews examples of both successful and unsuccessful person perception.

Social inference—making sense out of what we learn about others— begins with the collection of social data: social information like traits and names; physical appearances; nonverbal cues; and the evidence of others' actions. These many forms of social data are integrated and compiled to form impressions: social concepts are formed; impressions are organized; and social information is processed into social judgments.

SOURCES OF SOCIAL INFERENCE

Our first contacts with other people are not necessarily first-hand or personal encounters. Every day we receive mail and telephone contacts from people we have never met. Among our social networks, we near names and descriptions of others before we meet them ourselves. Experience has also taught us to draw rich conclusions from meager data: merely from another person's accent we might guess at his or her point of origin, temperament, and values.

Four common sources of social inference are reviewed here: social information about others; physical appearance; cues from nonverbal communication; and the implications of others' actions.

Social Information

Cognitive psychologists study the way humans function as information processors. Unique among the animal world, humans appear to have strong needs for information. Gestalt theories of perception describe the human search for meaning as powerfully influential in the way even inadequate or distorted data are interpreted.

We seem particularly hungry for information about other people. Aside from the evidence of our own senses and encounters with others, we rely heavily on several forms of social information: traits; names; and stereotypes.

TRAITS

A trait is a relatively stable and enduring personality tendency. It is a term or phrase that describes the way a person behaves across most situations. Allowing for occasional exceptions, a person described by the trait "generous" is assumed to behave in a giving and magnanimous way most of the time.

The importance of traits as a source of social information can be seen in the popularity and frequency of trait words in our language. Many different words can be used to conjure up similar impressions, each a shade distinct from its synonyms. For example, a generous person could be described as open, giving, free, unselfish, magnanimous, philanthropic, or excessive. The existence of so many terms in our language indicates a need for precision in social descriptions.

Traits are generalizations about behavior. Given exceptions and situational influences, it is unlikely that a generous person is generous all the time, or that an introvert never reaches out to others. Thus the attachment of a trait as a label involves some error: exceptions are ignored; extremes are expected. As will be seen in further discussion in this chapter (Impression Formation), these errors can be compounded when traits are organized as the major source of social inference about others.

NAMES

All names are not created equal. Research has confirmed that some names are considered more socially desirable and attractive than others. What is considered an attractive name also depends on the cultural and ethnic group in question. Names are considered more attractive if they sound familiar rather than unusual, and are easier rather than more difficult to pronounce.

Research suggests that when perceivers are given further, more important information about the named targets, the name-bias effects are diluted and disappear. That is, if you must choose between a candidate with an unattractive name who agrees with your values and one with an attractive name who disagrees, you will most likely favor the former. Names, then, do not appear to be lasting influences on others' impressions, although they can affect others' willingness to collect information beyond those names in the first place.

STEREOTYPES

A stereotype is a generalization about a category of people that sets them apart from other groups. For example, Americans may be stereotyped as loud and impolite by members of a culture that encounters tourist-class travelers from the United States. While there may be a kernel of truth in a stereotype, it is necessarily distorted by generalizing to new cases. For example, most of the Americans a hotel worker has encountered may well have been aggressive and poor tippers. But this does not guarantee that the next American she meets will have those qualities. Her stereotype of Americans will bias her new experiences—and possibly have the effect of a self-fulfilling prophecy, bringing about the very behaviors the perceiver expects.

Simplification and Social Judgment. A stereotype is a mental shortcut of the type reviewed in chapter 3. It simplifies social thinking because it summarizes experiences and associations with an entire group of people. It can lead to quicker and better social judgments if applied sensibly.

For example, a young woman has learned from her experience that young children like to get their way when challenged, and that they may cry when frustrated. She relies on this stereotype when caring for her neighbor's six-year-old daughter, finding ways to compromise at bathtime and bedtime, and not taking it personally or reacting angrily when the child cries.

Oversimplification and Prejudice. Because stereotypes are generalizations to new cases based on what may be limited experience, they can easily involve oversimplification. For example, a man who believes Southern Americans are not as intelligent as those from other regions may err in applying this stereotype to a new business acquaintance. Underestimating his colleague's intelligence, he may insult her or misjudge her ability to gain the advantage in negotiations.

Relying on a stereotype to make an inappropriate judgment about an individual is prejudice. Prejudices can technically be positive, but the term is usually applied only to negative evaluations of others without basis in experience. As will be discussed in chapter 12, prejudices can become the basis for unfair discrimination, behaving differently toward others solely on the basis of perceived group membership.

Prejudice and discrimination can result from the oversimplification of stereotypes. Because stereotypes are generalizations—not precise sets of data—they are only useful when considered in addition to, not as substitutes for, first-hand personal experience.

Appearances

Do appearances count for everything? Many cliches argue that clothes make the man or that a woman's looks are everything. Certainly, in first-hand encounters, physical appearance can be a powerful source of social data. Research has confirmed that socially desirable appearance usually has the effect of increasing attraction, while undesirable physical features can reduce or handicap attraction.

PHYSICAL ATTRACTION

While there are both individual and cultural differences in what features and combinations are considered good-looking, most people are attracted to those considered physically appealing. The appearance-attraction effect has consequences for person perception. Two forms of this effect are the halo effect and the physical attractiveness stereotype.

The Halo Effect. The detection of one important characteristic can bias the way other information about a person is interpreted. For example, if you like the way a new acquaintance looks, you may expect to like other things about him or her: stated attitudes, hobbies and preferred activities, style of interaction, and so on. As reviewed in the earlier discussion of self-fulfilling prophecy (see chapter 3), expecting other good things can lead you to distort your perceptions so that you only see what you expect.

The tendency of early social information to color the perception of later data is called the halo effect. Halo effects can be very strong in matters of personal appearance. Classic research has shown that attractive people are judged more generously and given lighter penalities for breaking rules, while those judged unattractive are judged more harshly and punitively.

The Physical Attractiveness Stereotype. Despite variability in what is considered attractive, within most cultures standards are agreed upon for determining who is or is not good-looking. In our culture as in many, what is beautiful is judged to be good, or better than what is not beautiful. This equation of looks with value is the physical attractiveness stereotype.

Research shows that this equation is indeed a stereotype—an unfounded generalization—rather than an accurate perception of how character is related to appearance. Individuals who are judged to be physically attractive have been found to be no more successful, intelligent, or benevolent than less attractive persons. There is, however, an expectancy effect that qualifies these findings. Because people are attracted to those who are good-looking, good-looking people may be more likely to experience social successes like early (not necessarily lasting) marriage, or the positive social judgments cited above.

STIGMA

Just as physically appealing people are given a desirable and attractive social label, those who are unattractive are often given an undesirable label. A social label that defines a person as deviant, flawed or undesirable is a stigma.

Examples. Examples of stigmas in modern society include obesity, terminal illness, physical and mental handicaps.

Not all stigmas are equal; some are "better" than others because they are easier to conceal, temporary, or nonthreatening to others. The worst stigmas are conditions that are obvious, unattractive, chosen rather than involuntary, disruptive and dangerous. Such stigmas are the source of severe social prejudice, and lead to social avoidance, ostracism, and discrimination.

For example, having AIDS (Acquired Immune Deficiency Syndrome) is generally considered a stigma. Although it is a complex illness with different symptoms and different sources, AIDS is often seen as such an important negative feature that a sufferer may be seen purely in terms of the illness.

Inferences. Why does the perception of stigma result in such irrational behavior as avoiding eye contact with a person using a wheelchair or denying civil rights to AIDS victims? One theory cites the power of stigmas to remind perceivers of their own vulnerability and mortality. To deny such threats, we distance ourselves from stigmatized individuals.

A related social inference about stigma is that victims must have deserved or brought upon themselves their difficulties. This is one result of the just world bias, a belief tendency that is correlated with prejudiced attitudes (see chapter 12). Unfortunately such irrational social judgments deny help and compassion to those in society who most need it.

Nonverbal Communication

Another aspect of interaction that can be processed for social information is nonverbal communication. While the vast majority of cultures rely on verbal and symbolic communication, other sources of information are contributed by nonverbal forms of behavior and expression. Different forms, combinations, and expressions vary in their significance to the perceiver.

TYPES OF NONVERBAL CUES

While nonverbal cues can be found in most aspects of human behavior, the categories most researched include facial expression, eye contact, body position and posture, movement and gesture, and voice qualities.

Facial Expression. The face is used to communicate the expression of affect or emotion. Researchers have identified six emotions that are most accurately recognized worldwide: happiness, sadness, anger, fear, surprise, and disgust.

Studies of nonverbal skills have indicated that women are more expressive than men in sending facial signals, and more sensitive than men in receiving and correctly interpreting them on others' faces. Other research suggests that facial expressiveness is negatively related to physiological arousal: those whose faces show what they are feeling do not register emotional arousal as highly as those who remain unexpressive or "poker-faced."

Eye Contact. When people's spatial relationships do not match their social intentions, they use eye-contact to mediate the difference. For example, if a stranger is sitting very close to you on a crowded bus or subway, you will probably avoid eye contact with him or her. This protects your privacy behaviorally if not geographically. Conversely, if the object of your affections is across a crowded room, you and the other person will probably make much more eye contact—to compensate for the separation—than you would if you were closer together.

The size and gaze of a person's eyes are judged in forming impressions. Wide eyes and dilated pupils are judged more attractive or receptive; this may have a factual basis, since arousal due to interest results in slightly widened eyes and dilated pupils. A direct gaze is interpreted as a sign of liking—up to a point: constant, uninterrupted staring is interpreted as a threat.

Eye contact operates as a "distance closer" between interacting people. We stand closer to others when their eyes are shaded, closed, or averted, and farther apart when open and directed toward ours. Research shows that museum visitors similarly stand closer to portraits with closed eyes, but back up while viewing open-eyed, directly gazing portraits.

Body Language. Specific fine-motor movements—like hand signals and sign language—are interpreted distinctively across subcultures. However, general large-body movements and postures are more freely interpreted. Some meanings are obvious: erect postures suggest alertness, while slumped postures look fatigued. Others are inferred: open postures may indicate approval or acceptance, while closed postures suggest rejection or disagreement.

For example, a saleswoman may feel encouraged to talk to a customer whose arms are relaxed and open, and who leans slightly forward while she extols the product's virtues. She might feel less effective and even rejected if the customer leaned away from her with his arms tightly crossed.

Symmetry of the arms can indicate attention or tension, while asymmetry can show relaxation. Depending on the context, either posture might be appropriate or not. For example, if you are talking to a friend, asymmetrically resting one arm behind your chair shows your comfort with your friend; sitting that way while talking with your supervisor or professor might seem disrespectful.

It is important to remember that body "language" is really a collection of movements, postures, and positions that may have less to do with a message than such goals as comfort or efficient movement. Patterns can only be meaningfully interpreted within a specific context, and when the target person has been observed over a wide variety of circumstances. Thus a given person crossing her arms while you talk to her may be indicating rejection—or simply the choice of a more comfortable physical position for the moment.

Gestures. Finer motor movements of the fingers, hands, and arms relative to the body can have specific meanings in different cultures. Some meanings symbolize words or sentences, as in making a V-for-victory shape with the fingers of one hand. Others are meaningful in the context of interaction, as when a hand is held up to halt the speaker's comments, or a student raises her hand to ask a question.

The use of gestures varies across cultures. Some ethnic groups and nationalities may "talk with their hands" more than others. In such contexts the gestures add important information to words that, alone, could be interpreted several different ways.

Voice. Even when you cannot hear another person's words clearly, you may be able to judge the emotion or intention of the speaker. The study of how tone and pace of voice contribute to communication is called paralinguistics. Research in paralinguistics has identified nonverbal voice qualities like pitch, loudness, and pacing that are associated with different emotions and situations. For instance, a loud or raised voice speaking quickly and abruptly can sound angry, while a hesitant, whispering one seems afraid.

SIGNIFICANCE AND FUNCTIONS OF NONVERBAL CUES

Nonverbal cues provide information along several dimensions of communication and impression formation. Three such dimensions include immediacy, affect, and modification of communication.

Immediacy. Immediacy refers to the closeness or presence of another person. Greater immediacy can be signalled by moving the entire body closer to another, or by making increased eye contact. Depending on the context, increased immediacy can indicate liking or dominance, while reduced immediacy can indicate dislike or submissiveness.

Increased immediacy can indicate liking, as when one person moves closer to another to be more accessible. It can also indicate dominance, as when a teacher stands over a student he is criticizing to intimidate or impress him.

An example of reduced immediacy to connote dislike would be moving to the sidelines at a party to avoid conversation with someone who is being too forward with you. An example of reduced immediacy in social status relations is bowing or curtsying—lowering one's posture and averting gaze before an authority figure—to indicate respect.

Affect. Less specific than liking or dominance are general expressions of one's emotions—happiness, anger, sadness, or such. Involuntary facial expressions can reveal the wearer's feelings if they are expressive enough or if the viewer is sensitive enough to read them. Nonverbal expressions of affect can be controlled somewhat, as when tearful mourners stiffen their faces and refrain from crying in public.

Many emotional experiences are combinations of feelings and are hard to decipher in others' nonverbal expressions and cues. For example, research shows that while some emotions are almost universally expressed and interpreted (see above, Facial Expression), others are displayed differently for different groups and individuals, and thus interpreted inaccurately.

Some nonverbal behaviors function as *adaptors,* unconsciously reflecting our emotional states. A confused or worried student may rub her forehead while she studies new material. A mechanic searching for engine problems may purse his lips while he investigates. A person on a date may betray both nervousness and attraction by fidgeting, tugging an earlobe, or brushing hair back with the fingers. While these involuntary actions all suggest conflict or distraction, the actions and patterns of adaptors differ widely from one individual to the next.

Modifying Communication. Researchers have classified several categories of nonverbal cues according to their communication uses. *Emblems* are gestures that symbolize specific definitions, like the hand signals for "V-for-victory" and "A-okay." These can vary and the same gesture may have dramatically different meanings across cultures.

Illustrators assist verbal communication by demonstrating actions or physical relationships. For example, snapping the fingers can illustrate that something happened quickly, and a rolling motion of hand and wrist can illustrate that a story went "on and on."

While speaking, we sometimes use *regulators* to signal pacing and turn-taking with our conversational partners. Nodding, holding the hands palm up, and leaning forward all indicate attention and encouragement to a speaker, while shaking the head, raising the hand palm outward, and turning away all signal discouragement or ending the interaction.

The fact that some cues are involuntary and others deliberate, some universal and others culture-specific, suggests that nonverbal behaviors can be both learned and biologically innate or influenced. Despite the diversity of cues available and their range of meanings (or meaninglessness), it is impressive that we rely on nonverbal behaviors so often and so effectively in forming impressions of others.

ACTIONS

To review, much information is collected before one ever meets the target person; other data are collected in the earliest moments of first interaction. In all fairness, however, in forming impressions, most people pay closest attention to others' behavior. Impressions are seldom frozen at an early point; new experiences and first-hand observations are weighted strongly in making social judgments of others.

Attribution. When perceiving others' behavior, we are most concerned with understanding the reasons or causes for their actions. This process of inferring causes to behavior is termed attribution. Attribution is such an important process in social behavior it will be discussed in detail in chapter 6.

In general, attributions about others' actions locate causes in either one's disposition (personality, mood, or traits) or in one's situation (the immediate circumstances surrounding the behavior). Situational attributions for someone's behavior leave such behavior unpredictable. Dispositional attributions suggest that future action can be predicted from present explanations.

For example, if you are a passenger in a new friend's car, how do you interpret her fast and reckless driving? If you make a situational attribution—she is in a hurry because you are late in departing for your destination—you may expect that, in the future, she will drive more carefully. But if you make a dispositional attribution—she is not a very attentive or careful person in general—you may decide not to ride with her in the future. Attributions thus have consequences for social judgments and experiences.

Attributional Bias. The consequences of attribution seem more poignant given the biases that may distort interpretations of behavior. For example, in explaining others' actions, especially when the behavior is unexpected or negative, people seem prone to make dispositional rather than situational attributions. Because this is done without sure knowledge of the cause, such a tendency is a bias, frequently an error. Knowledge of attributional biases can reduce distortion in social perceptions and judgments.

IMPRESSION FORMATION

Once different sources have been consulted, how do people combine information to make social inferences and judgments? Researchers have identified three kinds of processes involved in applying person perception: forming social concepts, organizing impressions, and processing social information.

Social Concepts

Is the social world something that is "out there" and is our job merely to observe it accurately? Some theorists argue that, on the contrary, our social experiences are constructed by us as we interpret our experiences and attach meanings to them. For example, we commonly sort the people we encounter into different age groups—distinguishing children from grown-ups, for instance. However, in most situations individuals of all different ages interact, rather than keeping strictly within their age-determined boundaries. Thus age groups are concepts—ideas we have that help us to organize the social world—rather than real qualities of the individuals we encounter.

Categories or groups of qualities that help us to think about people are social concepts. Such social concepts as age group, race, gender, and familiarity help us to distinguish between friends and enemies, men and women, and other distinctions in how we might judge and behave with each other.

CONCEPT DEVELOPMENT

Social concepts are developed through natural experience, learning, and language.

Experience. In the course of experience, people develop ways to distinguish among different types or categories of others they encounter. Some experiences are different in the way they are first processed by our senses. These lead to the development of *natural categories*. Natural categories in person perception occur among diferent kinds of *action,* not necessarily different groups of people. For example, a woman who is talking to a classroom full of students is naturally different from a woman who is running on an outdoor track. The same woman may engage in actions at different times and places; an observer would notice the change in her movement, and categorize her actions differently.

People may also be organized by patterns of behavior and characteristics. A general category into which many individuals might fit is a prototype. Some prototypes are more vivid—like "soldier"—while others are more diffuse—like "mother." There are some ways in which all soldiers are similar, and these may be imagined or pictures. But mothers can be so different from each other that it is not possible to picture a "typical" mother without costly distortion.

Learning. Social concepts are also learned through associations, reinforcement, and hypothesis testing. Thus a child is likely to acquire and use similar social concepts as his parents, by associating labels with meanings, or being rewarded for adopting the parents' language. Older children and adults use hypothesis testing by guessing at a concept to categorize someone, and having this guess confirmed by subsequent experience. For example, is your new teacher dressed strangely because she has no taste in clothing, or because she wants to make a value statement? By guessing that her attire is deliberate, and asking about it, you can discover something important about her that can influence your future interactions.

Language. Some words specifically describe people rather than objects or events. For example, a new coworker might be meaningfully described as diligent or energetic—but not as edible or hollow. The words our language uses to describe people can influence the qualities we perceive about them. Thus language shapes concepts as well as it articulates them.

For example, a newspaper article might refer to a 19-year-old male as a "youth" or a "man" but to a 19-year-old female as a "girl." The use of "girl" instead of "woman" influences the way readers think about this person and her reported actions. Habits of language can result in powerful social labels with effects on social judgment and interactions.

CONCEPT APPLICATION

Once categories are developed, how are labels applied to specific people? Three criteria for labeling are resemblance, motivation, and context.

Resemblance. When a new social experience has elements in common with a past one, the previous label will be applied. For example, if you have previously applied the label "bore" to an acquaintance who told long, pointless stories at a party, you may extend the same label to a professor whose lectures are long and hard to follow.

Motivation. Just as self-serving biases can distort self-perception, so likewise can such biases alter impressions of others. For example, if you receive a low grade on a class assignment, you may prefer to judge your professor as unfair and unreasonable. Similarly, if your favorite team is beaten in a close match with a rival, you may prefer to judge the opponents to be cheaters who play rough.

Context. Behaviors mean different things in different contexts. For example, a parent's smile means one thing if the parent is listening to a child's story and quite another if the parent is spanking the child. In the former context, the smile suggests patient affection, whereas in the latter it suggests cruelty.

Contexts are not equally salient to observers. If you receive a disappointing grade in class, you may be too distracted by your own disappointment to pay much attention to how the teacher or other students are behaving. You may not perceive the context of the teacher's comments accurately as a result.

*Cognitive
Processing*

Another view of impression formation focuses on the quantity and diversity of social information that must be comprehended in a meaningful whole. Humans are information processors and organize impressions according to specific perception processes. Research has identified several strategies people use to make sense of social data: centrality; primacy versus recency; and salience.

CENTRALITY

Classic research by social psychologist Solomon Asch (b. 1907) showed that some traits influence the way others are interpreted. For example, if a person is described as "warm" and "intelligent," a different kind of intelligence is inferred than if one is described as "cold" and "intelligent." The warm-cold dimension is central to the impression formed, in that it colors interpretations of all other traits provided. Such influential characteristics are termed central traits.

Other research has suggested that all traits can be categorized along two dimensions: the value of the trait (bad or good) and the orientation or nature of the trait (social or intellectual). For example, a good-social trait like "warm" provides important context for an intellectual trait like "intelligent"—warm intelligence is different from other kinds of intelligence. Thus a "central" trait is one that provides additional context for impression formation.

PRIMACY VERSUS RECENCY

If social information like a list of traits is acquired over time, the order of information may affect each trait's value in the overall impression.

Most research on person perception and persuasive communication suggests that first impressions are strongest. Giving greater weight to early or first information received is the primacy effect.

In some circumstances the last information can have a lingering influence on the impression formed. For example, if you are warned that a new acquaintance makes a good first impression but may be untrustworthy, you may reserve judgment until you have proof of his treachery. Such reliance on last information as more influential is the recency effect.

While circumstances like forewarnings can make recency more influential, in the absence of such special considerations most people appear to trust primacy as an organizing principle of social impressions.

SALIENCE

Salience is noticeability, especially within a particular context. Conditions that make a social stimulus salient include brightness, noisiness, motion, and novelty.

For example, we are more likely to notice a loud person in a quiet group, and people who are moving rather than those sitting still nearby. We are more likely to notice the lone man in a group of women, and the only black person in an otherwise white group. Anything that makes a person unusual in the social context makes him or her salient.

Salient people draw more attention. Salient people are seen as causing events around them. We evaluate salient persons more extremely than those around them. If a salient person is also a member of a stereotyped social category, he or she will be judged more similar to the stereotype.

Applying Social Information

Social information provides the basis for social behavior. Research reveals two specific processes people employ in moving from impressions to actions: impression integration, and social judgment.

IMPRESSION INTEGRATION

How are different meanings about one person pulled together into a coherent impression? Strategies in impression integration include evaluation, averaging, consistency, and positivity.

Evaluation. The most important decision we make about others is whether we like or dislike them. This subjective judgment of goodness or badness is evaluation. Once you have decided whether you like someone, other information about him or her falls into place.

Averaging. When impressions of someone are mixed—some likable and others less so, some that suggest competence and others that question it—do they cancel each other out? Research suggests that such contradictory impressions are integrated by an unconscious process of averaging. Specifically, different qualities are not only evaluated (good or bad, positive or negative) but also weighted (important or not important). These values and weights are then combined, and their average impression is calculated.

Consistency. As impressions are collected about someone, they are simplified so that they agree with each other. This is an example of the value of consistency in social cognition, as discussed in chapter 3. The halo effect discussed above (Physical Attraction) is an example of a consistency bias in impression formation. For example, if early information about someone is judged to be positive, later impressions will be interpreted to be consistent with this judgment.

Positivity. Similar to the self-serving biases that incline people to support their self-esteem, people also appear to see others in the best possible light. Research indicates that people tend to rate others as above average, and are inclined to change only in the same (positive) direction. One explanation for this person-positivity bias is that it is an extension of a general desire to have good experiences, what has been dubbed the "Pollyanna principle" (after the fictional heroine who liked to see the good in everyone). Another view maintains that such positivity is a specific outcome of judging the similar humanity in others.

SOCIAL JUDGMENT

Before we act, we make social decisions. The most important of these decisions rests on our judgment of other people. How accurate are our social judgments? Research has examined two applications of social judgment: personality, and deception.

Personality. How good are people at judging others' personalities? This question is complicated by the lack of agreement about how to measure personality, and what kinds of behavior reflect it. The social relations model of personality perception posits that your judgment of someone you know will be determined by three things: you, the person you are rating, and the relationship between the two of you. Thus there is no such thing as an "objective" judgment of another's personality.

Research cited earlier (Centrality) concluded that judgments of others' personalities are made along two dimensions: good-bad, and social-intellectual. Other research argues that in judging others' personalities, people use a more precise model based on five factors: extroversion (outgoingness); agreeableness; conscientiousness; anxiety; and intelligence or culturedness. It can be seen that these five factors are more detailed versions of the two-dimension model cited earlier.

Deception. Do we always trust the information we get from and about others? Is trust warranted? Research has examined how accurately people detect deception, cues to deception and beliefs about deception.

In general researchers have found that perceivers are only slightly better than chance at judging whether others are deceiving them.

When perceivers are accurate in spotting deception, they seem to have relied on cues about the deceiver's body rather than face. Apparently the face is easier for liars to disguise than is the body. Perceivers are even more accurate when they consult voice cues as well as body cues to deception. Words as well as voice quality appear to betray deception.

Perceivers who are deceived may put their faith in baseless clues to deception. Researchers have found that perceivers think that such cues as eye contact, reduced smiling, and shifting in one's seat are all clues to lying—when in fact none of them are.

*S*ocial thinking is usually focused on understanding other people. Social information is gathered, interpreted, and acted upon. Social inference draws on information about others' characteristics, physical appearance, nonverbal cues, and the evidence of their actions.

Information about others includes traits, names, and the simplified information provided by stereotypes. Appearances count, and research confirms that physical appeal leads to interpersonal attraction. Physical appearance can cause halo effects when other positive qualities are expected on the basis of attractiveness. The physical attractiveness stereotype biases perceivers to believe that what is beautiful is also good in other ways. In contrast, negative impressions can be traced to stigma, features deemed socially undesirable by perceivers. Stigmas can lead others to blame, ostracize and punish stigmatized individuals.

Social inferences are made about nonverbal cues, including facial expression, eye contact, body language, gestures, and qualities of voice. Patterns of nonverbal communication, whether involuntary or deliberate, can convey information about immediacy in attraction or dominance, affect, and modifications of verbal communication.

Others' actions are interpreted for clues to their dispositions and future behavior. Attributions are explanations for others' behavior, and can identify causality within the actor's personality or as part of the surrounding situation. Biases in attribution may erroneously blame disposition and ignore situational influences, with important consequences for social experience.

Once social information is collected, impressions are formed as the basis for social behavior. Social concepts are categories of social qualities by which perceivers structure their experience of the social world. Such concepts are developed through experience, learning, and language. Concepts are applied to specific individuals on the basis of resemblance to past experiences, the motivation of the perceiver, and the context of the social information.

Social concepts are processed similarly to other forms of cognition. Certain features of people and events shape the impressions we form of them. Important qualities of social stimuli are centrality of the information or trait, primacy or recency of the order of information, and salience of the persons perceived.

Social information is applied in impression integration and social judgment. Impressions are integrated according to such criteria as evaluation of the target person, averaging of traits, consistency of an individual's characteristics, and positivity of impressions people usually form of others.

Social judgments of personality are difficult to assess because of lack of consensus about objective personality measurement. Judgments of personality are influenced by several factors, including the judge's characteristics and the relationship with the target person. As important as it is to detect deception, people appear to be little better at it than they would be by chance. Research shows that actual clues to deceptive behavior differ significantly from those which perceivers think are clues to deception.

Selected
Readings

Buck, R. (1984). *The Communication of Emotions*. New York: Guilford.

Hall, E. T. ((1966). *The Hidden Dimension*. Garden City, NY: Doubleday.

Henley, N. (1977). *Body Politics: Power, Sex, and Nonverbal Communication*. Englewood Cliffs, NJ: Prentice Hall.

Huston, T. L. (Ed.). (1974). *Foundations of Interpersonal Attraction*. New York: Academic Press.

Jones, E. G. (1990). *Interpersonal Perception*. New York: W. H. Freeman.

Jones, E. E., D. E. Kanouse, H. H. Kelley, R. E. Nisbett, S. Valins, and B. Weiner. (1972). *Attribution: Perceiving the Causes of Behavior*. Morristown, NJ: General Learning Press.

Kleinke, C. L. (1975). *First Impressions: The Psychology of Encountering Others*. Englewood Cliffs, NJ: Prentice Hall.

Rosenthal, R. (Ed.). (1979). *Skill in Nonverbal Communication: Individual Differences*. Cambridge, MA: Oelgleschlager, Gunn and Hain.

Ross, M. and G. J. O. Fletcher. (1985). Attribution and Social Perception. In G. Lindzey and E. Aronson, (Eds.), *Handbook of Social Psychology*. New York: Random House.

Scheflen, A. E. (1972). *Body Language and Social Order*. Englewood Cliffs, NJ: Prentice Hall.

Schneider, D., A. Hastorf, and P. Ellsworth. (1979). *Person Perception,* 2nd edition. Reading, MA: Addison-Wesley.

Siegman, A. W. and S. Feldstein. (Eds.). (1987). *Nonverbal Behavior and Communication*. Hillsdale, NJ: Lawrence Erlbaum Associates.

6

Attribution

*A*s interested as people are in understanding the world—and especially each other—we are not guaranteed the answers to our questions. The most common social question is "Why?" We want to know why we and others act—or don't act—in certain ways. We want reasons for behavior, we expect excuses and apologies for disappointments and errors.

The process of explaining behavior is termed attribution. The word refers to the process of attributing action to various causes and influences. Causal attribution—explaining why—is important because it helps us to predict and somewhat control our social experience. Once we believe we understand the causes of behavior, we react with certain thoughts, feelings, and responses of our own. Finally, attributions about past events influence our expectations of the future.

This chapter examines theories of attribution, forms of attributional bias, and ways attribution theory can be applied to real life.

THEORIES OF ATTRIBUTION

The basic principles according to which attribution is conducted make up various attribution theories. Three broad approaches are reviewed here: naive psychology; correspondent inference theory; and causal analysis or covariance theory.

Naive Psychology

Fritz Heider, cited earlier as an important theorist in social cognition and the developer of balance theory (see chapter 4), began modern theorizing about attributions with his 1958 work, *The Psychology of Interpersonal Relations*. In this work, Heider introduced an alternative to earlier theories that behavior in everyday life was motivated by deep and hidden forces.

EVERYDAY BEHAVIORAL ANALYSIS

On the contrary, Heider argued, most people behave as if the reasons for their own and others' behavior were relatively simple to identify and understand. It is important, he argued, for people to understand the world and to control how the environment affects them. Therefore people make predictions about how others will behave, and form expectations about them.

Because even normal, everyday people are able to speculate about the causes of behavior—not just psychologists who understand deep motivations—Heider dubbed this process naive psychology (as opposed to depth psychology).

DIMENSIONS OF CAUSALITY

Naive psychology, the casual and automatic effort to understand behavior, identifies important dimensions of causality. Heider originally cited the dimension of locus or place of causality—whether the cause was internal or external. Later research has identified three additional dimensions of causality: stable or unstable, controllable or uncontrollable, and specific or global attributions.

Internal versus External. Behavior can be attributed to internal causes like the actor's (behaver's) mood, personality, abililities, state of health, or desires. Alternatively it can be attributed to external causes like outside pressures, bribery, threat, specific components of the social situation like how many people or which specific people are present, weather conditions, and environmental influences.

Stable versus Unstable. Behavior can be caused by factors that are relatively stable or unchanging, whether they are internal or external. For example, the actor's intelligence is a stable internal factor, but her mood may be unstable and changeable.

A speed limit is a relatively stable external factor influencing driving behavior, while the weather is relatively unstable since it varies over time.

Controllable versus Uncontrollable. Some causes are perceived as being in the actor's control, like effort or attention. Other causes are seen as less controllable, such as luck or natural talent (or lack of talent).

Specific versus Global. The effects of some causes are very specific, while those of others are global. For example, not getting enough sleep the night before a math test might have the specific effect of hindering one's performance on this particular test. However, not having any understanding of mathematics will have the more general effect of hindering all mathematics performance, on this test as well as in other forms of computation. Insufficient sleep is a cause with a specific effect, while poor ability in math is a cause with a more global effect.

Correspondent Inference Theory

If you watch a stranger acting a certain way and wonder about the reasons, you will have only limited information with which to reason. The attribution theory developed by researchers Edward E. Jones and Keith E. Davis in 1965 argues that, in explaining such "one-shot" observations, you will likely take the behavior at face value. You will infer that the actor's intentions correspond to his or her behavior. In other words, in making attributions with limited information, you will make a correspondent inference.

MAKING CORRESPONDENT INFERENCES

For example, on your way to class one day you observe a man and woman arguing. You notice that the man is raising his voice, and the woman is crying. Why are they acting this way? If you make a correspondent inference, you will conclude that the man intended to make the woman cry, and that he is expressing anger to punish or control her.

Correspondent inference theory further suggests that such attributions are seen as stable, internal dispositions. For example, you will conclude that the man you saw is generally angry and cruel, not that he is normally good-natured but you happened to see him on a bad day. He acted aggressive and punitive; a correspondent inference is that he *is* an aggressive, punitive person.

QUALIFICATIONS

Such quick judgment of a stranger on the basis of a single observation seems like jumping to conclusions. How can we be sure we are being fair or accurate? Several qualifications seem to be considered when people draw correspondent inferences: freedom of choice; noncommon effects; social desirability; and hedonic relevance; and personalism.

Choice. If a robber threatens a bank teller with a gun and orders her to hand him cash, why is she cooperating with him? Is it because she is secretly tempted to steal the cash herself? Of course not: she is acting under duress, and is only cooperating because she is being forced to act this way.

Correspondent inferences are not drawn in circumstances that involve obvious coercion or force. Observers only make correspondent inferences if the actor appears to have acted freely.

Noncommon Effects. Behaviors only tell us something about the actor if they produce distinctive or noncommon effects. Behaviors that produce common or predictable effects will not lead to a correspondent inference.

For example, if you observe a customer in a restaurant waving her hand at the waitress, you may conclude that this is simply a good way to get the waitress's attention (a common effect of waving)—action that would work just as well for any other customer who waved. However, if you observe a customer waving at the chef, to get his attention (a noncommon effect), you will probably conclude that this particular customer must be either exceptionally friendly, or a personal friend of this restaurant's chef. The noncommon effects of the actor's behavior—the appearance of expressing friendliness rather than calling for service—warrant your making an inference about the actor herself.

Social Desirability. Socially undesirable behaviors are seen as more "informative" for correspondent inferences than desirable behaviors. For example, if a stranger collides with you as you enter a room, and quickly says, "Excuse me," (a socially desirable response), you do not necessarily label the person as polite. After all, his apology was reasonable, and not at all surprising.

However, if a stranger collided with you and said nothing, moving wordlessly along as if you were not there, you would notice and probably label that behavior—and that person—as "rude." The fact that this person did a socially undesirable thing appears to be more *informative* about the person himself.

This reliance on undesirable actions as informative, while desirable ones are not, creates an unfortunate bias. When people are at their best we may attribute their good behavior to "living up to others' expectations," and only make personal inferences about them when they are at their worst.

Hedonic Relevance. We do not analyze or make inferences about all others' behavior. We particularly scrutinize those behaviors that are relevant to our own pleasure or pain—in other words, that are high in *hedonic relevance*. Hedonism is the practice of pursuing pleasure and avoiding pain; "hedonic" behavior follows this principle. Thus a military veteran might condemn a political protestor who burns the national flag, because it seems to insult the veteran's values, while a nonveteran might more easily dismiss the protestor's action.

Personalism. We are more likely to make correspondent inferences about actions that are *directed at* us personally, and are thus high in *personalism*. For example, a salesperson who sells bad merchandise to a friend of yours is unethical, but one who sells such a product to you is "a thief." The higher the personalism of the action, the more extreme the judgment of the attribution.

Causal Analysis Theory

Modern social behavior involves many interactions with and observations of strangers. Correspondent inference theory explains such one-shot opportunities in terms of the apparent characteristics of the action in question.

Most everyday attribution, however, involves not strangers but acquaintances, people with whom we have interacted before, and whose behavior patterns may be somewhat familiar. These are the people who are most likely to affect our own experiences. An attribution theory that addresses multiple events—like the behaviors of people we know—has been developed by Harold H. Kelley.

Kelley's theory examines the causal analysis or analysis of covariance an observer undertakes. In Kelley's theory, the observer acts like a naive scientist, collecting information (data) about behavior, and analyzing the pattern in order to understand what it means. At the conclusion of this analysis, the observer determines what attribution to make. Instead of making a "correspondent inference"—an inference that personality corresponds to action—the observer may attribute the behavior in question to some other cause, as a result of this analysis.

WHAT STIMULATES CAUSAL ANALYSIS

If we know people well, or even if we know them somewhat, what would cause us to be concerned about their motives? Knowing others implies some familiarity with their behavior, and some ability to explain it.

Several kinds of behavior are likely to precipitate a searching causal analysis. Researchers have identified five conditions or motivations that prompt people to ask the question, "Why?" These include unexpected events, negative events, extreme stressors, events with outcome dependency for the observer, and the need to preserve one's social schemata.

Unexpected Events. The most common stimulus for attribution is an unexpected event. For example, if a friend refuses to grant you a simple request, if your partner or spouse suddenly refuses to speak to you, or if someone who had planned to visit you suddenly cancels the trip, you face unexpected—and unexplained—consequences. To the extent that these discoveries might affect future experiences, you will need to know what they mean. It is the search for meaning, then, that prompts the question "Why?" and the subsequent causal analysis.

For example, if your friend has refused to do you a favor because she has an emergency to deal with, perhaps you can help her, and secure your friendship. If your spouse or partner is not speaking to you because of anger, this signifies the existence of conflict that must be faced and dealt with. Unexpected events and surprises—even when they are not unpleasant—raise questions about our ability to predict future experiences. Research shows that relationship partners engage in more attribution at times of relationship change—when intimacy increases, for example, or suddenly deteriorates. We seem to engage in attribution to reassert some control and competency over our social experience.

Negative Events. Even when events are not unexpected, if they are unpleasant we will engage in a search for reasons. This is related to hedonic motives—the desire to avoid pain and ensure pleasure. If we can understand what causes disappointments and failures, we may be able to prevent them, or to turn our luck around.

Extreme Stressors. The most ardent searches for causal explanations are prompted by extremely distressing events. Researchers have confirmed that seemingly incessant attributional analyses are engaged in by cancer patients, accident victims, victims of trauma like criminal assault and sexual molestation, parents who have lost a child, and individuals who are separated or divorced. In some cases the search for reasons might be applied to coping processes like recovery and grief. In others, however, the causal analysis can become an obsessive review, as when broken-hearted survivors disrupt sleep with thoughts of "Why?" and "If only . . ."

Outcome Dependency. We are not causally curious about all people's behavior. We are more likely to question the reasons for the actions of people who have some impact on our lives—people on whom we depend for important outcomes. Children may pay more attention to and wonder about their parents' behavior, for example, than vice versa. Employees need to be able to predict supervisors' treatment of them, and students try harder to figure out their teachers' priorities.

Preserving Schemata. Schemata are sets of ideas about experiences and events. When we encounter new information that violates or contradicts our schemata, we work harder to analyze and understand it. We are particularly motivated to fit the new information into the preexisting schema, and resist changing the schema to fit the data.

For example, if you have a high opinion of a friend, it will surprise you to learn that someone you respect, like a trusted teacher, dislikes that same friend. This teacher's disapproval violates your schema about your friend. It is threatening to consider that you might be wrong; the contradiction creates a state of cognitive imbalance (see chapter 4). Your causal analysis will seek to rationalize the contradiction while preserving your schema. One way to do this would be to assume that the teacher has only had one bad experience or has only seen your friend under unusual circumstances (an external attribution). If she gave your friend a chance, she would revise her opinion.

CAUSAL OPTIONS

In Kelley's theory, we conduct causal analyses of others' actions in order to determine which of two kinds of attributions to make: dispositional or situational. A dispositional attribution is an internal attribution about a person's stable characteristics and tendencies. A situational attribution finds cause in the external circumstances surrounding the actor.

In general, dispositional attributions promise greater predictive power than situational attributions. Ideally we will form dispositional attributions only when appropriate, and will not jump to conclusions about others' motives or personalities when behavior is situationally influenced. We engage in causal analysis in order to identify which behavior patterns are probably dispositional and which are probably situational in origin.

DIMENSIONS OF ANALYSIS

Causes and effects are observed to occur together (or covary). Patterns of covariance are analyzed for best explanations. Every behavioral event involves an actor in a particular situation. Observers analyze this actor-situation combination according to three dimensions of behavioral events in determining how to make attritibutions: distinctiveness; consensus; and consistency.

Distinctiveness. If the actor's behavioral reaction occurs only in this particular situation, the behavior is said to be high in distinctiveness. If it occurs in other situations, however, it is low in distinctiveness.

For example, why did Lee refuse to do a favor for Terry? If Lee usually agrees to do things for other people, then refusing Terry is unusual, and therefore high in distinctiveness. On the other hand, if Lee usually refuses to do favors for people, then refusing Terry is part of that pattern and is low in distinctiveness.

Consensus. If other people act similarly to the actor, the behavior is high in consensus. If the actor's behavior is unusual compared to other actors, it is low in consensus.

For example, if most people refuse to do favors for Terry, then Lee's refusal is high in consensus. But if other people usually do what Terry asks, then Lee's refusal is low in consensus.

Consistency. The actor-situation pattern over time reveals the consistency of the behavior. If the actor usually behaves this way in this situation, then this particular instance of the behavior is highly consistent with the pattern. If on the other hand the actor usually reacts differently in this situation, then this particular actor-behavior event is low in consistency.

For example, if Lee usually refuses to do favors for Terry, then this particular refusal is high in consistency. But if Lee usually does what Terry asks, then Lee's behavior is low in consistency.

Applying the Analysis. Once the observer has judged the distinctiveness, consensus and consistency of the actor-situation event, a causal attribution can be made. If all three dimensions are judged to be high, the observer will make a situational attribution.

For example, if Lee's refusal of Terry's request is highly distinctive (Lee usually grants requests), high in consensus (other people refuse Terry's requests), and high in consistency (Lee usually refuses Terry this way), then the cause of this event is something about Terry or Terry's request.

Alternatively, if distinctiveness and consensus are low, an observer will make a dispositional attribution about the actor. For example, if Lee usually refuses requests (low distinctiveness) but other people usually grant Terry's requests (so that Lee's behavior is low in consensus), then this particular event is attributable to Lee: something about Lee led to this event.

Finally, if consistency is judged to be low—if Lee does not usually refuse Terry—then the attribution may focus on the interaction between the actor and the situation, or to some other unique aspect of this particular instance. Low consistency indicates low stability in the event. Things do not usually happen this way. The other dimensions must be examined for clues about what kind of attribution to make.

CONTEXT EFFECTS

Obviously, causal analysis of an event's dimensions takes an observer both effort and time. It is important to remember that attributional processes are engaged only by special events, like the unpleasant surprises and stressors mentioned above.

Additionally, causal analyses seldom restrict consideration to the dimensions of distinctiveness, consensus and consistency if other information is available. Attributions consider the context in which behaviors occur. Context provides information about background, perspectives, and motives. Context effects can take the form of either discounting certain attributional factors, or augmenting explanations for behavior.

Discounting. When context offers plausible explanations for a behavior, other factors are discounted. Discounting applies a *subtraction* rule by eliminating alternative causes in favor of those that make more sense.

For example, if you see a usually mild-mannered friend arguing angrily with someone, you may initially attribute his bad temper to some provocation or insult by his opponent. However if you later learn that your friend had just received bad news, you might discount the opponent's influence in favor of blaming the bad news for your friend's bad mood.

Augmenting. Augmenting involves adding greater weight to a factor that seems always to account for a behavior. For example, if you meet someone at a party who seems both obnoxious and drunk, you might wonder whether her obnoxiousness is produced by her disposition or by the effects of alcohol. However, if you later encounter her while she is sober, and she still behaves obnoxiously, you will augment the causal power of her personality: whatever her sobriety, her behavior is obnoxious, so it must be part of her disposition.

ATTRIBUTIONAL BIASES

Although attribution endeavors to be a logical process of analyzing behvioral causes, it is as susceptible to error and bias as other forms of social cognition. Common attributional biases include the fundamental attribution error and misattributions about emotional arousal, motivation, failure, and undesirable behavior.

The Fundamental Attribution Error

Although the specific cause of a behavioral event may be either internal (dispositional) or external (situational), observers tend to overestimate dispositional influence and underestimate situational influence in others' actions. This biased tendency has been dubbed the fundamental attribution error. Because it involves inferring a disposition that corresponds to the event's outcome, it is also known as the correspondence bias.

For example, a student arriving late to class may have several reasons, both internal and external, for her tardiness: she may have overslept, or forgotten what day it was; she may have had car trouble, or been delayed by a phone call or traffic jam on the way. If her teacher commits the fundamental attribution error, he may simply assume the lateness is a disposition problem: the student has a bad attitude or does not take the class seriously, and is personally to blame for the problem. This can have unfortunate consequences, especially if the attribution is erroneous.

EXPLAINING THE FUNDAMENTAL ATTRIBUTION ERROR

Several explanations for the persistence of the fundamental attribution error have been offered: salience of events; the different perspectives of the actor and the observer; self-serving biases in social cognition; and cultural biases in attribution.

Salience. We overreact to salient or noticeable stimuli. In attribution this means that we "blame" the more noticeable or obvious features of a situation for its outcome. In most behavioral events, the salient component is the actor himself or herself. For example, if you observe an acquaintance screaming loudly at several people, your first reaction will probably be to wonder, "What is wrong with *her*?" rather than "What has *happened* to her?"

Actor-Observer Effects. The fundamental attribution error afflicts the conclusions drawn by observers, but not by actors. The difference between the two perspectives accounts for their different conclusions. This *divergent perspectives hypothesis* points out that an actor's perspective emphasizes the power of the situation, while that of the observer characterizes the actor as the agent of action.

For example, you feel frustrated in traffic because the car ahead of you is moving far below the speed limit. From your (observer's) perspective, it is the driver (actor) who is deliberately driving too slowly. Alternatively, from the driver's perspective, it may be situational factors like road hazards or pedestrians—interruptions you cannot see—that require him to slow down.

Research shows that the correspondence bias can be reversed by reversing participants' perspectives. When an actor can review her behavior on videotape from an observer's perspective, she may see herself as more influential. And when an observer considers the perspective of the actor—the situational factors catching the actor's attention—he is less likely to overestimate internal causes for behavior.

Self-Serving Biases. It may support an observer's self-image to hold an actor personally responsible for a negative outcome. In such cases, the fundamental attribution error is a function of the same self-serving tendencies that characterize so much social and self-cognition.

For example, if a teacher criticizes a paper you have written, it is more self-serving to conclude that the teacher is being unfairly critical (an internal attribution) than that the paper deserved such disparagement (an external attribution). Thus self-serving tendencies may lead us to commit the fundamental attribution error when explaining other's negative reactions to us.

Cultural Biases. In some cultures—especially Western and industrialized nations—a rationalist bias dominates attributional processes. Humans are considered more powerful agents of change than nonhuman forces like weather and the environment. For example, instead of recognizing a hurricane as a natural disaster, members of a stricken American community may seek to blame human agents like weather forecasters, insurance companies, or construction companies for the pain and destruction they have experienced.

CRITIQUE OF THE FUNDAMENTAL ATTRIBUTION ERROR

In light of research on the fundamental attribution error, it is wise to ask questions about its nature and its effects.

Is It Fundamental? The fundamental attribution error may not be "fundamental" at all if fundamental means "universal." Research on cultural biases suggests that North Americans have a person-disposition bias that is not found in other cultures.

Is It an Error? Attributing causes to dispositions may be a bias—but in cases where disposition is indeed "to blame" for behavior, this is not an error. For example, holding a student responsible for being late to class is an error if a situational factor caused the tardiness, but if the student genuinely neglected her attendance, the dispositional attribution is accurate.

In a nutshell, it may be best to remember that "the fundamental attribution error" is an early label for the tendency better thought of as *correspondence bias*. This removes confusion about whether or not the tendency is fundamental (universal) or erroneous.

Misattributions

Inasmuch as attribution involves making a guess about a behavior's true causes, there is always a chance that it will be mistaken. Besides the fundamental attribution error or correspondence bias, other forms of attributional error are possible. Misattributions can involve misperceiving the nature of emotional experience, the sources of arousal, one's own motives for action, and one's personal responsibility for outcomes.

EMOTIONAL MISATTRIBUTION

Self-perception theory (see chapter 4) asserts that people learn about their own dispositions by considering their actions. By extension, people also appear to make inferences about their own emotions in the same way.

Two-Factor Theory. Classic research by Stanley Schachter and Jerome Singer in 1962 examined the structure of emotional experience. Subjects were given injections of what they believed was a vitamin supplement; after the injections they were placed in the company of confederates who acted out extreme emotional states, like anger or euphoria. In reality the subjects' injections were not vitamins, but were either a form of adrenaline, which causes sensations of arousal, or an inert saline solution. Consequently, those who were aroused by adrenaline (but had not expected such side effects) took on the behavior of their angry or euphoric companions. These results showed that subjects who were aroused by adrenaline but did not attribute the arousal to the "vitamin" adopted the interpretations and labels of their emotional companions. Schachter and Singer concluded that emotional experience is composed of two factors: a physiological state of arousal, and a cognitive label that explains the arousal.

Subjects in Schachter and Singer's research had made misattributions about the true nature of their experience, falsely labeling it as emotion when it was merely an induced arousal state. Later research confirmed similar misattribution effects with other forms of arousal. In a 1974 study by Donald Dutton and Arthur Aron, subjects who were interviewed on a high bridge tended to misattribute their fear arousal to the attractiveness of the interviewer.

People appear to consult their own responses in interpreting the causes of emotional or emotion-like arousal. When distracted or misinformed, they can make misattributions about those causes.

Arousal and False Feedback. In 1966 researcher Stuart Valins asked male students to rate the attractiveness of photographs of women. Those who believed that the audible background sounds they were hearing signalled their own heartrates gave higher sex-appeal ratings to the specific photographs that "caused" the sounds to speed up.

In 1971, Dolf Zillmann found that subjects who were aroused by exercise reacted more angrily to frustration than those who had not been exercising.

Studies like these indicate that misattribution about the source of arousal can take the form of exaggerated reactions—misperceiving the degree of one's actual attraction or anger—even when the nature of the emotion is not misconstrued.

OVERJUSTIFICATION

Research on self-perception reviewed in chapter 4 confirms that, when overjustified for doing an enjoyable task, actors can mistakenly conclude that it is less enjoyable. In this case misattribution involves the intentions of the actor—oneself—rather than the locus of causality or the stimulus of emotional arousal.

DEFENSIVE ATTRIBUTION

As interested as we are in other people, we may sometimes get too close to their experiences. If we witness a tragic accident, for example, our ability to analyze it objectively is impaired by our fear that it might happen to us. In such experiences of vicarious threat, we distance ourselves from the pain of empathy by making defensive attributions.

The simplest form of defensive attribution holds the victim responsible for the tragedy. On learning that a woman has been raped, we might wonder if she "asked for it" by dressing provocatively or walking alone in a dangerous neighborhood. It is not uncommon, if you have been victimized, to be disappointed when friends react by criticizing your failure to prevent the crime: Why was your car unlocked? Why did you leave your home empty or unguarded for such a long time?

This pattern of blaming the victim is also predicted by the just world bias, a prejudice that people get what they deserve. As an attributional bias, however, it is focused on preventing the painful realization that what happened to the victim could happen to the observer.

Self-handicapping, making excuses for ourselves, and blaming circumstances for our failures are all forms of defensive attribution. They attest to the difficulty of being impartial in our observations of the social world. We want to understand, predict, and control our social experience—but fears, biases, and wishful thinking can sometimes distort our efforts at attribution.

APPLICATIONS OF ATTRIBUTION THEORY

Attribution theory and research has been put to work in a variety of practical applications, including understanding and reducing attributional biases, and in making therapeutic changes in attributional style.

Understanding Attributional Biases

By better understanding patterns and sources of attributional biases, we may be able to reduce our own susceptibility to such distorted thinking. This is particularly important in our dealings with significant others, people with whom we have close relationships. Two examples include clarifying marital dissatisfaction and interpersonal conflict.

MARITAL DISSATISFACTION

Is there any way to predict the success of a particular marriage? Research suggests that marital satisfaction or dissatisfaction is related to how partners make attributions about negative experiences. In dissatisfied couples, partners attribute bad experiences to each others' stable traits and personalities. Conversely, in happy couples, bad experiences are blamed on external, temporary causes.

For example, in an unhappy marriage, a wife may conclude that her husband forgot their anniversary because he takes their relationship for granted. In a happy marriage, the same oversight may be attributed to recent deadline pressure at work. In the latter case, the temporary nature of the cause allows the couple to postpone the anniversary celebration and stay on good terms. It may be possible to change partners' attributional patterns to bring about better relationship maintenance strategies.

INTERPERSONAL CONFLICT

Conflict is a common experience and an inevitable part of interpersonal relationships (see chapter 14). Research indicates that conflict is worsened when opponents make negative attributions about each other's intentions. For example, heads of rival companies may see competitive behavior as caused by treachery or bad faith. Such dispositional biases can be corrected, for example, by having each party to a negotiation offer reasonable explanations for his or her actions. A more complete understanding of the causes of behavior will make jumping to conclusions less likely, and can ease the way to conflict resolution and peacemaking.

Attributional Style

Individuals may develop attributional biases as a result of experience and self-fulfilling prophecy. For example, a student who believes she will always be poor at math may attribute a high score on a math test to luck or an unusually easy test. This attribution, distorted by her biased self-esteem, leads her to fail to prepare for the next test—on which she gets the "expected" low score.

Patterns in such self-attributions are referred to as attributional style. Attributional style has been studied with respect to its relationship with depression, and its application in psychotherapy.

DEPRESSIVE ATTRIBUTION

Depression is the most common affective (emotional) disorder. It is characterized by negative affect (e.g., sadness, anger), lack of energy (e.g., lethargy, low motivation), and avoidant behavior (e.g., oversleeping, social withdrawal). People suffering from depression tend to employ a self-defeating attributional style. When bad things happen to depressed people, they make internal, stable, global attributions about them.

For example, a depressed woman receives a call from a man saying he must break their date for dinner. In her disappointment, she attributes the cancellation to an internal cause ("I'm just not very attractive to him after all") that is stable ("I might as well face it: I'm not pretty and I never will be") and has global consequences ("No one will ever love someone as plain as I am"). Obviously such a pattern of self-attribution can lead to a self-perpetuating cycle of depressing experiences and explanations.

In contrast, a non-depressed woman would be more likely to make external, stable, specific attributions about the cancellation of the date: "I'm disappointed that he broke the date, but something must have come up. We can probably get together another time. Although I was looking forward to the date, there are other things I can still enjoy doing instead."

ATTRIBUTION THERAPY

Therapy for depression might usefully include a review and reworking of a client's attributional style. This attributional "retraining" can be accomplished by having the client keep a diary documenting personal credit for success but environmental blame for failure—thus reversing the depressive atributional style.

Attribution therapy can also be applied in students' academic performance. Poor students may erroneously attribute their failures to stable, internal factors ("I can't think analytically, I'll never learn this material"). Students can be retrained and encouraged to attribute failure to temporary, external factors ("Most students perform relatively poorly during freshman year"). Such habits can improve students' effort and feelings of self-efficacy, and assist in improving academic performance.

*O**ur interest in understanding people is particularly focused on the reasons for their actions. The process of explaining our own and others' behavior is attribution. Fritz Heider's naive psychology argued that attribution is an* *ongoing, everyday activity. Causality is analyzed in terms of several dimensions: whether the cause is internal or external; whether the cause and effect relationship is stable or unstable; whether the outcome is controllable or uncontrollable; and whether the effects are specific or global.*

Jones and Davis's correspondent inference theory argues that, in analyzing single instances of behavior, an observer draws a causal inference that corresponds to the event's outcome. Such simplistic attributions are qualified by considerations of whether the action was coerced or freely chosen; whether the behavior produced noncommon effects; whether the action could be considered socially desirable; whether the event has hedonic relevance for the observer; and whether it was directed at the observer personally.

Harold Kelley's causal analysis theory of attribution proposes that when people are motivated to explain specific events, they analyze several dimensions and context factors in arriving at conclusions. Specific kinds of events stimulate such efforts to explain: unexpected events, negative events, extreme stressors, the actions of those on whom we depend for certain outcomes, and events that challenge or threaten our preexisting schemata.

An observer analyzes an event to decide whether it is attributable to internal factors like the actor's disposition or rather to external factors like aspects of the situation. The actor-situation combination is analyzed in terms of three dimensions: distinctiveness; consensus, and consistency. High and low values of these dimensions are associated with attributions to the actor, the situation, the interaction between them, or other factors. If contextual information is available, it may discount or augment attributions to other factors.

Attribution is prone to distortion by various influences. One persistent form of bias is the fundamental attribution error, also termed the correspondence bias. The fundamental attribution error overestimates dispositional and underestimates situation influences on events, especially in explaining others' behavior. The error has been explained as a result of the salience of the actor to the observer, the differences between the actor's and the observer's perspectives, self-serving distortions on the part of the observer, and cultural biases that favor blaming human agents for various events. Critics have questioned whether the fundamental attribution error is really fundamental, since it does not occur in the absence of such cultural and cognitive biases. Moreover, it is not really an error if dispositional explanations are accurate.

Other attributional errors involve misattribution, misperceiving the true causes of events and experiences. Misattribution has been identified in classic research on emotional experience and labeling. Other research has shown that subjects given false feedback about their own arousal levels have responded in mistaken or exaggerated ways. Overjustification involves misattribution of one's motivations for goal-directed behavior. Defensive attributions are also undertaken to protect observers from the threatening perception that other people's tragedies might just as easily happen to them.

Attribution theory has been applied in various contexts. An understanding of attributional biases can relieve patterns of dissatisfaction in marriage and the escalation of interpersonal conflict. Research has also identified the effects of attributional style. The internal, stable, global attributional style of depressive persons can be retrained in favor of the external, unstable, specific pattern characteristic of non-depressed individuals. Attribution therapy has also been used to rework the way students explain their successes and failures, to encourage poor performers to take control and try harder in their academic work.

Selected Readings

Harvey, J. H. and G. Weary. (1981). *Perspectives on Attribution Processes.* Dubuque, IA: Wm. C. Brown.

Harvey, J. H. and G. Weary. (Eds.). (1985). *Attribution: Basic Issues and Applications.* New York: Academic Press.

Harvey, J. H., A. L. Weber, and T. L. Orbuch. (1990). *Interpersonal Accounts: A Social Psychological Perspective.* Cambridge, MA: Basil Blackwell.

Heider, F. (1958/1980). *The Psychology of Interpersonal Relations.* New York: Wiley.

Hewstone, M. (1989). *Causal Attribution.* Cambridge, MA: Basil Blackwell.

Jones, E. E., D. E. Kanouse, H. H. Kelley, R. E. Nisbett, S. Valins, and B. Weiner. (1972). *Attribution: Perceiving the Causes of Behavior.* Morristown, NJ: General Learning Press.

Kelley, H. H. (1979). *Personal Relationships: Their Structures and Processes.* Hillsdale, NJ: Erlbaum.

Seligman, M. E. P. (1975). *Helplessness.* San Francisco: Freeman.

Seligman, M. E. P. (1990). *Learned Optimism.* New York: Alfred Knopf.

Semin, G. and A. S. R. Manstead. (1983). *The Accountability of Conduct.* London: Academic Press.

Snyder, C. R., R. L. Higgins, and R. J. Stucky. (1983). *Excuses: Masquerades in Search of Grace.* New York: Wiley.

Weary, G. and H. L. Mirels. (1982). *Integrations of Clinical and Social Psychology.* New York: Oxford University Press.

Weary, G., M. A. Stanley, and J. H. Harvey. (1989). *Attribution.* New York: Springer-Verlag.

Weiner, B. (1986). *An Attributional Theory of Motivation and Emotion.* New York: Springer-Verlag.

7

Gender and Social Behavior

The overwhelming business of understanding ourselves and other people is simplified somewhat by such social devices as norms and roles. Norms are guidelines for socially accepted and expected behavior, and are more specifically addressed in chapter 10. Groups of related norms are organized into social roles, guidelines for behavior appropriate to a specific position or status. Some roles (e.g., pedestrian, defendant) involve only temporary constraints and situations. Others are more pervasive and enduring. The most powerful social roles are generally thought to be gender roles, the guidelines constraining behavior according to one's gender identity.

In this chapter we distinguish between sex, a term that connotes biological distinctions (male or female), and gender, which refers to the social and behavioral meaning of being either female or male. While casual conversation uses these words interchangeably, social scientists have found it helpful to be precise in referring to sex, gender, and gender roles.

Additionally, we will distinguish between gender (female or male) and gender role (feminine or masculine). People whose gender is female are expected to behave in feminine ways; those who are male are expected to behave in masculine ways. Gender (female or male) describes biology, while gender role conveys corresponding behaviors (feminine or masculine), whether norms or stereotypes.

Gender differences are fascinating, and our interest in them can obscure the fact that similarities between males' and females' behavior vastly outnumber the documented differences. Accordingly, this chapter examines first the few observable differences that have been identified between the genders. Secondly, we consider the origins of both differences and similarities in the process of gender socialization.

GENDER DIFFERENCES

Cognitive psychologists have noted that human attention is attracted by novelty rather than what is familiar. This may explain why, while gender differences in social behavior are relatively rare, they draw so much popular interest and controversy. Is one gender really stronger and more fit for military service than the other? Is one gender more suited for parenthood than the other? These complex social questions are deceptively simplified when reduced to either-or terms. Research evidence suggests that while some differences have been consistently identified by years of careful study, they are rare and their origins are by no means simple.

Patterns of Gender Difference

Social research has identified a few specific aspects of social behavior in which the behavior of males and females consistently differs: social power; interpersonal communication; sexual behavior; helping behavior; aggression; conformity; and intellectual abilities.

SOCIAL POWER

In most times and regions studied, males exhibit more social power than females. On one hand, people perceive men to be more dominant than women. On the other hand, in terms of control, influence, status, law, and well-being, in every society studied men *are* more dominant than women.

Authority and Status. Although women make up slightly more than half the adult population, men vastly outnumber women in positions of political and corporate leadership. In mixed-gender groupings, like juries, men are far more likely than women to be elected foreperson or credited with influencing deliberations.

Interesting research suggests that women may be more likely to suffer from *fear of success,* since success is considered more appropriate to the male than the female gender role. Learned aspects of the gender role, then, may perpetuate gender differences in some forms of social power.

Work and Money. Women expect and receive less pay for comparable work. In the United States, a female's average salary is 60% of a male's. Although women make up almost half the work force, they are vastly underrepresented in management positions. Single-parent households are more likely supported by working mothers than working fathers; those headed by women are more likely to be below government standards for poverty.

Language. The gender difference in social power is reflected in and maintained by language. Women are more likely than men to stammer, hesitate, and use hedges (e.g., "sort of," "I guess") in speech. Men interrupt women, and women are interrupted by men, more often than alternative patterns of interruption. Women are more likely to attach "tag questions" to statements; that is, they more often tag questions onto assertions of fact. For example, a man might say, "It looks like it will rain soon" while a woman might say "It looks like it will rain soon, doesn't it?" Such automatic modifications of speech may reflect females' stronger need for social approval.

In nonverbal communication, women have been found to avert gaze and avoid eye contact more than men. Men are more likely to physically touch others during communication, while women are more likely to be touched. Social critics note that these gender patterns in language parallel general social distinctions between dominant and submissive groups or classes. It has also been observed that the decision of which extreme—dominant or submissive—is considered "normal" may be arbitrary. Instead of seeing women's language as reflecting weakness or insecurity, an alternative interpretation might see men's language as unreasonably aggressive and insensitive.

INTERPERSONAL COMMUNICATION

Observations of different language patterns extend to the broader phenomenon of social communication. Cross-cultural studies of both sending and receiving nonverbal "messages" have concluded that women are better skilled in both conveying and interpreting information via posture, position, and facial expression. Women have also been found to smile at others more than men do. In group contexts, women are more likely to make emotional contributions, by giving help or support, while men are more likely to make task-specific contributions, like information or instruction.

Such differences in communication skill and emphasis have led some observers to conclude that women are more empathetic and sensitive than men. As shall be reviewed below, this may be better attributable to different life experiences than different inborn abilities.

SEXUAL BEHAVIOR

A gender gap—significant difference between males and females—has also been found in sexual attitudes. Women tend to be conservative in attitudes about casual sex, while men tend to be permissive.

This gender gap extends into sexual behavior. Similar to their counterparts in other species, male humans tend to be less selective about partners and more likely to intitiate sexual contact than females. Males are also more likely to initiate courtship, dating, self-disclosure, and touching.

HELPING

Reviews of studies of prosocial (helping) behavior indicate that, in the forms studied, men are more likely to offer help than women. However, most such research examines crisis intervention, or offering help to strangers during emergencies. Bystander assistance is only one form of help. It may be that such aid is an extension of social norms that expect men to be more heroic and risk-taking than women.

Little research has been conducted on other forms of help, such as nurturing friends and fostering family care. While some research suggests that women are more helpful than men in such contexts, data are insufficient to be more conclusive.

AGGRESSION

Through various times, places, populations, and methods of research, males are found to be consistently more aggressive than females. Acts of war and violent crime are attributable to more men than women. Boys and men are also found to be more aggressive than girls and women in socially acceptable play and competition.

Men are more aggressive than women both verbally and physically, although gender differences are greater for physical aggression. Differences are also greater in natural settings (e.g., playgrounds, homes) than controlled settings (e.g., laboratories, games).

Accentuating this gender difference in aggression is the fact that females generally learn to feel more anxious and guilty than males about behaving aggressively. Whatever a child's initial aggressive tendencies, therefore, social learning may result in very different lessons about whether it pays to behave aggressively.

CONFORMITY

Interest in social influence has led researchers to examine whether there are gender differences in conformity (willingness to change behavior as a result of social pressure). Most studies of conformity do not reveal gender differences; the few that do consistently show women to be more easily influenced. It is important to note that the emergence of gender differences in conformity depends strongly on the nature of the influential situation, the task and individuals involved. Such qualifications may make general conclusions about gender differences premature.

INTELLECTUAL ABILITIES

Gender differences have been identified in only three areas of intellectual performance: females have excelled in verbal ability; males have done better in mathematics; and males have outperformed females in certain visual-spatial tasks. Given the many different forms of these skills that can be tested and demonstrated, however, it is not possible to predict the outcomes of any particular comparison. Moreover, research techniques yield smaller and smaller differences over time. This suggests that better methods of testing behavior yield smaller differences. Therefore it is best to consider evidence on gender differences in intelligence as being as inconclusive as it is controversial.

Origins of Gender Differences

As interesting as the fact of differences is, the question of their origins is more compelling: are males and females different from the start, or do we learn to behave differently? Most research and speculation on the origins of gender differences has focused on the issue of "nature versus nurture," or whether biological influences (nature) outweigh those of learning and culture (nurture). Modern research is less simplistic, and considers several different, mutually influential processes: biology; childhood socialization; social roles; social situations; and distinctions between gender and sex.

BIOLOGY

Biology has an indisputable effect on gender differences. Males and females are relatively different in height, weight, and muscle mass; they are absolutely different in physical capacity to bear and nurse children. Sex hormones may influence prenatal development just as they affect physical changes during adolescent and adult life. Correlational evidence suggests, for example, the role of the male hormone testosterone in aggressive behavior.

Complicating biological explanations for gender differences is the power of experience in human development and behavior. Biological variations can be enhanced by culture well beyond their original influence. For example, men may have assumed the role of warriors in most societies because of greater upper-body strength, useful for such tasks as throwing spears and engaging in hand-to-hand combat. This equation of masculinity with military ability persists even today, although modern warfare involves high-technology skills like pushing buttons and operating aircraft—in which upper-body strength does not provide any advantage, and women may perform no differently from men.

The greatest problem with ascertaining the role of biology in gender differences is the role of learning in human behavior. Humans begin learning at birth; any gender differences in behavior may be attributable to differences in lessons learned. For example, if a three-year-old girl plays more with dolls than with toy guns, is this a reflection of her biology or the social lessons she has already learned? As young as she is, she is old enough to have been treated differently from her brothers (e.g., different toys, different instructions for play) from the moment of her birth. It may not be possible, when studying humans, to separate the observable effects of biology on behavior from those of one's culture.

CHILDHOOD SOCIALIZATION

As suggested above, children are categorized and treated differently by gender from the moment they are born. During childhood, socialization involves the transmission of lessons about social behavior through observation and operant conditioning like reinforcement and punishment.

Children learn about gender-appropriate actions by simply observing their parents and other family members, and learning vicariously through their experiences. For example, a large family may have one bedroom for the sisters and another for the brothers; toddlers new to this arrangement will look for clues to which siblings "belong" together.

Children are also directly reinforced or punished for their spontaneous actions. For example, a four-year-old girl who tries on her mother's makeup and jewelry may be rewarded with smiles and laughter; a four-year-old boy is more likely to be ridiculed or criticized for the same experiment.

The power and impact of socialization warrants a more detailed examination of this process, provided in the second half of this chapter (below).

SOCIAL ROLES

Most roles are constructed around relationships: a leader needs followers; drivers must yield to pedestrians; parents both protect and control children. For a given role (e.g., parent, spouse), the expectations and standards may be quite different for the two genders (e.g., mother versus father, wife versus husband). Our expectations about social roles for one gender or the other can powerfully influence our subsequent behavior and feelings. Recall the self-fulfilling prophecy discussed earlier (chapter 3): if we expect a female to be more interested in being a nurse than a doctor, we will give her information and encouragement that steers her in the direction we "predict."

Although many social roles are "gender-typed," or distinguished by different stereotypes for the two genders, changing roles and experiences are blurring these distinctions. For example, a person described as an "attorney" could be either a woman or a man; a telephone call to an "executive secretary" could be answered by either a man or a woman. Assumptions that were once made about which gender "belongs" in particular positions or occupations are no longer safe or accurate. Changes in roles lead to changes in expectations—which lead back to further changes in roles. The nature of these changes in gender roles is examined further at the end of this chapter (below).

GENDER SOCIALIZATION

Gender socialization—teaching and learning lessons about the behaviors that are considered socially appropriate and desirable for either gender—can enhance or modify biological influences as well as foster gender differences by itself. Interestingly, socialization can be as influenced by fiction as by fact. Thus, we will first examine the mythical and exaggerated expectations contained in gender stereotypes. Then we will examine scientific theories about how gender roles are learned, transmitted, and structured.

Gender Stereotypes

A stereotype is a generalization that distinguishes one category of people from another (see chapter 5). A gender stereotype is a generalization that sets one gender apart from the other. Gender stereotypes may be accurate reflections of general behavior (e.g., women are better interpersonal communicators than men; men interrupt more than women do), but as generalizations they may also simplify to an inaccurate degree. Gender stereotypes may also be based less in reality than in myth or tradition; for example, contrary to stereotypes of women pursuing men in romantic relationships, researchers have found that women tend to be more hesitant in making commitments and more willing to end an unsatisfactory relationship than men (see chapter 16).

To review the role of gender stereotypes in gender socialization, we will examine gender typing, gender schemata, media stereotypes, and the effects of gender stereotypes.

GENDER TYPING

The earliest stage in developing gender stereotypes is gender typing. Gender typing involves categorizing things and people as masculine or feminine; it happens comewhat automatically (with little conscious thought or attention). While children must learn how to gender-type, they usually manage to do so fairly early and quickly, and to use this information in self-presentation and personal preferences. For example, gender typing explains why girls prefer clothing in pastel shades like pink; pink is gender-typed as a "feminine" color. Toys can also be gender-typed (guns and cars are masculine, dolls and kitchen tools are feminine); so can jobs (police officers and firefighters are judged masculine, while teachers and nurses are considered feminine).

Gender typing has obvious consequences for education and professional advancement. Men may be discouraged from pursuing careers in nursing and teaching. Women may not aspire to male-dominated professions although there is no reason they cannot become distinguished as Supreme Court justices or shuttle astronauts. Both men and women deprive themselves of the emotional and financial satisfactions of work when their choices are limited by illogical stereotypes.

The ultimate extension of gender-typing may be to consider some basic skills and activities as feminine and others as masculine—despite the fact that either gender could perform these tasks equally well or often. For example, men can learn to be award-winning chefs, and women can be trained as automotive engineers, but in most American households women do the cooking and men attend to automobile maintenance. These household chores have been gender-typed, and individuals of different genders grow up with correspondingly different expectations and experiences.

GENDER SCHEMATA

At the subtler level of individual social cognition, each of us has ideas and feelings about the qualities and behaviors that "fit" one gender or the other. When we reflect privately on our social world, as individuals we usually tolerate more diversity and less consistency than social stereotypes demand. For example, while we may think of shopping and cooking as something mothers, not fathers, are "supposed" to do, we also know that not all women are "typical" mothers. Feminine gender schemata—clusters of ideas about feminine roles and qualities that go together—may include such diverse types as beauty queens, career women, tomboys, and spinsters. Masculine gender schemata may include jocks, hardhats, white-collar executives, and sissies. The terms and images employed fit *within* a particular gender role in the mind of the evaluator. While each schema comprises its own stereotype, it may cross rigid lines of more socially accepted stereotypes. For example, the gender schema of "beauty queen" includes masculine traits like ambition and competitiveness as well as feminine ones like emotionality and appearance-consciousness.

Schemata vary from one individual to the next; agreement among different people's schemata takes the form of social stereotypes. Stereotyped schemata are a necessary but insufficient step in prejudiced behavior like sexism. For example, a personnel director considers whether to interview a woman, a single mother, for a management position. The director's schema for "working mother" includes giving children's schedules priority over job requirements. Whether this is fair or not in the case of a particular job applicant, the personnel director may elect not to interview the woman based on this prejudice. In this manner sexist behavior (denying fair consideration to an applicant on the basis of gender or gender-related expectations) can be based on schemata.

MEDIA STEREOTYPES

Within a culture, similarities among individuals' gender schemata are often taken for granted as valid and propagated by media like newspapers, popular literature, television, and films. In television commercials, for example, women are more often portrayed as consumers obsessed with their own appearance, the cleanliness of their homes, and the happiness of their spouses and children. Men are more often depicted as experts and advisors—knowledgeable professionals offering direction to confused female consumers.

Various studies of media stereotypes have found that, in both artistic and commercial media, men are portrayed as engaging in active, varied, dominant activities, while women are shown as passive, domestic, and subordinate. Women are also generally less likely than men even to be portrayed in the media.

EFFECTS OF GENDER STEREOTYPES

As discussed above, individuals' gender stereotypes and schemata can prompt sexist behavior and feed self-fulfilling prophecies about gender-related achievements. Research specifically examining media sexism has also shown that exposure to television images can influence individuals' acceptance of the stereotyped messages they convey. Researchers speculate on the long-term effects of such media "numbing" and whether media, rather than reflecting a society's existing biases, actually create and perpetuate them.

Gender Roles

While one's gender is clearly inborn, one's gender role is not. Gender involves being female or male, and all the biological and psychological implications that entails. In contrast, one's gender role involves behaving in ways that are considered feminine or masculine. Human social behavior is never so simple as to be a matter of inborn forces or instincts. At least some experience, learning, and cultural shaping is required. Evidence indicates that gender roles are significantly a function of social learning, whatever biological predispositions might once have existed.

The complex system of learning involved in developing roles is known as socialization. In this section we review major theories of how gender roles are socialized, and identify primary agents of socialization. Finally we examine traditional and contemporary models of gender roles, and how changes in society and experience are affecting what it means to be feminine or masculine.

THEORIES OF SOCIALIZATION

An individual is socialized when he or she learns, directly and indirectly, how to act and think, and what to value within his or her social world. Socialization therefore affects internal processes like reasoning and the development of social schemata; it also affects behavior patterns and tendencies like personality traits.

Three broad kinds of theories address the ways in which gender roles are socialized: psychodynamic theories; social learning theories; and developmental theories.

Psychodynamic Theories. Psychodynamic theories argue that behavior and thought are the result of dynamic internal motives. The best known psychodynamic theory is psychoanalysis, developed by the Viennese physician Sigmund Freud (1856–1939). Freudian theory argues that, as infants grow into childhood, they experience conflicts over their affections for their opposite-sex parents. To resolve these crises of psychosexual development, young children unconsciously identify with their same-sex parents: little girls attach themselves to their mothers, and little boys imitate their fathers. As a result of this process, called identification, boys and girls internalize certain behavior patterns and values into their self-schemata.

Social Learning Theories. Many psychologists, unable to accept the primacy of unconscious motivation in so much social behavior, favor social learning theories over the concepts of psychoanalysis. Social learning applies basic processes of learning, like operant conditioning and observational learning, to social experience. Thus gender roles, argue social learning theorists, are developed through direct reinforcement or punishment, and through modeling.

Children who behave in ways considered appropriate to their gender will be reinforced by parents, teachers, and others who reward them for such actions. For example, a girl who chooses a dress instead of denim jeans as party attire may be complimented by her mother for looking like a "lady." Alternatively, children may be punished for violating gender roles. For example, if a boy runs from a fight with a playground bully, his father may ridicule him for being a coward or sissy. Both examples involve applying direct reward or punishment as a result of a child's spontaneous behavior.

Role modeling is a good example of observational learning of gender roles. Whenever a child imitates another's behavior in expectation of positive consequences, he or she is modeling. Gender role modeling can thus be shaped by live models, like parents and teachers, as well as by media models, including characters and figures from art, television, and the news. For example, if a girl looks through her mother's copy of a "women's magazine" she will observe the importance of things like beauty, fashion, youthfulness, cooking, and keeping house. Another example would be a young boy who observes that his older brother is praised more for his athletic abilities than his talent as an artist. In both examples children are learning about gender roles by watching the actions and preferences of other people, rather than through the consequences of their own behavior.

Developmental Theories. Social learning theories often portray the learning child as a passive recipient of powerful gender-role lessons. In contrast, social and cognitive developmental theories characterize children as active seekers of information. Children are considered to be strongly motivated to learn what to do and how to behave in order to succeed in their social world.

In brief, children want to be good members of society, so they try to identify the "good" behaviors to emulate as well as the "bad" examples to discard. This process of trying to perfect one's own behavior is termed self-socialization. For example, a boy may observe that most of his friends' fathers work outside the home, while most mothers work inside. His self-socialization conclusion, therefore, is that men work outside the home, and women work inside the home. However, if his own father works as a graphic artist from a home office, while his mother is an attorney with an office elsewhere, how will he determine his own "best" way to be masculine?

Young children—up to about age eleven or twelve—are strongly influenced by gender-role stereotypes, and tend to form rigid concepts of what is and is not appropriate for one or the other gender role. Thus it is only when they are older—around the time of puberty and adolescence—that most children are capable of gender-role transcendence, the ability to overcome stereotyped images and personal goals. In the example above, a boy who is eight years old may protest that his father is "acting too much like a mommy" by working at home, while one who is twelve or thirteen may more easily recognize that, while this is not a common arrangement, his parents' occupations do not actually hurt or change their broader gender roles.

AGENTS OF SOCIALIZATION

Controversies about child care, daycare, children's television programming and other entertainment generally revolve around concern about the agents of socialization. Who teaches children how to behave? Which agents are most influential? Research has yielded some conclusions about the key players in gender-role socialization: family experiences; schooling; peers; and adult social supports.

Family Experiences. The family interacts most with the child from the beginning of his or her life. First parents and then siblings and other family members have primary opportunities to provide both direct and indirect influences on socialization.

Regardless of family composition—the number and nature of household members—every family embodies a distinctive child-rearing climate. Child-rearing practices are seldom formally learned and vary for different families—and for different children within the same family. However, according to researchers of one model, varying child-rearing practices can be described along two dimensions: control and responsiveness.

Parents or caregivers can vary from high to low control of children's behavior. High-control parents or caregivers are demanding of their children and insist on high standards for their behavior. Low-control parents are undemanding and inconsistent in disciplining their children.

Parents can also vary in terms of responsiveness to their children's needs. High-responsive parents are very attentive to their children's needs, centering their interactions on the child. Low-responsive parents pay little attention to their children, ignoring or neglecting their needs.

Combinations of the extremes of these two dimensions yield four classifications of parenting or childrearing style. High control and high responsiveness characterize authoritative parents, who are demanding but democratic in their childcare. High control and low responsiveness distinguish authoritarian parents, who are demanding but not nurturing. Low control and high responsiveness lead to permissive childrearing, a pattern of being attentive to children while encouraging their early independence. Finally, low control and low responsiveness are hallmarks of uninvolved parents, who are detached from both their children and their parenting roles.

Regardless of the general childrearing climate, children have unique patterns of interaction with their parents, and these can lead to both gender-role opportunities and barriers. As noted above, children draw conclusions about gender roles by observing their parents and learning which behaviors are rewarded or punished. Research also indicates that boys are more harshly instructed to behave within the boundaries of masculinity than girls are encouraged to be feminine. For example, a boy who dresses like a girl will be more immediately and strictly criticized than a girl who dresses or acts boyishly. Parents also make gender-role-biased attributions about children's talents and skills; boys are encouraged to do well in mathematics, for example, while girls are warned they might do poorly. Such attributions have inevitable expectancy effects (see chapter 3), and children make similar prophecies about their own goals and talents.

Schools. After family contact and childrearing climate, children are most likely to receive gender-role socialization as a result of school experiences. School brings children in contact with non-parent adults (teachers) and peers who likely share common gender-role stereotypes. Additionally, the curriculum itself may lead to gender-role differentiation: boys may receive more instruction in science and mathematics, while girls are directed to spend more time on reading.

Specific teacher-student interactions can foster gender-role transcendence, as when a gifted girl is encouraged to pursue courses in mathematics and engineering, or a talented boy is given special instruction in drawing and painting. While such breaks from stereotyping are possible, they are rare, and most research indicates that classrooms embody prevailing gender-role prejudices in both content and social experience. For example, instead of creating mixed-gender teams, teachers often pit "the boys against the girls" in performance competitions. If boys are ridiculed for losing to girls, or girls are pitied for being brainy but not popular, gender-role stereotypes are rigidified, transcendence is less likely for any class member to achieve.

Peers. While children are young, peers (age-mates) begin to become more influential in their gender-role socialization. Children may be more likely than parents to tease (punish) boys for being sissies and girls for being tomboys. Likewise, peers may bestow the reward of social approval more generously to those whose behavior is gender-role appropriate. Research on older children, adolescents, and young adults confirms that peers have the power to make or break decisions about career paths that are nontraditional for one's gender role. As intangible as it may seem, social acceptance or popularity may be the greatest goal of much gender-role socialization.

Adult Social Supports. Is the child parent to the adult? In other words, is one's adult destiny an inevitable outcome of one's childhood influences? Research argues against this fatalistic conclusion but points out the difficulty of breaking from familiar and habitual patterns. People do continue to grow and change, and new experiences (e.g., contact with nontraditional gender-role models, like women who are attorneys and men who are childcare professionals) can alter expectations and schemata about oneself.

A critical factor in adults' success with gender-role transcendence is social support. A single mother who seeks a career in business management needs support and approval from many people: family members who assist in household labor; friends who have similar roles and aspirations; employers and colleagues who accept her nontraditional priorities; and social institutions, like daycare centers and grocery stores with extended hours. As long as such social supports are rare or unreliable, gender-role transcendence and personal fulfillment will be difficult or impossible, however enlightened the individual may be.

MODELS OF GENDER ROLES

Up to now gender roles have been described but not explicitly defined. What constitutes masculinity or femininity in modern society? Gender stereotypes provide some clues to the essence of gender roles. "Nurturant," "gentle," "talkative," "dependent," "tactful," "sensitive to others' feelings," and "neat" are all terms commonly considered to describe feminine behavior in this culture today. Conversely, masculine behavior is described by such adjectives as "competitive," "aggressive," "logical," "independent," "ambitious," "dominant," and "worldly." To a large extent the exact qualities deemed appropriate to either gender role are a matter of fashion and culture; when deciding what is feminine or masculine, it is important to consider the immediate context.

Different models to describe and interrelate gender roles have been proposed, and will be reviewed here. Finally, the impact of recent social change on gender roles will be assessed.

The One-Dimensional Model. Traditional views of gender role have characterized femininity and masculinity as polar opposites, or opposite extremes of a single dimension. According to this one-dimensional model, anyone who is high in masculinity is, by definition, low in femininity. Conversely, a very feminine person would have very few masculine characteristics. As narrow and limiting as this view of human nature may be, it does explain why some individuals might feel that a lack of one gender role's characteristics implies the presence of the other gender role. For example, a woman who does not wear her hair long (a feminine style), but rather keeps it cropped short, might be described as "boyish" in appearance. Alternatively, a young boy who prefers reading to playing competitive sports might be criticized as having "feminine" habits.

A Two-Dimensional Model. Social scientists have long rejected the one-dimensional model of gender roles in favor of a more comprehensive, two-dimensional system. In this model, femininity (high or low) represents one dimension, while masculinity (high or low) represents another. Every individual is conceived as having two values (e.g., scores on a gender-role measure): one on her or his femininity, and another on masculinity.

The two-dimensional system offers the advantage of conceptualizing a broader range of human possibilities than the one-dimensional system. Individual differences range from low to high femininity *and* low to high masculinity. By combining the extremes, clusters or patterns of traits can be recognized and identified.

Someone who is high on feminine and low on masculine characteristics is traditionally feminine, while someone who is high on masculine and low on feminine traits is traditionally masculine. Someone who is rated high on both gender roles is considered androgynous (from the Greek *andro,* "male," and *gyne,* "female"). Finally, an individual who has low instances of both feminine and masculine qualities is considered undifferentiated. Research on real-life self-reports of gender role combinations confirms that, while most men describe themselves as masculine and most women characterize themselves as feminine, sizable minorities claim qualities of both gender roles—or neither.

Changing Roles. Social changes in family structure and economic conditions have led to a revolution in gender-role identification and aspiration. Very few modern families fit the "traditional ideal" of working father, stay-at-home mother, and children. The workforce has begun to accommodate some of the needs of single parents and parents who want more family time. Domestic law has begun to consider the term "family" to include nonmarried partners. Couples are marrying later if at all, and more adults are living alone. Rigid ideas about femininity and masculinity in work and household roles are increasingly outdated and useless.

Research suggests that these social changes will lead to broader and more flexible gender schemata. For example, women will be able to pursue careers in business or science without having their femininity threatened; men will not be considered less masculine because they value domestic skills and spend time caring for children.

Some research has confirmed that androgynous people—individuals who have many feminine *and* masculine qualities—are more flexible and competent in a wide variety of tasks and endeavors. Androgynous people are also more satisfied in heterosexual marriages than traditionally feminine women or masculine men. Studies of self-esteem are less conclusive; people seem to feel better about themselves if they have more masculine qualities—regardless of their gender—not if they are more gender-appropriate (e.g., feminine females, masculine males) or androgynous (strong on both gender roles). Perhaps in this culture self-confidence still depends largely on the competence and ambition that characterize the masculine role model, not simply establishing a good fit between one's gender and one's gender role.

In conclusion, it is wise to recall that the study of gender differences in social behavior artificially exaggerates those differences. As noted earlier, most researchers conclude that, in the complex realm of human social behavior, where learning and experience interact with biological resources and predispositions, the similarities between the genders vastly outweigh the differences. Distinct gender roles may help simplify our social thinking, but they are merely vivid (and sometimes distorted) guidelines—not foolproof blueprints for individual potential and expression.

*P*eople *are generally interested in understanding individual differences in themselves and others. This has led to a focus on gender differences in social behavior, ways in which the behavior of females differs from that of males.*

While researchers generally agree that the genders are more similar than different in terms of social behavior, some gender differences have been identified. Men generally exhibit greater social power than women. Men occupy more positions of authority and command greater status. In the same or similar areas of performance, men receive higher pay and greater advancement. In both verbal and nonverbal language, men display greater dominance than women.

Women have been found to demonstrate greater skills in interpersonal communication, both in sending and receiving. Men have been found more likely to help in responding to emergency or crisis intervention, but studies of less heroic helping contexts are rare and thus a gender difference is not clear.

Women have been found to be more sexually conservative than men, who are more permissive, less selective, and more likely to initiate sexual contact than women.

Men are consistently identified as behaving more aggressively than women, who are more likely to experience guilt in the wake of aggressive action.

Studies of conformity are more frequently inconclusive about gender differences, but when a difference does emerge it is women who are more likely to conform to social influence.

Intellectually, men generally outperform women in mathematics and visual-spatial tasks, while women do better than men in verbal performance.

Research indicates that gender differences in social behavior are not attributable to simple biological determinants, but are the result of complex interactions between culture and learning and any biological factors. Gender differences in complex behavior can be traced to processes of childhood socialization, and the evolution and development of social roles.

Gender socialization begins with the recognition of prevailing gender stereotypes within one's culture and social environment. Young children develop such stereotypes first by gender typing ideas and items as being either feminine or masculine. They then develop broader gender schemata about different forms of feminine or masculine roles. Roles are also shaped by images popularized in stereotyped media portrayals. While personal experiences can soften the impact of media stereotypes, it is common for stereotyped thinking to foster and support sexism.

Gender roles—patterns of thought and action that are considered appropriate for females or males—are developed as a result of gender socialization. Three different traditions characterize theories of gender socialization. Psychodynamic theories favor the influence of gender identification in resolving unconscious conflicts in early childhood. Social learning theories argue for the power of operant learning (e.g., reinforcement and punishment) and observational learning (e.g., modeling) in gender socialization. Finally, social and cognitive developmental theories describe the processes by which children actively seek information about gender roles they can emulate.

The agents of gender socialization include family, schools, peers, and adult social supports. Family influences include both parental interaction and general childrearing climate. Schools provide both peer and teacher modeling and direct curricular guidelines for gender-role expectations. Peers can provide either acceptance or rejection to shape individual gender socialization. Older children are more likely than younger ones to achieve gender-role transcendence, but adults are most likely to succeed, and only with the aid of individual and institutional social supports that support their efforts.

Traditional models of gender roles were one-dimensional, positing femininity at one extreme and masculinity at the other. Recent research favors a two-dimensional model, in which each individual's behavior can be characterized as high or low feminine and high or low masculine. The two-dimensional model permits characterization of gender-role combinations as traditionally feminine, traditionally masculine, androgynous, or undifferentiated.

Social changes in recent decades have prompted speculation about redefinition of gender roles. Greater behavioral flexibility may be possible for androgynous than for traditional gender-typed individuals. However, such change is still new and its effects inconclusive. Moreover, a research focus on gender differences may obscure recognizing that similarities between the genders outweigh the differences that can be documented.

Selected Readings

Ashmore, R. D. and F. K. Del Boca. (Eds.). (1987). *The Social Psychology of Male-Female Relations*. New York: Academic Press.

Basow, S. (1986). *Gender Stereotypes: Traditions and Alternatives*. Pacific Grove, CA: Brooks/Cole.

Bleier, R. (1984). *Science and Gender*. New York: Pergamon.

Brownmiller, S. (1984). *Femininity*. New York: Linden Press.

Carter, D. B. (Ed.). (1987). *Current Conceptions of Sex Roles and Sex Typing*. New York: Praeger.

Doyle, J. A. (1983). *The Male Experience*. Dubuque, IA: Wm. C. Brown.

Eagly, A. H. (1987). *Sex Differences in Social Behavior: A Social Role interpretation*. Hillsdale, NJ: Erlbaum.

Fausto-Sterling, A. (1985). *Myths of Gender: Biological Theories About Women and Men*. New York: Basic Books.

Gilligan, C. (1982). *In a Different Voice: Psychological Theory and Women's Development*. Cambridge, MA: Harvard University Press.

Gutek, B. A. (1985). *Sex and the Workplace*. San Francisco: Jossey-Bass.

Guttentag, M. and P. F. Secord. (1982). *Too Many Women: The Sex Ratio Question*. Beverly Hills, CA: Sage.

Henley, N. M. (1977). *Body Politics: Power, Sex, and Nonverbal Communication*. Englewood Cliffs, NJ: Prentice Hall.

Hochschild, A. (1989). *The Second Shift: Working Parents and the Revolution at Home*. New York: Viking.

Matlin, M. W. (1987). *The Psychology of Women*. New York: Holt, Rinehart and Winston.

Miller, J. B. (1986). *Toward a New Psychology of Women*, 2nd edition. Boston: Beacon Press.

Pleck, J. H. (1981). *The Myth of Masculinity*. Cambridge, MA: MIT Press.

Shaver, P.. and C. Hendrick. (Eds.). (1987). *Sex and Gender*. Newbury Park, CA: Sage.

Tavris, C. and C. Wade. (1984). *The Longest War: Sex Differences in Perspective*. New York: Harcourt Brace Jovanovich.

8

Attitudes and Behavior

All humans seek to understand, predict, and control events in their lives. Psychologists apply the scientific method to this quest, and social psychologists focus in particular on social events and experiences. Early in its history, social psychology was consumed by the study of attitudes. Attitudes and opinions are formed in the course of our social experiences and predispose us to enter or avoid new experiences. More importantly, however, attitudes provide information about likely behavior. Thus attitude research is of interest to advertisers and consumers, politicians and voters, and others who hope to predict behavior.

Decades of research on attitudes led to greater caution in psychologists' attempts to predict behavior. More recently, evidence suggests that attitudes may even be the outcomes—rather than the predictors—of many actions. This chapter reviews the structure and relevance of attitudes today, how attitudes are formed, theories of how attitudes are related to behavior, and ways to apply our knowledge about these relationships.

DEFINING ATTITUDES

Attitudes and Related Concepts

An attitude is an evaluative reaction—a judgment regarding one's liking or disliking—of a person, event, or other aspect of the environment. As an evaluation, an attitude is a non-neutral position about the attitude object; it is either positive (good, approving) or negative (bad, rejecting), but never neutral. An attitude can range in its intensity, however; it can be slight, moderate, or extreme. For example, you may like vanilla ice cream, strongly prefer chocolate, and slightly dislike strawberry; all are attitudes, because they all involve evaluations.

Attitudes are formed to summarize experience and simplify behavior choices. Your attitudes about sex, violence, and movie stars, for example, will help you decide which movies to see and which to avoid. Attitudes develop from experience, and guide future behavior.

MODELS OF ATTITUDES

Attitude models attempt to account for the components and uses of attitudes.

One-Dimensional Model. The simplest model defines attitudes strictly in terms of liking or disliking for a particular object. Thus your dislike of movie violence (a negative attitude about violence in movies) generally will lead you to avoid movies you believe show too much violence on screen.

Three-Component Model. More useful are models that expand the effects of attitudes to a broader range of psychological experience. The popular three-part model argues that a single attitude involves three dimensions: cognitive experience (like beliefs), affective experience (emotions), and behavior (choices and actions).

For example, according to the three-part model, your dislike of movie violence will have developed from three kinds of information: ideas and beliefs you have about violence in movies; feelings you have experienced when you watch violent films; and your own behaviors and choices regarding such movies.

Moreover, your current negative evaluation of violent films includes three specific kinds of consequences: you probably have negative beliefs about violent movies; you experience unpleasant emotions when you watch them; and when you know a movie is considered to be violent, you will choose not to see it.

This last component—the behavioral intentions or consequences of an attitude—is especially important, since it implies that a person's attitudes predict her or his future behaviors. For example, if your friends know you have a negative attitude about violent movies, they can predict whether you will want to see a particular movie with them, based on its reputation for violence.

RELATED CONCEPTS

The term *attitude* can generally be used interchangeably with *opinion*; both refer to a person's evaluations of an attitude object or *referent* (the thing that is being evaluated).

Beliefs. A *belief* can be a part of an attitude, but it does not encompass the same experience. A belief is knowledge one accepts about a referent, it serves a cognitive function by providing information. A belief does not include the emotional or behavioral consequences of that information. Believing that bananas are tasty and edible, for example, is not the same as feeling happy to find a banana when you are hungry.

Nonattitudes. One's knowledge about a referent may include awareness of how many people feel, but this is not an attitude unless the evaluator shares that reaction. For example, in response to a political opinion survey, you may report that many people were offended by a candidate's prejudiced remarks, but this does not express your own attitude unless you feel offended too. Such knowledge—which includes beliefs and ideas about feelings and others' behavior—is best described as a *nonattitude*.

Attitude Measurement

One source of the attitude's appeal for social psychologists has been its accessibility to measurement. If an attitude can be measured, researchers can assess how it influences behavior, and is influenced by factors like time and social pressure.

SELF-REPORT TECHNIQUES

The most widely used form of attitude measurement involves asking individuals to report their own attitudes, a class of techniques known as self-report. Different self-report techniques, usually named for their developers, involve providing different kinds of answers or ratings.

Thurstone Scales. L. L. Thurstone (1887–1955) developed the first statistically useful approach to measuring attitudes. For a Thurstone scale, a researcher develops a set of statements about the attitude object. Each statement is then reviewed by judges who assign it a numerical rating according to a positive-negative scale. For example, imagine a 1 to 10 point scale of attitudes about President George Bush, where 1 indicates strongly positive attitudes and 10 indicates strongly negative attitudes. Thus, the statement "George Bush is the greatest president the United States has ever had" might probably be rated 1; "George Bush is a good person who does his best" might be rated 3; and "George Bush is the worst president the United States has ever had" might be rated 10.

A Thurstone scale is administered by asking respondents simply to read the list of statements, checking those with which they agree. The ratings assigned the checked statements are averaged to obtain an attitude score. Using the above example, a respondent whose average agreement rating is 2.5 obviously maintains a more positive attitude about George Bush than one whose average score is 8.6.

Likert Scales. Because Thurstone scales require so many steps (composing statements, judging them, administering and computing averages), they are used only rarely for attitude measurement. More common are Likert scales, named for developer Rensis Likert (1903–1981). Likert scales (pronounced LICK-ert), also known as summated rating scales, typically include several attitude statements. A respondent chooses a number from a scale of agreement to disagreement. The sum of the numbers chosen makes up the respondent's attitude to the referent in question.

For example, in completing a Likert scale on your attitude about cigarette advertising, you might read a series of statements in support of or against such advertising. Each statement is followed by a numbered scale indicating agreement or disagreement. Such a five-point scale might look like this:

Strongly Agree 1 2 3 4 5 Strongly Disagree

If you oppose cigarette advertising, you will choose low numbers for statements against such advertising, and high numbers for statements in favor of it. Summing numbers for the two different kinds of statements yields numerical measures of your attitude and its intensity.

Semantic Differential Scales. A single attitude includes different meanings or qualities of evaluation. For example, a negative attitude about cigarette advertising might include believing that such advertisements tell lies, and feeling angry at seeing a deceptive cigarette advertisement in a magazine or on an outdoor sign. A self-report technique that addresses these differences in meaning is the use of semantic differential scales. A respondent is asked to rate an attitude object on several scales whose meanings (semantics) differ.

For example, you might rate cigarette advertising along each of the following scales:

Good	1 2 3 4 5	Bad
Beautiful	1 2 3 4 5	Ugly
Honest	1 2 3 4 5	Dishonest
Healthy	1 2 3 4 5	Unhealthy

After rating, connecting the numbers will show a profile or pattern of ratings that is distinct from every other respondent's. As with other rating scales, your attitude can still be summarized in a numerical average. Semantic differential scales thus offer both summarized values and qualitative distinctions.

ALTERNATIVE MEASURES

A central problem with self-report techniques is response bias, the tendency of respondents to distort their responses to portray themselves as more knowledgeable or socially desirable. Another problem is that respondents may not have considered some attitudes carefully enough to rate them or express them verbally. In light of such concerns, researchers have developed alternative measures of attitude valence (positive or negative value) and intensity.

Physiological Measures. The affective or emotional component of an attitude may show up in physiological arousal. A more direct assessment of some attitudes may be achieved by measuring a respondent's arousal through such indications as pupil dilation, heart rate, and galvanic skin response (GSR, referring to the electrical conductivity of perspiration), and facial muscle activity. Such measures offer the advantage of being difficult for a respondent to control or disguise. Their major disadvantage is their inability to indicate the valence or direction of the respondent's attitude. For example, if a person's jaw muscles tighten at the mention of nuclear arms control, does that indicate that she favors or opposes such legislation?

The Bogus Pipeline Technique. Respondents may be less biased if they believe their efforts to deceive researchers are useless. For example, researchers arranged to record physiological arousal measures from subjects who also provided self-reports of their attitudes. The respondents were told that their "true" attitudes would be revealed by the arousal measures. In these circumstances, believing deception would be impossible, subjects were more likely to admit having unpopular or "politically incorrect" opinions. Thus the "cover story" about recording physiological responses tricked subjects into being more truthful.

Because arousal biofeedback is too general to serve as a "lie detector" or genuine attitude meter, this strategy is known as the *bogus pipeline* or false-feedback technique. When used to reduce subjects' response bias, it is really a self-report attitude measurement. As such, it works only if subjects believe such lie detection is possible; the bogus pipeline itself cannot really measure attitudes, but it may reduce deception or distortion in respondents' self-reports.

Alternately, the bogus pipeline can serve as a *non*-self-report technique if, once convinced such arousal measures work, subjects are asked to guess the attitudes these measures will reveal. In this way the subjects act as relatively objective observers of their own attitudes, rather than sources of self-descriptions they might be tempted to disguise.

Behavioral Measures. Ideally one's attitudes are reflected in one's behaviors. Thus a fair way to assess attitudes would be to observe an individual's actions, and make correspondent inferences (see also this theory of attribution in chapter 6). For example, suppose a researcher wishes to measure attitudes relevant to a major behavioral choice, like voting in an election. In order to assess attitudes *before* the election, the researcher might study related pre-election behaviors, like attending rallies in support of the candidates or contributing money to the candidates' campaigns. The numbers of people who attend rallies or the amount of money contributed to campaigns provide behavioral measures of attitudes toward the candidates.

Unobtrusive Measures. Observing people's behavior is a simple but reactive way to learn about attitudes. If people know their behavior is being studied, they may behave in distorted or deceptive ways. Therefore many researchers advise using unobtrusive measures, hidden or less obvious ways of learning what people do by studying the evidence or aftereffects of their actions (see Chapter 2). A simple example of how to measure political attitudes via unobtrusive measures would be to count partisan bumper stickers on cars in different businesses' parking lots.

One way to measure the popularity of different flavors of ice cream at a restaurant or concession would be to note the levels of ice cream remaining in containers after customers have been served. Because this equates popularity with low levels of ice cream, it is a measure of *erosion*.

An examination of the discarded napkins, bags, and paper cups strewn in a neighborhood with several different fast-food restaurants might indicate the source of most of the litter. This could suggest which restaurant is most popular—or merely that the patrons of that restaurant are most likely to litter. Such an unobtrusive measure, because it studies the artifacts and materials people leave behind, is a measure of *accretion*.

Some unobtrusive measures are ingeniously designed to gauge more specific attitudes than merely popularity. One intriguing strategy is the *lost-letter technique,* in which researchers leave stamped, addressed envelopes in various locations in the region being studied. Some are addressed in ways that support one side of an issue (e.g., "Committee to Re-Elect Senator Holt") while others suggest the opposite position (e.g., "Defeat Holt Committee"). Presumably a bystander who comes across such a "lost letter" will be more likely to mail it if she or he agrees with its apparent sentiment. Thus researchers wait to see which side gets more of its letters mailed; the final percentage provides a rough estimate of prevailing community opinion. While such a technique may reduce respondent bias, it also measures only community attitudes about the referents, not individual opinions.

ATTITUDE FORMATION

Ideally, attitudes are formed from one's experiences to serve as guides for future behavior. Researchers have identified three broad approaches to understanding how attitudes are formed: learning approaches; cognitive consistency approaches; and motivational approaches.

Learning Approaches

Attitudes are most commonly formed through learning, the process whereby experience and practice leads to relatively permanent behavior change. Three general learning processes have been identified in attitude formation: association; reinforcement; and social learning.

ASSOCIATION

Association involves making connections between experiences that are close together in time, space, or circumstances. Two forms of attitude formation through association are classical conditioning and mere exposure.

Classical Conditioning. Although most attitudes are complex collections of ideas, feelings, and intentions, some may be built on associating one experience with another, and making a common response. Learning to make the same response to a new stimulus that is associated with the original stimulus is termed *classical conditioning*. For simple emotional experiences, classical conditioning may lead to attitude formation.

For example, if a young child is required to attend church with her parents, and the church itself is usually hot and uncomfortable, she may come to think of "going to church" as synonymous with "being physically uncomfortable for an hour." Since discomfort is something she tries to avoid whenever possible, she may find herself looking for ways to avoid attending church. Over time, if her experiences are not broadened or corrected, she may develop a negative attitude about church attendance and faith in general.

Mere Exposure. A more subtle form of attitude formation can be built on repeated experiences with attitude objects, such as people or environmental features you encounter frequently over time. Social psychologist Robert Zajonc has documented the effects of such *mere exposure*. According to Zajonc (pronounced ZY-ence), repeated exposure to an object generally leads to positive feelings. For example, a television commercial you have seen many times may result in your liking the advertised product better than one you have never heard of. The mere exposure effect may occur because we associate familiarity (a result of frequent encounters) with reliability or attractiveness. This has important implications for interpersonal attraction (see chapter 15).

REINFORCEMENT

Most attitudes are too complex to develop from mere association. Attitudes can be learned from personal experience because of the consequences of that experience. For example, if you find that every time you take a psychology course, you enjoy the classes and earn high grades, you will be *reinforced* in developing a positive attitude toward psychology. Reinforcement is any consequence that increases a behavior, like a tendency to take certain kinds of courses or read certain kinds of books.

Family Influence. Parents and other family members are usually the first to provide reinforcement for an individual's attitudes. We are more likely to receive such rewards as praise, dessert, and social approval when we agree with our family members' expressed attitudes. Thus early parental reinforcement can shape attitudes that we carry with us into later life, including political and religious values and social opinions like racism or sexism.

Peers and Reference Groups. As we grow through childhood and adolescence, our peers become more important influences on our attitudes. As we spend more time with friends and age-mates and less with our families, our peers become a more important *reference group* by which to judge our opinions and values. The reinforcement provided by our reference groups usually takes the form of social acceptance and popularity. Thus teenagers and young adults may learn to express opinions that violate their parents' values, but are validated and supported—reinforced—by their friends, classmates, and coworkers.

SOCIAL LEARNING

Some attitudes may be acquired as a result of passive associations or the persuasive influence of reinforcing agents. More commonly, however, people actively seek information and experiences on which to base attitudes and behavioral intentions. This active quest characterizes the social learning approach to attitude formation. The most common forms of social learning involve vicarious learning (observing the consequences of others' behavior) and modeling (learning to imitate others' behavior).

Vicarious Learning. How do we learn new ways to act, dress, talk, buy, or vote? While we may experiment directly with some new behaviors, we can also learn by watching what happens to others. For example, a 14-year-old boy may not really understand what homosexuality is, but he sees that those who admit to being gay are criticized or persecuted by most of his classmates. He may thus learn vicariously—through watching what happens to the victims of such persecution—to express homophobic, anti-gay attitudes, and not to voice more tolerant or open-minded opinions.

Modeling. People whom we admire make up our *aspirational reference group* (in contrast with our *actual reference group,* the peer group with whom we currently identify). We may seek to improve our social lives by affecting and imitating the habits and tastes of those we admire. Thus if you admire a rock star who advocates legalizing marijuana, you may imitate her pro-legalization stance as one more way of "belonging" with her social group.

Cognitive Consistency Approaches

The cognitive tradition in psychology emphasizes people's desire to understand and acquire information about their world. One implication of the cognitive approach is that people need their beliefs and opinions to make sense. Since attitudes have a cognitive component (beliefs), we generally develop attitudes that make sense or are consistent (harmonious) with each other. Three cognitive consistency approaches specifically deal with the form and function of attitudes: balance theory, cognitive-affective consistency theory, and dissonance theory.

BALANCE THEORY

According to Gestalt theorist Fritz Heider (see chapter 4), cognitive elements like attitudes are in balance when they agree with each other. For example, if you (represented by P) like your best friend (O) and both you and your best friend like the same candidate for political office (represented by X), these three relationships are all in balance. They can be represented by the following triad (threesome) of notations:

P+ O, P+ X, and O+ X

Balance can also be maintained when attitudes are negative, as when both you and your best friend *dislike* the same candidate:

P+ O, P–X, and O–X

In its simplest terms, balance theory argues that an odd number of negative relationships (-) in a triad reveals an *imbalanced* set of cognitions. For example, if your best friend hates the same candidate whom you favor, this imbalanced state of affairs will create discomfort for you, and motivate you to change your opinion—either of your best friend, or of the candidate in question.

Balance theory accounts for attitude formation through a process of building on preexisting sentiments. For example, if you like your psychology professor, and she expresses a clear opinion about something you have not yet decided, you can best maintain balance by developing an attitude that agrees with hers.

COGNITIVE-AFFECTIVE CONSISTENCY

Sometimes we have evaluations—like feelings—about a person or thing before we have any real information. For example, you may be warned against someone you do not know personally by friends of yours who dislike him. Thus you have a negative affect—emotion—about this person, but no beliefs or information to back it up. According to the cognitive-affective consistency approach, you will collect information to "flesh out" your negative attitude about this person. For example, you may seek out examples of this person's social inadequacies, flaws, and crimes. In this way, your prejudiced emotion biases the kind of information you seek and remember about this person. You are most likely to seek and remember cognitive information that agrees—is consistent—with your established affect.

DISSONANCE THEORY

One of the most fascinating consistency approaches to attitude function is dissonance theory, developed by Leon Festinger (see chapter 4). Dissonance is an experience of discomfort created by disharmony among cognitive elements like attitudes. For example, if a woman believes herself to be open-minded and unprejudiced, she will experience cognitive dissonance if she finds herself unwilling to accept a date with someone of another race. Dissonance is theorized to be a motivating experience, an unpleasant experience one seeks to reduce by changing attitudes or behavior. The woman in the example above might reduce her dissonance, for example, either by accepting a date with someone of another race, confirming her original self-opinion, or by reformulating her opinion of herself to include her new-found prejudice. Either way, she will restore and maintain consistency among her existing constellation of attitudes.

Dissonance theory, like other cognitive consistency theories, is based on the assumption that harmony or consonance among cognitive elements like attitudes is important. It is particularly relevant to attitude change, as in the above example, and will be discussed in greater detail in chapter 9.

Motivational Approaches

Dissonance theory hints at another view of attitude formation, the idea that we may be more motivated to adopt some attitudes than others. Such motivational or incentive approaches assume that individuals assess the costs and benefits of making certain responses, including maintaining and expressing certain attitudes. Two kinds of models that fit this motivational characterization are evaluation models and processing models.

EVALUATION MODELS

Evaluation models characterize attitude formation as motivated by a desire to maximize positive outcomes. One model examines the importance of subjective evaluations of attitude objects, and another gives greater weight to expected value.

Cognitive Response Theory. One way we develop attitudes is by listening to those others express, and assessing whether we agree or disagree. Agreement is a positive cognitive response to a position statement, while disagreement is a negative cognitive response. The cognitive response approach suggests that, in determining whether you share a particular attitude, you will first assess whether your responses to the different parts of the attitude are mostly positive or negative.

For example, in deciding which of two cars you should buy, you will respond positively or negatively to each of several features about the two you are comparing. According to the cognitive response theory, you will form the preferential attitude toward the car that leaves you feeling more positive—even if those responses are not reasonable or fair. The essence of the cognitive response theory is that your subjective sense of agreement— *feeling* positive in your responses to the referent—determines your attitude, not a more objective assessment of your direct experience with the product.

Expectancy-Value Theory. Like cognitive response theory, expectancy-value theory argues that attitudes develop from an evaluation, a consideration of the positive and negative aspects of the attitude object.

Expectancy-value theory, however, includes the additional consideration of the *probability* that this attitude will lead one to good or bad outcomes. For example, you may find that, in deciding which of two cars to buy, you consider not only how each one looks, feels, and impresses you *now,* but also which one *will* seem like the better investment *later*. Thus, although the more expensive model is attractive and sporty, the less streamlined alternative offers more room for your possessions and your friends, and so you *expect* greater value from it in the future.

ELABORATION VERSUS HEURISTIC PROCESSING

The way an attitude is formed may depend on the importance of the attitude object, and the circumstances in which one's opinions take shape. Several theorists distinguish between attitudes formed as a result of elaboration or systematic cognitive processing and those acquired as a result of peripheral or heuristic processing.

Elaboration. The *elaboration-likelihood model* is an important theoretical understanding of how attitudes change in response to persuasive communication. Also termed the *central* or *systematic processing model,* this explanation has implications for both attitude development and change (see chapter 9). According to the elaboration-likelihood model, people are more likely to be thoughtful in deciding their attitudes in some circumstances than in others. Under ideal conditions, we think carefully about the arguments on both sides of a position before we take a stand. But when conditions are not ideal, we may be more influenced by peripheral factors like how attractive the source is or how we feel at the moment. (Thus *elaborate,* thoughtful attitude formation is more *likely* only when circumstances permit such thinking to develop).

Heuristic Processing. In contrast with the elaboration-likelihood model, the *heuristic* or *peripheral processing model* explains that many of our attitudes are formed rather quickly and easily, without apparent anguish or cost-benefit analysis. When we are distracted, uninvolved, or uninformed about an issue, we may pay more attention to superficial considerations, like how attractive the communicator is or whether we feel like being agreeable at the moment. Under such conditions, therefore, we rely on mental heuristics (rules of thumb or simple guidelines) or on peripheral cues to determine our final attitudes about the issues or objects in question.

Comparing the Models. The contrast between central, systematic processing or elaboration, and peripheral or heuristic processing is appealing, because it admits that human behavior is complex and varied: we do not form all our attitudes in the same way, or hold them all with equal intensity. Both the nature and the stability of our attitudes depends somewhat on the conditions and reasons that affected how we first formed them.

For example, your choice to join a particular social club at your school could be the result of either systematic/elaborative thought or peripheral/heuristic processing. If you were systematic, you would join because you have considered all the fraternities and sororities available and chosen that one above them all. As a result, your loyalty to this club if you become a member will probably be strong. In contrast, if you joined because of peripheral consideration—e.g., a casual friend urged you to join, and you had nothing else to do—you may find your loyalty quickly flagging if the costs of membership become too high.

ATTITUDES AND BEHAVIOR

From the beginning, attitude research has been intriguing because of its promise to predict future behavior. In recent years researchers have re-examined the exact relationship between attitudes and behavior. Traditional theories assumed that attitudes were formed first, and became the basis for behavioral intentions. More recent work has suggested that the relationship between attitudes and behavior is not unidirectional but rather one of mutual influence.

Do Attitudes Predict Behavior?

Do attitudes lead to behavioral intentions and ultimately to specific behaviors? If so, an advertiser or political campaigner need only measure a person's opinion to gauge the likelihood that he or she will buy or vote in a particular way. Early research suggested that expressed attitudes might not always predict related behavior. Later work has endeavored to identify the exact conditions in which attitudes do predict behavior.

EXPRESSED VERSUS IMPLICIT ATTITUDES

Most attitude measures rely on self-report, as reviewed above. Can such public descriptions be trusted, or are they too distorted by social desirability and other response biases? Classic research on the frailty of expressed attitudes has led to speculation about the reality of attitudes for most people.

LaPiere's Research. In 1934 researcher Richard LaPiere traveled across the United States with a Chinese couple, receiving service at hundreds of hotels and restaurants with very little evidence of anti-Chinese prejudice. Six months later, LaPiere wrote to the same establishments to inquire whether they *would* grant service to Chinese persons. Surprisingly, he received word that such service would be *refused* by over 90 percent of those responding. Did people's stated attitudes toward Chinese persons have so little correspondence to their actual behaviors?

LaPiere's surprising research was too flawed to be conclusive. Those granting service during his travels may have been different individuals from those who responded to his later letters of inquiry. It is important to examine the relationship between the attitudes and behavior of the same individual.

Are Attitudes Real? Some critics have speculated that attitudes do not really exist as "behavioral intentions" in people's minds, even if people are able to rate their agreement with various opinions in paper-and-pencil measures. Recent research makes important distinctions between attitudes, expressed attitudes, and behavior. If an attitude is real, it is only one of several influences on one's relevant behavior. For example, if you have an attitude in favor of ordering anchovies on pizza, you may order it if your friends agree; but if your friends contributing to a common pizza dislike anchovies, you may choose not to act on your pro-anchovy attitude at this particular time.

One's real attitude may not exactly match one's expressed attitude. For example, if you enjoyed a movie that your friends hated, you may refrain from openly disagreeing with them, for the sake of keeping peace. Your real attitude—"That was an enjoyable movie"—may go unexpressed, or may be kept secret while you express a popular opinion—"That was a terrible movie"—with which you secretly disagree.

WHEN DO ATTITUDES MATCH BEHAVIOR?

Researchers have found that the predictive power of attitudes depends on the way attitudes are formed, measured, and experienced.

Behavioral Specificity. The more specific an attitude is about behavior, the better it will predict related behavior. For example, how many people will attend a Saturday morning litter-collection drive? Measuring a very general attitude, like asking, "Do you believe it is important to keep our campus clean?," will probably not predict specific litter-pickup behavior. Many people will agree with the general question, but fail to show up for such a specific effort.

A better way to predict whether someone is likely to attend a litter collection drive is to ask specifically, "Will you show your support for a clean environment by attending a litter collection drive on campus this Saturday morning at ten o'clock?" Agreement with this behavior-specific statement is a better predictor of the action in question than expression of a more general value.

Attitude Potency. The stronger the attitude in one's thinking, the more it will influence subsequent behavior. Research shows that attitudes formed through *personal experience* are stronger than those based on second-hand information or less direct sources. For example, a man who has asked for and received help from his state legislator is more likely to support her for re-election than another supporter who has not had such a direct experience to validate his support. If several people have similar levels of agreement with an attitude, those whose attitudes are stronger because of more direct experience will be more likely to show their commitment in their behavior.

Attitudes are also stronger for those who have a *vested interest* in certain positions. For example, a 17-year-old may have a stronger commitment to protesting legislation to raise the age requirement for driver's licenses than a sympathetic 23-year-old. If the age requirement is raised to 18 years, the 17-year-old will lose a personal privilege, while the 23-year-old will not. The person with the vested interested—whose experience will be more strongly affected by the issue in question—is more likely to act on her anti-legislation attitude than the older, less affected one.

Attitude Salience. Related to attitude potency is the quality of attitude salience. Attitudes are more salient if they are more noticeable or prominent in our attention. Salient attitudes are more likely to be recalled and acted upon.

Attitudes can be made more salient by *priming*, using cues or reminders to bring them forward in one's memory. For example, a voter who has not made up his mind between two candidates may be influenced by the cries and banners of campaign workers near the polling center. The words of campaign workers may prime or retrieve the voter's earlier opinions; once recalled, these attitudes are more likely to be acted on.

Attitudes can also be made more salient by increasing an individual's *self-awareness*. Self-awareness focuses one's attention on oneself, including one's attitudes. For example, campaigns to reduce littering may employ posters with slogans like "People Who Litter Are Trash." Such slogans prompt the would-be litterer to reconsider—"I'm not trash, am I?"—creating self-awareness, including (it is hoped!) an anti-littering attitude.

Does Behavior Influence Attitudes?

Since attitudes only seem to predict behavior when, as described above, attitudes are particularly potent or salient, is the connection between attitudes and behavior really a weak one? On the contrary, there appears to be a strong attitude-behavior link if it is assumed to go in either direction. Specifically, it appears that not only can people use attitudes as the basis for behavior, we can also form attitudes on the basis of behaviors. Several research findings illustrate the tendency for actions to beget attitudes.

ROLE PLAYING

Acting as if you believe something can lead you to that belief. Research has explored several examples of how playing a part can create role-related attitudes.

Behavior Change. Research has shown that people who pretend to be lung-cancer victims are more likely to succeed in later efforts to quit smoking. Presumably the role made it easier to internalize the relevant attitude—regret at not having quit—which then made the behavioral commitment easier as well.

Self-Attribution. As reviewed in chapter 4, behaving in a certain way can lead one to make correspondent inferences about oneself. For example, smiling—for no reason—can apparently *induce* a good mood, or increase one's willingness to laugh at humorous material. Apparently, even when we know we are playing a part, we internalize the attitudes or moods that maintain that role.

The Foot-in-the-Door Effect

Studies of interpersonal influence have confirmed that people are more likely to acquiesce to a large request if they have previously agreed to a smaller, related request. This tendency, the *foot-in-the-door effect,* works because the first agreement (a behavior) led to the formation of an agreeable attitude, which in turn increased compliance with the second request.

For example, if an acquaintance asks you for a dollar, and you agree, your gift establishes your willingness (an attitude) to give money. If the same person later asks you for ten dollars, you may find it hard to refuse, since you would have to violate your willing-to-give-money attitude to do so.

Momentum of Compliance. The foot-in-the-door technique depends on several factors to be effective. First, the respondent's behaviors must be freely committed, not coerced. Second, subsequent demands or requests must increase the level of commitment required. Together these factors create a *momentum of compliance,* an increasing tendency to comply or behave in accordance with the requester's demands. The power of this strategy has been demonstrated in many forms of social influence, as will be discussed later in this chapter and chapters 9 and 10.

The Low-Ball Technique. A specific application of the foot-in-the-door principle is the *low-ball technique,* a persuasive strategy some salespersons use. In low-balling, a salesperson offers a customer merchandise for a bargain price (i.e., "pitches a low ball") but later raises the price before closing the sale. The customer, instead of refusing the deal, may feel committed to purchasing the *merchandise* even though the *price* has increased. Thus the customer has been induced to develop an attitude favorable to the specific merchandise rather than to the original terms of the sale.

The foot-in-the-door technique and its offspring depends on the power of behavior to develop a sense of commitment. Once an individual has acted in a self-committing way, he or she will be more reluctant to change a related attitude or behave differently in the future.

INDOCTRINATION

Fascinating research confirming the power of behavior to shape attitudes has examined real-world cases of indoctrination, such as recruitment or conversion. Two specific kinds of indoctrination illustrate the power of behavior to shape attitudes: brainwashing and cult recruitment.

Brainwashing. Popular images of brainwashing—converting fighters or campaigners to their enemies' causes—often suggest that victims cave in under the pressure of torture and threat. In fact, research confirms that such threats or bribes bring about short-term compliance but not long-term acceptance. True conversion is only possible when pressures are withheld, and instead victims are induced, step-by-step, to behave more and more in agreement with their captors.

For example, when American heiress Patricia Hearst was kidnapped and held prisoner by terrorists in the early 1970s, she was induced to join them not through coercion but through gradual invitations to participate in their revolutionary work. Repeatedly assured that she was "free to leave," she came to infer that she stayed not out of fear but out of commitment. Thus brainwashing employs a technique similar to foot-in-the-door persuasion: invite first small and then larger behavioral commitments from the target person, and she will develop attitudes that sustain this behavior.

Cult Recruitment. Cults are difficult to distinguish from mainstream social groups like organized religions or political parties. An important distinction appears to be cults' tendencies to isolate their members, protecting them from outside perspectives and influences, and controlling members' interpretations of events. Researchers have identified common attitude-shaping techniques employed by cult recruiters. For example, prospective members may first be invited to inquiry meetings, and then asked gradually to make stronger commitments by attending education sessions, doing favors for other members, or tithing larger amounts to cult support. In this way a "momentum of compliance" is established, from which it is difficult for the recruit to depart.

It should be noted that, while cult recruitment techniques seem devious because their purposes are suspect, many of the same general practices prevail in mainstream organizations. Political causes recruit support with smaller and then larger requests for involvement and support. Respected churches bring new members "into the fold" through a staggered series of requests, involvements, and commitments. Whatever the application, the attitude-shaping principles are basically the same: once a behavior pattern is established, the actor develops attitudes that will support and maintain it.

Theories of Attitude-Behavior Relationships

Several theories or models are broad enough to address why attitudes prompt behavior and how behaviors shape attitudes: the reasoned action model; self-presentation; self-perception; and self-justification.

THE REASONED ACTION MODEL

Researchers Icek Ajzen and Martin Fishbein have developed a very influential model of attitude-behavior relationships. Their *reasoned action model* argues that attitudes are important in forming behavioral intentions, and that people generally seek to behave in accordance with such intentions. This model assumes that human thought and action are rational: we behave only when we have reasons, and when we have good reasons we act on them. The reasoned action model can be applied to explain a wide variety of behaviors and attitudes, and so has maintained popularity among researchers and applied practitioners.

A major problem with the reasoned action model is its exclusion of non-rational factors that can influence behavior. Such factors may include limited abilities or resources, perceived control, and external constraints and opportunities. For example, if you are impressed by a television commercial and form a behavioral intention to buy the product advertised, will you inevitably act on this intention? Not if you cannot find the product, or cannot pay the price, or find a satisfying alternative.

SELF-PRESENTATION

Cognitive consistency theories maintain that people value the experience and the appearance of being consistent. Self-presentation arguments extend this by pointing out that people will try to act in attitude-consistent ways, presumably in order to seem reasonable and stable. According to self-presentation theories, we consider how attitude-behavior connections will affect *impression management* efforts, attempts to control others' perceptions of us. In some cases we will try to appear consistent, and so act out our stated attitudes. In others we may "go with the flow" of social pressures and act like those around us, perhaps violating some unexpressed attitudes. In either extreme, the relationship between particular attitudes and behavior is determined by the actor's concerns with self-presentation.

Self-presentation theories address the *appearance* of attitude-behavior agreement rather than their genuine mutual influences. We may act or talk "as if" our attitudes and our behaviors agree, depending on our assessment of how others will view us. Two other theoretical traditions—self-perception and self-justification—more directly address the real connections between attitudes and behavior.

SELF-PERCEPTION

The essence of self-perception theory, already reviewed in chapter 4, is that we make inferences about ourselves—our abilities, moods, and attitudes—by first observing our own behaviors. Thus we sometimes act first and ask questions later, drawing conclusions about intentions and attitudes only after the fact. Self-perception theory explains such seeming counterintuitive findings as the fact that we can affect our emotions by altering our facial expressions, or mistakenly think we are angry or in love because of arousal caused by frightening or intoxicating stimuli. Self-perception theory seems best suited to explaining *newly-forming* connections between attitudes and behaviors. If one's behavior is made salient, and one's attitudes are not yet clearly formed, behavior will shape new attitudes more than any pre-existing attitudes will prevail.

SELF-JUSTIFICATION

A fascinating tradition of research argues that, whether or not action is truly reasoned, we are motivated to rationalize it or make it appear to be reasonable. We have, in other words, a need to justify our actions, and to act justifiably. The strongest evidence in favor of self-justification comes from research on cognitive dissonance, reviewed in chapter 4 and earlier in this chapter.

Dissonance Reduction. Dissonance theory argues that mismatches among cognitive elements create dissonance, an arousing tension we are motivated to reduce. Unjustified behaviors are difficult to disguise and impossible to change once they have been enacted. Dissonant attitudes, however, are easier to alter: one need only change one's mind, and the new attitude can be brought into line with the unalterable behavior.

For example, if you have agreed to do a favor, like babysitting, for an acquaintance, you may feel uncomfortable with the idea that your friend has taken advantage of your good nature by imposing on your time longer than promised, and then not offering to pay you. The behavior—"I babysat this person's child for an entire evening without compensation"—may seem dissonant with a preferred self-attitude, "I am a strong person whom others cannot take advantage of." You cannot change the fact that you granted the favor, but you can change your imputed *reasons* for that behavior: "I enjoyed myself because I like children." This attitude manipulation reduces dissonance—and also sets up a new attitude, a commitment to be willing to babysit again in the future.

Attitude Formation versus Attitude Change. Dissonance is created only when existing cognitive elements clash; thus a behavior will cause discomfort only if it violates an existing attitude. The likely outcome of dissonance reduction will be attitude change or replacement, motivated by rationalization. For these reasons, self-justification theory seems better to explain attitude *change* than attitude formation. Self-justification motives are often targeted by advertisers and other persuasive communicators, as will be discussed in chapter 9, "Attitude Change."

*A*ttitudes are evaluative judgments of people or things (attitude objects or referents). One-dimensional views of how particular attitudes lead to related behavior have been replaced by three-dimensional models of the affective, cognitive, and behavioral components of attitudes. Attitudes may include beliefs as well as feelings and intentions. Neutral positions without evaluation are considered nonattitudes.

Attitude measurement relies heavily on self-report, either through Thurstone scales (attitude statements that vary in intensity), Likert scales (statements rated for agreement or disagreement), or semantic differential scales (including scales measuring different meanings of an attitude). Alternative attitude measures may involve recording physiological arousal, asking subjects to guess what arousal measures indicate (the bogus pipeline technique), behavioral measures, and unobtrusive observation.

Attitudes are generally formed through learning, maintenance of cognitive consistency, or motivational incentives. Within learning theories, association processes include classical conditioning and the effects of mere exposure. Reinforcement accounts for the power of family members and reference groups to shape attitudes through rewards like social approval. Social learning approaches review the effects of vicarious learning and modeling or imitation in attitude development.

Cognitive consistency—agreement among cognitive elements—includes balance theory, cognitive-affective consistency, and dissonance theory. Attitudes may be acquired in attempts to maintain balance among existing preferences. According to cognitive-affective consistency theory, emotional responses may lead to compatible cognitions and beliefs. Dissonance theory argues that disharmony among cognitive elements creates tension that is best reduced by developing consonant or harmonious attitudes.

Motivational approaches argue that various incentives govern which attitudes are developed. Evaluation models propose that attitudes are formed to accommodate one's cognitive responses to a referent, or because certain attitudes are expected to have greater value. Other models examine the thoughtfulness given to attitude formation. Under ideal conditions, one may pay close attention to arguments central to an attitude, and be more likely to elaborate its details. When pressured or distracted, one may process information more superficially, relying on heuristics or peripheral cues to shape final attitudes.

Traditional theories assumed that attitudes underlay behavioral intentions, and that attitudes provided good prediction of action. While many factors have been identified to disrupt the relationship among attitudes, expressed attitudes, and actions, the conditions that promote attitude-behavior correspondence have also been identified. Attitudes are more likely to predict behavior when attitudes are specific to the behavior in question, when attitudes are strong, and when one's attitudes are salient. Other research suggests that the connection between attitudes and behaviors is mutual. Role playing, the foot-in-the-door effect, and indoctrination case studies all demonstrate the power of behavior to shape attitudes.

The theory of reasoned action proposes that attitudes are a necessary but insufficient factor in behavior intentions and ultimate action. Self-presentation research suggests that attitudes and behavior may either correspond or not, depending on the actor's skills or goals in impression management. Self-perception theory suggests that, for new or unformed attitudes, behavioral commitment may precede and cause one's preferences. Finally, self-justification theories argue that action may not be reasoned but rather rationalized. In this view, dissonant behavior prompts a reevaluation and change of pre-existing attitudes in order to restore one's sense of order and cognitive consistency.

Selected Readings

Abelson, R. P., E. Aronson, W. J. McGuire, T. M. Newcomb, M. J. Rosenberg, and P. O. Tannenbaum, (1968). *Theories of Cognitive Consistency: A Sourcebook.* Chicago: Rand McNally.

Ajzen, I. and M. Fishbein, (1980). *Understanding Attitudes and Predicting Social Behavior.* Englewood Cliffs, NJ: Prentice Hall.

Eiser, J. R. (Ed.). (1984). *Attitudinal Judgment.* New York: Springer Verlag.

Festinger, L. (1957). *A Theory of Cognitive Dissonance.* Stanford, CA: Stanford University Press.

Hovland, C., I. Janis, and H. Kelley, (1953). *Communication and Persuasion.* New Haven, CT: Yale University Press.

Newcomb, T. S., K. Koenig, R. Flacks, and D. Warwick, (1967). *Persistence and Change: Bennington College and Its Students After 25 Years.* New York: Wiley.

Oskamp, S. (1977). *Attitudes and Opinions.* Englewood Cliffs, NJ: Prentice Hall.

Petty, R. E. and J. T. Cacioppo, (1986). *Attitudes and Persuasion: Classic and Contemporary Approaches.* Dubuque, IA: Wm. C. Brown.

Pratkanis, A. K., S. J. Breckler, and A. G. Greenwald, (Eds.). (1989). *Attitude Structure and Function.* Hillsdale, NJ: Erlbaum.

Rajecki, D. W. (1989). *Attitudes,* 2nd edition. Sunderland, MA: Sinauer Associates.

Snyder, M. (1987). *Public Appearances/Private Realities: The Psychology of Self-Monitoring.* New York: Freeman.

Zimbardo, P., E. G. Ebbesen, and C. Maslach, (1977). *Influencing Attitudes and Changing Behavior*, 2nd edition. Reading, MA: Addison-Wesley.

9

Changing Attitudes

Once attitudes are formed or in place, how are they changed? Insofar as attitudes are developed through experience, then new experiences and discoveries are likely to modify them, or cause some to be rejected in favor of new ones. Alternatively, attitudes may be changed as a direct result of persuasion, a form of social influence aimed at changing people's beliefs, feelings, and behaviors.

This chapter first examines the factors in persuasive communication identified by an influential research tradition in social psychology. Different theories about attitude change are then evaluated. Finally, research on various strategies for resisting persuasion is reviewed.

PERSUASIVE COMMUNICATION

In the wake of the social changes wrought and revealed by World War II, an influential tradition of research on attitude change developed at Yale University. The model developed by this so-called Yale group, under the leadership of Carl Hovland (1912–1961), characterizes attitude change as the result of persuasive communication. The effectiveness of persuasion is determined by the qualities of the source or communicator, the content and presentation of the persuasive message, and the motives and abilities of the audience.

Source Effects

The first information one usually receives about a persuasive message involves characteristics of the source or communicator of that message. Research confirms that two communicator variables are especially important in effective persuasion: credibility and attractiveness.

CREDIBILITY

Messages are more persuasive—result in greater attitude change—when communicators are perceived as believable or *credible*. Although distortion and biases can lessen their influence, communicators are likely to be seen as more credible if they are seen as high in either *expertise* or *trustworthiness*.

Expertise. Experts and people who seem to know what they are talking about are more persuasive than admitted nonexperts or novices. Similarly, communicators who have established expertise in one area may be able to transfer their influence to another, related domain. For example, although a racing-car driver may not be an expert in non-racing automotive technology, his advice about which car to buy may be persuasive because of the general automobile expertise he seems to possess.

Expert influence may account for the greater persuasiveness of *rapid speech*: quickly spoken messages have been found to cause greater attitude change than normal or slow speech. Fast talk implies knowledge (expertise) on the part of the speaker, while slower speech may convey uncertainty, ignorance, or efforts to deceive.

Trustworthiness. Communicators are more credible if they are perceived as trustworthy. Trustworthy sources are those perceived to have sincere, honest intentions. Because of the value of trustworthiness, even nonexperts can be credible communicators.

Politicians who are uninformed can still be admired for their friendly good will; they can leverage this image into greater persuasive power. Celebrities admired for their talents as performers can be persuasive communicators because their audience trusts and admires them. An actress best known for her role as a detective cannot claim to be an expert about pain relief, but she is a credible—and thus a persuasive—communicator because her audience sees her as honest and trustworthy.

Biases. Credibility is important to audience members as an index of a message's validity or truth. Audience members are less influenced by communicators they believe to be biased. *Knowledge bias* results when a source relies on inaccurate information, and is most damaging to a communicator's reputed expertise. *Reporting bias* results when the communicator withholds correct or complete information, and jeopardizes a communicator's trustworthiness.

ATTRACTIVENESS

Even a casual perusal of print and television advertising reveals the importance of communicators' attractiveness. Celebrities whose reputations are based in entertainment, sports, politics, and even scholarship are filmed, photographed and quoted as they endorse products. Even unknown actors and models appear to be chosen for their attractiveness to the message's intended audience. In general, the better we like a communicator, the more persuaded we are by the message.

Disliked communicators may not only be ineffective persuaders, they may actually convince audience members to adopt the attitude opposite the one they espouse. This is known as a *boomerang effect*. For example, if a celebrity you personally dislike endorses a particular brand of breakfast cereal, you may decide never again to buy it, simply on the strength of your dislike for the endorser. (Consider also how the effects of liking and disliking are predicted by *balance theories* of attitude consistency, reviewed in chapter 8).

Researchers have identified three kinds of attractiveness that make a communicator more likable and persuasive: physical appeal; power; and similarity to the audience.

Physical Appeal. Good-looking people have greater persuasive power than those with average looks. In some cases the attractive person may not actually deliver the message but merely accompanies the sales pitch, as when an attractive man or woman is shown enjoying the use of an advertised product while an unseen narrator extols its virtues. In such presentation the advertisers are relying on the effects of attractiveness by association.

Power. Communicators who are seen as powerful are more persuasive than ineffective or unknown sources. Typically communicators must have reward power or coercive power—the power to reward or punish—to have such persuasive effects. For example, if a coworker or classmate urges you to be a blood donor at an upcoming community donation drive, you may be unpersuaded. But if your professor or boss urges you to attend, implying how pleased she will be with those who participate, you may be more persuaded to join the effort.

Similarity to the Audience. Communicators can be likable for other reasons than perceived physical appeal or power. An important factor in interpersonal attraction is perceived similarity. If a communicator first establishes similarity by arguing, "I am just like you," then he or she will be more persuasive in recommending products, services, or political candidates. For example, television commercials may precede product descriptions with "testimony" or dramatic accounts of characters who needed and used the product. A beer commercial typically features a young adult male enjoying beer with his friends after a hard working day or an exciting sports event. Advertisements for nonprescription medication depict characters suffering from various ailments until they achieve relief with the sponsor's product. Viewers will be more persuaded by such sales pitches if they perceive the characters as similar to themselves, identifying with their concerns and willing to try their remedies.

In some cases a message will be persuasive if the communicator is perceived not as similar to the audience member, but as someone to whom the recipient would *like* to be similar. People whom we aspire to be like and belong with make up our *aspirational reference group,* as opposed to the *actual reference group* to which we already belong. For example, a television commercial for a particular brand of designer jeans may portray several attractive men and women, beautiful people living a good life, and wearing the product. If you know you are not like these people but would *like* to be like them, you may feel encouraged to pay the "admission price" and dress like them until you belong.

SOURCE EFFECTS IN CONTEXT

Will both credibility and attractiveness make a communicator more persuasive in all circumstances? Researchers caution that the most effective source qualities depend on the content of the message and the nature of the audience.

Factual Messages. When a persuasive message is based on facts or information, a expert communicator is more persuasive than an attractive one. For example, in an advertisement about the power of a new pain relief medication, a communicator who looks and talks like a physician will be more persuasive than a good-looking person grinning at the product.

Value Messages. When the message is about matters of opinion and taste instead of fact, a communicator who seems similar to the audience will be more persuasive than one who talks like an expert. For example, which brand of soft drink should you buy? A communicator is more likely to influence your choice by dressing and talking like you and your friends, than by listing the results of recent scientific analyses of the top brands.

Source-Message Interactions. The impact of a source may depend on the content of the message. Some messages purport to be "about" the communicator or some aspect of the situation, rather than aimed at attitude change. For example, arguments against self-interest and "soft sell" approaches, reviewed below (see Self-Interest), combine message and source effects to be persuasive.

Message Effects

In a market economy, the many products, services, and politicians being advertised may seem indistinguishable, so persuasion relies heavily on communicator variables. In general, however, the communication model of attitude change identifies many more message variables than communicator variables as having persuasive effect. Qualities of a persuasive message that have been found to affect attitude change include the position the message advocates, the content and composition of the message, the order and balance of its presentation, and the channel or medium through which the message is communicated.

POSITION

The closer a message is to the recipient's current position, the more readily he or she will accept it.

Acceptance and Rejection. In one theory, the attitudes most similar to a recipient's current position are considered with that person's *latitude of acceptance*. Attitudes that are irrelevant make up a *latitude of noncommitment*, and those that are unacceptable are in the recipient's *latitude of rejection*. A persuasive message is more effective if it falls within a recipient's latitude of acceptance, and will probably fail if it lies within the recipient's latitude of rejection.

For example, a woman who is strongly in favor of reproductive choice, including the choice of legal abortion, listens to a political candidate explain his position on such rights. He claims to favor reproductive freedom although he expresses concerns about whether the state should pay for all medical procedures. This moderate pro-choice stance probably falls within the listening woman's latitude of acceptance. Thus she would probably accept and support his campaign for office. In contrast, pro-life candidates who opposed legal abortion would clearly fall into her latitude of rejection, and she would oppose their election on this issue.

Credibility and Discrepancy. Message position interacts with communicator credibility in some cases of persuasion. Typically, a recipient will not be persuaded by a message that is highly *discrepant* (different) from his or her current stance, as reviewed above. However, the more *credible* a communicator is perceived to be, the more effective he or she will be with a discrepant message.

The lesson of such research seems to be that, if the position you advocate is extremely different from most of your audience's views, have it delivered by a highly credible communicator. If the chosen communicator is seen as attractive but not credible, keep the message closer to the audience's current position. Credibility appears to "buy" a wider latitude of acceptance in the minds of critical recipients.

CONTENT

In a consumer culture, the language of advertising is pervasive. Commercial jingles and slogans are a familiar part of what we hear and see every day. Does the wording and emphasis of such familiar messages influence our acceptance of them? Three sets of message factors seem to be related to their persuasive power: message complexity, emotional appeal, and self-interest.

Simplicity. More complex messages are harder to comprehend, and less likely to lead to behavioral intentions. Thus the simpler the message, the more persuasive its impact. A catchy slogan that associates a product brand name with an implied effect—like "Pepsi, the Choice of a New Generation!"—is easier to remember, and not difficult to act on.

Simple messages, however, may be self-limiting. Many important behaviors cannot be urged or taught through simple slogans. For example, the anti-drug slogan, "Just Say No!," was found to be popular to recite but not particularly effective in changing people's long-term drug use behaviors. Resisting social pressure, overcoming personal habits, and developing alternative strategies are complex endeavors not effectively encouraged through the recitation of slogans.

Emotional Appeal. Messages can be more effective if they arouse strong emotional responses in recipients. Most research has examined the particular effectiveness in *fear appeals,* messages that warn of danger or difficulty if recipients are not persuaded. Results suggest that moderate fear-arousal works best, while extremely frightening messages may paralyze recipients into inaction or denial. Most effective are fear appeals immediately followed by specific behavioral recommendations to *prevent* the frightening possibilities.

For example, a message persuading pregnant women to seek medical care early and regularly will be more effective if it warns of the dangers—to mother and infant—of neglecting prenatal care, *and* offers specific recommendations for how and where to find low-cost medical attention. The dangers cited will arouse recipients' fear but not too much, and the behavioral recommendations will enable them to take immediate practical steps to prevent those frightening consequences.

Self-Interest. Audiences can usually detect whether a communicator is the true source of the message or a mere spokesperson using a prepared script. The latter is not necessarily less persuasive, especially if he or she seems credible or attractive. However, a communicator who stands to gain if the audience accepts the message may seem suspect because of this self-interest. Conversely, if a communicator delivers a message that either provides no such gain or *contradicts* his or her self-interest, the message will be more persuasive.

For example, a political advertisement might feature a voter who claims, "I voted for President X, and I'm sorry I did. He was bad for the country, and I do not support his re-election." Not only is this communicator not gloating, he is announcing his fallibility. His message is not self-interested, because it does not make him look good or self-satisfied. Ironically, it seems that much more sincere and genuine. Such messages that violate communicators' apparent self-interest are often more persuasive.

A related message effect is the "soft sell," a persuasive message that denies any persuasive intent. For example, a car salesperson may argue, "I don't care whether you buy a car from me, as long as you shop carefully and get a good deal." This message may be more persuasive of the hidden agenda—selling the customer a car, regardless of denying such intent—because the communicator insists she has nobler interests at heart.

PRESENTATION

The way a message is presented can affect its persuasive power. Research findings have found three effects of message presentation: order, delay, and balance.

Order: Primacy and Recency Effects. Persuasive messages often compete with each other for audience attention and loyalty. Persuasion may depend on the order in which recipients encountered a particular message. For example, if you are to debate an opponent before an audience, will you be more persuasive if you present your side first or last?

Research on person perception (see chapter 5) confirms that the sequence of information processing influences final impressions. Generally such research supports the prevailing power of the *primacy effect*: first impressions usually count strongest. Thus in the example above, if you and your opponent have equally strong arguments, you may be slightly more persuasive if you present your side first.

However, under some conditions the latest message will be the one that is best remembered and adhered to. Research suggests that this *recency effect*—last impressions leaving lasting impressions—prevails only under specific conditions: when an audience is convinced that first impressions would be erroneous, or when so much time has passed since the first message that the more recent information is more useful in planning behavior.

Delay: The Sleeper Effect. Most research indicates that, the fresher the message is in the recipient's mind, the more powerful its effects. Interesting contradictory findings, however, pointed to the occasional influence of a *sleeper effect:* some messages were more persuasive weeks or months later then immediately after they had been delivered. Why does delay have such counterintuitive effects?

For example, a classmate of yours might casually mention hearing a rumor that a particular psychology professor, "Dr. Jones," is very tough on his students. If you don't know or trust this classmate well, you may dismiss her comments at the time. Weeks later, consulting the next semester's course schedule, you find that Dr. Jones is teaching a course you might want to take, and you recall the warning—but not the source. You have forgotten the *discounting cues* (a low opinion of the classmate) and remembered only the *argument* against Dr. Jones. Thus your new negative attitude about Dr.

Jones seems to have been "sleeping," only emerging long after the first persuasive communicating.

Two explanations have been proposed for the sleeper effect. One, the *dissociation explanation,* argues that the association between the persuasive conclusion ("Don't take a class with Dr. Jones") and the *discounting cues* (hints that this message is weak, like your judgment that the communicator is not credible) become weakened. This *dissociation* or weakening of connections increases over time. Eventually only the connection between the conclusion and the persuasive arguments is retained.

An alternative explanation is that impressions of the communicator ("She is not credible") and the message ("Dr. Jones is difficult") decay in memory (are forgotten) at different rates. This *differential decay* explanation explains why we might remember a rumor but forget exactly where and from whom we heard it. "What" is forgotten more slowly than "where" and "from whom."

Balance: One Side versus Two Sides. Many persuasive arguments take sides: an issue presented simplistically as having only two positions, for example, "for" and "against." Should a persuasive communicator acknowledge an opposing point of view—or is it more expedient to concentrate on presenting only one side?

Research confirms that the effectiveness of a message's balance—whether it presents one or both sides—depends on the audience. Recipients who are knowledgeable about the issue, involved in it, or opposed to the source's position are more likely to be persuaded by a two-sided than a one-sided approach. Such audience members know that another side (their own) exists; acknowledging that fact and honoring their leanings makes a communicator more credible and an opposing message more persuasive.

For example, a speaker who favors wilderness protection may anticipate resistance or hostility from an audience of lumber workers. Audience members may fear that conservation measures will restrict their work and cost them jobs. Instead of speaking exclusively about the importance of wilderness protection, the spokesperson should acknowledge the importance of securing the local economy, protecting incomes and jobs, and establishing compromise between the region's human and nonhuman inhabitants. This two-sided approach will be more persuasive because it blends its arguments with sympathy for the opposition.

CHANNEL

Consumers are inundated with advertisements in seemingly every medium, from print like newspapers and magazines to audio and video media like radio and television commercials. Marketers invest huge amounts of money in producing such persuasive messages. Is it a given fact such appeals work? Are consumers simply driven by the latest, slickest, or loudest exhortations to behave as the advertisers wish? The answer from research is, "It depends."

Mass Media. The media have a distinct advantage in volume: newspapers and television can deliver persuasive messages to more people per message than personal contacts. Mass media campaigns have the disadvantage of relying on *passive* communication: they can only send messages one way, they cannot interact or argue with the recipients.

Research suggests that media channels differ in the kinds of messages they sell best. Printed messages are better comprehended—they can be more detailed, and the audience can reread them—but they are also more critically considered. Audio and audiovisual messages are more easily accepted *if* they can be simplified sufficiently for shorter presentation.

Media channels also interact with likability of the source: *likable* communicators are more persuasive in *audio* or *audiovisual* form than written; *unlikable* communicators are more convincing in *written* appeals. Thus the choice of vehicle may depend on communicator characteristics. Attractive, influential communicators will be more effective on radio and television; those who rely more on logic than celebrity appeal may do better in print media.

Personal Contact. As a form of social influence, persuasion is most assured when the communicator has personal contact with the recipient. A friend who recommends a product is more likely to influence your buying behavior than a television commercial you can turn off or forget. This explains the enduring success of door-to-door marketing: it is easier to turn off a radio or turn a magazine page than turn away a live person, perhaps a neighbor, who comes calling to sell her wares.

An increasingly popular channel is direct-mail marketing. This approach—mass mailings to individuals identified on address lists—attempts to combine the volume of mass media with the more direct contact of a "personal" letter. Preliminary research suggests that such "junk mail" persuasion is more effective than passive media channels but still far less effective than live, face-to-face contact.

Two-Step Communication. Finally, persuasive messages increasingly rely on an interaction between media channels and social contact. The friend who recommends you buy a certain brand of product may have initially been influenced by a magazine advertisement. A family member urges you to check out a "big sale" at a neighborhood retailer, which she learned about from a radio announcement. This *two-step flow* of persuasive communication relies on combining the advantages of mass media (volume, expediency) with those of personal contact (social influence, reference group appeal).

Audience Effects

Throughout this discussion of the "power" of communicators and persuasive messages, the active role of the audience has been implicated. Audience characteristics determine which communicators will seem credible or attractive, which messages will seem reasonable, memorable, or balanced. What else do we know about the recipient's role in persuasive communication?

ATTENTION

Especially in mass media appeals, audiences who do not pay attention cannot be persuaded. Further, those who attend but do not comprehend or agree will not form the hoped-for behavioral intention.

Selective Exposure. People tend to form connections with and stay close to people and experiences that support their attitudes and values. By such natural associations, we usually miss arguments that challenge or oppose us. This *selective exposure* may take the form of watching only certain television programming and reading only specific kinds of print material. We thus expose ourselves to information very selectively, encountering the ideas that "fit" our views and avoiding those that do not.

Ego-Involvement. Some of our attitudes are more important to us than others. A campaign worker is clearly more personally involved in whether his candidate is elected than a voter who supports the candidate from a distance. The more *ego-involved* a recipient is with a preexisting attitude, the less receptive he or she will be to other positions, and the more attention he or she will pay to compatible arguments.

One factor in ego-involvement is *issue involvement,* or the degree to which a recipient is personally affected by the attitude object. For example, you will probably pay more attention to proposed tuition increases at schools in your geographic area than in another state. The immediacy of the consequences makes local tuition increases a more involving issue for you, and so you pay more attention to the arguments for or against them.

Another factor in ego-involvement is *commitment* to an attitude, a promise of future action that is not easily revoked. Commitments can take the form of *behavior;* sending a non-refundable contribution to a candidate's election campaign will reduce your finances and increase your support for the candidate in other ways. Commitment can also take the form of a public *contract,* such as announcing to your friends that you plan to quit smoking on your birthday. Finally, commitment is only effective in ego-involvement if it is a *free choice.* If no one has coerced or pressured you into contributing time to a cause, like helping out at a homeless shelter, your attitude toward this cause will be stronger and more resistant to change.

PERSONAL CHARACTERISTICS

Advertising is big business; advertisers invest in research to learn all they can about their prospective audiences. Some of this research has attempted to gauge people's receptivity to persuasive messages based on age, needs, and mood.

Age. Popular culture often portrays children and adolescents as gullible and labile—quickly changing their loyalties, open to new ideas. In contrast, older adults are imagined to be set in their ways, conservative, and resistant to innovation. If there were any factual basis to such images, we might expect young people to be more easily persuaded than older ones.

Research on this question supports an *impressionable-years hypothesis,* explaining that children and young adults (18 to 25 years of age) have less stable attitudes than older individuals. This means that their attitudes are more likely to change, in response to new experiences as well as social influences like persuasion.

No evidence, however, supports the notion that the ageing process causes increased attitude rigidity, or by itself creates resistance to persuasion. Instead, differences between one age group's attitudes and another's seem more due to differences in their experiences in their life and times. The age-group or cohort that grew up in the 1960s and 1970s have different memories and anchoring experiences from those who grew up in the 1980s and 1990s. Thus age differences in attitudes and attitude change are better accounted for by a *generational explanation* (each generation has unique formative experiences) than a *life-cycle explanation* (specific attitudes depend on one's age). For example, your grandparents' tastes in music may seem "conservative" compared to your own; this may be because they prefer the music popular when their generation grew up, and not because ageing has altered their openness to new sounds and trends.

Needs. A message will be more persuasive if you need what it purports to offer. Advertisers and campaigners try to identify audience members' needs, and tailor their messages to make the appropriate promises. A shampoo commercial, for example, may open with a question like, "Is your hair dull and lifeless?" A recipient who tacitly responds, "Yes, it is!" is more likely to be persuaded to buy the brand of shampoo being advertised.

Some persuasive messages will also try to *arouse* needs, connect them to a simple problem, and promise a solution with a particular product or action. For example, an advertisement may depict a person as suffering from social rejection, argue that the problem is simply due to bad breath, and suggest a particular brand of mouthwash as the elegant solution. In this case, the persuasive message first arouses concern about social acceptance ("Do people like me as much as I want them to?"), creating a sense of need that the product will "simply" satisfy.

People with relatively low *self-esteem* have been found to be more easily persuaded than more secure, self-confident individuals. This is a general finding with other forms of social influence besides persuasion, as well.

Research shows that some people have a higher *need for cognition* than others. Such individuals seek more information and spend more time and effort processing it than others. Those with a low need for cognition use more mental shortcuts and do not consider messages as thoughtfully. People with a high need for cognition are more persuaded by strong arguments and less persuaded by weak arguments compared to those low in this need.

Finally, common sense approaches to social influence recommend that you "butter up" an individual whom you wish to persuade. Why would a good *mood* make one easier to persuade? Research indicates that people in a good mood (e.g., from receiving good news or an unexpected bonus) are less likely to process a message carefully and critically, and thus accept it more readily.

Situational Effects

Persuasion is not merely the sum of its parts—communicator, message, and audience. Some effects are due to the many processes that overlap and interact during persuasive communication. Three such processes that have important consequences for attitude change are message density, repetition, and distraction.

PROCESSES THAT EFFECT ATTITUDE

Message Density. People are bombarded with persuasive messages in many media, and promoting many different products, services, and people. Research indicates that such *message density* interferes with individual persuasive communications. Recipients may remember a general attitude ("I would enjoy drinking that product") but not a specific brand. Another result is that praise for one brand can be diluted by criticism from a competitor, so that persuasion in general is less effective. One conclusion may be that "brand loyalties"—consumer preferences for a favorite brand—cannot be developed via short, passive messages amid so much competition.

Repetition. Many common social influence practices involve repetition. Schoolchildren repeat rote lessons, church members recite familiar prayers, and advertisers replay commercials—with the assumption that what is repeated will become accepted. Does it work? Research suggests that it does.

The repetition-persuasion effect is largely due to the effects of *mere exposure* to a stimulus (see Learning Approaches, chapter 8). Repeated exposure to a pattern of sights or sounds makes that pattern familiar, and familiarity leads to liking. Repetition of a persuasive message represents a kind of investment the source makes: if an advertiser has been reciting her brand's name and slogan to you for years, then when you finally consider buying such a product, the favorable attitude you have developed will be put into action.

Distraction. Recipients of a persuasive message, in considering its arguments, can tacitly develop criticisms (*counterarguments,* discussed below) that lessen its persuasive power. Any process that interferes with such counterargument can stall this resistance and increase the recipient's susceptibility. Some communicators and messages will therefore employ *distraction* to consume the recipient's attention, leaving little ability to resist. For example, as you stand in an automobile showroom and listen to a sales pitch, you are free to consider the flaws and deceptions in what you are hearing. However, if the salesperson invites you to test drive the vehicle, continuing the sales pitch while you drive, you may be too distracted by the effort of safe driving to counterargue. Besides the experience of driving the car, you may only be able to remember what the salesperson said, and not your silent doubts and concerns.

THEORIES OF ATTITUDE CHANGE

Why do people change their attitudes? The communication model of persuasion, reviewed above, specifies the components in the persuasion process: communicator, message, and recipient. As you have read, however, research has yielded a bounty of information regarding which components—and interactions among them—lead to most effective persuasion. Two kinds of theories have developed hypotheses to account for what persuades whom, when, and how: the elaboration-likelihood model and self-justification theories.

The Elaboration Likelihood Model

By extension from the communication model of persuasion, attitude change may be the result of the various factors involved in transmitting the message: source, message, and audience variables. But these factors may not always work together. For example, what happens if a communicator is credible and attractive, but a message is highly discrepant with the recipient's preexisting position? It is important to be able to predict not only what factors influence persuasion, but when and how different factors will be most influential.

The *elaboration-likelihood model* of persuasion, developed by researchers Richard E. Petty and John T. Cacioppo, depicts attitude change as the result of information processing. In this model, an audience member may either apply very little *elaboration* (scrutiny) to the message received, or a great deal. Messages given low elaboration will be effective for different reasons from those given high elaboration.

CENTRAL PROCESSING

When conditions permit the recipient to concentrate on the arguments in the persuasive message, he or she engages in *central* or *systematic processing*. How logical are the arguments? Do they make sense to the recipient? Do they overcome the recipient's objections and concerns? The answers the recipient hears and infers to these questions will determine whether persuasion is effective.

For example, in deciding whether to spend money on a vacation trip with friends, you might listen to their plans and encouragement, and then decide privately what to do. In the course of central processing you will be able to consider the expense involved, the time necessary, what you will be able to do, and what you might miss or sacrifice—both if you make the trip, and if you stay home. Under these conditions, you are most likely to be persuaded to go *if* you are convinced that the trip will be enjoyable, the plans are careful, and the cost is reasonable.

PERIPHERAL PROCESSING

If conditions prevent careful, elaborative consideration of the message, Petty and Cacioppo's model predicts that persuasion will depend on *peripheral* or *heuristic processing*. In this case, the recipient's persuasion depends on peripheral cues—factors that are not central to the arguments themselves—like characteristics of the communicator, message presentation, or the audience.

Continuing with the example above, if you are unable (or unwilling) to devote elaborative thought to whether to take the vacation trip with your friends, you will consider peripheral cues and heuristics (rules of thumb) in making your decision. Thus you are more likely to be persuaded to take the trip if your friends are attractive and convincing, and if you were in a good mood when they proposed the trip to you. Conversely, if these are not your favorite companions, or you are too worried about money to consider paying for a vacation trip (for example, a heuristic like "Money saved is money earned"), these considerations may cause you to decline.

Self-Justification Theories

As reviewed in chapter 8, self-justification theories propose that people have a need to justify their actions, and to maintain consistency among their attitudes and behaviors. In this model, attitudes are changed when doing so restores harmony and justification to one's thoughts and feelings. Two processes translate self-justification into attitude change: dissonance reduction and commitment.

DISSONANCE REDUCTION

Leon Festinger's cognitive dissonance theory asserts that a mismatch between a new action and an old attitude creates *dissonance,* an uncomfortable tension we are motivated to reduce. Since the action cannot be retrieved or undone, the attitude—the more malleable cognitive element—is changed to match the action. For example, a student who has always hated competitive sports is encouraged to try out for the track team by a teacher she admires. Having tried out and been accepted, she experiences dissonance: "I always thought I hated sports, but this was fun and I felt good doing it." She can either repudiate the action—"I shouldn't have tried out, I'm sorry I did"—or revise her attitude—"I may have been wrong, sports aren't all bad." Of the two, the easier in terms of self-esteem and practicality is attitude change. The dissonance reduction process explains how and why new experiences cause us to revise our opinions of people and things.

THE POWER OF COMMITMENT

Behaviors Lead to Attitudes. Not all attitudes are *ego-involving;* some may be easier to change than others. As discussed in chapter 8, attitudes formed through personal experience tend to be more potent than those acquired through second-hand or passive means. Thus a persuader's best chance for achieving attitude change comes from inducing the recipient to make a behavioral *commitment* in the desired direction. Self-justification processes will subsequently lead the actor to convince himself or herself of the corresponding attitude.

Inducements. For example, would you change your brand of breakfast cereal from now on simply to save 25 cents? If while shopping you notice that a brand comparable to your usual favorite costs somewhat less, you might impulsively decide to purchase the new brand on this occasion. This brief act represents a behavioral commitment. When you run out of cereal and shop for more, you may find the new brand no less expensive than your former favorite. What will you do?

This depends on how you feel when you realize how fickle you have been. If you are shopping primarily for bargains, you may simply bypass all brands, old and new, in favor of whatever costs least. On the other hand, you may feel tension—dissonance—about having switched brands for so little savings. If you wish to *justify* your unusual behavior—buying the new brand instead of your old favorite—you may "realize" that your attitude has changed, and you "really" like the new brand better. "I bought it once because it saved me money," you may conclude, "but I keep buying it because I really like it." The one-time price reduction has induced a behavioral commitment; this commitment in turn resulted in attitude change.

The success of such inducement techniques has resulted in regular price cuts, trial-sized packages, and cost rebates—all designed to bring about a single behavioral commitment, in the hope that this action will beget a change in recipients' attitudes.

RESISTING PERSUASION

The persuasive communication model might leave you with the impression that strategies for persuasion vastly outnumber your options for resisting. Research has contradicted this impression by identifying several effective strategies for such resistance: the effects of forewarning, defensive behaviors, and attitude inoculation.

Forewarning Effects

Many persuasive messages are overtly designed to change our attitudes. We know that television commercials, for example, intend to influence us, not merely to inform or entertain us. Research indicates that such knowledge—*forewarning* of persuasive intent—helps us to be less influenced by the persuasion that follows.

COUNTERARGUING

When forewarned, we most commonly engage in active counterarguing against the persuasive message. Typically we do this silently, considering the arguments and counterattacking them in sequence. For example, when a car salesperson tells you, "This model was rated in the top ten by professional racers" and "The engine runs smoothly even at 120 miles per hour," you might counterargue by thinking or saying, "But I'm not a professional racer" and "I never drive faster than 65 miles per hour!"

The effectiveness of counterarguing can be undercut by distractions that prevent such thinking, as discussed above. Thus when forewarned, we can best plan to resist persuasion by ensuring our ability to formulate counterarguments and resisting distractions.

PSYCHOLOGICAL REACTANCE

Knowing that someone is trying to persuade you may cause you to assert your independence by resisting the message, however good its arguments. This reaction—seeking to do the opposite of what is urged—is termed *psychological reactance*. It is a common reaction to the "hard sell," overt, high-pressure persuasion tactics. Psychological reactance can be employed in everyday instances of social influence, where we know it as "reverse psychology." For example, a parent might induce a child to eat her spinach by feigning to take it away, announcing, "This is grown-up people's food, you're too young to have any." If this abrupt withdrawal creates psychological reactance in the child, she may attempt to reassert her will and freedom of choice by insisting, "I am not too young to have any! Give me that spinach!"

Psychological reactance is stimulated by persuasive efforts that threaten a recipient's freedom of choice and self-control. For this reason, dictatorial or tactless orders might backfire when people become reactant instead of cooperative. For example, "Keep Off the Grass!" might prompt some pedestrians to pound the turf in defiance of such orders, while a subtler request like "Please Help the Grass by Walking on the Footpath" wins more converts.

Defensive Behaviors

Even when we are not forewarned, we may resist or weaken attempts to change our attitudes by avoiding sales pitches, putting off behavioral commitments, and denying "obligations" to persuasive communicators. For example, you might receive a sweepstakes entry form in the mail, promising "No Purchase Necessary!" but inviting you to order magazine subscriptions. The expectation that you might win could tempt you to feel you "ought" to order a subscription or two. By adopting a defensive perspective, you can remind yourself that no purchase *is* necessary for winning, and that you have no obligation to order something you did not ask for.

SELECTIVE AVOIDANCE

Just as belonging to certain social organizations and reference groups brings us naturally into contact with certain persuasive messages, it also takes us away from others. This results in *selective avoidance,* a tendency to avoid sources and messages that challenge our current opinions. This form of defensive behavior is simplest for passive channels of persuasion: we can change channels, lower the volume, use the "mute" function or turn off the set to avoid unwanted commercials.

Advertisers anticipate the ease of selective avoidance, and try to make their messages harder to avoid, by raising the volume to capture listeners' attention, or by offering material—glimpses of celebrities, or interesting stories—that we cannot resist.

SOURCE DEROGATION

We can defend against attempts to persuade us by criticizing or *derogating the source* of the message. In its simplest form, this means discrediting an opponent to weaken his or her argument. This can happen naturally, as when you find yourself ready to reject anything a disliked or mistrusted person says. It can also be employed deliberately, as when we reduce the pressure of an argument by responding, "That must be a lie."

Attitude Inoculation

Resistance to persuasion can be facilitated if the intended recipients are not only forewarned, but are also allowed to develop their own arguments against the persuasive message. This can be achieved by presenting audience members with a mild form of a persuasive message, and allowing them to consider their own counterarguments. Once these are developed, the recipients will more easily resist stronger persuasive arguments.

This process is termed *attitude inoculation,* after the medical process of inducing a mild form of an illness so the body will develop natural immunities against the more dangerous disease. Attitude inoculation is most effective in strengthening preexisting attitudes by challenging them. Once the challenge is met and rebuffed, an individual has both strategies and practice in resisting persuasion in the future.

Parents may try to instill enduring attitudes in their children by challenging them to respond. For example, parents could ask their children to consider what to do if they were tempted to cheat on a test. Children who can produce thoughtful, realistic responses will be stronger in resisting such temptation alone; their earlier thoughts will have "inoculated" them against later threats to their honesty.

Once formed, attitudes may be modified by new experience, information, or the form of social influence known as persuasion. The communication model of persuasion characterizes attitude change as the result of a process involving three sets of variables: the source of the message, the message itself, and the recipients or audience.

Persuasion depends on source effects like credibility and attractiveness. A communicator is perceived as more credible if high in expertise or trustworthiness. A communicator's attractiveness can be enhanced by greater physical appeal, power over the recipient, or perceived similarity to the audience. Source factors may interact with persuasive context: factual messages are more persuasive if the communicator is high in expertise, while value messages are more readily accepted if the communicator seems similar to the audience.

Message effects include the position the message advocates, its content, the way it is presented, and the channel through which it is communicated. Recipients tend to accept messages that are not too discrepant from their current attitudes; a discrepant message is more persuasively communicated by a credible source. In terms of content, messages are more readily accepted if they are simple rather than complex, moderately emotion-arousing (especially if accompanied by behavioral recommendations), and seen as contrary to the self-interest of the source. Presentation effects include the primacy effect, although recency effects are obtained in certain conditions; the sleeper effect if time has elapsed since the original communication; and the persuasiveness of balanced (two-sided) arguments for involved or knowledgeable audiences.

A final message variable is the channel of communication. While personal contact is generally the most effective form of social influence, media persuasion can be effective with different messages and communicators. Media messages may be transformed into personal contact through a two-step process of communication flow, from media to significant others to the final recipients of the message.

Audience effects include factors affecting attention to the message and personal characteristics of the recipients. Recipients pay greater attention to attitudes compatible with their social experiences, creating a selective exposure effect. A recipient's ego-involvement with an issue will affect persuasion, as determined by issue involvement and behavioral commitment. Other audience effects may depend on personal characteristics like the age of the audience and needs like need for cognition, low self-esteem, and current mood.

Situational effects on persuasive communication include processes like message density, repetition, and distraction. Message density may dilute persuasion, but repetition may increase the familiarity and thus the acceptability of a message. Distraction may increase persuasion because it interferes with a recipient's ability to counterargue.

Two broad theories of attitude change are the elaboration-likelihood model and self-justification theory. The elaboration-likelihood model characterizes persuasion as the result of cognitive processes that may be either elaborative (scrutinizing) or superficial (influenced by peripheral cues or heuristics). When elaboration is possible, persuasion is determined by the arguments of the persuasive message. When processing is peripheral, persuasion is affected by variables such as source effects and channel factors.

Self-justification theory argues that attitudes will change if they are brought into conflict with other cognitive elements, like induced behaviors. When attitudes and behaviors conflict, resulting dissonance creates tension that is best reduced by changing the attitude to fit the behavior. Thus attitudes may be changed through inducements to behave differently.

Persuasion can be resisted through the effects of forewarning, defensive behavior, and attitude inoculation. Forewarning prompts counterarguing, so that recipients defuse the persuasive messages themselves. It may also create the experience of psychological reactance, in which recipients reject the persuasive message by behaving in the opposite manner.

A recipient can engage in defensive behaviors, weakening persuasion by denying or distancing the message. Selective avoidance is possible by relying on our social experiences to reduce contact with challenging or threatening positions. If confronted with a challenge, recipients can derogate the source, judging the communicator to be a liar or noncredible.

Attitude inoculation strengthens resistance to persuasion by permitting recipients to develop counterarguments. Recipients are exposed to a mild dose of a persuasive message, after which they formulate responses to reject the message and strengthen preexisting attitudes.

Selected Readings

Alwitt, L. F. and A. A. Mitchell, (Eds.). (1985). *Psychological Processes and Advertising Effects: Theory, Research, and Application.* Hillsdale, NJ: Erlbaum.

Brehm, J. W. (1966). *A Theory of Psychological Reactance.* New York: Academic Press.

Cialdini, R. B. (1988). *Influence: Science and Practice.* Glenview, IL: Scott, Foresman.

Festinger, L. (1957). *A Theory of Cognitive Dissonance.* Palo Alto, CA: Stanford University Press.

Hovland, C. I., I. L. Janis, and H. H. Kelley, (1953). *Communication and Persuasion.* New Haven, CT: Yale University Press.

Howitt, D. (1982). *Mass Media and Social Problems.* New York: Pergamon Press.

Newcomb, T. S. (1943). *Personality and Social Change.* New York: Dryden Press.

Petty, R. E. and J. T. Cacioppo, (1980). *Attitude Change: Central and Peripheral Routes to Persuasion.* New York: Springer Verlag.

Petty, R. E., T. M. Ostrom, and T. C. Brock, (Eds.). (1981). *Cognitive Responses in Persuasion.* Hillsdale, NJ: Erlbaum.

Varela, J. A. (1971). *Psychological Solutions to Social Problems: An Introduction to Social Technology.* New York: Academic Press.

Wicklund, R. A. and J. W. Brehm, (1976). *Perspectives on Cognitive Dissonance.* Hillsdale, NJ: Erlbaum.

Zimbardo, P. G., E. B. Ebbesen, and C. Maslach, (1977). *Influencing Attitudes and Changing Behavior,* 2nd edition. Reading, MA: Addison-Wesley.

Zimbardo, P. G. and M. R. Leippe, (1991). *The Psychology of Attitude Change and Social Influence.* New York: McGraw-Hill.

10

Social Influence

At the core of most social psychology is the observation that people influence each other: we seek and often get what we want from each other, in both direct and indirect ways.

In the twentieth century, interest in social influence peaked after World War II. The effects of propaganda, military authority, and social status all involve understanding forms and processes of social influence.

In this chapter we examine the forms and processes of social influence, including conformity, obedience, and power. We also review effective strategies for resisting or defying such influence.

DEFINING SOCIAL INFLUENCE

Social influence refers to a change in attitude or behavior as a result of interactions with others.

Levels of Social Influence

There are different degrees of social influence: you may completely accept someone's influence, or you may merely go through the motions of cooperating. It is helpful to understand the different processes involved in different levels of influence.

ACCEPTANCE

Sincere, inward change as a result of social influence is termed *acceptance*. If a person or group convinces you to believe—as well as to act—in the desired direction, your conversion is based on inner processes.

Identification. Influence may be accepted because one identifies with a group, cause, or individual. *Identification* helps to maintain a personal relationship between them. In this kind of acceptance, the content of the behavior or belief change is less important than its social results. For example, you may identify with a social club, and accept their rules, even though you do not yet know what all the rules are.

Internalization. A deeper form of acceptance occurs when one is convinced to believe in the changed attitude. In this case, one has *internalized* the new belief, accepting both its meaning and its social form. For example, you may join a social club because you agree with its standards (internalization), not just because you feel the members are like you (identification).

COMPLIANCE

In some cases, social influence does not extend very deeply, and does not completely transform attitudes. When one changes behavior or the expression of an attitude, but does not accept the change completely, *compliance* has occurred. By observing others we can often find examples of compliance without being certain whether there is also acceptance. For this reason, researchers are more likely to discuss *compliance effects:* compliance changes behavior, and can be observed and measured, whereas acceptance can only be revealed through honest self-report—and may not be revealed by a given study.

Conformity. By far the most widely researched form of compliance is *conformity,* a change in attitude or behavior as a result of group pressure. Research on conformity has concentrated on the conditions that cause such change, and the processes that account for it, as will be reviewed below.

Obedience. A fascinating form of compliance is *obedience,* in which one person influences a behavior change in another as a result of a direct request or command. Classic research on obedience, reviewed below, has sought to identify the extent of social obedience, and the factors that affect its influence.

Standards for Influence

Why do we comply with—and sometimes accept—others' influence? Theorists suggest two different reasons or standards: normative influence and informational influence.

NORMATIVE INFLUENCE

Recall the theory of social comparison (see chapter 4): in order to validate our social beliefs, we consult the behavior of others. If our observation of others suggests guidelines for behavior—norms—we may be influenced to copy their actions. This reliance on others as providing social standards leads to *normative influence.* For example, when deciding which courses to take, you may ask friends for advice, relying on their suggestions rather than researching the options yourself. It is as if you conclude "all those people cannot be wrong." Normative influence is particularly dependent on social cues like the size of the social group or the status of the person influencing behavior.

INFORMATIONAL INFLUENCE

It is important to acknowledge that social influence is as likely to be constructive as it is to be damaging. Sometimes we change our minds and our actions because others have taught us a better way, or brought useful information to our attention. This *informational influence* results in not only compliance, but acceptance. For example, while working on a research project, you discuss your plans to analyze your data with members of your research team. When several of them point out a more efficient procedure for analyzing the data, you realize they are right, and change your plans. Your plans have changed because you have been influenced by the *information* they have provided, not merely to "go along" with the group (as in normative influence).

Many experiences of conformity involve both informational and normative influence. The nature of many social groups and relationships is such that other people provide us with both normative standards and new information, both of which can affect our thinking and behavior.

FORMS OF SOCIAL INFLUENCE

Important examples of social influence have already been reviewed in this book: impression management (see chapter 5) and persuasion (chapter 9) are both common forms of social influence. In this chapter we examine three forms of social influence that have constituted important research traditions in their own right: conformity, obedience, and power.

Conformity

It is not surprising that people "go along with" the thoughts and actions of their friends and coworkers. We rely on such relationships for many benefits, including standards for change. What is intriguing is whether people will conform in the presence of strangers. Why would people we do not know have the power to influence us? Classic research has examined the impact of the mere presence of others—strangers or friends—on two processes: norm formation, and performance under group pressure.

NORM FORMATION

Norms are behavioral guidelines: they shape and influence the actions of those who consult them. But norms are also the *result* of social interaction: the behavior of many people *determines* what is popular, fashionable, or "normal." This means that norms can and will change, and that people must continue to study each other to determine what the norms are and how to conduct themselves.

Sherif's Research. In a classic series of studies undertaken in the late 1930s, Muzafer Sherif (1906–1988) examined the power of perceived norms in influencing behavior. Small groups of strangers were assembled in a darkened room, and asked to watch and judge the movement of a small point of light. (In fact, the light itself never moved, although it appeared to, an illusion termed the *autokinetic effect*). When subjects were able to share their judgments with each other, their judgments of the light's "movement" tended to converge upon a group norm. In other words, although they were strangers, group members relied on each other's "perceptions" to determine a norm, and then conformed their own judgments to that norm.

Norm formation within the groups not only yielded standards for immediate behavior (estimates of the light's movement), but also influenced individual subjects' judgments for up to a year later. Further, as new group members replaced old ones, the older norms persisted and influenced new members' judgments. The endurance of social norms may explain the persistence of traditions many generations after the original conditions and people who developed them. The norm formation Sherif identified is best explained by social comparison processes: group members, in order to perform well, relied on the patterns they perceived in each other's judgments, thus both creating and consulting a social norm.

Social Contagion. Once norms are formed, they can be transmitted widely and rapidly. You may have wondered how rumors, popular fads, and even jokes spread so quickly from one region to the next. After all, these are interesting social phenomena, but not really valuable ideas or knowledge that improve task performance. Research suggests a number of events that provoke *social contagion,* the spreading of a behavior pattern across many people as a result of their interactions.

For example, factory workers who feel underpaid and unwell may "catch" an imaginary disease they attribute to a dangerous substance or pest. As each individual succumbs to the symptoms, his or her coworkers look for—and often find—those same symptoms in themselves. When the illness itself is imagined, and the "symptoms" are emotional and behavioral, the best explanation of the "contagion" is modeling. As coworkers and friends identified and sympathized with those who were stricken, they copied those symptoms themselves.

GROUP PRESSURE

Most studies of conformity have examined the effects of group presence on individuals. Sometimes the group is present—one is in the physical presence of other members. Other times the group may be imaginary, as when one enters a darkened movie theater and assumes that other audience members are already seated. The most influential research on group pressure has been that conducted by social psychologist Solomon Asch (b. 1907). In the 1940s and 1950s, Asch studied the effects of group pressure on individual judgments and behavior. Later research examined the effects of pressure from imaginary groups.

Asch's Research. In the simplest form of Asch's experiment, a group of subjects was gathered in a room to participate in a study of visual perception. Cards were displayed with vertical lines of various lengths. Each subject was to call out his judgment about which line best matched the length of that on a second card.

In reality, only one member of the group was really a subject, the only subject. Other members were confederates working with the experimenter; on prearranged trials these confederates unanimously called out obviously inaccurate judgments. The question was whether subjects would conform by calling out the same wrong answers. Across all subjects and trials, Asch found that subjects' responses conformed 37 percent of the time. Although some never conformed ("independents") and some always conformed ("yielders"), most conformed at least once.

Asch's study indicated that, even among strangers, individuals were socially influenced to conform to norms, even in matters of fact, when subjects could see reality for themselves.

Crutchfield's Variations. In the 1950s social psychologist Richard Crutchfield automated Asch's procedure. In Crutchfield's variation of the conformity experiment, several real subjects at a time viewed questions from privacy booths, and answered in sequence. Each subject answered last, after being deceived about how others had responded. Consequently, their own responses were more likely to conform, even to answers that should have seemed obviously wrong.

Asch's research had confirmed that the visible and physical presence of others creates group pressure to conform. Crutchfield's variation indicates that, even when evidence of others is indirect and individuals do not face the rest of the group, trends in group behavior create influence to conform.

SITUATIONAL FACTORS AFFECTING CONFORMITY

Research by Asch and others has identified several factors that determine conformity: group size, unanimity, cohesiveness, and public commitment.

Group Size. As group size increases to three to five people, so does the likelihood that members will conform. Beyond five members, size of group has less effect on individuals' conformity.

Unanimity. A unanimous group elicits greater conformity from any individual than a nonunanimous group. The presence of a single deviate makes it easier for any individual member not to conform. This conformity-breaking effect is probably due to modeling; once a deviate has voiced his or her dissent, others have an example of nonconformity to follow.

Cohesiveness. The extent to which group members bond together and value belonging is termed its *cohesiveness*. Conformity is greater among members of cohesive than noncohesive groups. Liking each other and enjoying each other's company make it harder for you to deviate from group opinion.

Public Commitment. Conformity is higher among groups in which judgments and votes are made in public. For example, a written (anonymous) ballot may show a pattern of voting different from a hand count of the same group. In showing support or opposition, group members will feel more pressure to conform to certain others' opinions. When voting anonymously, each will feel more secure and less vulnerable to criticism by opponents.

INDIVIDUAL DIFFERENCES AFFECTING CONFORMITY

Research has identified ways in which some individuals differ from others in their tendency to conform. Influential factors include status, gender, personality traits, and culture.

Status. People with low or relatively lower status are more likely to conform than those who are high. Well-dressed people are more likely to be "copied" when they provide a bad example. People in high-status professions are more likely to question authority and break from the norms, while those in lower-status occupations are more likely to seek guidance from their "superiors."

Gender. As reported earlier (see chapter 7), while most conformity studies reveal no gender difference, the few that do suggest that women may conform more than men in certain conditions. Critics observe that this gender difference is more likely to be mentioned in earlier studies—usually conducted by male investigators—than in more recent ones. Others note that women may not be more "conformist"—a pejorative interpretation—but rather more "socially oriented" than men. Finally, gender differences in conformity may be caused by attributions of power: men generally have more social power (and status) than women. The gender "effect" may be merely another form of the status effect already noted.

Personality. Personality differences in social behavior are fascinating; casual investigators are more likely to ask "What kind of people conform?" than "What kinds of conditions make almost anyone conform?" However, endeavors to find stable connections between personality and conformity have yielded only weak conclusions. Some studies suggested that people who have a stronger need for social approval are more likely to conform.

In general, research on "conforming personalities" indicates that, when conformist situations are "strong"—structured and influential—personality differences make little difference in behavior. But when situations are "weak"—ambiguous and not constraining—an actor's tendency to conform may be related to other behavior patterns or personality tendencies.

Culture. Different cultures and nationalities engender different values and goals. Americans are more punctual and time-obsessed than Spaniards or Italians; the Japanese value work and education more than most Americans. Conformity may also be a tendency that varies across cultures.

Social psychologist Stanley Milgram conducted a variation of Asch's conformity experiment in two cultures he had determined to vary in conformity: France (expected to conform less) and Norway (expected to conform more). Results confirmed a significant effect of cultural difference: in the same experimental arrangement, far more Norwegian students conformed with confederates' wrong answers than did French students. French students in fact repudiated the apparently mindless conformity of other group members. If cultures differ in conformity, it is likely that subcultural differences are also influential: some geographic or ethnic traditions may encourage conformity while others discourage it.

Obedience to Authority

During and after periods of international conflict, people become more interested in how nations and peoples differ. After World War II, many Americans felt a smug assurance that what happened in Nazi Germany "could never happen here"—because Germans were more likely than Americans blindly to follow the orders of their leaders, even of mad dictators like Adolf Hitler. Was this true? Yale social psychologist Stanley Milgram (1933–1984), who had studied with Solomon Asch, constructed an ingenious and controversial experiment to establish a baseline of obedience: how far will an individual go to obey the orders of an otherwise unknown authority figure?

MILGRAM'S RESEARCH

In Milgram's original study, subjects were recruited to participate in what was advertised as a study of the effects of punishment on learning. As a subject arrived, he was introduced to another "subject" (actually a confederate who acted a prearranged role); after drawing lots (rigged), the subject took the role of "teacher" and the confederate that of "learner." The experimenter, clad in a laboratory coat, explained that the teacher was to recite word pairs to the learner, who would listen via intercom from the next room. The teacher was to test the learner's recall of word pairs, punishing each mistake with a shock from an electric shock generator, increasing the intensity by 15 volts for each mistake. The generator displayed shock intensities from 15 to 450 volts; how far would each "teacher" go in punishing the "learner," simply on the order of the experimenter?

Prior to conducting the experiment, Milgram had solicited estimates from professionals and average citizens, who guessed that they themselves would not exceed 300 volts, and that "other people" would not go as far as 450 volts. In fact, 63% of Milgram's subjects administered "shocks" (there were no actual shocks; the "learner" acted his responses of pain and protest) to the 450-volt level without stopping. In a second series, Milgram had the "learner" complain of a heart condition, but this had no effect on obedience: 65% of subjects complied to the 450-volt level.

Subjects did not blithely obey to the limit in most cases, but usually expressed some discomfort or concern about shocking the learner. If subjects protested, the experimenter offered only reminders that the experiment required them to go on. Subjects were not otherwise bribed, threatened, or bullied.

Through employment of deception (about experiment's purpose and the "learner's" experiences), Milgram was able to ascertain that a majority of subjects obeyed an authority figure to the extreme of inflicting what they believed was real pain on an innocent victim. The use of deception and the disillusioning findings created enduring controversy surrounding Milgram's research.

An important conclusion about Milgram's research is that social situations can be powerful. Most people considering or learning about the experiment judge themselves as likely to disobey; yet most subjects in the original series did obey. The reality of the experimental situation—its experimental realism (see chapter 2)—construed a powerful situation that was difficult for most subjects to resist. Despite the temptation to ask "What kind of person would obey orders to hurt innocent people?," it is more instructive in social psychology to ask rather, "What aspects of the situation make it difficult for most people to disobey?"

FACTORS AFFECTING OBEDIENCE

Further research by Milgram and colleagues identified important factors influencing subjects willingness to obey versus their ability to disobey: victim proximity, proximity of the authority figure, nature of the authority, and group support.

Victim Proximity. The greater the distance between the subject ("teacher") and the victim ("learner"), the greater the percentage of subjects who obeyed to the limit. When the victim was in a separate room, over 60% of subjects obeyed; 40% obeyed to the limit when the victim was in the same room; 30% obeyed when the subject sat beside the victim and held his hand onto a shock plate to deliver punishment. The closer the victim, the harder it is for the subject to deny the effects of obedience.

Authority Figure Proximity. The closer the authority figure (the experimenter) was to the subject, the greater the percentage of subjects who obeyed to the limit. In Milgram's original series (63-65% obedience), the experimenter remained in the same room with the subject. When the experimenter delivered instructions by telephone, only 21% of subjects actually obeyed to 450 volts.

Nature of the Authority. Milgram's original series were conducted at Yale University, a prestigious institution whose status carries social influence. When the same experiment was conducted in a nearby town with no university authority or affiliation, obedience dropped to 48% of subjects.

In one variation, the experimenter left the laboratory on a pretext; a "clerk" remaining behind (actually a confederate) ordered the subject to increase the shock level for each punishment. Eighty percent of subjects refused to comply with orders from this "illegitimate" authority figure. Obedience is not apparently transferred easily to those who supplant an authority figure's position.

Finally, the vestiges of authority may communicate information about who is or is not to be obeyed. Results of some studies indicate that subjects may comply with those they believe to be persons "in authority," judging by attire (e.g., a uniform) or other clues (e.g., badges, language, or titles).

Group Support. In one variation of Milgram's original paradigm, threesomes of "subjects" (one subject plus two confederates) were ordered to administer shocks to a "learner." When the confederates jointly defied the experimenter's orders, 90% of the subjects joined them.

Social Power

Studies of conformity and obedience differ in not only arrangement but in the nature of power: pressure to conform comes from the "power" of a social group; pressure to obey derives from the "power" of an authority figure. *Power* is defined as the force an influencer can use to cause change in a person's attitude or behavior. Thus power constitutes an important category of social influence. Social psychologists have identified several different types and effects of power.

TYPES OF POWER

Bertram Raven and his colleagues have identified six types of power, distinguished by the basis of social influence involved in each: coercive power, reward power, legitimate power, referent power, expert power and informational power.

Reward Power. *Reward power* is influence based on affluence, on the ability to give others something they want (e.g., money, approval), or take away something they dislike (e.g., discomfort, inconvenience). Reward power has the disadvantage of requiring the influencer to monitor the target's behavior, to know if and when to reward the target for complying.

Coercive Power. *Coercive power* is the power to punish. For example, if someone has coercive power over you, he or she may try to influence you by threatening to take something away from you (e.g., wages, affection) or inflict harm (e.g., public criticism, suffering). One disadvantage of coercive power is that it requires the influencer to monitor the target's behavior for signs of influence or defiance. Another problem is that coercive power demoralizes and antagonizes its targets; people who cooperate only out of fear tend to comply without acceptance.

Legitimate Power. Some people influence us because we recognize they have the right to do so, because of their authority, status, or social position. This is social influence based on *legitimate power*. For example, a professor has the legitimate power to decide when the deadlines are for a student's work. Legitimate power is limited by its role. For example, a professor does not have the legitimate power to ask a student to run errands for her.

Referent Power. Other kinds of relationships besides professional roles can have social influence. Under the influence of *referent power,* the target identifies with (wishes to be similar to) the influencer, and so complies. Referent power accounts for the pervasive indirect social influence our friends and family members can have on us. But referent power is fragile, since dislike or disrespect can break the "hold" an influencer has on a target.

Expert Power. *Expert power* is based on the target's belief that an influencer has generally superior knowledge or expertise in a relevant area. For example, if your physician advises you to lose weight, you are more likely to take this advice than if your dry cleaner tells you the same thing. The physician is seen as possessing expertise about your health, and about health in general. This gives him or her expert power in influencing your health-related habits.

Informational Power. Even a non-expert can exert social influence if she or he possesses specific information to support the change proposed. Facts that impress or convince the target comprise the influencer's *informational power*. For example, your best friend may not know much about cars in general, but may insist he or she remembers that a leading consumer magazine awarded a very low rating to the model you have considered buying. This knowledge may be relevant enough to your needs that you are persuaded to reject that model, as your friend advises.

All the types of power identified by French are *socially dependent*. This means that they depend on some quality, strategy, or asset of the *influencer* in order to be effective. If a would-be influencer cannot reward or punish you, is not someone you respect or like, and possesses neither expertise nor relevant information, he or she will not wield sufficient power to influence you.

EFFECTS OF POWER

Power is an experience that has effects both for the target of the social influence—who is relatively powerless—and the wielder—who is relatively powerful.

On The Powerless. Someone who is regularly influenced to behave in a particular way may initially yield by mere compliance. For example, you may salute a superior officer or address a supervisor politely, while secretly despising or disliking him or her. This may seem like an ideal solution to the problem of resented power: you modify your behavior to deceive your influencers, but never actually change your underlying attitudes.

Ironically, research suggests that programs of compliant behavior, over time, can generate internal acceptance. For example, after daily standing to recite the Pledge of Allegiance, you are likely to come to believe and accept what you are pledging, although initially you may not comprehend such concepts as "pledging" or "allegiance."

Two processes seem to account for this tendency: *a momentum of compliance*, and *behavioral commitment*. Acting as though you believe something may evolve into increasing demonstrations of your support. Such demonstrations create a momentum of compliance, a powerful tendency to lean in the influenced direction. Secondly, if your actions are so alien to your real feelings, they will create a feeling of dissonance. Because every influenced action represents a behavioral commitment, you cannot undo your actions but may still rework your attitude. The effects of power on the powerless, therefore, may ultimately be effective, even if met initially with resistance, false cooperation, or hypocrisy.

Another possible effect of power on the powerless is that the target loses a sense of competence of self-efficacy. People who act only on orders or advice from others—like hospital patients, nursing home residents, or prisoners of war—may gradually relinquish their own independence or sense of capability. This state of *learned helplessness* (discussed in chapter 4) has been linked to poor health, low self-esteem, and unwillingness to change or escape difficult conditions.

Most social roles require one to be both influencer and target at different times, so that few individuals are *always* powerful—or powerless. For example, a supervisor who usually barks orders at her employees may defer, when she is at home, to the domineering ways of a parent or spouse. Research confirms that different bases of power interact and mesh in personal and social relationships. Some studies of heterosexual couples indicate that wives and husbands use different kinds of power. Others show that men use different social influence strategies than women do with their intimate partners. The effects of power therefore depend somewhat on particular relationships and interactions, as well as on characteristics like gender.

Effects on the Powerful. Having power and successfully wielding social influence may have observable effects on people. A simulation of prison roles and regulations showed that young men playing the part of prison guards developed exaggerated patterns of dominant behavior, abusing and disparaging those playing the part of prisoners. Researchers examining whether "power corrupts" have argued that access to power increases the chances that it will be used, that social influencers come to control and devalue their targets, and that feeling powerful becomes essential to influencers' self-esteem. These processes and tendencies make unchallenged power an addictive and destructive habit.

Explanations of Social Influence

In some cases social influence is not hard to understand: if your boss asks you to do something fairly easy, and you know that she has the power to reward or punish you, you may conduct a very simple cost-benefit analysis to conclude that it would be best to comply. But other forms of social influence are harder to understand. Why would anyone agree to obey orders to hurt an innocent victim, especially if the person issuing the orders offers neither bribes nor threats as inducements? A broad theory—social impact theory—has been developed to explain a wide range of social influence. In addition, a number of processes have been proposed to account for individual cases of compliance.

SOCIAL IMPACT THEORY

According to social impact theory, the *social impact,* or force to comply, that is felt by a target is determined by three factors: the *strength* of influence, the *immediacy* of the influence, and the *number* of influence sources present. Impact will be greater, and the target more likely to comply, when influences are strong, immediate (close), and numerous.

For example, in Milgram's original experiments on obedience to authority, there was only one source of influence (the experimenter) and he was only moderately strong (perceived as a scientist, an authority figure). However, the source had very great immediacy: the experimenter remained close to the subject, and regularly prodded him with reminders of the experiment's requirements. The victim's original position (the next room) was low in immediacy; when immediacy was increased, obedience dropped.

Other research has confirmed the value of the other factors in social impact theory. For example, a news story about the death of fifty people (high number) in your neighborhood (high immediacy) in a dramatic apartment building fire (high strength) will have much greater impact on you than a story about the death of two people (low number) in Peru (low immediacy) in an outbreak of cholera (low strength). As a result of the first story, you may take action by contributing to a relief fund or doing volunteer work; the latter story may provoke only a slight frown, if you notice it at all.

SOCIAL INFLUENCE PROCESSES

Social psychologist Robert Cialdini has identified six techniques used by would-be social influencers: authority, social proof, scarcity, liking, reciprocity, and commitment-consistency.

Authority. People with one or more forms of power (reviewed above) will wield that power to establish their authority over the target. In addition to utilitarian considerations by the target about the costs and benefits of complying, norms encouraging respect for authority encourage this process of social influence. Most people are educated to behave as instructed, by parents, teachers and other authority figures. Thus it may not be necessary for an influencer to wield power; presenting oneself as an authority may be sufficient to effect change.

Social Proof. Social proof is provided when others provide standards for an individual's behavior. Essentially, social proof is the outcome of the social comparison process, in which one consults others' actions to validate one's own beliefs or plans. For example, if you and several classmates are late for class but the others assure you that this professor "will not care" and that being tardy will be "all right," you will feel pressure to join them rather than hurrying ahead. Their numbers and agreement will provide a form of "proof" that they must be right.

Scarcity. According to the principle of *scarcity,* desire for a commodity increases as the supply decreases. This affects social influence when an individual imagines that others are competing with him or her for a scarce resource. This creates a form of imagined group pressure to take action that will beat the competition. For example, a salesperson will encourage customers to buy now by reminding them that there are "only three days left in this sale!" or urging them to "buy now while they last!" Scarcity may interact with feelings of psychological reactance (see chapter 9): you may feel that scarcity of resources threatens your free choice; to reassert your freedom, you take action rather than delaying.

Liking. People we like have more influence with us than those we dislike. This common-sense maxim bears review in an analysis of social influence. Given the persuasive power of communicators who are seen as informed, trustworthy, attractive, and similar to ourselves (see chapter 9), it is not surprising that such people are effective in other forms of social influence as well.

Reciprocity. One good turn deserves another; this summarizes the principle of *reciprocity,* the rule that favors should be returned. Reciprocity has been identified as the motivating influence in prosocial acts like helping behavior (see chapter 17). When applied deliberately to elicit such actions, it is a process of social influence. For example, if a classmate you do not know well compliments you on the way you answered a question in class, you may feel flattered. If she then asks you to lend her your notes to copy, you may find it difficult to refuse, out of sense that this simple favor "repays" or reciprocates her compliment.

Reciprocity has been found to take different forms in social influence. *Guilt inducement* involves first making a target feel guilty about some error or failing, then making a request while he or she is still "vulnerable." For example, if you felt you had disappointed a friend by arriving late for an appointment, you might readily agree to "make up" for your lateness by paying for his lunch.

Another effective reciprocity strategy is the *door-in-the-face* technique. In this tactic, the influencer first makes an unreasonably large request of the target, one the target must refuse. The influencer then immediately makes a smaller, related request, which the target is almost relieved to grant. Having had to say no—slamming the door in the requester's face—the target is anxious to be able to open the door again, and show how reasonable and giving he or she is.

Finally, social influence is more successful if the influencer, having made the original request or sales pitch, appears to compromise or sweeten the deal before the target complies. This is termed the *that's-not-all* technique, because as the target is considering the request, the influencer adds that "that's not all" he or she will offer you if you accede. For example, someone deciding whether to buy an appliance on sale is promised that, in addition to the sale price, he will be given a free set of accessory attachments. Research suggests that he will be more likely to agree than if the additional offer had not been made. The target's agreement may be made out of a sense of reciprocity, since the "extra" offer seems like a greater concession on the influencer's part.

Commitment-Consistency. Finally, as reviewed above and in previous chapters, influencers may win cooperation by inducing an initial behavioral commitment from a target. In order to be consistent with this initial action, the target develops an attitude in favor of changing in the requested direction. For example, an exhibit salesperson may urge you to "complete this entry blank" requesting a home visit by someone who will tell you all about the product and bring you a free gift ("no obligation"). While the promise of a free gift may have induced the easy initial behavior (completing an entry blank), the presence of a salesperson in your home—at your request—may create a sense of dissonance that is best reduced by promising to buy the product line. In order to be consistent with your initial commitment, you agree to the larger, related commitment. (You will also recognize this as the basic process of the *foot-in-the-door* technique, reviewed in chapter 8).

RESISTING SOCIAL INFLUENCE

Thus far material in this and earlier chapters may suggest that social influence can be powerful and inescapable. However, research confirms that many strategies can enable a target to resist an influencer's advances. Some are deliberate, others are side effects of personal and situational effects. The forms of resistance reviewed here include processes that lead to deviance and strategies for minority influence.

Deviance

Conformity is sometimes portrayed in pejorative or negative terms, like mindless or sheeplike behavior, giving in to others instead of holding out for what is right. However, the alternative—deviance or nonconformity—is more often considered a negative pattern. Deviants—people who do not conform—are likely to be criticized or ostracized by other group members. Deviants are not "team players," they do not "go along," and threaten the group's sense of consensus and cohesiveness.

DEVIANCE IN GROUP CONTEXT

When the agent of social influence is a group—two or more people who are mutually influential—deviance may take two forms: independence and anticonformity.

Independence. In his original series of experiments on conformity, Solomon Asch distinguished between subjects who always conformed—"yielders"—and those who never conformed—"independents." He found three reasons for the independents' nonconformity: some were confident of their own accuracy despite the others' unanimity; some felt duty-bound to answer as instructed, as they judged the task, although the others' disagreement shook their self-confidence; and finally, some were simply detached from the other group members, only paying attention long enough to answer, and otherwise oblivious to the confederates' glares of disapproval.

Other research has characterized true independence as behavior that deliberately ignores group pressures and norms. Truly independent group members adhere to their own beliefs and standards, and are not shaken or lured by the consensus of group sentiment.

Anticonformity. Some who resist group pressures have a history of resisting or defying authority. These *anticonformists* are less guided by their own standards than driven to oppose the group's. Their actions are influenced more by reactance—"No one tells me what to do!"—than normative or informational influence.

DEVIANCE AND IDENTITY

As noted in chapter 4, many processes of self-development are essentially social. We define ourselves in terms of whom we belong with—and how we are different from others. Thus deviance may be a matter of identity as well as group involvement.

Psychological Reactance. Psychological reactance has already been described as a repudiation of social influence motivated by self-control. When one is told what to do, one may react by feeling unduly controlled, and rebel in order to reestablish a sense of free choice. To some extent psychological reactance is a process of self-efficacy, demonstrating to ourselves (and to would-be influencers) that we govern our own behavior and set our own goals. As noted in chapter 9, reactance can also backfire when it is anticipated and used in "reverse psychology" by a persuasive communicator.

Reactance can also be the first step in broader social rebellion. Those who experience reactance and reject social influence have several influence-breaking effects: as deviates, they deprive the group of unanimity; they model nonconformity for other group members who may follow their example; and they express the reservations that others may also be experiencing.

Personal Uniqueness. To some extent individuals may have a need to feel unique. Research indicates that, when people are experimentally manipulated into conformist behavior, they may find ways to assert their uniqueness by other forms of nonconformity. Research on *spontaneous self-concepts* also shows that people's self-descriptions are composed to distinguish them from their group context. For example, a person from Southern United States in a group of people from the North may begin her self-description with, "I'm from the South."

Minority Influence

In cases of social influence through group pressure, those who resist majority influence become *de facto* members of the minority group. Minority group membership need not be synonymous with defeat. Research confirms three strategies that enable a minority to exert influence on the rest of the group: consistency, confidence, and deviations from the majority.

CONSISTENCY

Whatever the size of the minority, the more consistent its behavior with past expressions and actions, the stronger and more influential it will be. In other words, rather than vacillating and adopting a variety of nonconformist positions, a minority is likely to be effective by adopting and sticking to an original position.

CONFIDENCE

Any display of self-confidence will distinguish the minority and make it more influential. For example, entering the deliberation room ahead of the majority, smiling, taking the head seat at the table, and speaking with calm reassurance all convey stability—and power.

DEFECTIONS FROM THE MAJORITY

Just as deviates model nonconformity to other group members, minority group members model disagreement to wavering members of the majority. If members of the minority can anticipate and respond to the unspoken doubts of some members of the majority, they may win defections. Every defector weakens the social impact (by reducing the number) of the majority. A defector also paves the way for further defections, by modeling departures from the majority. While a minority by definition has relatively less social impact (smaller numbers) than a majority, other social processes can compensate for strength and immediacy, creating a momentum that might shift the balance in the reverse direction as the group evolves and interacts.

In social influence, an individual or group causes a target to change attitudes or behavior. There are two broad levels of social influence: acceptance and compliance. Acceptance involves complete change in accordance with the influence, and may be achieved through identification or internalization. Compliance involves only an observable change in behavior, and is usually what is studied in research on conformity or obedience. Social influence usually involve adhering to one of two standards: normative influence, or compliance with group norms, and informational influence, or conversion due to education.

Three types of social influence reviewed here are conformity, obedience, and social power. Classic research on conformity can be traced to Muzafer Sherif's original studies of norm formation. This research demonstrated that group members will modify their behavior in order to converge onto a group norm. Research on social contagion suggests that other forms of normative influence may be fostered through modeling.

Conformity due to group pressure was investigated in research by Solomon Asch, who identified the impact of immediate group pressure. Variations on Asch's work by Crutchfield demonstrated the impact of implied or imagined group presence. Conformity is greatest when the group is large, unanimous, and cohesive, and when conformity entails public commitment. Individual differences also affect conformity: research suggests that low status individuals conform more than high status persons, that women may conform more than men, that conformity may be greater for those who need social approval, and that cultures may influence individuals' willingness to conform.

Stanley Milgram's classic research on obedience to authority demonstrated that most subjects, deceived about the nature of their experimental participation, were induced to obey an authority figure's orders to administer "shocks" to a victim (actually a confederate). Obedience was greatest when the victim was distant, the authority figure was close, the authority was validated by a prestigious institution and the authority figure was perceived to be legitimate. Obedience was reduced when the victim was close, the authority figure distant or illegitimate, and when the subject had group support in defying the experimenter.

Social power involves the force one agent has in influencing another. Power may be based on ability to reward, ability to punish, legitimate authority, likability or similarity to the target, possession of expertise or of relevant information. The effects of power on the powerless include increasing likelihood of acceptance, and in extreme cases, learned helplessness. Effects on the powerful include exaggeratedly dominant behavior and depersonalization of the target.

Social influence has been explained in terms of social impact theory. According to social impact theory, impact is greatest when the sources of influence are strong, immediate, and numerous. Studies of social influence have also identified several specific strategies and techniques. People are more influential if they represent authority, offer social proof to the target, threaten scarcity if the target does not act, are likable, engage the target in reciprocal favors, or induce the target to make an initial commitment that prompts consistency in subsequent action.

Social influence can be successfully resisted through both deviance and minority influence. Deviance in group context may be produced through independence or anticonformity. Deviance may also serve in identity development. For example, psychological reactance supports self-control, and individuals compensate for excessive conformity by reasserting personal uniqueness. Minorities may exert influence in groups by behaving consistently, maintaining self-confidence, and winning defections from the majority.

Selected Readings

Cialdini, R. B. (1984). *Influence: How and Why People Agree to Do Things*. New York: Morrow.

Cialdini, R. B. (1988). *Influence: Science and Practice*. Glenview, IL: Scott, Foresman.

Freeman, J. L. and A. N. Doob, (1968). *Deviancy*. New York: Academic Press.

Kelman, H. C. and V. L. Hamilton, (1988). *Crimes of Obedience: Toward a Social Psychology of Authority and Responsibility*. New Haven, CT: Yale University Press.

Kerckhoff, A. C. and K. W. Back, (1968). *The June Bug: A Study of Hysterical Contagion*. New York: Appleton-Century-Crofts.

Kipnis, D. (1976). *The Powerholders*. Chicago: University of Chicago Press.

Milgram, S. (1974). *Obedience to Authority*. New York: Harper and Row.

Milgram, S. (1977). *The Individual in a Social World*. Reading, MA: Addison-Wesley.

Miller, A. G. (1986). *The Obedience Experiments: A Case Study of Controversy in Social Science*. New York: Praeger.

Moscovici, S. (1976). *Social Influence and Social Change*. London: Academic Press.

Staub, E. (1989). *Roots of Evil: The Psychological and Cultural Sources of Genocide*. New York: Cambridge University Press.

Schopler, J. and B. D. Layton, (1972). *Attributions of Interpersonal Power and Influence*. New York: General Learning Corporation.

Tedeschi, J. (Ed.). (1974). *Perspectives on Social Power*. Chicago: Aldine.

Wheeler, L., E. Deci, H. Reis, and M. Zuckerman, (1978). *Interpersonal Influence*, 2nd edition. Boston: Allyn and Bacon.

11

Group Behavior

Humans are social animals, seeking and developing each other's company. We also organize our company together into groups. Group membership offers personal benefits, and group participation achieves goals that solitary individuals may not. In this chapter we examine the nature of psychological groups, the dynamics of group performance, and the role of group leader.

THE NATURE OF GROUPS

Not all collections of people make up true psychological groups. A group is defined by functional qualities, not physical properties.

Definition of a Psychological Group

For social psychologists, a *group* consists of a minimum of two or more people who interact, communicate with, and influence each other for a period of time.

GROUPS VERSUS NONGROUPS

As broad as this definition seems, it restricts our consideration of group psychology, especially in terms of behavior. To comprise a group, a collection of people must share more than circumstances. They must share perceptions and goals. Group members must be aware of each other, interact with each other, and exert influence on each other. To communicate with each other, they must both send and receive messages. And they must be engaged in these processes for more than a few moments.

For example, a collection of six persons who board and ride an elevator together for several floors do not *per se* make up a group. However, if a common stimulus were to unite their attention—such as the elevator's sudden, unscheduled stop between floors—they might quickly *become* a group.

Aggregates. A collection of people who do not interact or influence each other is more correctly thought of as a nongroup assembly or *aggregate* of individuals. As noted in the example above, an aggregate can quickly become—and just as quickly cease to be—a group.

Reasons for Group Involvement. Why do people join or participate in groups? In some cases, "joining" is not an issue. For example, if the elevator you are riding becomes jammed between floors, your cooperation with fellow passengers will develop quickly, and not as a result of any formal initiation or "joining" procedure.

Formal or otherwise, there are two common reasons why people join groups: goal attainment and need gratification. By working together, people can accomplish *goals* that might be difficult or impossible for solitary individuals to achieve. For example, you may realize that moving to a new house or apartment will take all your time for several days—and that some items will be too heavy for you to budge. By inviting a group of friends to help you, you will accomplish the task must more quickly, efficiently, and probably safely.

Additionally, group participation addresses many social *needs*. These may include access to approval, a sense of belonging, friendship and love.

INDIVIDUALS IN GROUP CONTEXT

People do not inevitably lose their individuality in groups, although groups may help lessen self-awareness and produce a state of deindividuation (discussed below). In fact, group membership can heighten certain aspects of individual experience. Three important effects of the group on the individual are identity, deviance, and social impact.

Identity. Belonging to a group is a form of social categorization: the group becomes one aspect of social identity. For example, in introducing yourself to others you may mention being a student, a member of a particular class or program of study. Reference groups, mentioned in earlier chapters, are particularly important in defining not only identity but aspirations. When groups come into contact with each other, individuals may compare their own group (the *in-group*) favorably to the alternatives (*out-groups*).

Deviance. Group goals can sometimes override or conflict with individual members' personal goals. When a member breaks with the group's norms to satisfy personal needs, he or she becomes a *deviate* (or *deviant*). According to social comparison theory (reviewed in chapter 4), members of a group are important in validating each other's beliefs. A deviate threatens that validation by defecting and reducing consensus. Therefore, up to a point, the rest of the group will communicate with the deviate in an effort to restore consensus. Beyond that point—when cooperation seems unlikely, for example—the group stops working *with* the deviate and begins to reject him or her. Ultimately the deviate will most likely be pushed out of the group, thus restoring consensus with one fewer member.

Social Impact. The previous chapter reviewed *social impact theory*, an explanation of social influence. According to this theory, the degree to which a targeted individual is influenced depends on three factors: the strength of the source of influence, the immediacy of the influence, and the number of sources.

Group membership can be seen as having social impact on an indidivual. Taken factor by factor, a group will have greater influence on each member if it is strong (e.g., important to the membership); if the group's influence is immediate (e.g., the group meets frequently, or the members live near each other); and if the group is large in number (e.g., the group is more populous than alternative organizations).

Group Structure and Function

Harvard social psychologist Robert Bales has distinguished two important functions of group behavior: the *task agenda* and the *social agenda*. The task agenda involves doing work, like solving problems and making decisions. The social agenda involves meeting the emotional needs and social roles of the group's members. Groups meet these two agendas through several key processes and structures: norms, roles, and cohesiveness.

NORMS

Norms have already been defined as rules or guidelines for accepted and expected behavior. As shown in chapter 10, groups develop norms—even unconsciously, as in Sherif's norm formation research—whenever they rely on each other for judgments. In social groups, some norms are explicit: members know what they are and can explain them to newcomers. Others are implicit or subtle, occasionally taken for granted until a deviate unwittingly "crosses the line" and attracts attention.

For example, most groups have a norm for *how* decisions are made. A small circle of teenagers, deciding how to spend the weekend, may have a norm of deferring to the opinions and wishes of the one or two members who drive and have access to cars. Differently, a group of coworkers in a small business may agree that important contracts are to be voted on by all members, with a simple majority (more than half) ruling. In these examples, the teenager who suggests taking a vote and the coworker who tries to play dictator will be violating norms, and may be treated as deviates until the group restores consensus—or pushes the deviate out.

ROLES

As noted in chapter 7, roles are sets of norms defining behavior appropriate to particular social positions. Groups usually involve roles; some are broad, like leaders and followers, while others are more specific. Roles differentiate members' functions and contributions within the group. Roles may be organized according to individual talents. Roles can be a source of reward, as well as a source of problems within a group.

Defining Roles. Given the two functions of groups, it is not surprising that some members of a group be considered *task specialists* while others are viewed as *socioemotional specialists,* respectively members who are focused on those complementary concerns.

Roles may differ in not only function but value to the group. Roles associated with greater prestige or respect are said to have higher *status*— position or rank. Status affects the way members of the group communicate and work with each other. For example, high-status members like bosses and managers may initiate communication with lower-status members, but not vice versa. A professor can interrupt a student worker to ask a question, but a student worker is not free to enter a professor's office and ask questions without permission. Status can be a reward for specific members, but it is not without cost, since differences in status can be a source of resentment or competition among members.

Problems. In social groups, two kinds of *role conflict* commonly occur. One type is *person-role* conflict, in which a person finds his or her group role difficult to perform. For example, a committee member may be required to criticize other members' work but feel unconfortable with having to do this.

Another type of role conflict is *inter-role* conflict, in which memberships in different groups compete with each other. For example, a church member may feel conflicted when her company schedules a workshop on a date with church significance. To be a good church member, she should skip the workshop; to be a good employee, she must violate church standards. Since each of us may belong to many different groups, inter-role conflict can be a familiar—if not minor—problem.

When one's responsibilities within a group are unclear or unstable, the individual suffers the difficulty of *role ambiguity*. Roles are likely to be ambiguous when a member first joins a group, or when task performance changes. For example, if a small service company shifts from paper record-keeping to the use of computers, the roles of the file clerk may become ambiguous. It is not yet clear what—if any—function he will have in the organization from this point on.

COHESIVENESS

Perhaps the most influential quality of group interaction is *cohesiveness,* feelings of attraction and loyalty that motivate members to stay in the group. When members want to stay in a group, they are more likely to acquiesce or give in to its influences. Members of cohesive groups like each other more and support common goals more strongly than members of less cohesive groups. High cohesiveness can be a source of both benefits and liabilities. Members of highly cohesive groups enjoy their membership and interaction more, but are also prone to make mistakes by giving group feeling a higher priority than other group goals (see Groupthink, below).

Factors in Cohesiveness. Anything that makes a group more valuable to its members increases cohesiveness. This includes past history of success in group efforts, threat from outside forces and competition with out-groups.

Barriers to Cohesiveness. Competition *within* the group can reduce cohesiveness, since members fear threat from each other. Another barrier to fellowship is disliking or special preferences among members. When members are drawn to and away from each other, subgroups form which break down organizational unity.

The tendency for a group to polarize into subgroups can be revealed by a *sociogram,* a diagram illustrating members' preferred associations. Sometimes preferences balance out and unify all group members, but it is easy to imagine how some individuals may be liked or disliked by several others. When attractions are unequally distributed, subgroups are more likely to form, and cohesiveness is undermined.

Preferential differences in members' feelings are more likely to develop in large groups, and thus group size is negatively related to cohesiveness: the larger the organization, the harder it is to maintain attraction, loyalty, and fairness evenly among all members.

CLASSIFYING GROUPS AND TASKS

Groups differ not only in size and internal dynamics, but also in terms of the way they perform their tasks. Group researcher Ivan Steiner has provided a comprehensive analysis of work groups, identifying four categories of groups and tasks: additive, conjunctive, disjunctive, and divisible.

Additive. Additive tasks require all members to pool their efforts toward a common, shared product. Members of such groups add their efforts together in pursuit of a common outcome, hence the description "additive." For example, in a group tug-of-war competition, no one member takes a lead role; the winning team beats the opposition because of the combined efforts of all members.

Because additive tasks do not permit individuals or their contributions to be singled out, additive tasks are especially vulnerable to the problem of *social loafing*. Research shows that individuals actually contribute less effort to additive tasks than when they work alone or are individually monitored. For example, a team of three students assigned to produce a joint paper for a single grade are vulnerable to social loafing. The student who is least motivated may take a "free ride" on her teammates' efforts; the others may feel demoralized and not work as hard as they normally would. Poor performance is possible because the group causes *diffusion of responsibility*: the fault for a poorer grade is diffused or shared equally among the group members. Teachers and supervisors should be warned of the dangers of social loafing, whose effects can be reduced by monitoring individual contributions, or making the task conjunctive instead of additive.

Conjunctive. Many teams involve members working together by complementing each other, not simply adding effort. These groups are involved in *conjunctive* tasks, by definition working together but doing so by performing separate subtasks. Although each member performs a task separate in time and nature, all are interdependent in pursuing a common goal.

For example, four classmates may work conjunctively in conducting psychological research and writing a final report: one student reviews the literature, a second designs and conducts the experiment, the third statistically analyzes the data, and the fourth composes a discussion of the findings and what they mean.

Conjunctive groups are only as good as their weakest members, since the quality of the total product will be hurt by any single flawed or weak performance. In the above example, the research team's chances for a good grade will be harmed if the experiment was poorly designed or the discussion badly written.

Disjunctive. *Disjunctive* tasks permit group members to work independently on tasks but share in group outcomes, either success or failure. For example, members of a jury deliberate after a trial to arrive at a verdict. They collaborate to arrive at an "either-or" decision—their work will not be judged for the quality of their results, but only for which of two views they have agreed to accept. One problem with disjunctive groups is that majorities can be wrong and can overrule or influence accurate minorities or deviates. Juries can and do sometimes acquit guilty parties—and convict the innocent.

Divisible. When a group task is broken into different components, and each completed by a different member, their work (and the group) is termed *divisible*. Divisible groups are common, including many sports teams, corporate structures, and bureaucratic organizations. For example, a college or university is made up of several divisions with different goals: academic officers oversee instruction and research; student services attend to resident life, health care, and security; and financial affairs range from developing grant support to collecting tuition. As different as these goals and their subtasks must be, each of them contributes to making—or breaking—the larger institution.

The problems of divisible groups like bureaucracies are familiar: members feel alienated, subgroups fail to communicate or cooperate, and weak links are hard to identify and fix. Much of management research and theory focuses on strategies for streamlining complex, divisible organizations.

Group Processes

Individuals in group context can behave differently from people acting independently. To understand the effects—good or ill—of group involvements, it is important to review key effects and processes of group involvement: deindividuation, social facilitation, and group socialization.

EFFECTS ON SELF-AWARENESS: DEINDIVIDUATION

What happens to individuals when they become part of a larger group? Research suggests that, in important ways, they may lose their individuality. Specifically, group immersion and involvement may reduce self-awareness, creating a state of *deindividuation*. This condition of lessened self-awareness has been found to reduce deliberation and produce disinhibited, impulsive behavior. For example, deindividuation may account for urban vandalism, crowd violence, and a "lynch-mob" mentality.

Research indicates that deindividuation is the product of several causes or antecedent conditions: anonymity, group immersion, and arousal or distraction. The outcomes of deindividuation include, as a result of reduced self-awareness, actions that are not consistent with the individuals' attitudes, and absorption of apparent group norms. For example, an excited fan at a rock concert may become deindividuated by being socially anonymous in the enormous, raucous crowd. As a result, although she is normally shy and nonviolent, she may more easily be caught up in the crowd's protests when there is no encore, screaming obscenities or battling security officers trying to clear the building.

One need not be in a psychological group to experience deindividuation. Deindividuation can be caused by the mere presence of many others, whether they interact or not. However it is important to recognize the effects of group immersion on individual self-awareness, since this byproduct of membership may undermine both group and individual goals.

EFFECTS ON PERFORMANCE: SOCIAL FACILITATION

The mere presence of others has also been found to have a systematic effect on performance. Others may be present as either *co-actors* (persons performing the same task as the actor) or *audience* members (observing or receiving the actors' behavior).

Helping or Hindering Performance. In some cases, the mere presence of others—whether they are co-actors or in the audience—has been found to boost performance. This was first termed the *social facilitation* effect, because the social presence of others seemed to facilitate performance. For example, a woman doing aerobic exercise finds she works harder and for a longer period of time when she participates in an exercise class than when she works out alone.

Further research on social facilitation identified another, contradictory pattern: for some tasks, the presence of co-actors or audience hindered performance. For example, a reporter for a campus newspaper finds it difficult to type accurately if others seem to be watching him at the keyboard.

Explaining Social Facilitation. Analysis confirms that the effects of social presence depend on task complexity: the presence of others boosts performance of simple (easy or familiar) tasks, but hurts performance of complex (new or difficult) tasks. Apparently the presence of others causes arousal, which slightly improves performance of simple tasks but generally hurts performance of complex tasks. In either case, a *dominant response* is being "facilitated": when performing a simple task, one's dominant or most likely response is to perform well; when performing a complex task, one's dominant response is to work slowly and make mistakes.

Why does the presence of others create arousal? One explanation is the *evaluation-apprehension* hypothesis. In this view, the presence of others makes us apprehensive about being evaluated by them. For example, you work harder in your aerobics class because you worry you will be judged "unfit" by your classmates.

Another explanation is the *distraction-conflict* hypothesis. This argues that the presence of others distracts us: being social creatures, we want to pay attention to the others who have come to compete or watch. This conflict in our attention—between the others present and the task at hand—creates arousal, which produces the social facilitation effect.

Both explanations may be valid in different circumstances. The distraction-conflict hypothesis additionally explains why social facilitation has been observed among non-human species, like birds and insects. Unless we accept that animals "worry" about how they will look to other animals, it makes more sense to explain their arousal in terms of distraction and conflict.

GROUP SOCIALIZATION

The process by which newcomers to a group become integrated members is *group socialization*. Group socialization proceeds in a series of stages, similar to the phases of interpersonal attraction and relationships (see chapters 15 and 16): investigation, socialization, maintenance, and sometimes resocialization and remembrance.

For example, if you became interested in a student political organization, you and the members of the group would first *investigate* each other to learn whether it would be mutually desirable for you to join. Once you had met their requirements, your entry would introduce you to other members and opportunities for you to participate. In the course of your *socialization,* you would discover group norms and how to abide by them, while group members taught you values and methods. Socialization might include a formal initiation, with a preset schedule of activities to involve you as well as enhance your loyalty to the group. Ultimately you would gain acceptance as a full-fledged member.

Group membership takes effort, since such affiliations do not "come naturally." If you are strongly committed, you will do whatever is necessary for *maintenance*.

However, you might lose interest as other roles or groups take priority in your life. You may also reevaluate your membership if you disagree with a group position or action. This divergence may be either subtle (e.g., skipping meetings) or more noticeable (e.g., deviant behavior or vocal opposition). *Resocialization* efforts might involve fellow members' encouraging you to "come back" or "come around," or your establishment of a new form of participation. If this is not successful, however, you exit the group; as an ex-member, your only connection the group is one of *remembrance*.

GROUP PERFORMANCE

Most research on groups has focused on what groups do, especially work (rather than play) like solving problems and making decisions. Even informal groups like friends and coworkers spend time making decisions—where to have lunch, how to pay for recreation. Many formal groups are charged with decision-making, such as developing company or agency policy, or representing the wishes and needs of the constituency who elected them. Because of the importance of group decision-making, research has been conducted to identify factors that can facilitate and bias such work, problems unique to group problem-solving, and recommendations for improving group performance.

Decision-Making

The basic concern about group decision-making is whether it is better or worse than individual decision-making. For example, is it better to charge a single individual—like a president, supervisor, or commanding officer—with responsibility for deciding how to spend resources or invest effort? Or will results be fairer and of higher quality if a group—like a cabinet, task force, or advisory board—makes that decision?

FACTORS AFFECTING GROUP DECISION-MAKING

Five factors have been identified as affecting the quality of a group's decision: acceptance of common goals, divisibility of task, status structure, group size, and group heterogeneity.

Common Goals. A decision will be better if all members of the group accept common goals. For example, a group of friends deciding where to spend a vacation together will have a better time if they already agree about how much they can afford and whether they prefer the city or the shore.

Task Divisibility. Some tasks are more easily divided up than others. Those which are divisible will lead to better delegation within the group, and a better final result. For example, the different arrangements involved in vacation planning can be divided and handled separately. In contrast, a committee drafting a constitution for a professional society cannot so easily separate the various ideas and goals they must address.

Communication and Status. Higher-status members talk more and wield more influence, while lower-status members defer to their superiors. This is not necessarily a problem. For example, a group of coworkers may be comfortable asking the supervisor among them to make a final decision between two alternatives. Alternatively, if there is friction among friends because of status differences, there may be bickering about different standards and less consensus about the one "best way" to spend their resources and time.

Group Size. The smaller the group, the more efficient its work. Larger groups represent a wider range of opinion, but each member contributes less to the final result. Smaller groups also keep a tighter rein on individual differences in dominance: no one person can easily "take over" a meeting of five people, since theirs is a small audience not likely to remain passive. Recognizing this, for example, a large group of friends might appoint a smaller subset to make travel arrangements, with the understanding that everyone will cooperate with their final plan.

Group Heterogeneity. Heterogeneous groups include many different kinds—e.g., races, genders, ages, occupations—of people; homogeneous groups' members are more similar to each other. Research confirms that decision-making is faster among homogeneous groups, but may be of lower quality because of the social categories and opinions that are not considered. In general, heterogeneity makes for better results only if differences among members are not divisive or reduced to stereotypes.

BIASES IN GROUP DECISION-MAKING

Three sources may contribute biases or prejudices in group efforts to make decisions: members' predispositions, minimal solutions, and choice shifts.

Predispositions. Group members bring individual prejudices and opinions to their deliberations. If such predispositions were admitted and discussed, the differences could cancel each other out. However, research indicates that, as deliberations proceed, individual prejudices intensify, and distort the final decision. For example, studies of jury deliberations show that, when the evidence presented is weak or ambiguous, jurors may rely on their prejudices to influence the final verdict.

Minimal Solutions. It is difficult for most people to accept criticism comfortably, yet that is exactly what confronts every member of a decision-making group. Consequently members may refuse to discuss or reveal their opinions, keeping back possibly influential information. When a minimally acceptable solution is suggested, members may support it to terminate conflicted discussions. Self-justification theory (see chapters 4, 8, and 9) suggests that, once a decision has been reached, members will be able to rationalize it more easily than they will criticize it or offer alternatives.

Choice Shifts. If group members are anxious to agree with each other, why does one solution gain acceptance before another? Research shows that group deliberation processes build on members' pre-existing leanings, exaggerating them in their original direction. For example, if everyone in a vacation-planning group initially favors a beach trip over a city excursion, deliberations will exaggerate their "pro-beach" tendencies. As a result they may overlook practical problems and alternatives, such as the discomfort of beach weather in August, or the economy offered by city-resort price breaks. These choice shifts represent a much-studied problem known as *group polarization,* considered in detail below.

Group Polarization

By combining the factors that may qualify and bias group decision-making, we recognize that group deliberation is more than the sum of its members' individual choices. One example of this group enhancement or exaggeration is group polarization, originally dubbed the risky shift.

THE RISKY SHIFT

The question of whether groups make better or worse decisions than individuals was provocatively answered by research on an apparent *risky shift*. In the early 1960s, researcher James Stoner had groups consider what level of risk to recommend as "acceptable" for various plans and choices. Stoner found that groups found higher levels of risk acceptable than individual members did before deliberation. Group deliberations apparently resulted in a shift to more risk, dubbed the "risky shift."

ALTERNATIVE EXPLANATIONS

Stoner's findings prompted several years of research, which suggested a contradictory pattern: some groups displayed a risky shift, but others revealed a *cautious shift*—with group decisions favoring a more conservative choice than individual members. In both cases, however, group deliberations reflected the kinds of *choice shifts* reviewed above as a source of group bias.

Present theory favors the conclusion that both risky shift and cautious shift are the results of *group polarization*. In the course of discussion together, group members more strongly support their initial inclinations. Their attitudes polarize—shift more closely to the poles or extremes—as a result of talking together. Thus if members were originally somewhat pro-risk, they shift to greater risk; if originally conservative, they shift to greater caution.

Group polarization can be explained by both normative influence and informational influence. In terms of normative influence, group members may rely on discussion to reveal tendencies, interpreting these as norms on which they converge. Informational influence may occur when discussion produces facts and arguments members can use to rationalize their positions.

Groupthink

Recall that groups have two agendas: task-oriented, and socioemotional. Within cohesive groups, problem-solving may be complicated by fear of criticizing or questioning each other's positions. As a result, a group may engage in defensive avoidance, denying there are problems with their chosen course of action. This in turn can lead to *groupthink,* a pattern of group decision-making that protects cohesion at the cost of decision quality.

For example, members of the executive committee of campus student government must decide which of several petitioning organizations to provide with funding. The executive members are good friends as well as colleagues and hestitate to contradict each other. As each promotes his or her pet project as deserving funding, it becomes harder for the group to reject any one request. If a well-liked member or the chair of the committee proposes a minimal "solution," like giving a little funding to everyone, it will be hard for anyone else to protest that suggestion as weak or avoiding responsibility. For the sake of protecting group feelings and avoiding stress or dissonance, groupthink prevails, and the final decision is haphazard, shortsighted, or of poor quality.

SYMPTOMS

Original work on groupthink was conducted by researcher Irving L. Janis, who identified eight primary symptoms within three categories: overestimating the in-group, closed-mindedness, and pressures toward uniformity.

Overestimating the In-Group. In the course of groupthink, members display two illusory beliefs: the *illusion of invulnerability* and the *illusion of morality*. Group members believe they cannot be hurt or attacked for their work. For example, student government members may assert that "no one would dare criticize our plan, since, after all, they elected us." They also justify their decision on moral grounds. For example, the student executives might reassure each other that what they are doing is "for the good of the entire student body."

Closed-Mindedness. Groupthink participants engage in *collective rationalizations*. As they articulate their plans, they offer arguments that justify their decisions, like "we have to give these groups funding, they wouldn't have asked if they didn't need the money." Members also support and strengthen each other's *stereotyped views* of out-groups and their leaders. For example, if a student executive points out that the campus newspaper could portray their decision in a poor light, others might argue that "everyone knows the editor is a crackpot, no one takes the newspaper seriously."

Pressures Toward Uniformity. Members engage in *self-censorship*, keeping to themselves any misgivings or criticisms. Some will even apply *direct pressure on dissenters to conform*, either with "friendly" cajoling or harsh criticism. Specific members may take particular responsibility for applying such pressure, appointing themselves as *mindguards*—comparable to bodyguards—with the job of protecting the group from contrary information. Finally, as all these pressures toward uniformity converge, no one speaks except in support of the plan, creating the *illusion of unanimity*: if no one opposes, then everyone must agree.

ANTECEDENTS OF GROUPTHINK

As already noted, groupthink is a likelier danger for groups who value their cohesiveness and fear the threat of dissension. Janis's model suggests several factors that foster a groupthink mentality: cohesion, isolation, homogeneity, the lack of impartial leadership, and high stress.

Cohesion. Groups high in cohesion—that "we feeling"—have something to lose if there is dissension among the ranks. The socioemotional agenda may seem to be in conflict with the task agenda.

Isolation. When a group is relatively isolated—cut off from other colleagues, responsibilities, or ideas—they are more vulnerable to the errors and illusions of groupthink.

Homogeneity. The more similar the group members are to each other, the less likely any will be to introduce novel or alternate perspectives.

Lack of Impartial Leadership. Impartial leadership may be lacking for two reasons: either an opinionated leader is in place, or there is no clear leadership among the group. In the former case, a directive leader can send messages, subtle and overt, that discourage contradiction. In the latter case, strongly opinionated group members may exert undue influence, shifting discussion as they prefer.

High Stress. Cohesive, friendly, leaderless groups make decisions all the time without falling prey to illusory thinking. Groupthink is usually prompted by circumstances that exaggerate the importance of difficulty in decision-making. When the stakes are high or the issue seems critical, fear of failure or threat brings the other factors to a focus. For example, if student executives making budget decisions are pressured by deadlines or the threat that campus administrators will interfere "if you fail to establish a budget by yourselves," their stress will increase their tendencies to groupthink.

PREVENTING GROUPTHINK

Once the factors leading to groupthink had been specified, strategies for preventing groupthink were more easily developed. Janis recommends ten prescriptions for preventing groupthink, detailed below.

1. Group members should be educated about groupthink.

2. The group leader should remain impartial and not promote any position.

3. The group leader should encourage members to criticize, evaluate, and voice their doubts.

4. At least one member should be assigned the role of *devil's advocate,* arguing against the group's prevailing opinion.

5. Divide the group into subgroups, each meeting and making recommendations independently.

6. Consider out-groups' opinions and possible actions.

7. After making a decision, hold a "second-chance" meeting to reevaluate and criticize it.

8. Invite outsiders to attend meetings and challenge the group's assumptions.

9. Reduce isolation by consulting with nonmembers and reporting their reactions to the group.

10. Charge more than one group with deliberating simultaneously.

Improving
Group
Performance

Aside from specific recommendations for preventing groupthink, what other strategies are available to help groups do good work? Researchers have offered four emphases for improving group performance: brainstorming; group communication; membership; and planning.

BRAINSTORMING

Problem-solving groups can sometimes do better work by using a technique called *brainstorming,* a procedure for increasing group creativity.

Ground Rules. This approach to group activity involves four subgoals:

1. Members must voice their ideas freely and without withholding or criticizing them first.

2. Postpone criticizing their own or each other's contributions.

3. Produce as many ideas as possible.

4. Enhance and enlarge each other's contributions.

A good strategy for brainstorming involves first explaining these goals, and then encouraging members to offer their ideas in a free discussion, while a group secretary records every suggestion made. After all comments have been offered, a group leader can invite criticism of each one, ruling out those that are considered inferior or impractical.

The Nominal Group Technique. Although brainstorming is popular it may still be handicapped by social loafing, evaluation apprehension, and social arousal interfering with members' thinking. An alternative approach is the *nominal group technique,* in which ideas are first generated privately, then shared with the group, and once more privately evaluated and voted for. Once votes are tallied, the group may deliberate on the results.

Group members work as individuals first, so they are a group in name only (nominally). By reducing criticism and social stimulation, this technique may reduce social loafing and other forms of interference. However, although the nominal group technique avoids some of the pitfalls of brainstorming, it is too structured to produce the same kind of creative atmosphere.

GROUP COMMUNICATION

Different groups involve different *communication structures,* which can be distinguished as either centralized or decentralized. Centrality has different effects under different working conditions.

Centralized versus Decentralized Communication. *Centralized* communication structures require all or most members to communicate only through a central individual, like a team leader. *Decentralized* structures allow members to communicate freely with each other without go-betweens. Research indicates that centralized groups perform better on simple tasks, while decentralized groups do better with complex tasks.

Productivity versus Personal Satisfaction. As efficient as centralized structures may be, their members experience less satisfaction than those in decentralized groups. This interaction suggests that groups may maximize both productivity and satisfaction by remaining flexible, adopting a centralized structure for certain tasks and a decentralized plan for others.

MEMBERSHIP

While a group is more than the sum of its parts (members), individual differences among members are still important.

Selection. Researcher Robert Bales recommends that members be selected in terms of three personality dimensions: activity level, sociability, and group interest. For example, a member who is active, friendly, and concerned with group goals would seem to be an ideal group member. In contrast, one who is inactive, unsociable, and self-interested may be a source of difficulty or antagonism.

Task Accomplishment. Members' accomplishments depend not only on their individual personalities but on how they work together to accomplish tasks. Therefore a varied membership, including some diversity along the three dimensions mentioned above, offers the best opportunities for a range of tasks and obligations.

PLANNING

Like individuals, groups solve problems better if they first plan a strategy. Research confirms that, the more groups discuss *how* to solve the problem at hand, the better the final *result* will be. In addition, the following specific strategies seem to pay off for problem-solving groups:

1. Long-term groups should resist forming habits and consider innovative approaches.

2. Costs and benefits of possible solutions should be itemized.

3. Decisions and likely outcomes should be role-played before the group commits to them.

4. If decisions have been difficult or low-quality, call in consultants and counselors to assist the group's work.

LEADERSHIP

Many of the problems and solutions of group performance reviewed above focus on the leader's role. In this section we review the functions of leaders, characteristics of leadership style, and theories about what makes leaders effective.

Defining Leadership

Leaders are influential group members who guide, direct, and motivate group effort. Leadership is a function of four factors: the leader's qualities, the nature of the group, the group setting, and the group's regard for the leader.

LEADERSHIP BEHAVIOR

Leaders engage in two main sets of behavior: task-oriented actions and socioemotional actions.

Specialists. Some leaders are competent in both roles and can balance these agendas. Others are better at one than the other: *task-specialists* are better in their focus on the group's work, while *maintenance specialists* are better socioemotional leaders.

Hybrid Leadership. While leaders are as different as their groups, the most effective leaders are those who bring out the best in their groups. Research on team effectiveness indicates that such leaders are people who are concerned with *both* their people (socioemotional leadership) *and* production (task-orientation). This combination has been dubbed *hybrid leadership* since it combines the leader's two primary agendas.

FUNCTIONS OF A LEADER

A group leader's most important functions are goal-attainment, group maintenance, symbolic identity, group representation, and group transformation.

Goal-Attainment. The leader defines goals and helps formulate a plan to attain them.

Group Maintenance. The leader oversees group structure and interaction, reducing conflict and promoting harmony among members.

Symbolic Identity. Groups are often identified with their leaders, as in terms like "the President's Commission on Crime" or "Rev. Jackson's coalition." A leader provides a group with a symbol the members can identify with, increasing group unity.

Group Representation. The leader represents the group's wishes and requirements in negotiation with other groups and outsiders.

Group Transformation. A leader can enable specific members to develop or change their roles, developing their own influence and leadership, and can enable the group itself to grow and improve.

Leadership Effectiveness

The effectiveness of leadership has been studied through both analysis and theory. Leadership analysts have focused on the sources and effects of different *styles* of leadership. Leadership *theories* offer explanations for leadership in terms of leaders' characteristics, groups, situations, and interactions among these factors.

LEADERSHIP STYLE

Research on leadership first developed just before World War II. After the war, worldwide interest in international conflict prompted a closer look at how leaders and groups interact.

Governmental Style. Early research focused on three different governmental structures: autocratic, democratic, and laissez-faire leadership. *Autocratic* or *authoritarian* leaders act as dictators, setting group goals and policy, assigning tasks and teams, and keeping their distance. Members of such groups exhibit extreme aggression (especially against scapegoats), and productivity decreases in the leader's absence.

Democratic leaders offer guidance but permit group members to set policies and goals and determine task and team assignments. Such team members exhibit little aggression, and productivity tends to remain constant regardless of the leader's whereabouts.

Laissez-faire leaders (French for "to allow (them) to do") give their groups complete freedom and do not participate in group tasks. Laissez-faire groups are neither particularly productive nor aggressive.

Initial conclusions about these three governmental styles favored democratic leadership as most effective. However later research revealed powerful situational interactions: the effectiveness of a form of government depends on the group's circumstances. For example, in times of peace democracy flourishes because there is time for the debate and deliberation necessary. But in times of stress, split-second decisions cannot be postponed to conduct opinion polls, and talented autocratic leaders may better provide what is necessary.

More recently, *normative theory* argues that effectiveness depends on how much a leader allows followers to participate in decision-making. Whether the decision should be leader- or follower-generated depends on three considerations: how high the stakes are, how much expertise the leader has, and how essential followers' acceptance is. For example, if a committee's decision is critical, the chair knows all the important facts, and members' support is not necessary, the chair may safely make an *autocratic* decision. In contrast, if the decision is critical and the chair well-informed, but the support of group members is vital to the plan's success, the chair is best advised to adopt a more participative style of leadership.

Management Style. Recent leadership research focuses on more commonplace leadership like business management. Researchers have argued that managers' styles are influenced by leaders' assumptions about human nature and the meaning of work. A prevalent viewpoint among managers, dubbed *Theory X,* asserts that most people dislike work and responsibility, value only safety and security, and must be coerced into working with threats of punishment and promises of incentives. For example, a Theory X professor will assume her students are lazy and inattentive, and will dispense good or poor grades to influence their cooperation.

In contrast, *Theory Y* managers assume that people enjoy doing challenging work and making creative contributions. The Theory Y manager's job is to help workers realize their potential, not to motivate them from the "outside" with rewards or punishments. An example of a Theory Y manager would be a professor who encourages students not only to develop their own projects, but to help plan and teach the class.

The self-determination theory argues that leaders' effectiveness depends on how they provide feedback to their followers. Feedback can either control and direct workers or inform them and support increased autonomy. Research confirms that managers promote workers' self-determination when they allow workers to make choices, offer noncontrolling positive feedback, and acknowledge others' perspectives.

THEORIES OF LEADERSHIP

Are great leaders born or made? Different theories have explained leadership as a result of personal characteristics or how personal qualities interact with situations.

Trait Theories. The *great person theory* of leadership argues that successful leaders share specific features and talents. Early research, however, generated a long and contradictory list of "leadership qualities" collected from the biographies of such great persons. More strongly supported today, therefore, is the conclusion that leaders do not differ in important or systematic ways from their followers.

Recent research has focused on traits common among those who emerge as leaders, those who are encouraged by early support and success. *Emergent leaders* have been found to possess three kinds of personality traits: intelligence, dominance, and masculine role characteristics. For example, a presidential candidate appears more promising if she is bright and informed (intelligent), confident and charismatic (dominant), and perceived to be aggressive, decisive, and unemotional (masculine). Recent research suggests that personal adjustment is another important quality, which explains why political candidates' backgrounds are sometimes investigated for signs of licentiousness or disorder.

Contingency Theories. According to the best-supported models, leader effectiveness depends on how well a leader's characteristics fit the demands of the situation. Since success is contingent on the interaction of traits with circumstances, these models are referred to as *contingency theories* of leadership.

The best known contingency theory is Fred Fiedler's least-preferred coworker (LPC) model. According to Fiedler, every leader can identify his or her LPC—the group member he or she least wishes to work with. The leader's attitudes toward the LPC predict leadership effectiveness: a leader who rates the LPC positively will favor group relationships, whereas one who rates the LPC negatively will have a stronger task-orientation.

Moreover, LPC ratings interact with situations to predict leader effectiveness. Pro-LPC, socioemotional leaders fare best when they have only moderate control over the group. Socially sensitive leaders are especially helpful when the group has some problems and the way is not clear. In contrast, anti-LPC, task-oriented leaders do best when they have either high control or low control. When events are going smoothly, a considerate leader is not necessary. And when the group is plagued with difficulties, only a task-oriented leader can keep everyone on track.

In sum Fiedler's work portrays leadership effectiveness as a matter of finding the right person at the right time. As a group grows and develops, it will encounter different demands and situations. Leadership should be kept a flexible matter, and potential leaders—with both task and social skills—should be regularly cultivated within the group's membership. In the right circumstances, every group member has the potential to be a great leader.

A group consists of a minimum of two people who interact with and influence each other. A nongroup or aggregate can become a group if it shares perceptions and interacts. People join groups to attain goals and meet social needs. Group context can provide members with a sense of social identity. Deviates threaten group consensus and will either be converted or rejected. Social impact theory predicts that group influence over members is a function of group strength, immediacy, and size.

Groups provide their members with norms that guide behavior. Norms may be assembled into roles. Roles help differentiate group members' functions, but can cause problems in cases of person-role and inter-role conflict, and when roles become ambiguous. Group cohesiveness can be increased by inter-member liking and threats from outside groups or competition. Cohesiveness can be undermined by internal competition and preferential differences among members.

Groups can be distinguished by task performance. Additive groups combine efforts for shared goals, and are vulnerable to social loafing. Conjunctive groups collaborate by performing subtasks separately. Disjunctive groups work together on either-or decisions. Divisible tasks are performed by bureaucratic groups with separate subtasks and responsibilities.

Participation in large, involving groups can reduce members' self-awareness and create deindividuation. The mere presence of others can facilitate a performer's dominant response, improving simple performance and hindering complex performance. Social facilitation is caused by arousal, as the result of evaluation-apprehension or distraction and conflict. Structured groups socialize their members from investigation, to socialization and maintenance. If a member strays, he or she may be resocialized, or after exiting, is kept only in remembrance.

Studies of group performance have concentrated on group decision-making. The quality of group decisions is affected by acceptance of common goals, task divisibility, communication and status, group size, and group heterogeneity. Group decision-making can be biased by members predispositions, hasty acceptance of minimal solutions, and shifts in choice toward opinion extremes.

Group polarization research began with observation of a choice shift to risk. Other research revealed a shift to caution, suggesting that group deliberation was polarizing members' initial leanings. Another problem in decision-making is groupthink, whose symptoms include overestimating the in-group, closed-mindedness, and pressures toward uniformity. The antecedents of groupthink include cohesion, isolation, homogeneity of membership, lack of impartial leadership, and a high-stress situation. Research has yielded several prescriptions for preventing groupthink.

Group performance in general can be improved in several ways. Brainstorming is a popular way to increase group creativity, and pitfalls may be corrected through the nominal group technique. Studies of group communication show that centralized communication structures do better with simple tasks, while decentralized structures do better with complex tasks. Flexibility of communication structures may maximize both productivity and member satisfaction. Group performance can be affected by members' personal characteristics and skills in task performance. Finally, groups make better decisions if they plan their strategies.

Leaders are influential group members who guide goal-attainment. Some leaders are task specialists focused on group work, others are maintenance specialists focused on the socioemotional agenda, and some are hybrids—good at both agendas. A leader's functions include goal-attainment, group maintenance, providing a symbol to identify with, representing the group, and transforming the group and its goals.

Leadership effectiveness is affected by style, leaders' qualities, and situational pressures. Governmental styles include autocratic or authoritarian, democratic, and laissez-faire leadership. Their effects differ and depend on the group's situation. Normative theory proposes that leader effectiveness depends on matching tasks with member participation. Management styles include Theory X which disparages workers' motivation, Theory Y which favors actualizing workers' potential, and self-determination which favors managers' encouraging workers' autonomy.

Traditional theories explained leadership as a function of traits. Recent research identifies characteristics that encourage emergent leaders. Most widely accepted are contingency theories, depicting leadership as resulting from an interaction of leader's qualities and situational demands. Such theories suggest that, in the right circumstances, any member can be a leader.

Selected Readings

Beebe, S. A. and J. T. Masterson, (1986). *Communicating in Small Groups*, 2nd edition. Glenview, IL: Scott, Foresman.

Brown, R. (1988). *Group Processes: Dynamics Within and Between Groups.* Oxford, England: Blackwell.

Doise, W. (1978). *Groups and Individuals: Explanations in Social Psychology.* New York: Cambridge University Press.

Festinger, L., S. Schachter, and K. Back, (1950). *Social Pressures in Informal Groups.* Stanford, CA: Stanford University Press.

Fiedler, F. E. and J. E. Garcia, (1987). *New Approaches to Effective Leadership: Cognitive Resources and Organizational Performance.* New York: John Wiley.

Forsyth, D. R. (1983). *An Introduction to Group Dynamics.* Monterey, CA: Brooks/Cole.

Hendrick, C. (Ed.). (1987). *Group Processes.* Newbury Park, CA: Sage.

Hogg, M. A. and D. Abrams, (1988). *A Social Psychology of Intergroup Relations and Group Processes.* New York: Routledge.

Janis, I. L. (1982). *Groupthink: Psychological Studies of Policy Decisions and Fiascoes,* 2nd edition. Boston: Houghton Mifflin.

Janis, I. L. (1982). *Victims of Groupthink.* Boston: Houghton Mifflin.

Janis, I. L. (1989). *Crucial Decisions: Leadership in Policy Making and Crisis Management.* New York: Free Press.

McGrath, J. E. (1984). *Groups: Interaction and Performance.* Englewood Cliffs, NJ: Prentice-Hall.

Mullen, B. and G. R. Goethals, (Eds.). (1987). *Theories of Group Behavior.* New York: Springer-Verlag.

Paulus, P. D. (Ed.). (1989). *The Psychology of Group Influence,* 2nd edition. Hillsdale, NJ: Erlbaum.

Rosnow, R. L. and G. A. Fine, (1976). *Rumor and Gossip: The Psychology of Hearsay.* New York: Elsevier.

Shaw, M. E. (1975). *Group Dynamics: The Psychology of Small Group Behavior,* 2nd edition. New York: McGraw-Hill.

Swap, W. (1983). *Decisions in Groups.* Beverly Hills, CA: Sage.

Wheeler, D. D. and I. L. Janis, (1980). *A Practical Guide for Making Decisions.* New York: Free Press.

Steiner, I. (1972). *Group Process and Productivity.* New York: Academic Press.

12

Prejudice and Discrimination

Prejudice and its consequences are problems apparently as old as the human tendency to separate into groups. Once they have been cognitively categorized as separate, social groups are less easily brought together to collaborate on common human endeavors.

In this chapter we examine the forms and effects of prejudice, its sources in human experience, and strategies for reducing prejudice and discrimination.

FORMS OF PREJUDICE

Prejudice involves the formation of both attitudes and behaviors, with related but different social consequences.

Attitudes

A prejudice is an attitude (usually negative) about people based on their membership in a particular social group. The term comes from "prejudgment," implying that the attitude is not based on broad experience. While it is possible to be positively biased toward someone—for example, prepared to like someone your best friend has told you about—the term "prejudice" is usually reserved for negative prejudgments.

COMPONENTS OF PREJUDICE

Like other attitudes, prejudices include components like specific thoughts and beliefs, feelings, and behavior patterns. The most important of these are stereotypes, social categories, and social norms.

Stereotypes. As discussed in chapter 5, a stereotype is a generalization about a category of people that sets them apart from other groups. A stereotype simplifies social perception memory; as a mental shortcut, it unfairly ignores individual differences and exaggerates the salience of group membership. For example, a stereotype of a British citizen as a conservative white male in formal attire—including hat and umbrella—ignores the likelihood that British citizens include nonaristocrats, liberals, and persons of Asian and African ancestry.

Social Categorization. Stereotypes are the result of social categorization, the process of perceiving individuals as "belonging" in different social groups. Social categorization magnifies differences between groups, and minimizes differences among members within a particular group.

Social categorization involves two processes that make stereotyped thinking more likely: assimilation and contrast. Assimilation is the perception that all members of a group are more alike than not in other ways. For example, a young woman is assimilating if she thinks that all older adults are poor drivers, and becomes irritated when she sees that the driver ahead of her is older.

Contrast involves believing that differences between groups are greater than they really are. In the example above, if the woman believes that older adults are generally worse drivers than members of her age group, she is contrasting the age groups.

Social Norms. Prejudicial attitudes include ideas about social norms, such as popular opinions about how one's own group evaluates other groups. For example, a newcomer to a community may discover that, for obscure reasons, a particular ethnic minority group is regarded as inferior and undesirable by the majority of local residents. If the newcomer is to "fit in" with the majority, she will try to conform with this norm of prejudice.

ACQUIRING PREJUDICE

Like all attitudes, prejudices are acquired through experience. Two explanations for prejudice acquisition are social learning theory and social identity theory.

Social Learning Theory. In social learning, behavior is changed through social forms of association, reinforcement, and observation. Many lessons about prejudice are acquired through socialization. For example, a boy who hears his father use disparaging remarks about a minority group will learn that his father's behavior is acceptable, and may emulate it. Other lessons may be absorbed from the media. For example, magazine and television advertisements in the United States overwhelmingly depict Caucasians, as actors or consumers, and very rarely show actors who appear to be of African or Asian descent. Even a very young child viewing such images will be influenced by such exaggerated "ideals."

Social Identity Theory. One's self-esteem—sense of self-worth—has two components: personal identity and social identity. Social identity is the part of self-esteem one derives from group membership. This evaluation begins with making a distinction between one's in-group (the group one belongs to) and all out-groups (rival or alternative groups).

According to social identity theory, developed by researcher Henri Tajfel, once group memberships are distinguished, people develop attitudes and behaviors that benefit their in-groups relative to their out-groups. For example, if you are a new member in a social club at school, you will think and act in ways that promote the welfare of your club—participating in fundraising activities, for example—but not for other groups or nonmembers. This preference for members of the in-group is termed *ethnocentrism*.

Tajfel's research revealed that social identity processes developed even "minimal groups"—groupings of people whose "membership" involved no interaction with other members. Simply knowing you are in a category with other people predisposes you to liking them and favoring that category over others. For example, if your section of a college course meets at 10:00 a.m. and the other section meets at 11:00 a.m., you would already like to think that the 10 o'clock section is "better" in various ways.

Discrimination

Discrimination refers to behavior that results from prejudice. Treating one group of people differently because of one's prejudice is discriminatory behavior. For example, thinking that all African-Americans are less qualified to be teachers than Caucasians is a prejudice; consequently refusing to hire a specific African-American candidate for a teaching position is discrimination. Discrimination takes many forms, some old and familiar, some new, and others very subtle.

RACISM

Racism is discrimination based on racial prejudice. The most common form of racism in the United States and other white European cultures is based on prejudice against African-Americans. Other common forms of racism discriminate against those of Native American ("American Indian"), Hispanic, and Asian (e.g., Indian, Japanese, Vietnamese) descent.

Old-Fashioned Racism. Old-fashioned racists based such policies as segregation on bigotry: prejudice that characterizes the target group as inferior to their own group.

Modern Racism. Modern racists are more ambivalent about minority groups like African-Americans. They value freedom, equal opportunity, and fair play—but resent the attention and "advantages" they feel the minority group has been awarded. Modern racism—also termed *symbolic racism*—is subtler than old-fashioned racism, but just as powerfully discriminatory in its effects.

SEXISM

As reviewed in chapter 7, although women make up more than half the world's population, in most of the world women hold inferior status, have less power, less social freedom, and fewer opportunities than men. Since few differences have been identified in men's and women's social behavior, and none that explain such disparity (see chapter 7), this gender difference in social value has been largely blamed on sexism. Sexism is discrimination based on prejudice against another gender; it typically refers to prejudice against females.

Sexism is based on stereotypes that have little or no foundation in fact. Because gender roles are an important social categorization, we seem to develop more extensive stereotypes of gender than of other group distinctions. Within a culture these stereotypes are likely to be shared and supported. Sexism and its consequences are therefore difficult but not impossible to correct.

OTHER FORMS OF DISCRIMINATION

Modern technology and mass communication have brought many diverse groups of people into contact or awareness with each other. Not surprisingly, many group distinctions have developed into other forms of discrimination.

Ageism. Discrimination against individuals on the basis of their membership in particular age group is ageism. Its most common form targets older adults, especially persons over the age of 60, but ageist policies also discriminate against other groups like adolescents and school-age children. For example, refusing to hire a teenager because he seems like "an irresponsible kid" or a 62-year-old woman because "her memory probably isn't reliable" illustrates different forms of ageism.

Homophobia. Prejudice and discrimination against gay or homosexual individuals, especially males, has been attributed to homophobia, literally an irrational fear of homosexuals. Such antigay and antilesbian discrimination can range from subtle forms like job barriers and mandatory AIDS testing to overt violence like "gay bashing" (unprovoked aggression against persons believed to be homosexual.)

The roots of homophobia are both social and personal. Sexual norms are important but seldom openly discussed; deviants threaten such norms and suffer social sanctions and penalties. Homophobia is also more likely among individuals who are personally insecure or conflicted about gender identity issues. Such individuals may feel threatened by the presence or existence of persons with nonnormative preferences, and may feel encouraged to act on such prejudice by the existence of homophobic social institutions, policies, and practices.

Effects of Prejudice and Discrimination

Prejudice and discrimination are considered social problems because of their destructive effects on both those who wield such attitudes and behaviors and their victims.

EFFECTS ON THE PREJUDICED

People who hold prejudices rely on stereotypes in their social thinking. Stereotyped thinkers are better and faster at both perceiving and remembering information that conforms with their prejudices. For example, a man who is prejudiced against African-Americans is more likely to notice and remember meeting a black person whom he considers unintelligent and lazy. In other words, prejudiced thinking helps to process ideas that maintain the prejudice, not information that challenges it. Prejudices tend to be self-perpetuating.

EFFECTS ON THE TARGETS OF PREJUDICE

The more obvious problem with prejudice is its impact on its victims, those who are prejudiced and discriminated against. Research has identified several ways in which targets suffer, as well as important considerations in interpreting the extent and nature of prejudice.

Socialized Discrimination. A broad but subtle problem with discrimination is that, like any behavior, it cultivates attitudes that support it. Specifically, as people employ and adapt to discrimination, they get used to it and find it more acceptable, a "fact of life." Such social acceptance both maintains the underlying prejudices and makes it more difficult to change discriminatory practices. For example, resistance to employing women in traditionally masculine roles—like military combat pilots—both increases characterizations of women as "unfit" for such work and prevents serious discussion of changing such discriminatory policies.

One example of socialized discrimination is social Darwinism, an exaggerated application of some evolutionary ideas to justify social policies. One idea promoted by Charles Darwin (1809-1882) was that biological features are passed on if they promote "survival of the fittest." Social Darwinism takes the view that those cultures and ethnic groups which have best survived—e.g., by being dominant—are by definition "fittest." For example, controversial arguments have been based on research that claims to show a hereditary basis for racial differences in I.Q. (intelligence quotient, a theoretical measure of intellectual ability). If African-Americans earn consistently lower I.Q. scores than Caucasians, and if the origin of this difference is racially genetic rather than environmental, this conclusion would both "explain" and "justify" continuing discrimination in hiring, education, and economics.

An alternative interpretation of I.Q. differences between the races is that they are due to differences in experience. As a group, African-Americans have significantly fewer economic opportunities, lower socioeconomic status, and less education than Caucasians. The plausibility of such alternative explanations makes policies based on social Darwinism both premature and blatantly discriminatory.

Psychological Damage. Individual members of targeted groups suffer in several ways from discrimination. Such persons suffer demoralization and damaged self-esteem: they think of themselves as worthless and inferior. Persons who have been discriminated against also may develop the will to fail, a phenomenon identified among women as "fear of success." Finally, discrimination may be a self-fulfilling judgment: those who are predicted to fail "because" they belong to a targeted group may fail as a result of this condemnation. For example, a teacher who believes that athletes are stupid may expect less of students who are known to belong to athletic teams, discouraging them so that ultimately they perform poorly, confirming the teacher's "prophecy."

Criticisms of Research. Social research is difficult because it seeks to explain practices and processes that have already begun. Research on the causes and effects of prejudice and discrimination generally focuses on existing social groups rather than creating new social distinctions. Critics caution that research on prejudice and discrimination may be limited by other findings.

For example, critics note that not all members of a targeted minority group are equally affected by discrimination. Many African-Americans, for example, have been found to have much higher self-esteem than many Caucasians; differences may have more to do with status or education than race.

Moreover, the effects of discrimination depend on the historical context of the prejudice. For example, the psychological damage of racism was more obvious among African-Americans living in the 1950s than in the 1990s. The value placed on feminine qualities is measurably higher today than it was decades earlier. The effects of prejudice and discrimination must be interpreted with culture and history in mind.

SOURCES OF PREJUDICE

Prejudice is acquired through learning and socialization. Three sources develop and sustain prejudice and discrimination: cognitive, emotional, and social processes.

Cognitive Sources of Prejudice

Prejudiced attitudes rely on prejudiced beliefs and biased perceptions and memories. Four kinds of information are used to develop prejudice: social categorization, stereotypes, attributional processes, and social beliefs.

SOCIAL CATEGORIZATION

Prejudice depends on perceiving people as belonging to different groups or social categories. Such social categorization begins with making superficial distinctions between in-groups and outgroups, and extending those to more important differences.

In-Groups versus Out-Groups. One's social identity depends on one's group membership. It is natural for us to think of people as having different social descriptions or categories. By extension, your own category is your in-group; people in the other categories are—to you—members of out-groups.

As noted earlier, even members of "minimal groups" develop an ethnocentric preference for in-group members. The distinction between in-groups and out-groups is further exaggerated by assimilation (assuming that members of a group are alike) and contrast (assuming that differences between groups are greater than they really are).

Dissimilar Beliefs. Research also indicates that racial distinctions are interpreted as signalling belief distinctions. That is, prejudiced Caucasians perceive African-Americans as being similar to each other in beliefs and values as well as skin color; they also perceive them to be dissimilar to themselves in beliefs and values. This research suggests that the "real" source of racial prejudice is the mistaken assumption that a person's race signals his or her belief system.

THE POWER OF STEREOTYPES

You may know about stereotypes without believing in them. For example, you may be able to describe a stereotype about a social group you belong to, yet as a member of that group reject the stereotype as simplistic and misleading. Stereotypes may bias perception and recall, but they are not immune to the effects of experience. How and why do stereotypes influence social thinking?

Illusory Correlation. Illusory correlation is the mistaken perception of an association between variables that are actually unrelated (see chapter 3). It is likely to occur when we perceive the co-ocurrence of noticeable events or conditions. For example, if you come across the name of an old acquaintance in a letter one day, and that night receive a phone call from the same person—both unusual events—you may be tempted to think that the experiences are connected, or that one caused the other.

Contact with members of out-groups is rare. If an out-group member does something noticeable and unusual—e.g., is charged with committing a crime—we are likely to associate out-group *membership* with the charged *criminal* behavior. Such illusory correlations can easily foster and sustain prejudice.

Shared Infrequency. Illusory correlation could be defused if contact with out-group members were a more frequent and therefore less noticeable or unusual experience. However, members of in-groups "keep to themselves," keeping contact with out-group members rare. Because this avoidance is mutual—members of both groups avoid outside contact—it is referred to as shared infrequency. Shared infrequency permits illusory correlations and stereotypes to persist since contradictory contacts are never made.

Heterogeneity versus Homogeneity. Stereotypes are also sustained by the belief that members of one's in-group are distinct individuals while members of the out-group are "all alike." These parallel biases—in-group heterogeneity and out-group homogeneity—have been found to distort perception as well as cognition. For example, you may find it harder to describe a member of another race than one of your own race, because "they all look alike" to you. This so-called *own-race bias* turns out to afflict even non-prejudiced persons, probably because even non-racist persons typically have less contact with members of racial groups other than their own.

SOCIAL ATTRIBUTION

As reviewed in chapter 6, attribution is the process of explaining behavior. Efforts to explain surprising or negative events can be distorted by stereotyped thinking. Two important consequences are biased labeling and the ultimate attribution error.

Biased Labeling. Even when the behavior of out-group members seems similar to one's own, it is possible to describe the two actions differently. For example, if you pride yourself on being a hard worker, you may resent thinking that a member of a disliked group is also hardworking. Instead, you think of your behavior as "diligent" while the other person is "mindlessly driven." This is biased labeling. In its most common form, a biased label describes the same behavior favorably for the in-group, and unfavorably for the out-group.

The Ultimate Attribution Error. Recall from chapter 6 that the fundamental attribution error involves overestimating dispositional influences and underestimating situational influences in explaining behavior. We are more likely to commit the fundamental attribution error in explaining others' behavior than our own. When this bias is extended to distinguish out-group members' actions from those of in-group members, it is termed the *ultimate attribution error*. For example, suppose your team competes with a rival team in two games, with the result that your team wins one game and your opponents win the other. You would be committing the ultimate attribution error if you claimed credit for your own team's (the in-group's) victory, but attributed your loss to cheating or rough play by the other team (the out-group).

SOCIAL BELIEFS

Beliefs are an important part of prejudiced attitudes. Some prejudices are based on religious or political ideologies. Prejudice may also be supported by broad beliefs that the world is a just place.

Ideological Beliefs. Research has detected a link between conservative political ideologies and some forms of prejudice. This may be explained in terms of compatible (balanced) right-wing values: free enterprise, personal initiative, and no governmental intervention. Other research has detected a correlation between certain measures of religiousness (e.g., church membership) and prejudice. This may be explained in terms of religion's role as a social regulator. The religion-prejudice link disappears when religion is defined in terms of ethical commitment rather than church membership or orthodoxy. It is also important to recall that correlation does not verify causation: it may be that prejudices lead to certain political or religious affiliations, rather than that ideologies support prejudice.

Belief in a Just World. Research by psychologist Melvin Lerner and his colleagues indicates that people vary in their belief that the world is a just place, where people get what they deserve (and deserve what they get). People with high scores on measures of this *just-world bias* have been found to believe that victims—e.g., of rape, spouse abuse, or poverty—must have brought about their own suffering. They are thus more likely to *blame the victim,* a bias that supports many forms of prejudice.

Emotional Sources of Prejudice

Beliefs cross over into feelings, so that prejudice is sustained by needs and emotions. Psychodynamic theories explain prejudice in terms of aggressive drive and displacement. Other research has indicated the possibility of a "prejudiced personality."

PSYCHODYNAMIC THEORIES OF PREJUDICE

Psychodynamic theories explain behavior and personality in terms of inner forces like instincts and motives. The best known of these, psychoanalytic theory, argues that aggression is an expression of an unconscious death instinct (see chapter 13). Because every individual also has a life instinct, this hidden "death wish" is usually deflected outward onto a target other than oneself, a process called *displacement*.

Displacement explains the development of prejudices aimed at *scapegoats*, individuals and groups who are safer or more accessible targets than the true sources of one's anger. For example, German Nazis in the 1930s and 1940s focused their prejudice on scapegoats—primarily Jews—whom they blamed for such widespread ills as unemployment and a depressed economy.

THE PREJUDICED PERSONALITY

After World War II, a group of researchers at Stanford University sought to identify the characteristics of anti-Semitism (prejudice against Jews). They concluded that such prejudice was but one aspect of a constellation of prejudices, fears, and beliefs making up the *authoritarian personality*.

The authoritarian personality rigidly adheres to conventional values and behavior patterns, and advocates severe punishment for deviates. Such a person also exaggeratedly respects and obeys strong authority figures (like dictators and disciplinarians). Not surprisingly, authoritarians are generally hostile, suspicious of intellectuals, and, interestingly, extremely superstitious.

Subsequent research on authoritarianism failed to clarify whether this personality pattern characterized a disorder or merely the result of prejudiced socialization. For example, if a child is raised in an anti-Semitic environment, he or she would most likely develop anti-Semitic prejudices as well. Because of such ambiguity, theories of prejudiced personalities are no longer considered credible.

Social Sources of Prejudice

Social experiences that may sustain prejudice include relative deprivation, group conflict, and institutional supports.

RELATIVE DEPRIVATION

Feeling that we are deprived relative to others—relative deprivation—can lead us to resent feeling victimized. However, instead of directing resentment against those who are relatively better off—those whom we envy—we may displace this resentment, just as we displace aggression, onto a safer target. Thus relative deprivation explains both the rebellion of oppressed minorities, and the victimization of those same groups by others who are better off but similarly frustrated.

For example, in an economy with a large impoverished population, a strained middle class and an extremely affluent wealthy upper class, the poor may be angry at all those who are better off than they—and the middle class may harbor resentful prejudice against the poor.

GROUP CONFLICT

The most obvious source of intergroup prejudice is conflict between groups. According to *realistic conflict theory,* conflict between groups is caused by mutually exclusive goals (also, see chapter 14). The most common source of conflict is competition over scarce resources. Classic research by Muzafer Sherif and his colleagues examined the behavior of boys participating in a summer camp experience. After the boys were divided into teams competing for valuable prizes, their earlier cross-team friendships broke down; each boy now felt loyal to his in-group and prejudiced against all members of the out-group. Hostile feelings were so tenacious that researchers had to attempt several strategies to resolve the conflict before they could conclude the camp experience.

INSTITUTIONAL SUPPORTS FOR PREJUDICE

Many forms of discrimination are so historically rooted and familiar that they have become institutionalized. Examples include the racial segregation of American schools and other services prior to the 1960s, the long-entrenched policy of *apartheid* in South Africa, and restrictions barring women from joining civic organizations or country clubs.

Because such practices are socially pervasive, they may be widely accepted as "normal." Individuals and groups who challenge them are accused of making trouble or rocking the boat. Very often such challenges are thwarted by the subtlety of institutionalized prejudice. For example, unless our attention is so directed, we may not even notice how men outnumber women on television.

REDUCING PREJUDICE AND DISCRIMINATION

Because prejudice, though pervasive and enduring, is learned rather than innate, social psychologists are optimistic about the chances of reducing its effects in society. Strategies have been developed both to change prejudicial attitudes and to alter discriminatory behaviors.

Changing Attitudes

The most direct strategies for changing attitudes are those which target the building blocks of prejudice: stereotypes, social categories, and social learning.

DIRECT STRATEGIES

Counteracting Stereotypes. Since stereotypes prevail only when they are not challenged, researchers have explored ways to render stereotypes less useful. Findings indicate that people relay less on stereotypes when told to pay close attention to individuals of whom they form impressions. When perceivers are motivated to be accurate, they rely on data instead of stereotypes.

Changing Social Categories. The "us-them" distinction becomes useless when "us" includes "them." For example, science fiction films may portray world powers as forgetting their differences to combine forces in fighting hostile invaders from space. Instead of "America versus the Russians" the central conflict is "Earth versus the Aliens." Practical, everyday versions of this *recategorization* involve having antagonistic groups collaborate on mutual goals, as when battling neighborhoods join forces to fight street crime.

Nonprejudiced Lessons. Schools and teachers who advocate harmony and collaboration can be undone by parents and homes that encourage students to be prejudiced. Effective anti-prejudice programs must first win the cooperation and support of children's families. Additionally, lessons about alternatives to prejudice can be provided by models who demonstrate such models. Finally, prejudice "simulations"—games or demonstrations that assign students roles of oppressed or oppressor—have been found to be effective in clarifying the arbitrary and destructive nature of prejudice and discrimination.

Changing Behavior

Strategies for changing discrimination patterns include changing social policy, increasing intergroup contact, and establishing cooperative programs.

CHANGING SOCIAL POLICY

It is said that "you cannot legislate morality," but we have already observed that compliance leads to acceptance (see chapter 10). This is the rationale for attacking prejudice by changing its consequences.

Desegregation. The best example of changing discriminatory social policy is desegregation, legislated as a result of civil rights efforts in the United States in the 1960s.

Affirmative Action. Related legislation encourages affirmative action to undo the effects of discrimination by boosting opportunities to members of traditionally oppressed groups.

Critics argue that affirmative action creates a policy of *reverse discrimination,* because benefits for one group entail a "loss" (e.g., not getting a job) for the other. This view depends on structuring hiring in terms of competition; if competitive hiring remains the norm, anyone's gain symbolizes another's loss.

Behavior Begets Attitudes. Changing the law to penalize discrimination like segregation and unfair hiring practices has the effect of pulling away institutional supports for prejudice. In addition, when people do not *behave* as if they are prejudiced (because they cannot legally do so), they will eventually cease to *think* as if they are prejudiced.

THE CONTACT HYPOTHESIS

An important complement to desegregation is integration: not only are barriers between groups removed, but members of both groups are encouraged to mix in pursuing common goals. The philosophy of integration is based in part on the *contact hypothesis,* the expectation that, as groups get to know each other through contact, their stereotypes will break down and their prejudices will dissolve.

Conditions for Effective Contact. Original hopes for the contact hypothesis have been tempered by the slight gains integration has made. Researchers now conclude that, for contact between groups to succeed in reducing prejudice, several conditions must be met:

1. Those in contact must have equal status.

2. The situation should encourage participants to depend on and cooperate with each other.

3. Social norms should promote individual personal relationships among participants.

4. Authorities should approve of contact and acceptance.

5. Participants should contradict stereotypes of their groups.

6. Participants should generalize their tolerant attitudes to new situations and groups.

COLLABORATION

The most successful strategy for reducing conflict in Sherif's boys camp study was establishing superordinate goals. When both teams collaborated in order to achieve joint goals, their prejudices became self-defeating and were discarded.

Rewarding Cooperation. Research on group performance shows that outcomes can be encouraged by rewarding cooperation instead of competition as a "winning" strategy.

The Jigsaw Technique. A cooperative program that can be established in schools is the *jigsaw technique,* so named because each child in a work team provides one piece of the "puzzle" they are working on: the team cannot meet its goal (e.g., mastering a lesson) unless each member masters his or her own unit *and* teaches it to the others. Thus the team is rewarded not for additive effort (see chapter 11), but for helping each other cooperatively.

*P*rejudice is a negative attitude toward people based on their group membership. It involves stereotyping, social categorization of people, and acceptance of social norms that favor prejudice. Prejudice is acquired through learning, as part of normal socialization, and in developing social identity through group membership.

Discrimination is behavior based on prejudice. Racism, whether based on bigotry or ambivalence, and sexism are the most common forms of discrimination. Other forms include ageism and homophobia.

Prejudice affects those with prejudiced attitudes by distorting their perception and memory for social information. Effects on the targets of prejudice include socialized discrimination and psychological damage.

Cognitive sources of prejudice include social categorization, stereotyping, attribution, and social beliefs. Social categorization involves distinguishing between in-group and out-group, and exaggerating differences in their beliefs. Stereotypes can be fostered by illusory correlations, and supported by shared infrequency of contact, as well as exaggerated perception of in-group heterogeneity and out-group homogeneity.

Social attribution includes biased labeling and the ultimate attribution error, both distorted interpretations of out-group members' behavior. Social beliefs that support prejudice may be derived from political and religious ideology. People who believe in a just world may be more likely to blame the victims of prejudice.

One emotional source of prejudice is the displacement of aggression onto a scapegoat group. Some research has also identified a prejudiced personality, the authoritarian, who is more likely to advocate discrimination and punishment for deviates.

Social sources of prejudice include relative deprivation, group conflict, and social supports for prejudice. Relative deprivation may explain both social rebellion and displacement of prejudice onto the least powerful. Group conflict resulting from competition may lead to prejudice against rivals. Institutional supports for prejudice include traditional policies and subtle practices suggesting that prejudice is acceptable.

Prejudice and its consequences may be reduced by changing both attitudes and behaviors. Prejudiced attitudes may be changed by countering stereotypes, changing social categorization, and developing lessons that teach alternatives to prejudice. Behavior can be changed through changing social policies, encouraging meaningful contact between groups, and establishing rewards for collaboration and cooperation.

Selected Readings

Adorno, T. W., E. Frenkel-Brunswik, D. J. Levinson, and R. N. Sanford, (1950). *The Authoritarian Personality*. New York: Harper and Row.

Allport, G. W. (1954). *The Nature of Prejudice*. Reading, MA: Addison-Wesley.

Amir, Y. and J. Sharan, (1984). *School Desegregation*. Hillsdale, NJ: Erlbaum.

Dovidio, J. F. and S. L. Gaertner, (Eds.). (1986). *Prejudice, Discrimination, and Racism: Theory and Research*. New York: Academic Press.

Gutek, B. A. (1985). *Sex and the Workplace*. San Francisco: Jossey-Bass.

Jones, J. M. (1972). *Prejudice and Racism*. Reading, MA: Addison-Wesley.

Katz, P. (Ed.). (1976). *Towards the Elimination of Racism*. Elmsford, NY: Pergamon.

Katz, P. and D. A. Taylor, (Eds.). (1988). *Eliminating Racism: Profiles in Controversy*. New York: Plenum.

Kidder, L. H. and V. M. Stewart, (1975). *The Psychology of Intergroup Relations: Conflict and Consciousness*. New York: McGraw-Hill.

Lerner, M. J. (1980). *The Belief in a Just World: A Fundamental Delusion*. New York: Plenum.

Miller, N. and M. B. Brewer, (Eds.). (1984). *Groups in Contact: The Psychology of Desegregation*. Orlando, FL: Academic Press.

Schuman, H., C. Steeh, and L. Bobo, (1985). *Racial Attitudes in America: Trends and Interpretations*. Cambridge, MA: Harvard University Press.

Tajfel, H. (1982). *Social Identity and Intergroup Relations*. Cambridge, England: Cambridge University Press.

Turner, J. C. and H. Giles, (1981). *Intergroup Behaviour*. Oxford, England: Blackwell.

Worchel, S. and W. G. Austin, (Eds.). (1986). *The Psychology of Intergroup Relations,* 2nd edition. Chicago: Nelson-Hall.

13

Aggression

*A*ggression has been a topic of central interest to social psychology since the early days of the discipline. The social problems of aggression—war, interpersonal hostilities, and violence—keep this topic current in the interest of amateurs and professionals alike.

This chapter reviews first the nature and components of aggression, and then major theories explaining its origins and function. We then consider the different shapes or manifestations of aggression: evidence about what provokes aggression, and how aggression figures in social issues like sexual violence, social problems, and modern life. We conclude with a consideration of strategies for controlling and reducing aggression.

THE NATURE OF AGGRESSION

Defining Aggression

Aggression is defined as behavior intending harm or negative consequences to others. The key to this definition is *intention*: intending but failing to do harm *is* aggressive; unintentionally causing harm is *not*. The many different forms of aggression can also be distinguished by purpose, social sanction, and form.

CATEGORIZING AGGRESSION

Hostile versus Instrumental. Aggression can be described as either instrumental or hostile. Instrumental aggression is aggression that intends harm as a means (instrument) to another goal. For example, yelling at a child to make her stop drawing on the walls is instrumental aggression.

Hostile aggression is aggression that intends harm as its primary goal. For example, yelling at a child to make her feel bad is hostile aggression.

Social Sanctions. Aggression can be either antisocial or prosocial in form. Antisocial aggression intends harm in violation of social norms and goals. For example, a robber who hits a clerk while robbing a store is committing antisocial aggression.

When aggression occurs in the course of promoting social good, it is considered to be prosocial aggression. For example, a police officer aggressively stopping a criminal suspect is committing prosocial aggression.

Sanctioned aggression involves aggressive acts that are not clearly either antisocial or prosocial. While they are not required for social goals, they do not violate social norms. For example, a victim defending herself against an attacker or a coach sending a rebellious player to the showers are both engaging in sanctioned aggression.

COMPONENTS OF AGGRESSION

Aggression is a complex process involving thoughts and feelings as well as behaviors.

Aggressive Behavior. Because only behavior can be observed, scientists study the variables affecting aggressive behavior. Most research has examined physical aggression, involving overt actions and damaging consequences. But the fact that words can hurt validates the power of verbal aggression. Especially in personal relationships, the meaning of verbal aggression can be painful and provocative, but not physically injurious or fatal.

Aggressive Affect. The affective or emotional aspect of aggression is obvious. Persons engaging in aggressive behavior are usually aroused, although dispassionate aggression—like "cold, calculating" aggression—is certainly possible.

Although *anger*, the aggressive emotion, is not directly observable, it has been characterized (by frustration-aggression theory) as a readiness to engage in aggressive behavior. According to self-reports, anger is a more common experience than aggressive behavior. Anger alone is not "enough" to create aggression.

Aggressive Cognition. Is there an angry style of thinking? According to one view, exposure to aversive events generates *negative affect,* which in turn activates a "fight or flight" response. That is, negative feelings can prompt you to anger and then aggression, *or* to fear and then escape.

The direction in which negative affect is channeled—anger or fear—depends on cognitive assessment of the circumstances. You must determine *why* you feel bad; your conclusion will determine your actions. For example, if you are shoved by a passer-by who apologizes for her clumsiness, you may feel annoyed but probably will not be angry or aggressive. But if you are pushed by an acquaintance during an argument, you will probably feel both angry and aggressive.

A related cognitive process is attribution, the process of explaining behavior. People are more likely to react with aggression if they have first attributed a provocation to hostile intent. Some individuals have a stronger tendency to make such *hostile attributions* of others' behavior, frequently in error.

Theories of Aggression

Different theories characterize aggression as an innately driven tendency, as the result of frustration, or as learned behavior.

MOTIVATION THEORIES

Motivation theories explain aggression as the expression of inborn forces or inherited predispositions that drive behavior. One such theory of aggression was proposed by psychoanalytic theory. Later work on animal behavior led to an ethological theory of aggression. Modern research has also indicated biological influences on aggressive behavior.

Psychoanalytic Theory. After the carnage and destruction of World War I, psychoanalytic theorists proposed that behavior is motivated by two unconscious forces: the life instinct (revealed in sexual behavior) and the death instinct (revealed in aggression). In this view, aggression is a natural and inevitable outcome of human conflict; the life instinct usually deflects aggression away from the self, victimizing others.

According to psychoanalytic theory, because aggression is the result of an unconscious drive, an individual's tendency to aggress will be reduced by releasing or expressing this urge. For example, if an angry man strikes out at an attacker, he will subsequently be less aggressive than before the act. Moreover, the theory argues that a vicarious release of aggression—e.g., watching others behave aggressively—will effectively release and reduce aggression. This process of releasing emotion is called *catharsis*.

Psychoanalytic theorists recommend catharsis as a strategy for reducing aggressive tendencies. For example, if you are angry at a member of your family, you can release this anger safely by fantasizing about retaliating, or by watching a violent film or television program. If you "get it off your chest" or "get it out of your system," remaining aggressiveness will be reduced and unlikely to explode without warning.

Ethological Theory. Another motivational theory of aggression that makes different assumptions is based on the research of Konrad Lorenz. Lorenz, an ethologist (who studies the evolution of behavior), studied the function of aggression in various species of territorial animals. Lorenz concluded that aggression is an instinctive pattern of behavior that is released to promote survival. For example, wolves (a territorial species) whose territory is invaded by another wolf will poise to attack. The invader may either stay and fight or signal intent to escape by exposing its throat (a gesture of surrender) and fleeing (with its tail between its legs). The other wolves' attack behavior will be released or not depending on the invader's "signal."

In ethological theory, human aggression is typically motivated by territorial protection. Property disputes, crimes of jealous passion, and international warfare are all forms of territorial conflict. In this view, aggression may be controlled but cannot be eliminated, since its survival value guarantees that it will be inherited.

Biological Influences. Biological mechanisms may underlie human aggression. Stimulation to certain parts of the brain within the limbic system results in violent or attacking behavior. Brain anomalies—like tumors and injuries—have sometimes been discovered in individuals who have behaved violently. The male sex hormone testosterone has also been implicated in violent behavior. While different lines of research all suggest a biological role in aggressive behavior, results have not been conclusive. No single biological factor has been found to "cause" human aggression, individually or collectively.

Other research has identified biochemical influences like drugs, especially alcohol, which disinhibits or reduces personal and social restraints on aggression. Low blood sugar has also been related to increased aggressiveness. While chemicals that are or are not introduced into the body may affect aggressive behavior, they do not explain the pervasiveness of human aggression across time and cultures.

FRUSTRATION-AGGRESSION THEORY

The first truly testable psychological theory of aggresion was frustration-aggression theory, proposed in the 1930s by a group of scientists working at Yale University.

The Original Theory. According to the original theory, frustration inevitably leads to some form of aggression. *Frustration* is anything that blocks goal-attainment; such a block can be external, as when someone else seizes the goal first, or internal, as when one does not have the resources to reach the goal. For example, a man who is cut off by another vehicle in heavy traffic (frustration) may react by swearing or blaring his horn at the offender (aggression). The target may be nonhuman, as when, after depositing coins in a vending machine and failing to get the desired item or her money back, the customer angrily pounds on the machine with her fists.

Aggression may also be *displaced* onto a safer or more accessible target. For example, a woman whose supervisor has harshly criticized her work may refrain from retaliating but later pick a fight with her roommate.

The Revised Theory. Mixed results in tests of frustration-aggression theory indicated many exceptions to the "rule": frustration did not always lead to aggression, and aggression could not always be traced to frustration.

After revision, the theory specified that frustration leads to anger, a *readiness to aggress*. Thereafter, specific cues or reminders may provoke the release of anger in aggressive behavior.

For example, a student who is frustrated at receiving a disappointing grade may feel angry on leaving the class but make no comment. When a classmate who did well on the test teases him, he may retaliate with an aggressive outburst.

Revised frustration-aggression theory also acknowledges that aggressive cues may provoke anger into aggression. Aggressive cues may be objects or experiences—e.g., weapons—that are not related to the frustrating experience but still remind the actor of aggressive options.

Research has demonstrated the power of such stimuli to provoke aggression from frustrated or competitive subjects, a consequence known as the *weapons effect*. For example, a man arguing with his wife may be more likely to strike her or shoot her if he sees a handgun nearby than if he sees a nonaggressive object like a spoon or kitchen appliance. Other aggressive cues include toy guns and black clothing (since "bad guys wear black hats").

Social Applications. If frustration leads to aggression, it may be possible to reduce social violence by correcting social injustices that lead to frustration. Studies confirm that aggression is more of a social problem in cultures and locales afflicted by *relative deprivation,* the sense within one social group that they are not as well off compared to another. However, aggression does not appear to be a correlate of *absolute deprivation*; that is, aggression occurs not where people really are more impoverished, but where the contrast between the haves and have-nots is more immediately perceived.

It may be impossible to prevent relative deprivation, because of the *adaptation-level phenomenon*. This effect describes people's tendency to adapt or become accustomed to their current levels of comfort or affluence. Thus, shortly after receiving a raise, an employee adapts to her higher income and no longer feels benefitted. Given the power of adaptation, it may be impossible to anticipate and meet people's needs before they feel deprived, and then frustrated, and finally aggressive.

SOCIAL LEARNING THEORY

According to the most widely accepted theory of the nature and causes of aggression, aggressive responses are learned as a result of direct experience and observation.

Direct Experience. From childhood most people learn that some kinds of aggression, in some situations, can be rewarding. Those who behave aggressively may win scarce or desirable resources from those whom they best. Peers, parents, and teachers may also reward aggression with social approval, encouragement, and praise. Children may infer the value of aggression from the fact that nonaggression—like refusing to fight when attacked by a bully—is scorned by others as a sign of weakness or cowardice.

Observational Learning. Aggression is powerfully learned from models. Children learn what to do and how to be aggressive by watching other children, adults—and media. Classic research conducted in the 1960s by social psychologist Albert Bandura confirmed that models need not be live or immediate to teach aggression. In Bandura's research, children who had watched a televised adult attacking an inflated doll exactly imitated the aggression when given the opportunity. Further research building on this study has confirmed that viewing televised violence increases aggressive behavior, numbs viewers to the impact of violence, and alters observers' ideas about the social world.

Aggressive Scripts. Some theorists have argued that aggressive behavior follows a social "script," a set of rules about how to respond to certain situations. For example, when arguing children are told to stop fighting, each may protest that the other one "started it." This reveals their belief that, if another individual provokes or starts the fight, there is no penalty for responding aggressively. This rationalistic bias—assuming that actions are excusable if good reasons are offered—is part of a common cultural script. Another guideline for aggressive scripts is the *negative reciprocity norm,* the principle that evil may be returned for evil. One example of this norm is judging that a woman who insults her husband "deserves" to be battered. Another example is the policy of building up a defensive nuclear arsenal "just in case" the enemy strikes first.

MANIFESTATIONS OF AGGRESSION

Aggression is a complex experience that is manifested in many forms, at different levels of psychological function, and in combination with other factors. While many of these considerations overlap, it is helpful to review two broad questions researchers have asked: What provokes aggression, and how is aggression related to other social issues?

What Provokes Aggression?

Frustration-aggression theory suggests that a frustrating experience leads to a readiness to aggress. General arousal and emotion may influence aggressive behavior. Specific stimuli and conditions can also provoke aggression. Finally, media images of violence may reduce inhibitions against aggressive behavior.

AROUSAL

According to the *two-factor theory* of emotion, emotional experience has two components: physiological arousal, and a cognitive label or interpretation of the source of the arousal. Arousal is necessary for the emotional feeling, but is not specific enough to channel it; a reason or label is necessary for appropriate action, but needs arousal to energize it. For example, being upset without knowing why is not an emotion, and having a reason but not feeling upset is not an emotion. But both feeling upset and attributing a reason for it constitute an emotional experience.

General Arousal. Many forms of strong arousal, whatever the cause, can increase subsequent aggression. For example, if a woman who has been jogging vigorously is blocked by an inconsiderate driver, her physical arousal makes her more likely to make an angry protest or gesture. According to the *excitation-transfer theory,* the arousal generated by one situation can activate behavior in another.

Aggression as Dominant Response. Arousal is most likely to trigger aggression if aggressive behavior is the *dominant response tendency* in that situation. For example, aggression is a likely (dominant) response to an insult but not to a joke. If you are aroused by your circumstances, and then insulted, you are more likely to aggress; if while aroused you are told a joke, you will probably laugh.

Attribution and Labeling. You are more likely to aggress if you label your arousal as due to anger than if you find another label. For example, if you are late for an appointment and irritated by the delay, you can attribute your arousal to lateness rather than provocation. However, if someone interrupts you in your hurry, you may attribute your arousal to being angry at the interrupter, and subsequently aggress against him or her.

PROVOCATIVE STIMULI

Once arousal is stimulated, interpretations or labels are most often based on stimuli in the immediate situation. Researchers have identified several stimuli that provoke aggression: pain, heat, crowding, threats and attacks.

Pain. Researcher Neil Azrin and colleagues found that animals receiving painful electric shocks consistently attacked each other, although the shocks were unrelated to other animals' presence. Further work confirms that, for both humans and nonhumans, psychological pain (like frustration) and physical comfort (e.g., heat) as well as physical pain will produce an aggressive attack response. The attack was found to occur only when the preferred response—escape from the aversive situation—was prevented. Thus the pain-attack response is rooted in the fight-or-flight stress reponse: when one response is impossible, the other is made.

Heat. The *long hot summer effect* predicts that urban tension (e.g., caused by racial tension or poverty) is more likely to erupt into violence during the hot summer season. While laboratory studies show that subjects in hot rooms express dislike and hostility toward others, real-world studies are correlational, and cannot separate the effects of heat from other factors like crowding.

Crowding. *Crowding* is the feeling of not having enough space. Studies of nonhumans confirm that animals in overpopulated environments do behave more aggressively than those in controlled settings. Among humans, crowding may first lead to fear—of crime or scarcity—or frustration, creating the arousal that fosters aggression.

Threats and Attacks. Attacks lead to retaliation, particularly when they seem intentional. Even perceiving another person as intending to attack—a threat—can increase the tendency to retaliate. Perceptions of intention and threat are important to attach an appropriate label to both the arousal and the context.

MEDIA VIOLENCE

Watching aggressive models can have a *disinhibiting* effect, reducing social restrictions on viewers' own behavior. Bandura's studies of observational learning (discussed above) confirm that models can be just as effective when they are depicted by media as when they are live. The power of media models is especially controversial, since media portrayals of violence have steadily increased in recent decades, in both frequency and intensity. Do such images provoke aggression by viewers? Various research programs have examined the role and effects of aggressive behavior as entertainment and as a game.

Violent Entertainment. Subjects who have watched violent movies are slower to report violent incidents they have witnessed. The more violence subjects have watched, the less physiological response they have to new exposures, evidence of a "numbing" effect. As violence becomes a bigger part of entertainment, it becomes less shocking and more acceptable to viewers.

More sobering results confirm that childhood exposure to media violence has longterm effects on those children's behavior, and younger viewers appear to be more vulnerable than adolescents. One explanation of this media effect is that entertaining portrayals of violence reinforce viewers'—especially children's—aggressive scripts. Stronger scripts are rehearsed through imitation and fantasy, and make more likely habitual aggressive responses to personal conflict. For example, children who get a steady diet of television violence incorporate images of violent heroes and plots into their play. When they experience real-life instances of frustration or anger, they are more likely to apply these well-rehearsed lessons, and respond with aggression.

Violent Games. Not all aggression is portrayed as violence. Games and sports, for example, involve instrumental aggression—physical or symbolic harm inflicted on opponents in competition. Is this an important distinction? Many theorists think not: aggressive sports promote aggressive behavior as a cultural norm and value. They also validate impressions that people have the right to be aggressive under certain conditions. When the messages of violent sports are combined with norms about negative reciprocity (above), it may be natural to conclude that competitors have the right to punish each other aggressively for the "injustice" of being threatened. Aggressive sports may also add to both viewers' and players' aggressive scripts.

Besides sports, violence is a popular feature of many video games. Research already confirms that both participating in and observing such violence—though "merely" symbolic and fantasized—does have the effect of increasing aggression in free play.

Aggression and Social Issues

How central is aggression to different social problems? Does modern social life itself contribute to individuals' aggressiveness? This section examines aggression's role in social issues like sexual violence and domestic abuse, and considers the relationship between aggression and personality.

SEXUAL VIOLENCE

Rape. Social scientists recognize the crime of rape as one of aggression rather than sex: sexual behavior is used to harm victims, not as an expression of interpersonal attraction. Studies comparing the incidence of rape in different cultures confirms that rape is most likely to occur in societies which condone violence, revere males as dominant, and separate the sexes. Only with this particular constellation of "values" will the rapist have learned that he has the right to commit rape and is protected by his culture. Rapists are more likely to be members of minority groups, victimized themselves in many ways, and to believe the "rape myth," the false impression that violent behavior is arousing and that women enjoy being brutalized.

Pornography. Correlational research has shown that rapists report significantly high exposure to pornography, media and materials depicting sexual violence. Research confirms that exposure to pornography can have the same effects on viewers as other violent media: numbing them to its shock value, increasing its acceptability, increasing arousal, and disinhibiting their behavior. Males who view pornography victimizing women are more likely to behave aggressively toward women than men, suggesting that pornographic media also influence viewers' aggressive scripts, including ideas about whom to attack.

Distraction versus Arousal. Consistent with the excitation-transfer effect (above), viewing pornography is found to increase aggression by rechanneling "erotic" arousal in angry directions. After viewing pornographic materials, subjects became angrier when provoked by unrelated stimuli. However, other research has suggested that, like laughter, genuine erotic arousal is incompatible with feelings of aggression. That is, a person who is truly aroused by attraction to someone should be too distracted to carry out an aggressive impulse. The *excitation-valence model* explains these contradictory findings by saying that it is the valence—positive or negative value—of the pornography that determines whether it will be distracting (reducing aggression) or generally arousing (increasing aggression). Research has confirmed that subjects who view pleasant pornography (without violence or victimization) are subsequently less aggressive, while those who view negative pornography (e.g., sadomasochism) display greater aggressiveness.

FAMILY VIOLENCE

Since aggressive scripts encourage us to seek aggressive "solutions" to personal conflicts, these are likely to emerge in domestic conflicts with those we love.

Learning Domestic Violence. Research shows that domestic violence may be "inherited" through experience: men and women who grew up in abusive homes are most likely to be physically violent toward their own families. Boys who see their fathers hit their mothers are more likely as adults to hit their own wives; men make up the majority of spouse abusers, although it is unclear which gender is "ahead" in spouse abuse.

Children who are neglected or abused are more likely—if they do grow up—to repeat the same cycle of violence with their own offspring, either by initiating or tolerating aggressive behavior. These findings suggest the power of social learning in shaping behavior: although victims may have resolved "never to be that way" themselves, violence in the home was a deeply absorbed lesson about social reality.

Frustration and Family Violence. Domestic abuse is also explained by the frustration-aggression theory. Once relative deprivation or aversive experiences have set up a readiness to aggress, the angry individual displaces aggression on family members as convenient targets. For example, a man who is frustrated about being unemployed may attack his wife, or a woman who is frightened by financial distress may batter her child. Although in either case the aggressor may feel remorse and guilt, he or she may also be reinforced by the influence and power that such aggression represents.

PERSONALITY

Are people more aggressive, personally and as a society, than we used to be? Research has examined several ways that modern living may increase our tendency to behave aggressively.

Deindividuation. Recall from earlier discussions (see chapters 4 and 11) that a reduction in self-awareness may produce a state of deindividuation. When deindividuated, a person is more likely to engage in behaviors that are normally inhibited—e.g., aggression, vandalism, or bullying. The antecedents of deindividuation include group immersion, physical and social anonymity, and activities that arouse and distract.

Researchers have argued that modern city life is naturally deindividuating, since urban centers are crowded, busy places where people can feel generally anonymous and alienated. Thus simply trying to live day to day in a stressful environment may create a readiness to aggress; once in this state, an individual may be provoked to aggression by even minor irritations.

In a reverse application, deindividuation may be deliberately induced to bring about aggression. For example, a group of would-be vandals may first disguise themselves with masks or by acting under cover of night. An example of socially sanctioned deindividuation and aggression is military service, which emphasizes anonymity (e.g., identical haircuts and uniforms) as well as group immersion and activity (e.g., drills, group responses, strict hierarchical ranking). In a sense, every member of a uniformed service is somewhat deindividuated, possibly ready to aggress if appropriately provoked. Military personnel can usually be controlled to displace such aggression against the enemy. However, their reduced self-awareness makes them less likely to violate unethical orders or act responsibly against group momentum.

Type A Behavior. Physicians and health psychologists have identified a stress-prone personality profile, the *Type A pattern,* associated with a greater risk of heart attack and cardiovascular illness. The Type A behavior pattern is characterized by impatience, obsession with time, perfectionism, competitiveness, irritability, and anger. (In contrast, individuals without such traits are described as *Type B*).

Types As have been found to be more likely than Type Bs to engage in hostile aggression, to initiate family violence, and to experience interpersonal conflict. While research continues, it is not yet clear whether Type As learn their dangerous and self-destructive behavior as a result of socialization. The stress and aggressiveness associated with Type A behavior may be the human consequences of placing so much social value on success, speed, ambition, perfection, and winning.

PREVENTING AND CONTROLLING AGGRESSION

Research and theory have suggested several strategies for reducing aggression. Some traditional approaches have had mixed results, while modern programs seem more promising.

Traditional views of aggression have emphasized its instinctive nature, and have advocated controlling or rechanneling rather than reducing it.

Catharsis. The psychoanalytic concept of catharsis has a common-sense appeal: aggression could be lessened if people were allowed to release their anger in a harmless way. For example, if someone angry at his boss can "get it out of his system" by watching a violent film, he should be less angry afterward, and less likely to speak or act in retaliation. Certainly the catharsis hypothesis is implicit in the notion that violence in children's television programming is harmless, or that it offers them an avenue for releasing their childish aggression.

In contrast to such expectations, however, catharsis does not appear to work. While physical exertion may lead to exhaustion and thus reduce aggressiveness, such effects are usually temporary. More often, viewing or fantasizing about aggressive retaliation maintains or increases aggressive tendencies.

For example, a woman who is angry at her sister tries to distract herself by watching a violent television show. While watching she identifies with the hero, who violently destroys all his enemies. After the show, she decides to call her sister and "have it out with her." It may be that vicariously viewing aggression, rather that offering catharsis, instead allows viewers to rehearse aggressive responses.

Punishment. Perhaps the worst "strategy" for controlling aggressive behavior is physical punishment. For example, if a young boy hits his little sister, his mother may scold him and strike him in hopes he will learn to behave differently. Unfortunately, this punishment has taught him that some forms of aggression (e.g., his mother striking him) are acceptable; further, his mother herself has modeled physical aggression. Punishment may eliminate a response immediately, but it does not complete the job by suggesting alternative behaviors. The boy who was struck by his mother may not hit his sister again, but neither has he learned how to react *nonaggressively* the next time his sister provokes him.

Punishment can be more successful if it does not involve physical attack (e.g., hitting) and if it removes the child from the rewards that often reinforce punishment. For example, if a child who has hit another child and taken his toy is physically punished, she may still enjoy the "reward" of attention from her peers and the disciplining adult. However, if instead she is immediately sentenced to "time out," such as a room nearby, she cannot observe or feel rewarded by the effects of her actions. Techniques like time out have proven much more effective in managing aggression than physical punishment.

RESEARCH-BASED STRATEGIES

Research on aggression has suggested effective strategies based on both frustration-aggression theory and modeling theory.

Cognitive Interventions. People are more likely to aggress not only when aroused, but when they interpret their arousal as anger and when they believe aggression is an appropriate response. Therefore, relabeling arousal as nonaggressive or determining that retaliation is not appropriate should reduce aggression. Research confirms both these effects.

For example, a frustrated driver in a summer traffic jam hears a radio announcer remarking that "on such a hot day, we're probably all irritable, so try to keep cool." Reinterpreting her arousal as due to heat rather than inconsiderate drivers, she is less likely to feel angry, and less likely to act in an aggressive or dangerous manner.

An angry individual can also be mollified with an apology. An apology signals a social script or heuristic that makes aggression inappropriate. If someone has insulted you, but then repented and apologized, it is *not* appropriate to retaliate. Moroever, apologies that give external, uncontrollable excuses are more effective at reducing aggression than those which blame internal, controllable causes. For example, if a friend is late meeting you for dinner, you will feel less angry if she explains, "I'm sorry, I got stuck in traffic" (external and uncontrollable excuse) than if she says, "Sorry I'm late, I forgot all about you" (internal and controllable). Apologies also restore justice by admitting error and correcting the initial frustration.

Modeling Alternatives to Aggression. Just as viewers learn how to aggress by watching violent models, we may learn nonaggressive alternatives by watching others respond more creatively. Several experiments indicate that watching nonaggressive models does lead to lower levels of aggression. Providing collaborative or cooperative models can also expand people's social scripts to include more constructive responses than aggression.

Reducing Television Violence. Television, especially children's programming, is somewhat easier to monitor and improve than other media like films. Networks and production companies are constrained not to exceed guidelines for aggression in the content of cartoon and live-action programs. Nonetheless the level of violence remaining is substantial. A better strategy may be to inoculate children against television violence.

Inoculation develops individuals' resistance to a message by giving them a small dose against which to build resistance. For example, a child who watches a violent cartoon with her parents is encouraged to talk with them about the silly parts and the unpleasant parts. Later when she sees such material on her own, she will be a more critical viewer, less likely to be numbed or tutored by entertaining portrayals of aggression. Research confirms that this approach, reducing the effects of violence, is more direct than attempting to reduce the amount of aggression displayed in various media.

Aggression is behavior that intends harm to others. Hostile aggression intends such harm as the goal itself, while instrumental aggression uses harm to achieve a different goal. Prosocial aggression is committed to uphold social norms or law, while antisocial aggresion violates such rules. Sanctioned aggression is aggression that is not required but is considered acceptable. The components of aggression include behaviors that are physical or verbal, affects like arousal and anger, and cognition such as one's assessments and attributions of the provocative situation.

Theories explain aggression as reflecting inborn motivations, a natural reaction to frustration, or a response learned through reinforcement and observation. Psychoanalysis explains aggression as the expression of the death instinct. In this view aggression can be released through experiences that provide catharsis. Ethological studies of nonhumans conclude that aggression is an instinctive response to territorial violations. Research on biological influences implicates brain function, biochemistry, and drug use in aggressive behavior but does not identify a biological cause.

Frustration-aggression theory originally postulated that aggression is the inevitable response to frustration. The revised theory further explained that frustration might rather lead to a readiness to aggress. Aggression is provoked by aversive stimuli or aggressive cues like weapons.

Social learning theory explains that aggression is directly and indirectly reinforced through social experience. People also learn to behave aggressively by copying the actions of others, including media figures as well as live models. Social learning also results in the development of aggressive scripts to guide behavior.

Aggression is manifested in provoked instances as well as many social problems. The excitation-transfer theory suggests that arousal caused by other stimuli can be transferred to aggressive behavior. This will occur when aggression is determined to be appropriate, or when arousal is attributed to aggressive conditions. Provocative stimuli include aversive experiences like pain, heat, crowding, and attacks. Images of violence in the media also portray aggression as entertaining and essential to competitive games.

Sexual violence like rape is an act of aggression rather than sexual expression. Sexual violence may be aroused by pornography, especially negative pornography, because it numbs the viewer, portrays sexual violence as acceptable, and increases arousal. Family violence may be the result of social learning, as children from abusive homes grow up to repeat the cycle with their own spouses and children. Family members may also be the targets of displaced aggression when other experiences have frustrated the aggressors.

Aspects of modern living may be related to increases in social aggression. Living in cities may cause residents to become deindividuated, with reduced inhibitions against aggression. Cultural values promoting success may encourage Type A behavior, characterized by anger and vulnerability to diseases of stress.

Traditional approaches to controlling aggression involved punishment and catharsis. Physical punishment techniques are ineffective because they model aggression and do not supplant aggressive behavior with alternative responses. Catharsis has not proven effective in long-term reduction of aggression. Fantasizing about or viewing aggression may actually provide a rehearsal that increases arousal and aggressive tendencies. Greater success is associated with techniques based on cognitive intervention and modeling. Nonaggressive attributions and apologies are both effective in reducing aggression. Children are also less aggressive when they have observed nonaggressive models and been inoculated against television violence.

Selected Readings

Archer, D. and R. Gartner, (1984). *Violence and Crime in Cross-National Perspective.* New Haven: Yale University Press.

Averill, J . (1983). *Anger and Aggression.* New York: Springer-Verlag.

Bandura, A. (1973). *Human Aggression: A Social Learning Analysis.* Englewood Cliffs, NJ: Prentice-Hall.

Bandura, A. and R. H. Walters, (1963). *Social Learning and Personality Development.* New York: Holt, Rinehart and Winston.

Baron, R. A. and D. R. Richardson, (1991). *Human Aggression,* 2nd edition. New York: Plenum.

Center for Research on Aggression. (1983). *Prevention and Control of Aggression.* New York: Pergamon.

Dollard, J., L. Doob, N. E. Miller, O. H. Mowrer, and R. R. Sears, (1939). *Frustration and Aggression.* New Haven, CT: Yale University Press.

Freud, S. (1955). *Civilization and Its Discontents.* London: Hogarth Press.

Geen, R. G. and E. Donnerstein, (Eds.). (1983). *Aggression: Theoretical and Empirical Reviews.* New York: Academic Press.

Goldstein, J. H. (1986). *Aggression and Crimes of Violence,* 2nd edition. New York: Oxford University Press.

Groebel, J., and R. Hinde, (Eds.). (1988). *Aggression and War: Their Biological and Social Bases.* New York: Cambridge University Press.

Gurr, T. R. (1970). *Why Men Rebel.* Princeton, NJ: Princeton University Press.

Huesmann, L. R. and L. D. Eron, (1986). *Television and the Aggressive Child: A Cross-National Comparison.* Hillsdale, NJ: Erlbaum.

Liebert, R. M., J. N. Sprafkin, and E. S. Davidson, (1989). *The Early Window: The Effects of Television on Children and Youth,* 3rd edition. New York: Pergamon.

Lorenz, K. (1968). *On Aggression.* New York: Bantam Books.

Malamuth, N. M. and E. Donnerstein, (Eds.). (1984). *Pornography and Sexual Aggression.* New York: Academic Press.

National Institute of Mental Health. (1982). *Television and Behavior: Ten Years of Scientific Progress and Implications for the Eighties.* Rockville, MD: National Institute of Health.

Oskamp, S. (Ed.). *Television as a Social Issue.* Newbury Park, CA: Sage.

Tavris, C. (1982). *Anger: The Misunderstood Emotion.* New York: Simon and Schuster.

Zillmann, D. (1979). *Hostility and Aggression.* New York: Halsted.

Zillmann, D. (1984). *Connections Between Sex and Aggression.* Hillsdale, NJ: Erlbaum.

Zillmann, D. and J. Bryant, (Eds.). (1989). *Pornography: Research Advances and Policy Considerations.* Hillsdale, NJ: Erlbaum.

14

Conflict

The social world is not perfect, and many identifiable social problems involve conflict. Is conflict inevitable? Must it entail destruction? Are peaceful relationships—both personal and international—ever possible?

Social psychologists have developed hopeful answers to these and other questions. In this chapter we review the nature of conflict, its processes and most common sources. We conclude by considering extensive research on how conflict can be resolved.

THE NATURE OF CONFLICT

Defining Conflict

Conflict is the experience of tension resulting from incompatible goals between two or more individuals or groups. For example, if you want to visit friends out of town this weekend, but your parents want you to stay and take care of their house while they leave town, you and they are in conflict. Initially at least, your goals are incompatible: if you achieve your goal, they cannot achieve theirs, and vice versa. But conflict is often complicated by considerations of different goals and consequences. Generally it is best to distinguish among different types of conflict, and to identify the processes and sources that create it.

TYPES OF CONFLICT

Conflicts can be distinguished in terms of whether they are clearly competitive or not, and are labeled as either zero-sum or mixed-motive.

Zero-Sum Conflict. A case of pure competition is a zero-sum conflict. It is so named because one party's gain is the other's loss; the sum of their outcomes is zero. For example, a sports context in which only one of two sides will be the winner is a zero-sum conflict.

Mixed-Motive Conflict. Most conflicts are not as simple or obvious as zero-sum arrangements. Instead, the parties involved are engaged in a win-versus-lose struggle in which the best solution is not clear. The solution one party favors has disadvantages for the others. Ultimately, the payoff or reward outcome will have either individual or joint benefits.

For example, in the earlier example, the decision about whether you should leave town, or stay so your parents can leave you in charge, is a mixed-motive conflict. Even if you stay this weekend, you can still leave on another date; but you may not have the same opportunities for friends or places to visit. Alternatively, if you stay you can please your parents, which is important in your ongoing relationship; if you leave, you may lose their respect or trust somewhat, and lose future opportunities for their help. This is a mixed-motive conflict because the "best" solution for you may not be the best for them, or for your relationship as a family. And there may be no solution that leaves everyone feeling happy and satisfied.

CAUSES OF CONFLICT

As complex as conflict is, the causes can be fit into four categories: scarcity, revenge, attributions, and miscommunication.

Scarcity. As noted earlier (see chapter 10), scarcity of a valued resource may influence a person to take action. If you believe your favorite cereal will soon be taken off the market, you may visit several local groceries to buy up the remaining boxes—an action you would otherwise not undertake. Likewise, much conflict can be traced to competition over scarce resources. For example, if you and several friends each would like the last piece of pie remaining after dinner, you may experience some tension in determining who gets it and why. Scarcity of resources like arable land, money, low-cost housing, and jobs underlies many powerful social and international conflicts.

Revenge. Reciprocity is a social norm dictating that actions should be returned in kind: kindness should be repaid with kindness, while harm may be revenged. Harm as a result of aggression or injustice can be the cause of social conflict when the wronged party (or the one who *feels* wronged) tries to get even. For example, if a coworker has lied about you to damage your reputation and get ahead, you may feel the situation is intolerable until you set the record straight and either reveal the lie or hurt her in return. A reasonable assessment of this tension reveals that vendettas seldom solve or end conflict; but the desire for revenge is not a rational experience.

Attributions. As reviewed in chapter 13, the victim of harm retaliates if he or she attributes the harm to the attacker's aggressive intentions. Likewise, if we perceive a problem as due to a party's insincerity or selfishness, we are more likely to experience conflict than if we blame uncontrollable circumstances. For example, if you drive in a carpool with other students, it is important to take turns and share the driving equally. Doing more than your share because your partner's car broke down can be annoying, but attributing your partner's request to laziness or miserliness about paying for gas will lead to conflict.

Miscommunication. Recent survey work blames faulty communication for many intergroup conflicts. This includes language barriers, mis-interpretations, a poor history of communicating, and insufficient exchange of information. For example, if your partner offers you advice about a project you are working on, it may sound patronizing or critical to you because you are sensitive about your talent in this area. What was intended to be helpful may actually seem like an attack. Which was it, and whose fault is it? The communication process involves both a sender, who may have been too blunt, and a receiver, who may have been biased or moody. It is difficult in resolving communication-based conflict to isolate blame or discover when the tension began.

Conflict Processes

The causes of conflict are really reflections of combinations of conflict processes. Several motives and social interactions set the stage for conflict: interdependence, competition, threat, escalation, and face-saving.

INTERDEPENDENCE

Social interdependence is a relationship between parties whose outcomes are jointly determined. For example, if your outcomes depend solely on *your* decisions and actions, you are independent. If you and your partner, however, experience the outcomes—happiness or misery—that your actions produce together, you are interdependent. Neither of you can take control of these outcomes, and neither can remain unaffected while the other acts.

For example, neighbors are interdependent in terms of how much they enjoy the neighborhood; if they work together to promote everyone's safety and aesthetic values, they can all be happy. But if they do not work together, or if any one of them "drops out" to do as he or she likes, everyone suffers: the surrounding neighbors are bothered by the deviate's disregard, and the deviate is ostracized by the others.

COMPETITION

When interdependence is competitive, conflict arises. When each party depends on the other for outcomes, and their outcomes are scarce, they work against each other instead of together, and the result is conflict. For example, two neighbors may disagree about how their properties should look: one prefers to relax on the weekends, enjoying silent surroundings and natural landscaping; the other likes the trim and tailored look, and prefers to rise early to run the power mower. Their goals compete: if the "natural" neighbor refuses to mow his lawn, the "tailored" neighbor will live next to an overgrown lot; if the "tailored" neighbor rises early to mow the lawn, the noise will prevent the "natural" neighbor from sleeping late. They are in competition because their goals are mutually exclusive, but they are interdependent because their enjoyment of their *neighborhood* is something neither can control individually.

THREAT

When the costs of being interdependent outweigh the benefits, a threat system develops. For example, two roommates split rent but have different schedules and preferences. Terry likes to stay up late and sleep late the next morning, while Lee is usually early to bed and early to rise. Each has the power to interfere with the other's sleep time—a reduction in resources. If Terry plays music too loud for Lee to sleep at night, Lee may threaten to do the same to Terry in the mornings.

Responding to Threat. Four responses are possible after a threat has been issued: submission, defiance, counterthreat, and flight. For example, after Lee has threatened to play the television loud in the mornings if Terry does not turn off the stereo after eleven o'clock, Terry may *submit* by agreeing to Lee's demands. Terry may be *defiant* by turning up the late-night volume and challenging further discussion. Terry may issue a *counterthreat*, like "If you deliberately wake me up early, I refuse to help you type your research papers." Finally, Terry can take *flight* by moving out to find a roommate with a compatible schedule. Which response the threatened party makes depends on factors like power, the size of the threat, participants' personalities, and the possibility of effective communication.

ESCALATION

The discussion of threat above implies that conflict can grow or escalate as parties respond to each other.

The Conflict Spiral. If threat is responded to with counterthreat, each exchange may lead to greater tension and promises of greater pain. Each response, rather than answering or satisfying the latest demand, increases the tension by raising the stakes. This pattern of escalation to greater tension is termed the *conflict spiral*: the vicious circle of argument escalates the tension between parties.

Debate, Game, and Fight. Another pattern of escalation has three stages: debate, game, and fight. Many conflicts start with a simple disagreement; the two parties *debate* their positions, each trying to persuade the others. If unresolved, the debate can become a *game,* each no longer trying to persuade but rather competing to "win" by making the better points. Finally if there is no clear winner, the game can become a *fight,* whose goal is no longer to persuade or win but to eliminate or *destroy the opponent.*

For example, two partners may be discussing how to spend the evening together. One wants to watch the movie "Rambo," but the other prefers "Bambi," so they debate about which to attend. Eventually, they argue more than persuade, and cite the opinions of friends and movie reviews to back up their preferences. Finally, their differences about movies lead to the airing of other differences, and they cancel plans to spend any part of the evening together. They are victims of conflict escalation: their interaction, once begun, has become too intense to manage or resolve.

FACE-SAVING

An important factor in social conflict is all parties' concern with not only their outcomes but with appearances.

Effects. Many social conflicts are played on a public stage, with on-lookers who form opinions about the issues and participants. Concern with evaluation-apprehension and social status in the future can complicate conflict beyond the issues and goals at stake. Concern with *face-saving* may make one party more likely to threaten the other, or refuse to concede out of fear of appearing to be weak.

Factors in Face-Saving. Research confirms that early experience with loss of face can motivate subjects to be unyielding or threatening in later conflicts. Face-saving is also more motivating to people who have invested heavily on the conflict. Spending resources or effort in a conflict situation may make one resistant to finding solutions, as though further conflict is needed to justify commitment up to now. Finally, face-saving may be an investment in itself: if you expect future conflict, and want to count on others' respect, you will work harder to win it by saving face now.

Sources of Social Conflict

Research on the sources of social conflict has focused on two situations: perceiving wrong or injustice, and experiencing entrapment in social dilemmas.

PERCEIVING WRONG

Many people pursue the same things in life: security, material well-being, popularity, and such. Opportunities for competition are numerous, yet for most times and people, conflict is a disruption rather than a normal experience. One experience that can turn an "ordinary" problem into a source of conflict is the perception of injustice or wrongdoing. For example, if you drive around a city block, vainly searching for a parking place, you may feel frustrated but move on to park elsewhere. However, if you find a parking space only to have it taken by another driver's illegal maneuvering, you will feel wronged and may pursue a conflict with the interloper.

Research into the perception of wrong has focused on three experiences: perceiving injustice, misperceptions, and mistrust.

Perceived Injustice. The justness of a relationship is a perception that the outcomes are distributed fairly. For most people, this means that the proportion of outcomes to inputs is equal for all involved, a condition known as *equity*. For example, two people invest in a small business and, one year later, must divide up their profits. If one person contributed 60% of the total investment, she should receive 60% of the total profit. This is an equitable distribution of outcomes.

Any other division would be inequitable, or unjust, and could lead to conflict. For example, if the profits are split equally, the one who invested more will be underbenefitted (by receiving only 50% instead of the 60% she is entitled to), and the other person will be overbenefitted (receiving 50% rather than the appropriate 40%). Underbenefitted persons usually feel angry and misused, while overbenefitted partners often feel guilty, until matters are set right.

Besides equity, another interpretation of justice can be *need-based*. This can take the form of a *social responsibility* norm, according to which those who have more are obligated to care for those who have less. In this conceptualization, injustice results when someone with ample resources fails or refuses to share them with another in need. This source of conflict is most likely to be pointed out by the needy parties, who may feel frustrated, hostile, and as if they have nothing to lose by protesting.

Misperceptions. Since conflict begins with one party's perception of incompatibility, any bias or error in perception can cause conflict to arise even from actual harmony. For example, suppose you and a friend had worked together on a project. If you hear a rumor that your friend will receive a greater reward than you, like a higher grade or bonus pay, you may feel angry—at your friend—and tempted to express your feelings before confirming what you heard. In this way misperceptions can breed conflict.

The most critical—and yet the most common—misperceptions are those formed of one's opponents. One such misperception is that one's own position is reasonable while the opponent's is extreme and unrealistic. Ironically, each party is likely to have formed this assessment; thus this pattern is termed the *mirror-image perception*. Perceptions and behaviors are mutually influential: perceiving the other as an enemy leads to challenges and threats, which usually reinforce perceptions of enmity and extremism.

Mistrust. Just as trust is important in making a communicator persuasive, it is essential in harmonious interdependence. If one party loses trust in the other, promises are likely to be broken and the conflict intensified. Trust is most simply defined as the expectation that others will do as they say; it has also been defined as the expectation that others will act to help rather than harm.

Trust itself is usually built up over time, and develops as a function of both personalities (e.g., some people are more trusting than others from childhood) and situational cues (e.g., knowing that one's opponent is invested in a peaceful outcome). Ironically, mistrust can develop quickly, as the result of a single act of betrayal, and is then resistant to change. One reason is the power of attributions: once a person's ingratiation is attributed to treacherous insincerity (a dispositional attribution), his or her subsequent actions are likely to be interpreted as equally unreliable and untrustworthy.

Mistrust can be reversed, but only if the betrayer admits doing wrong, shows remorse, and makes restitution to the wronged party. Because there are no guarantees of acceptance after such gestures, however, it is not surprising that some mistrusted persons would rather "save face" by refusing to admit wrongdoing rather than take the chances necessary to regain trust.

SOCIAL TRAPS

Much social psychological research has focused on the social and situational conditions that lead to conflict. Social traps are mixed-motive situations that tend to reward competitive rather than cooperative behavior, pitting the individual against his or her own community. The typical social trap multiplies the self-promotion of every participant with disastrous results for the community as a whole. Researchers have studied several social dilemmas (requiring either-or decisions) and games (mixing several goals) that illustrate the dynamics of social traps.

The Prisoner's Dilemma. The best-known dilemma used in laboratory studies of conflict is the *Prisoner's Dilemma,* a problem based on the plight of two criminals who have been caught working together but are being questioned separately. Isolated, each is offered the same deal: if you confess and your partner does not, you will be granted immunity and your partner will get the maximum sentence; if you both confess, you will each get a moderate sentence; if you both refuse to confess, you will both get light sentences. The terms and outcomes of the Prisoner's Dilemma are summarized in Table 14.1.

Imagine that you are one of the two prisoners, looking over this chart to determine what to do. In considering your options selfishly, you can see that your best outcome—going free—can be achieved only if *you* confess but *your partner* does not. Your *individual* outcome depends on the *combined* decisions you and your partner make. Unfortunately, your partner is considering the same set of options. You cannot confer before deciding whether to confess.

If Your Response Is:	And Your Partner's response Is:	
"I confess"	"I confess"	"I do not confess"
	Result will be:	*Result will be:*
	You get moderate sentence.	You go free.
	Partner gets moderate sentence.	Partner gets maximum sentence.
"I do not confess"	"I confess"	"I do not confess"
	Result will be:	*Result will be:*
	You get maximum sentence.	You get light sentence.
	Partner goes free.	Partner gets light sentence.
Not confessing is the *cooperative* choice: when both partners respond this way, they get the maximum mutual benefit.		
Confessing is the *noncooperative* choice: if you make this response, you betray your partner in hopes of personal benefit.		

Table 14.1 Payoff Matrix for the Prisoner's Dilemma

The essence of the Prisoner's Dilemma is that what is best for either prisoner is unlikely to occur: your partner is not likely to sacrifice himself or herself to let you go free; he or she probably knows that same thing about you. You would be unwise to confess in hopes that your partner does not confess. Perhaps you ought to *cooperate* with your unseen partner: if both of you *refuse to confess,* you will both receive light sentences. Thus *not confessing* is the "cooperative" choice, since if both prisoners choose it, they get maximum mutual benefit.

Unfortunately, your fate depends on what *both* of you do, and you cannot know exactly what your partner's decision will be. You might be unwise *not* to confess—since your partner might *confess,* and betray you. If you mistrust your partner, you are more likely to refuse to cooperate, hope to go free, and confess—which will backfire badly if your partner has anticipated and done the same thing. *Confessing* is thus the "noncooperative" choice, since it betrays one's partner.

The Commons Dilemma. The basis for another decision-making dilemma is what ecologist Garrett Hardin calls "the tragedy of the commons," referring to a farming community's common land. If each household grazes a few livestock on the commons, all can share the benefit of a slight reduction in grazing costs. However, if each member is tempted to use more than his or her share—and every member makes the same abusive decision—the multiplied consequence will be the destruction of the commons.

The commons is a metaphor for any shared, finite (non-renewable) resource: clear air or water, land, roadways, or a beautifully unlittered landscape. Each community member benefits somewhat from the combined agreement to use the commons properly; all suffer when anyone puts personal gain above community good. The dilemma is that individual benefit is only possible when *all* users respect the delicate balance between use and abuse. The "tragedy" is that temptation to abuse the commons becomes strong when one sees others doing it—the only way to "get one's share" is to join in the abuse. For example, a picnic area will be attractive only if every user removes his or her trash. But if you see the ground already littered, you feel your own trash would not add noticeably to the problem, whereas proper disposal will inconvenience you.

The Nuts Game. One game version of the commons dilemma has been developed by researcher Julian Edney, using a bowl of metal nuts. Players seated around the bowl are told that each is to maximize his or her own nut accumulation, and that every ten seconds the number remaining in the bowl will be doubled. It might seem obvious that all players should wait and let the nuts accumulate before dividing them up, most do not do so. Most players promote selfish gain over both group welfare and reason, depleting the nut supply *before* the first ten-second doubling. Unless groups are encouraged to plan conservation, they are more likely to be competitive than cooperative, and engage in collectively self-defeating behavior.

The Payoff Matrix. The critical determinant of behavior within any dilemma or game is the *payoff matrix*, the arrangement of rewards and penalties for cooperating as opposed to not cooperating with other players. (The term "matrix" refers to the divided square in which the various outcomes are usually portrayed). Note that the Prisoner's Dilemma *dictates* the payoff matrix to the prisoners; if a different set of outcomes were promised, it might be possible to increase prisoners' willingness to cooperate—or defect.

A real-world example of a payoff matrix would be social norms about competition. If our culture admired cooperation rather than competition, congratulating players for producing the best results rather than for being the fiercest winners, we might apply such values in other aspects of social life. To some extent governments and administrations attempt to control the payoff matrix, by determining whether an economy will encourage free enterprise (individual self-promotion) or communal endeavor (benefitting the collective).

RESOLVING CONFLICT

Understanding the essence of conflict—its causes, processes, and social sources—leads to the development of solutions. Generally, conflict resolution strategies focus on three types of changes: changes in existing rules or relationships, changes in the ways parties interact, and improvements in communication.

Changing the Rules

Conflict is often the result of circumstances or conditions affecting the participants' original relationship, such as prevailing norms and values, and the vulnerability of interdependent partners. Changing these conditions—in a sense, changing the rules—can alleviate tensions and reduce the potential for conflict.

CHANGING SOCIAL VALUES

As mentioned above, ours is a competitive culture: we like winners, and suspect cooperation to be a sign of weakness. But competition is only one of several possible social values a culture can promote.

Alternatives to Competition. Three alternatives are cooperation, altruism, and individualism. Each of these proposes a way of distributing the outcomes of participants' actions. *Competitive* values push the individual to outdo all others. *Individualism* promotes self without regard to others. *Altruism* promotes others' outcomes without regard to self. And *cooperation* promotes the joint outcomes of self and others.

Socialization of Alternatives. Individuals vary in the degree to which they favor any one of these four social values. To a great extent, we develop such values as a result of socialization. Socialization can become an agent of conflict resolution if parents and cultural institutions teach the benefits of altruism and cooperation—the two social values that promote helping, and for which social dilemmas do not develop.

For example, when confronted by a social trap, if you have been raised to believe the helpful response is the "right" response, you will quickly act cooperatively. If other players have been similarly educated, the conflict will be over before it has begun. In contrast, if you (and the other players or community members) have been raised to believe in self-promotion, whether by competition or individualism, you will lack the trust and cooperative experience necessary to avert disastrous conflict.

One example of how agents of socialization can change is the impact of the environmental movement on marketing and advertising. More products are being touted as environmentally "safe" or "recyclable," promoting the impression that such considerations of posterity are "good"—both morally and for business.

PROMOTING INTEGRATIVE RELATIONSHIPS

Exchange versus Integrative Relationships. Interdependent relationships themselves are a vulnerable context for both partners: each relies on the other for joint outcomes, yet neither holds a controlling interest. This is due to the fact that interdependent relationships are based on *exchange*—an expectation of short-term give-and-take. A simple example of an exchange relationship is that between you and a retailer: you pay your money, and the retailer sells you the chosen item; each of you gets what you want, in an even (you hope) exchange of value. In an exchange relationship, each party is motivated to maximize his or her personal resources. Obviously such motives feed conflict, since they do not value joint or cooperative outcomes.

The alternative is *integrative relationships,* in which each participant is motivated to help the other. Integrative relationships bring individuals' efforts together—integrate them—into the mutual *investments* of their relationship and their shared goals. For example, the relationship you have with your best friend is more likely integrative than exchanged-based. When you do a favor for or give a gift to your friend, you do so at least in part because it is good for your continuing relationship to support and please this person. In contrast, favors to exchange partners are done with an expectation of quick return, not any long-term investment. You expect your retailer (an exchange partner) to give you back your change; you do not keep strict "score" with your close friend, since trust and generosity are good for the long-term well-being of your friendship.

The Dual-Concern Model. How can exchange relationships be "moved" into integrative modes? One suggestion is that the two parties to a conflict be encouraged to adopt a *dual-concern model* for its solution. That is, each opponent should be made to see that the best outcome will be reached when each party feels concern for the other's needs as well as his or her own. For example, *problem-solving* concentrates not on how the parties struggle against each other but rather on how both might struggle together against the problem. Sensitivity to dual concerns may be enhanced by learning about each other, recognizing common concerns and vulnerabilities. Thus foreign exchange and travel experiences increase empathy between nations, making dual-concern, integrative models a more common basis for international relationships.

Changing Interactions

Rule-changing is effective if conflict can be anticipated and steps taken to prevent or lessen it. What about reducing conflict that has already been provoked? Research confirms the effectiveness of both changing the parties' cognitions and changing the context of the interaction.

CHANGING COGNITIONS

Conflict is defined by the perception or assessment of incompatible goals. If conflicted parties are induced to change these perceptions or attributions, conflict can be reduced or neutralized.

Perceptions. One or both parties may be wrong about the conflict: there may be no real conflict at all, or it may be about procedure rather than goals. Conflict resolution can begin by having each participant specify his or her goals but not the means to achieve them. This separates disagreement about outcomes from procedures. Only after discussing and agreeing on common goals should the parties go on to discuss methods. This strategy relies on the power of correct perceptions: rather than allow fear or mistrust to distort their perceptions of each other, participants are attending to facts and searching for convergence.

A strategy for reducing conflict escalation requires restricting conflict to debate, and not permitting it to spiral into a game or fight. The *debate technique* involves having each partner state, to the other's satisfaction, what the opponent's argument or position is.

For example, in the debate over which movie to see, one partner must explain why the *other* wants to see "Rambo," accepting correction until he or she can state it clearly. They then switch roles, the other explaining why the first wants to see "Bambi." In the course of this role-taking experience, each partner empathizes with the other, considering motives and goals. At this point they may discover agreement—"Sure, as long as we can see 'Bambi' later this week, maybe 'Rambo' would be fun after all"—or they may be able to collaborate on an alternative solution: "Since we really just want to spend the evening together, let's skip the movies and go out for ice cream. Then we can each order what we prefer and still be together!"

The debate technique requires one partner—either one—to be the first to stop the escalation and suggest the restatement procedure. Since the conflict has not yet escalated, face-saving may not be at risk, and further escalation can be forestalled.

Attributions. Conflict develops when one party attributes the other's actions to insincere or untrustworthy intentions. If these attributions can be corrected or softened, the mistrust and suspicion that fuels conflict can be prevented. Attributional education may best be accomplished through empathy, putting oneself in the other's position and considering the likely motives and goals. It may also be furthered with outside information, such as third-party references or assurances of good faith. At the very least, attributions should be kept free of bias from irrelevant personal experience. For example, the man who mistrusts his new coworker because the last one was treacherous is being unfair in his suspicions. Unless the new colleague took lessons from the last, there is little reason to expect a similar relationship or outcome.

CHANGING THE CONTEXT

Some aspects of the conflict situation may be amenable to change. These include the size of the group, conciliatory strategies, and establishing superordinate (higher) goals.

Size of the Group. The larger the group, the less impact each member may feel he or she will have on the outcome. For this reason voters in populous electoral districts may not bother to go to the polls. Researchers confirm that the larger the group, the less cooperative its members will be. This tendency can be undercut by keeping *each* member's potential cooperative benefit as high as possible—and advertising that fact. For example, to encourage high voter turnout, campaigners should remind voters of the individual benefits at stake in the election: "Don't let others vote away your benefits!" or "Your vote to Plan B could mean *you* get a raise in salary." In this way, no matter how large the group becomes, each participant keeps the same incentive to cooperate.

Conciliation. Since the exchange of threat intensifies conflict, it makes sense that reducing threat should have the opposite effect. Social psychologist Charles Osgood has since the early 1960s proposed such a plan for world-affairs concilation (from the Latin *conciliare*, "to bring together"). Osgood's strategy is titled Graduated Reciprocated Initiatives in Tension-Reduction, and abbreviated GRIT. GRIT works in three broad stages:

1. The initiator must announce its intent to be conciliatory.

2. The initiator then carries out several conciliatory acts.

3. The initiator retains its capacity to retaliate; if either party aggresses, the other reciprocates in kind.

Information on both laboratory and real-world versions of the GRIT strategy confirm that it works. Its effectiveness may rest on its simple tit-for-tat interaction: gestures of good will are returned in kind, as are acts of treachery. Neither side gives up its strength in order to effect peace; in fact, both sides may rush to outdo each other in generosity and largesse, as power is equated with reward rather than coercion.

Superordinate Goals. As Muzafer Sherif found in his study of competitive teams in boys' camps, competition over scarce resources can easily escalate into intergroup conflict and aggression (see chapter 12). Sherif and his colleagues also discovered, in trying to reconcile the boys to becoming friends again, that the most effective strategy was establishing *superordinate goals,* higher goals common to both teams. When both teams of boys were required to work together to achieve a joint goal—e.g., repairing a broken water line, or pulling a food truck from a ditch—their joint efforts (and success) overcame their in-group/out-group hostilities. Similarly, warring factions and quarreling partners may reduce their differences after considering their joint, superordinate goals: a safer working environment, or happy and healthy children.

Improving Communication

At the heart of much work on resolving *interpersonal conflict*—conflict between partners in close relationships—is an emphasis on the importance of better communication (see chapter 16). Communication can be improved either by the parties involved, or through the assistance of an agent like a mediator or arbitrator.

BARGAINING

Bargaining involves direct negotiation between the disagreeing parties. Research suggests that it may be wise to start "tough," asking for as much as possible. Ultimately, even though some retreat and concession will be necessary, you may end up with more than if you had been "softer." This may be because tough bargaining lowers the other party's expectations for the outcome.

However, taking a tough stand initially may jeopardize face-saving and make even reasonable concessions seem submissive. If initial positions are hardened and parties become intractable, both may become locked into the process of conflict with no dignified options for negotiation. Thus the best strategy might be to start tough but stay flexible.

THIRD-PARTY INTERVENTION

If positions have hardened and parties cannot negotiate in good faith, a third party may be able to resolve their dispute. Two common forms of third-party intervention are mediation and arbitration.

Mediation. In mediation, a neutral third party brings opponents closer to a solution by helping them to communicate and offering suggestions. A central aspect of the mediator's job may be to reestablish mutual trust between the parties. Mediators may also act as go-betweens when the quarrelers are separated, or as translators when they are close enough to communicate but fearful of misunderstandings.

Arbitration. If all efforts—direct and through mediators—to bring the opponents together fail, a third party may *arbitrate* the dispute by imposing a solution both agree to abide by. The arbitrator is usually chosen as someone mutually acceptable to both parties—a process that can be conflicted in itself. Moreover, the fear of what arbitration might impose—a settlement neither party really wants—may propel the combatants back to the bargaining table. If it has the opposite effect—if fear of arbitration freezes both parties into a war of the wills—dispute may be settled with "final-offer arbitration," in which each side makes it best reasonable-sounding final offer, and the arbitrator selects one. This gives each side the last word without entailing a fight.

*C*onflict is experienced when two parties have incompatible goals. In zero-sum conflict, one party's gain is the other's loss. In mixed-motive conflict, every mutual solution represents a mixture of costs and benefits for both parties. Conflict can be caused by scarcity of resources, a desire for revenge, negative attributions, and miscommunication.

An important process in conflict is interdependence in relationships, in which each party depends on joint outcomes. Competition also breeds conflict, when each party feels that to win requires making the opponent lose. Threats can prolong conflict as they provoke counterthreats and other debilitating responses. Conflict itself can escalate in a spiral, or from a debate to a game to a fight. Finally, an important goal for each participant is saving face in front of each other and spectators.

One source of social conflicts is the perception of wrong. One source of perceived injustice is inequity, a result of disproportionate outcomes. Misperceptions of each other also leads parties into conflict. Trust between opponents takes a long time and is difficult to develop, but can be quickly dissolved by betrayal.

Much research has focused on social traps, in which individuals are rewarded for promoting self over the larger community. One social trap is the Prisoner's Dilemma, in which each participant feels encouraged to make a noncooperative decision and betray the other. In the commons dilemma, each participant's overuse of a common resource leads to the destruction of the resource, or commons. The Nuts Game shows that inexperience in cooperative efforts can result in depletion of common resources. An important determinent of players' actions is the payoff matrix, or structure of rewards and penalties for cooperative versus selfish behavior.

Conflict may be resolved by changing the ground rules or the interactions of conflicted parties, and improving communication between them. Social values may be changed if the agents of socialization promote altruism and cooperation over individualism and competition. Integrative relationships can be promoted by educating parties to the dangers of exchange relationships and the value of dual concerns.

Interactions can be changed by influencing the way parties think and the context of their interaction. Perceptions should be corrected, and attributions based on fairness and reality. The context can be changed by controlling the size of the group and members' expectations of personal benefit. Conciliation programs like GRIT can be initiated to evoke cooperation from opponents. The imposition of superordinate goals has also been found to reduce conflict between groups.

Communication can be improved by direct negotiation as in tough but flexible bargaining. Third parties can intervene by acting as mediators helping the other two to communicate, or as arbitrators imposing a solution both agree to accept.

Selected Readings

Bacharach, S. and E. Lawler, (1981). *Bargaining*. San Francisco: Jossey-Bass.

Barner-Barry, C. and R. Rosenwein, (1985). *Psychological Perspectives on Politics*. Englewood Cliffs, NJ: Prentice Hall.

Blalock, H. M., Jr. (1989). *Power and Conflict*. Newbury Park, CA: Sage.

Brockner, J. and J. Z. Rubin, (1985). *Entrapment in Escalating Conflicts*. New York: Springer-Verlag.

Deutsch, M. (1973). *The Resolution of Conflict*. New Haven, CT: Yale University Press.

Druckman, D. (Ed.). (1977). *Negotiations: Social Perspectives*. Newbury Park, CA: Sage.

Jervis, R. (1976). *Perception and Misperception in International Politics*. Princeton, NJ: Princeton University Press.

Johnson, D. W. and R. T. Johnson, (1987). *Learning Together and Alone: Cooperative, Competitive and Individualistic Learning*, 2nd edition. Englewood Cliffs, NJ: Prentice-Hall.

Kohn, A. (1986). *No Contest: The Case Against Competition*. Boston: Houghton Mifflin Company.

Lewicki, R. J. and J. A. Litterer, (1985). *Negotiation*. Homewood, IL: Richard D. Irwin.

Pruitt, D. G. (1981). *Negotiation Behavior*. New York: Academic Press.

Pruitt, D. G. and J. Z. Rubin, (1986). *Social Conflict: Escalation, Stalemate, and Settlement*. New York: Random House.

Rubin, J. Z. and B. R. Brown, (1975). *The Social Psychology of Bargaining and Negotiations*. New York: Academic Press.

Rubin, J. Z. and C. Rubin, (1989). *When Families Fight: How to Manage Conflict With Those You Love*. New York: Arbor House/William Morrow.

Stroebe, W., A. Kruglanski, D. Bar-Tal, and M. Hewstone, (1988). *The Social Psychology of Intergroup Conflict: Theory, Research, and Applications*. Berlin: Springer-Verlag.

Taylor, D. M. and F. M. Moghaddam, (1987). *Themes of Intergroup Relations*. New York: Praeger.

Turner, J. and H. Giles, (1981). *Intergroup Behavior*. Chicago: University of Chicago Press.

White, R. K. (Ed.). (1986). *Psychology and the Prevention of Nuclear War*. New York: New York University Press.

Wollman, N. (Ed.). (1985). *Working for Peace: A Handbook of Practical Psychology and Other Tools*. San Luis Obispo, CA: Impact Publishers.

15

Interpersonal Attraction

---

*F*ew topics in social psychology are more provocative and relevant than the study of personal relationships: the attractions, friendships, loves, commitments, and often the losses we sustain with other people. Other disciplines like sociology, communication, and family studies have much to contribute to a thorough understanding of these experiences.

The social psychological perspective focuses more on processes that develop over time, like interpersonal attraction, than on social institutions like marriage or human functions like spoken conversation. The social psychological perspective is also distinctively situational: we seek to understand how factors in our social environment influence our involvement with others.

The social psychology of personal relationships begins with an examination of the general processes of interpersonal attraction: affiliation and its consequences, attraction, and interaction with others. In the next chapter, we continue to the processes of intimacy that characterize close relationships.

AFFILIATION

As has been noted previously, humans are social animals. Most of our experiences involve interacting with others in some way. This tendency to seek contact with one's own kind is affiliation. Other species are also affiliative, as can be inferred by their tendency to gather and travel in flocks, schools, swarms, herds, and gaggles.

Research has identified motives for human affiliation, as well as patterns of individual differences in affiliating. It is also important to consider the consequences of *not* affiliating, usually the condition we call loneliness.

Motives for Affiliation

The main reason people affiliate is to gain social rewards. Some affiliating may be coincidental to physical rewards—such as when people line up to see a movie or crowd into a restaurant like animals at a watering hole. But even when the presence of others can be bothersome or excessive—e.g., long lines into a theatre—it can be socially rewarding to be part of the crowd, since it confirms that we are in the "right" place (e.g., going to a popular movie or restaurant).

FEAR REDUCTION

According to the cliché, misery loves company. Researchers have confirmed that opportunities to affiliate may be sought out by those who are suffering or expect to be suffering.

Schachter's Experiment. A classic experiment on the benefits of affiliation was conducted in 1959 by social psychologist Stanley Schachter. College women who had volunteered to be subjects were told what to expect by a serious-looking "doctor" clad in laboratory coat and stethoscope. In all cases, the women were told they would be given electrical shocks and their physiological arousal would be measured. The women were asked to indicate where they would like to wait until the experiment began some time later: either privately in separate rooms, or together in a classroom. In actuality, this was the dependent variable.

There were two experimental conditions (levels of the independent variable) in this experiment: high fear and low fear. In the high-fear condition, the doctor acted sternly formal, telling the women their shocks would be extremely painful (although they would not cause permanent damage). The women in the low-fear condition were told by a pleasant, smiling doctor that their shocks would feel like a tingling or tickle, but would not be painful. The different presentations of instructions were meant to arouse either high or low fear in the subjects. (There were no actual shocks: after stating their waiting preferences, the women were assured the experiment was over and were debriefed).

Results confirmed that fear increases desire to affiliate: high-fear women overwhelmingly preferred to wait *with* other women, while low-fear women overwhelmingly stated *no* preference.

Explaining the Fear-Affiliation Connection. To some extent, waiting with others may promise to reduce one's fear. With others you may be able to ask questions about your experience, or simply distract yourself from what worries you. This *distraction hypothesis* implies that any "warm body" will help when we seek to affiliate, whether or not the other person has common interests or a common fate. Another explanation for the fear-affiliation connection is *social comparison*.

SOCIAL COMPARISON

As reviewed in earlier chapters (e.g., chapter 4), an important way to support our own beliefs is to compare them to others' for validation. This is social comparison, a powerful motive for affiliation.

Uncertainty. Thus we are motivated to affiliate whenever we are uncertain about what is normal, appropriate, or true. For example, research on gossip and rumors indicates that we are most likely to talk with others when the issue is important but our information is weak or unclear. This uncertainty increases our motivation to validate our conclusions socially.

Fear. When we are afraid, it is helpful to be with others so we can check out our reactions. However, in this case it is important that the others *also* be afraid; thus misery not only loves company, it loves *miserable* company.

For example, if you are waiting to keep an appointment with your dentist, you would probably prefer to have others in the waiting room rather than wait alone. But if you are nervous because you expect to receive painful treatment, you would most prefer the others waiting *also* to be expecting painful treatment. In your nervousness, you will not be alone, and may seek consolation in that fact.

Schachter confirmed this misery-loves-miserable-company effect in a follow-up study to the original, in which subjects were given two choices for "waiting with others": waiting with others who were fellow subjects (the *similar* condition) and waiting with others who were available but were not connected with the experiment. Results confirmed that high-fear subjects wanted *only* the company of fellow sufferers. This indicates that the fear-affiliation connection is explained more by social comparison than distraction.

Variations in Affiliation

Not all people have the same affiliative needs, either in general or when particularly aroused (e.g., frightened).

BIRTH ORDER

For example, some people learn early in life that the presence of others can be comforting in times of stress or anxiety. In this case, a factor like *birth-order*—the order of one's birth in the sequence of siblings—may be related to affiliation. Research has confirmed that firstborns are much more likely to affiliate when frightened than are later-borns, even as adults.

One explanation for this birth-order effect is that firstborn children are "experimental" children for their parents, who give them greater attention and nurturance than later-born children, who are treated more casually. Thus firstborns learn to seek comfort from others, while later-borns develop some ability to comfort themselves.

INFORMATION

Another factor affecting our affiliative choices relates to the information-value of being with others. If a lack of certainty or accuracy motivates us to seek the company of others, we should seek to affiliate more with those who promise to give the best information. Research confirms that people report greatest desire to have contact with those who are seen as honest and accurate, even if their information is critical or unpleasant. This information effect in affiliation hints at a finding (reviewed below) in attraction research: preferences for contact with *specific* individuals are affected by perceived qualities of those individuals.

ATTACHMENT

Our first life lessons may be about social affiliation. For the first year of life, infants tend to form an attachment—a strong preference for physical contact and social access—to the primary caregiver (e.g., mother). This attachment may be the basis for an individual's affiliation and relationship patterns in later life.

Three types of attachment have been identified in the behavior of infants and children. Most children have *secure attachments*, comfortable with contact and trusting of its rewards. The remaining *insecure attachments* are classified as either *anxious/ambivalent* or *avoidant*. Anxious/ambivalent individuals have mixed emotions about social contact: they may seek contact, then fear rejection and withdraw. Avoidant persons have difficulty forming close, trusting relationships with others. Research by Phillip Shaver and Cindy Hazan and colleagues has confirmed that the attachment patterns formed in childhood persist into adulthood, affecting both relationships and general lifestyle.

Loneliness

While most individuals have secure attachment patterns, there are many reasons to be wary of getting close to others. Others may reject or hurt you, and even good relationships can fail painfully. Nonetheless most people seek contact with others for the rewards it provides. Those who have inadequate or insufficient relations with others are defined as experiencing loneliness.

TYPES OF LONELINESS

Loneliness is not synonymous with being alone; it is possible and common to be alone, without feeling one's relationships are inadequate. It is possible to be lonely when not alone, a painful experience that is unfortunately not uncommon.

Situational versus Chronic Loneliness. Everyone experiences loneliness sometimes. For example, when you start school or move to a new residence, your lack of contacts may cause you some temporary loneliness.

This is loneliness as a *state, or situational loneliness,* a result of normal but transient (changing) conditions.

Others appear to suffer from *trait or chronic loneliness,* experiencing dissatisfaction about the number or quality of their relationships, irrespective of changes or circumstances.

Social versus Emotional Loneliness. Loneliness can also be distinguished in terms of the kinds of relationships one longs for. People who suffer from a loss of community or "belonging" are experiencing *social loneliness*. For example, when you move to a new town, you are separated from friends you know and not yet incorporated into a new network. The alienation and discomfort you feel are typical of social loneliness.

In contrast, loss of a specific intimate relationship results in *emotional loneliness*. For example, a woman who has recently lost her husband may have attentive, concerned friends, but still feel depressed over the lack of personal companionship and intimacy she shared with her husband. These are the symptoms of emotional loneliness.

FACTORS AFFECTING LONELINESS

Research has identified several factors affecting chronic loneliness.

Demographic Characteristics. Loneliness is related to age; teenagers and young adults (*not* older adults) are at greatest risk for loneliness. This is probably because young adults have higher expectations that are more easily disappointed.

People are more likely to feel lonely if they are poor, and if they are unmarried, although marriage is no guarantee against loneliness. Some research suggests that men are more likely than women to feel lonely, perhaps because females are socialized to seek and maintain relationships. Other work indicates that, because women value relationship success more than men do, women are at greater risk for loneliness when expectations are not met.

Personality Characteristics. Shyness and self-consciousness have been connected to loneliness, as have introversion (social withdrawal) and nonassertiveness. Most revealing are findings that loneliness is related to low self-esteem and poor social skills, like an inability to listen. While all these connections are correlations—connections that do not specify causality—it is possible that a bad self-concept and related unskilled behavior may cause failed relationships, and consequently lead to loneliness.

Loneliness may result from self-defeating attributions. If a person attributes his loneliness to internal, stable, global causes, he may cause his feelings to persist. For example, if a student feels he is lonely because he is boring to others and always will be, and that there is nothing interesting about him, he is condemning himself to a loneliness he cannot change or control. Alternatively, if a worker attributes her lonely feelings to missing her old friends, she can take action to change her experience: call them, or visit new friends, or do something interesting. In any event, her ability to make external, unstable, specific attributions about her loneliness gives her the power to change her feelings.

Finally, lonely people may commit the error of *false consensus,* assuming that others may think and act the same way they do. This makes them less likely to perceive alternatives for cognition or behavior. They are also in danger of assuming, if others are like themselves, that they do not have to overcome their shyness or explain themselves in order to get to people. Not making such efforts dooms them to remaining out of contact.

REDUCING LONELINESS

Strategies for reducing loneliness can involve both cognitive therapy and improving social skills.

Cognitive Therapy. As suggested above, loneliness may be alleviated by developing constructive, optimistic attributions for one's feelings. Additionally, lonely people can correct false comparison effects, and recognize that others are different from themselves in many ways. Finally, shyness can be changed if shy people realize that others are neither focusing on them nor evaluating their behavior.

Social Skills Training. Lonely people may need instruction in the kinds of social experiences that most people learn through trial and error. This may include conversational skills, including asking open-ended questions and active listening. Lonely people may be taught how to deal with social conflict and discomfort, and how to make a better impression. Instruction may include modeling, showing subjects good and better ways to engage in social interaction.

Research results confirm that both cognitive and social skills therapy can make a difference in the experience of formerly lonely individuals.

ATTRACTION

While affiliation provides social rewards, most of us form preferences to be with specific individuals, not "just" anyone. Such preferences for social contact indicate attraction rather than affiliation. Ample research suggests some basic models of human interpersonal attraction, identifying both situational and personal factors in its development.

Models of Attraction

Attraction has no single cause, but is a response prompted by many different motives and stimuli. Two models of attraction are based on the power of reward, and a third proposes a sequence by which rewards are evaluated.

HOMANS' REWARD MODEL

Every interaction has an associated cost; even brief business transactions take time or money. We consider such costs as well as possible benefits in selecting groceries, places to do business—and people to be with. According to theorist George Homans, humans are attracted by the promise of interactions that promise "profit," or more reward than cost. As long as the promised reward exceeds the apparent cost of an interaction, we will feel attracted to the person in question.

For example, if you have a classmate who seems both bright and attractive, you may wonder whether to befriend this person. Possible rewards include companionship, being associated with someone good-looking, even tutoring by an expert. Possible costs might include the time and other resources you might have to spend to get this person's attention, and the fact that you might be expected to return these favors and resources. If rewards exceed costs, you will feel attracted; if costs overwhelm rewards—even temporarily—you will not feel attracted enough to take action.

BYRNE'S LAW OF ATTRACTION

Theorist Donn Byrne has developed a model similar to Homans' principle of reward. According to Byrne's *law of attraction,* the more positive reinforcement (e.g., reward) you expect from a person, the more attracted you will feel. By emphasizing reinforcement rather than specific rewards, this model characterizes attraction as a *process* rather than a *state*. That is, interpersonal attraction is not like a magnetic force between two people, but an ongoing, changing experience dependent on how the two interact.

The law of attraction identifies several different experiences as important to reinforcement: similarity, positive evaluation, and compatibility (reviewed in detail below) are all factors in greater attraction.

MURSTEIN'S STAGE MODEL

Are all factors equally important to initial attraction? Bernard Murstein's *stimulus-value-role model* of attraction says no: according to Murstein, different qualities are important at different stages in interpersonal attraction. In the stimulus stage, first contacts with others highlight external features as most important. For example, you might first be attracted to someone similar to yourself in age, social background, and level of attractiveness.

In the second stage, the value stage, your interactions with the other person bring into consideration how similar your attitudes and values are. For example, you might find someone with the same religious or political ideas appealing, while someone who disagrees with you on such principles is less pleasant to be with.

Finally, in the role stage, what matters most is whether you and the other person develop compatible roles, ways of relating to each other. For example, if you are used to being dominant and making decisions, you may find someone equally dominant too competitive, and prefer someone more willing to let you be in charge. Conversely, though, you may find it easier to be with someone similar, who shares your decisiveness, since such a person appreciates those qualities in you.

Determinants of Attraction

The experiences that determine attraction can be distinguished as situational or personal. Situational determinants are circumstances that affect attraction but are not directly controllable. Personal determinants are qualities of the individuals involved and their interaction together.

SITUATIONAL DETERMINANTS

Situational factors in attraction may seem paradoxical; it is hard to imagine how a personal experience like attraction could be affected by circumstances beyond one's control. However, research confirms that at least two such situations do have a powerful impact on attractiveness: propinquity and familiarity.

Propinquity. Propinquity refers to proximity or nearness. In general the greater the propinquity of one person to another, the greater the attraction between them. Most people who end up being best friends or getting married started their relationships by being thrown together or put into contact, usually on a regular basis. For example, you are more likely to run into and form an opinion about someone who lives in your dormitory or neighborhood than someone who does not—no matter how much else you have in common. Propinquity research confirms that such nearness can act like a filter in early interactions, determining who does and does not eventually form an attraction.

Classic research on the effects of propinquity was conducted by Leon Festinger and colleagues at the Massachusetts Institute of Technology in the early 1950s. They found that, among older students assigned to dormitory housing complexes, friendships formed among those who lived nearest each other—rather than among those who had the same majors, or came from the same home towns, or other possible factors. This supported the power of *physical propinquity* or sheer geographic nearness.

Further research has clarified the greater power of *functional propinquity,* or behavioral contact. Even if you have several neighbors equally close to you, you will form the greatest attraction for those with whom you come into contact, especially regularly and spontaneously. For example, if you live next door to two roommates, and one of them regularly takes out the trash on the same mornings that you do, you will form a stronger attraction for that person than for the other roommate.

We are further attracted to people on the basis of anticipated contact. If we *expect* to run into others, we like them better than those we do not expect to encounter.

Certain living circumstances and architectural features affect functional propinquity. For example, since these locations are traveled by more people, you may be most likely to encounter others—and thus most likely to be popular—if you live on the ground floor of a building, near a stairwell or elevator, near an exit, or near a service room like laundry facilities or vending machines. In this way the "accidents" of our circumstances determine our social lives.

Familiarity. Another situational factor in attraction is familiarity, which has also been argued as the basis for the propinquity effect. Familiarity is based on frequency of experience: the more you have seen someone or done something, the more familiar it is to you. Researchers have found that familiarity generally increases attraction. This contradicts romantic myths about the allure of novel experiences or attractive strangers; by definition, novelty and strangeness involve unfamiliar experiences.

The familiarity effect is best explained by the power of mere exposure. Researcher Robert Zajonc has found that people rate as more positive or attractive those stimuli—whether faces, melodies, or abstract drawings—that they have been exposed to more frequently than others. Subjects have even been found to prefer the way they look in a mirror—the "self" they are most familiar with—to the reverse image others always see. Mere exposure may be enough to increase attraction because it reduces anxiety about novel stimuli. The more you see someone, the more predictable he or she seems to be; if uncertainty causes anxiety, such predictability can be relieving and pleasant.

Personal Determinants

Although propinquity and familiarity may filter out many other people we will not have the chance to be attracted to, those who remain will be evaluated by us—and we by them—on a number of personal factors: physical attractiveness, personal qualities, attitude similarity, and need complementarity.

PHYSICAL ATTRACTIVENESS

Although the proverb warns us not to judge a book by its cover, for most of us attraction is strongly affected by others' physical attractiveness. Since a person's appearance is usually the first "information" we receive about him or her, we may give it greater weight (the primacy effect), or form an expectation that his or her other qualities will be similarly evaluated (a halo effect). According to the physical attractiveness stereotype, what is beautiful is considered good, an expectation that biases person perception (see chapter 5). Finally, the association of certain features (e.g., youth, strength) with social value may be a vestige of our ancestors' emphasis on procreation in mate selection, although such a sociobiological view is difficult to verify.

In an influential study, researchers paired students who had volunteered for a blind-date dance, and asked them to rate their partners for skills, qualities, and physical attractiveness. Results indicated that the single greatest predictor of whether a subject wanted to see his or her date a second time was that person's physical attractiveness. For example, if a date was rated low on intelligence or conversational skills but high on physical appeal, the rater expressed a desire for a second date.

Physical attractiveness may be most influential when one has no fear of rejection, as in the assigned-date study above. Most social dating has no such guarantees, however; thus most people appear to choose dates and partners similar to their own level of attractiveness. This is known as the *matching effect*. Partners may also seek to "match" physical attractiveness with a similar level of another quality, such as self-esteem or competence. Research suggests that people who have suffered failure lower their standards for physical attractiveness, while successful people raise their standards. This indicates a form of exchange, in which qualities like physical beauty are "traded" for similar levels of other personal "commodities."

Standards for physical beauty vary across cultures and times. Mass media like television and print advertising bombard us with images of beautiful entertainers and models endorsing products. Compared to such images, average men and women may appear to fall unacceptably short of our standards, a result termed the *contrast effect*. Standards for attractiveness may also depend on personal bargaining power. Those who have little to offer or restricted opportunities for contact may settle for less attractive partners.

Research shows the reverse effects of negative physical attractiveness, a form of stigma (see chapter 5). People who are considered physically deformed, plain, or undesirable may not only be passed by but rejected both personally and socially. In our culture, for example, obesity is stigmatized, so that extremely overweight people may be discriminated against in the workplace as well as in their social lives.

OTHER BASES OF ATTRACTIVENESS

Other qualities considered attractive are dominance and competence. Dominance includes such behavior as assertiveness and competitiveness. Researchers have found that, in studies of heterosexuals, dominance increases the perceived attractiveness of men but not of women.

We tend to like competent people better than those who are incompetent or talentless. A qualification to this relationship is that extremely competent people are seen as more likable if they commit a blunder. For example, a very intelligent person who spills coffee on himself or herself may be seen as "smart but human," while a less intelligent coffee-spiller is seen as "a loser."

Similarity. One of the most consistent findings in the research is that we like people who are like us. We prefer people who are similar to us in age, height, intelligence, background and, particularly, attitudes and values. Early interactions offer opportunities to explore similarities; the higher the proportion of attitude similarity, the greater the attraction.

Similarity may be important because it maintains balance or consistency among our relationships. Relationships are balanced when their valences (positive or negative evaluations) are in agreement. Thus if you like social psychology and you like your friend Lindsay, your relationships with your studies and your friend will be in balance if Lindsey also likes social psychology; if Lindsey disagrees with you, your cognitive elements are imbalanced.

Another interpretation of the effects of similarity argues that we are not so much attracted to *similar* others as we are negatively affected by those who are *dissimilar* to us, an effect termed the *repulsion hypothesis*. Research has failed to confirm this effect, however. Evidence rather supports the view that we encounter others in social circumstances loaded with influence (e.g., biases, stereotypes) and base *additional* attraction to certain individuals on such experiences as perceived similarity.

Complementarity. Finally, folk wisdom has long argued that "opposites attract," but researchers have failed to confirm the reality of this advice. True opposites are unlikely even to meet, much less to attract each other. However, it is likely that we will be attracted to those who both share similar values *and* meet unique needs. Need gratification may take the form of complementary qualities. For example, a talkative person may be most comfortable with a good listener; they are not opposite, since they share the attitudes they converse about, but they have complementary skills and behavior patterns. Complementarity may be more important to relationship *development* than to initial attraction. But a person with specific needs may look for those qualities in another person, and find such individuals more attractive.

ATTRACTION AND INTERACTION

It should be apparent that it is difficult to separate attraction as a passive experience from interaction with others. Much of what we find attractive we will discover only after we make contact. Three interactive processes are therefore important in interpersonal attraction: expressing feelings, initiating interaction, and further developing the relationship.

Expressing Feelings

Feeling attraction for a person will not lead to a relationship unless that attraction is acted on. Theorists have explored the importance to relating of showing positive regard, reciprocating attraction, and being either too easy or too hard to get.

POSITIVE REGARD

There is evidence that a key factor in finding someone attractive is being regarded positively by that person. In other words, you will feel attracted to someone who expresses liking for you. One explanation for this comes from humanistic personality theory and client- or person-centered therapy: we associate reward and security with positive regard, and seek such regard from others.

Need for Positive Regard. Research suggests that attraction to those who give positive regard increases if one needs such regard. For example, if you have recently experienced failure and feel bad about yourself, you will be more attracted to someone who expresses interest in you than if you were more self-confident. This indicates that positive regard is a need-based reward and may fluctuate with our self-esteem.

Other research evidence extends this idea that attraction is based on need for self-regard. People with low self-esteem have been found to express greater attraction to the significant people in their lives, the people who provide them with positive regard. Needier people value it more highly, and experience greater attraction to those to promise it.

Ingratiation. Finally, an offer of positive regard may be an *ingratiation strategy* rather than a sincere compliment. Powerful people may know this and devalue much of the "praise" they receive from those who hope to win favor. Positive regard is meaningful only if it is honest, but honesty is not easily gauged. Being wary and dismissive may lead one to reject both sincere and insincere flattery. If you don't know whom to trust, you may trust no one, and experience loneliness despite your appeal to others.

RECIPROCAL LIKING

Expressions of positive regard are important because they imply liking or attraction. Researchers have found a reciprocity effect in attraction: we become attracted to those who behave as though they are attracted to us—in sum, if people like us, we like them back.

Perceived versus Actual Reciprocity. The behavior of the other person is essential for reciprocal liking: perceived reciprocity is more influential than actual reciprocity. For example, if someone acts attracted to you—you can infer attraction from the person's words and deeds—you will probably reciprocate the feeling. But if another person who actually likes you fails to express that clearly, you will make no attributions of attraction, and your own feelings will be unaffected.

Self-Fulfilling Prophecy. Why is perceived attraction reciprocated? Theorists speculate that people respond to perceiving "liking" differently from from other interactions. For example, if you know someone likes you, you may present a more likable side of yourself to him or her. As a result, the other person expresses more attraction to you—and the result is a self-fulfilling prophecy. Because someone believes you are likable, you become likable.

PLAYING HARD TO GET

Folk wisdom warns against wearing your heart on your sleeve: if you show you like someone, that person may take advantage of your feelings, or take you for granted. Far better to play "hard to get," implying that you are selective about those whom you like. Research does not support the wisdom of playing hard to get. In contrast, subjects in one study indicated greatest preference for a date who was only "selectively" hard to get. That is, a subject would feel most attracted to a woman who indicated she was attracted to *him*—who expressed liking for him—but *not* attracted to others. Such a strategy combines the selectivity of playing hard to get with the generosity of expressing liking.

Initiating Interaction

What are the most effective ways to initiate interaction with an attractive other? Researchers have examined the role of general social skills, and the power of compliments in building initial interactions.

SOCIAL SKILLS

Social skills are people's abilities to interact comfortably and successfully with others.

Listening. Most social skills involve conversation, both listening and expressive. Good listening involves providing cues of attentiveness, nodding or smiling in reaction to the other, and aligning nonverbal cues with active listening. For example, to show you are listening to someone, you should look at him or her, making regular eye contact (but not staring), react appropriately, and make sure your body faces the speaker in a comfortable but attentive way.

Opening Lines. An opening line can start conversation by making contact and drawing attention to the speaker. Research confirms that while good opening lines can improve later interaction, a bad choice can destroy chances for further contact.

One study categorized opening lines in three groups: cute-flippant, innocuous, and direct. An example of a cute-flippant remark would be "You light up the room so much, I need to put on sunglasses"; it seeks attention by flirting humorously. An innocuous remark would be "What do you think of this class?" A direct opener would be "You look interesting, can we get to know each other?" Results indicated both men and women preferred hearing innocuous or direct opening lines. Most subjects—especially women—disliked cute-flippant remarks; such efforts to impress are apparently self-defeating.

Other work confirms that the best openers are lines that really open conversation—by inviting interaction and mutual interest. The worst are lines that close it before it begins, perhaps by expressing extreme opinions, or asking closed-ended questions like "Do you come here often?" (A response of "No" effectively ends that conversation). In contrast, an open-ended question like "What do you like about living here?" gives the responder an opportunity for self-presentation and interaction.

REWARDS AND COMPLIMENTS

Whether flattery will get you nowhere, somewhere, or everywhere depends on the value of your flattery.

Effective Compliments. Research shows that compliments are most effective in developing positive interaction when they are seen as honest and unconditional. Compliments from powerful, popular, or high-status people are more likely to increase liking than praise from weak, unpopular, or low-status flatterers.

Gain/Loss Theory. Compliments are more powerful if the compliment-giver has not been complimentary in the past. For example, if a professor who normally never praises your work remarks to you that your latest paper or test performance was very good, you will value it more than if she doled out such praise on a regular basis.

Gain/loss theory argues that a contrasting history makes a comment more effective than a consistent one. Praise from a critic is more uplifting, and criticism from a fan more devastating, than comments consistent with a person's usual opinion of you. Such breaks with "tradition" make the comment seem more salient and sincere to the recipient. Research also indicates that the gain effect is greater than the loss effect: you will like a critic much more for a single compliment than you will condemn a fan for a single criticism.

Relationship Development

As attraction pervades interaction, when does one person's attraction to another become a mutual relationship? Two approaches are helpful in understanding how one-sided attraction may—or may not—proceed: intimacy development and exchange versus communality.

INTIMACY DEVELOPMENT

The essence of interaction is communication, and the development of closeness or intimacy depends on a qualitative change in communication. While no two relationships proceed in the same course, a common model of intimacy development has been charted by theorist George Levinger. According to Levinger, once two people have overcome separation (zero contact) they may proceed to each of three levels:

1. *Awareness* of each other, based on propinquity;

2. *Surface contact,* founded on physical attractiveness and perceived similarity; and

3. *Mutuality,* involving compatibility, self-disclosure, and empathy.

The goal of such development, mutuality, requires a balance between both partners' needs, resources, and ability to communicate. Levinger's theory depicts relationship development as two circles moving toward and intersecting with each other. Greater intimacy is associated with a greater area of intersection.

EXCHANGE VERSUS COMMUNALITY

If initial attraction is based on reward or reinforcement, then casual relationships involve exchange. However, intimate relationships appear to be based on interdependence rather than exchange. Researchers Margaret Clark and Judson Mills have confirmed that intimate relationships are based on *communality,* a mutual investment in joint goals, rather than a simple exchange of individual resources and goals.

For example, in a casual relationship, you expect and provide a tit-for-tat exchange. If an acquaintance asks you for a favor, like a ride to school, you feel you can (and probably should) ask for a return of the favor at some point. However, your relationship with your best friend is probably communal. If you gave your best friend a small gift, you would be surprised and probably hurt if he or she later gave you something "to pay you back." Such an even, short-term exchange would signal that the communality is not mutual; your friend does not see your gift as an investment, but rather as an obligation.

In times of severe conflict or deterioration, relationship partners may descend from communal to exchange interactions. For example, if partners are breaking up, they may hasten to return things like books and tapes to each other, a sign that they are again exchanging and "keeping score" rather than investing in joint goals.

Personal relationships begin with affiliation, the human preference to be with others. One motive for affiliation is fear reduction: frightened people draw comfort from others' presence. Another motive is social comparison: in times of uncertainty or anxiety, people look to others for information and guidance. Firstborns may have greater needs for affiliation than later-born individuals. We may also be more likely to seek affiliation with those who provide accurate or complete information.

Affiliation patterns may be affected by different attachment patterns. Most people form secure attachments, seeking satisfaction from social relationships. Some are insecure and anxious or ambivalent about others, hopeful for contact but worried about rejection. Finally, some are insecure and avoidant, withdrawing from others and unable to form intimate attachments.

Inability to affiliate can result in loneliness. Situational loneliness is the result of transient losses or separations, while chronic loneliness afflicts some individuals most of the time. Loss of community results in social loneliness, while loss of intimacy results in emotional loneliness. Loneliness is associated with certain demographic characteristics like age, and with personality characteristics like shyness. Loneliness may be reduced through a program of both cognitive therapy and social skills training.

Attraction involves the desire to affiliate with specific individuals. Homans' model argues that attraction is based on reward, while Byrne's law of attraction proposes the importance of reinforcing interactions. Murstein proposes a stage model of attraction, with attraction based on stimulus qualities, then values, and finally role development.

Situational determinants of attraction include propinquity and familiarity. According to the propinquity effect, people are more attracted to those whom they are near, especially those with whom they make regular contact (functional propinquity). Propinquity may be explained in terms of the value of familiarity. Familiarity increases through mere exposure, since more frequent experiences are predictable and preferable.

Personal determinants of attraction include physical attractiveness and other positive qualities, similarity, and need complementarity. According to the physical attractiveness stereotype, physically attractive people may be perceived as good in other ways. Most people seek partners with matching levels of attractiveness. Physical attractiveness may also be matched with other qualities like self-esteem, money, or talent. Other qualities affecting attraction are personal qualities like dominance and competence. We are more attracted to those who are similar to ourselves, especially in attitudes and values. Opposites do not appear to attract, although need complementarity may be a source of compatibility.

Once individuals interact, attraction is produced by expressing positive feelings, such as positive regard and reciprocal liking. We like people who like us, especially if they are selective but not hard (for us) to get. Interaction is better initiated by individuals who are socially skilled as good listeners. Good opening lines are those that are direct or innocuous, or ask open-ended questions. To be effective, compliments must be seen as genuine; compliments are more effective when they represent a "gain" in the flatterer's regard for the recipient.

Relationships develop through communication. One model of intimacy proposes that communication proceeds from initial contact to interaction and mutuality. Another explanation argues that partners must shift from an exchange basis to communality in order to achieve greater intimacy.

Selected Readings

Austrom, D. R. (1984). *The Consequences of Being Single*. New York: Peter Lang.

Berscheid, E. and E. H. Walster, (1978). *Interpersonal Attraction*, 2nd edition. Reading, MA: Addison-Wesley.

Burgess, R. L. and T. L. Huston, (Eds.). (1979). *Social Exchange in Developing Relationships*. New York: Academic Press.

Byrne, D. (1971). *The Attraction Paradigm*. New York: Academic Press.

Derlega, V. J. and A. L. Chaiken, (1975). *Sharing Intimacy: What We Reveal to Others and Why*. Englewood Cliffs, NJ: Prentice Hall.

Derlega, V. J. and B. A. Winstead, (Eds.). (1986). *Friendship and Social Interaction*. New York: Springer-Verlag.

Duck, S. (1983). *Friends, for Life*. New York: St. Martin's Press.

Duck, S. and D. Perlman, (Eds.). (1985). *Understanding Personal Relationships*. London: Sage.

Hatfield, E. and S. Sprecher, (1986). *Mirror, mirror... The Importance of Looks in Everyday Life*. Albany: State University of New York Press.

Hendrick, C. and S. Hendrick, (1983). *Liking, Loving and Relating*. Monterey, CA: Brooks/Cole.

Huston, T. L. (Ed.). (1974). *Foundations of Interpersonal Attraction*. New York: Academic Press.

Jones, E. E. and C. B. Wortman. (1973). *Ingratiation: An Attributional Approach*. Morristown, NJ: General Learning Press.

Kelley, H. H. (1979). *Personal Relationships: Their Structures and Processes*. Hillsdale, NJ: Erlbaum.

Marsh, P. (Ed.). (1988). *Eye to Eye: How People Interact*. Topsfield, MA: Salem House.

Peplau, L. A. and D. Perlman, (Eds.). *Loneliness: A Sourcebook of Current Theory*. New York: Wiley-Interscience.

Rubin, Z. (1973). *Liking and Loving: An Invitation to Social Psychology.* New York: Holt, Rinehart and Winston.

Rubin, Z. (1980). *Children's Friendships.* Cambridge, MA: Harvard University Press.

Sternberg, R. J. and M. Barnes, (Eds.). (1988). *The Psychology of Love.* New Haven, CT: Yale University Press.

16

Close Relationships

*P*ersonal relationships are based on more than interpersonal attraction. They are built of interactions and communication, change over time, and involve unique processes and experiences, not merely the combined actions of two partners. Most personal relationships may be casual rather than close, such as acquaintanceships, most involvements with coworkers, and people who are familiar but not well known.

In distinction from other personal relationships, close relationships involve a high degree of interdependence. This interdependence takes the form of four interrelated experiences between the two partners: the two persons have strong impact on each other, frequent interaction, involving diverse activities over a long period of time. A close relationship, in sum, is an influential relationship.

Social psychologists' interest in close relationships begins with a consideration of the history, forms, and experience of love. We go on to review stages and processes in relationship development, including communication, maintenance, and conflict. Finally, we review what is known about the common experience of relationship termination, including the reasons for breakdown, the process itself, and strategies for coping.

LOVE

Love has not been easy to study. It is a popular topic but one laden with "common sense" and folk wisdom. Efforts to study scientifically the dynamics of love have met with political resistance as well as practical challenges like what to measure and whom to study. Despite these difficulties, researchers have provided insights into the history and importance of love and different forms and expressions of love.

The Idea of Love

Love is a new idea in the history of human relationships. Researchers have explored the evolution of this idea and its importance in modern relationships.

THE HISTORY OF LOVE

Evolutionary Origins. Familial love probably evolved because of its survival value. Pair bonds who loved or cared for each other were more likely to produce surviving offspring. Infants born to loving parents were more likely to survive and pass on to their descendants any genetic basis for such feelngs. Similarly, love within the clan and tribe strengthened early humans' ability to combat the elements and cooperate to hunt and gather. As human communities grew larger and became more formally organized, the expression and forms of love seem to have adapted to reflect these changes.

Romantic Love. For most of history and most civilizations, marriage has been regarded as an important alliance based on family and economic responsibility. The idea of marriage as a love match only developed late in the Western world. In the late twelfth century, troubadours carried new songs into France and England by way of Moorish Spain and the Crusades in the Middle East. Their stories blended Western ideas about partnership and Christian idealism with Eastern concepts of consciousness and love. The result was a hybrid ideal of love independent of mating, marriage, or physical expression—a higher love that we call "romantic" because of its celebration in romance language and song.

The idea of basing an important union like marriage and family on essentially transient emotions was slowly popularized in Western Europe. Blended with ideas of liberty and personal freedom, it flourished in early America. The modern result is a popular (though not universal) conviction that love is the single most important basis for mate selection.

THE IMPORTANCE OF LOVE

Love in various forms undoubtedly is the basis for many friendships, although women are more likely to use the word "love" in describing their same-gender friendships than are men. The importance of love to many relationships researchers is probably its influence in mate selection: most heterosexuals people today cite love as the most important factor in deciding whether and whom to marry. (Research on homosexual relationships indicates similar patterns for commitment decisions, although homosexual couples in most places cannot legally marry). Men (who have traditionally had more affluence and thus more choosing power) have valued love more than women. As women have gained independence and power in comparison with men, however, they are increasingly naming love—rather than, for example, financial security—as the critical element in planning marriage.

Typologies of Love

Several theories explain the difference between love and liking, different basic styles of love, and the essential components of love in its many forms.

FRIENDSHIP AND LOVE

Several theories have explained love by distinguishing it from liking or the less emotional positive regard we feel for friends. In contrast, these models seek to identify the ideas and feelings that make love a matter of intense passion or arousal.

Rubin's Attitude Theory. Social psychologist Zick Rubin distinguished between love and liking as two different attitudes. In Rubin's attitude theory, love is distinguished by three components: *attachment* (e.g., need to be together), *intimacy* (in communication), and *caring* (e.g, making the person's welfare a high priority). In contrast, liking is characterized by feelings of affection (a warm positive regard) and respect (positive evaluation on the basis of talent or status), and assessments that another person is very similar to oneself. Rubin constructed scales of both attitudes and confirmed that attitudes predicted behavior: subjects who scored high in love made more eye contact and stood or sat closer to their partners. Other research confirmed that, for men, love but not liking scores were related to feelings of sexual arousal.

Companionate versus Passionate Love. Researchers Ellen Berscheid and Elaine Hatfield have distinguished between calm companionate love and more arousing passionate love. *Passionate* or *romantic love* is characterized by an intense longing for union with one's partner. It is intense but short-lived, and involves both positive emotions like euphoria and negative experiences like conflict, jealousy, and insecurity.

In contrast, *companionate* or *compassionate love* is the deep, lasting, affectionate attachment of two people. According to Berscheid and Hatfield, love that begins as intense passion eventually subsides into a calmer but more enduring companionship.

COMPONENTS OF LOVE

Several theorists have preferred to identify the essential components of different kinds of love, including characteristic sets of ideas, feelings, and behaviors.

Rubin's Love Scale. Zick Rubin's theory of love as an attitude (above) proposes that love's essential components are attachment, intimacy, and caring. A reanalysis of Rubin's love scale led theorist Harold Kelley to conclude that love includes four components: caring, needing, trust, and tolerance for the other's faults. Kelley's subjects identified first caring and then needing as the most important of these.

Davis's Cluster Model. According to theorist Keith Davis, love has many qualities in common with close friendship: trust, companionship, acceptance, respect, helping, confiding, understanding, and spontaneity. In addition to this "friendship" base, love has two more sets of experiences: the "passion cluster" and the "caring cluster." The passion cluster includes fascination, exclusivity, and sexual desire. The caring cluster includes selfless giving and acting as the other's advocate or champion. Other research has supported the importance—especially to lovers—of the caring cluster in particular; subjects often rate passion as more peripheral to lasting intimacy.

Love as Emotional Expression. Another explanation of love is based on Schachter's two-factor theory of emotion. In this view, passionate love involves three sets of conditions:

1. The presence of a stimulus person with the appropriate characteristics;

2. A cultural background supporting the experience of passionate love; and

3. The emotional experience of love, including physiological arousal plus a label interpreting it as "love."

For example, if you live in a culture (e.g., the modern United States) that supports the idea of love, and you encounter an individual who is the right age and appearance to be attractive to you, you will likely interpret ongoing arousal as due to your love for this person. In less romantic terms, love is a product of learned beliefs, situational cues, and mislabeled arousal.

Sternberg's Triarchic Theory. Yale psychologist Robert Sternberg has proposed that love is composed of one or more of three basic components: intimacy, passion, and commitment. Combinations of these components yield different experiences or kinds of love, as follows:

Intimacy =	*Liking*
Passion =	*Infatuation*
Commitment =	*Empty Love*
Intimacy + Passion =	*Romantic Love*
Intimacy + Commitment =	*Companionate Love*
Passion + Commitment =	*Fatuous Love*
Intimacy+ Passion+ Commitment =	*Consummate Love*

Other research argues that commitment is not an integral aspect of love, although it is important in certain kinds of relationship development.

STYLES OF LOVE

Sternberg's triarchic or triangular theory bridges discussions of the components of love and the different forms or styles of love. Sternberg explains different forms as the result of different combinations of components. Two other theories, related to each other, argue that there are different *kinds* of love, which can blend to form distinctive experiences for different individuals or couples.

Colors of Love. Researcher John Alan Lee has identified six styles or "colors" of love, listing them both by their ancient Greek labels and modern terminology:

Eros = Romantic or passionate love

Agape = Altruism or brotherly love

Ludus = Playful or flirtatious love

Mania = Possessive or obsessive love

Storge = Companionate love

Pragma = Practical love

Primary and Secondary Styles of Love. Lee's survey findings were followed up by researchers Clyde Hendrick and Susan Hendrick, who propose that three styles are primary: Eros, Ludus, and Storge. The other three are combinations of two primary "colors": Storge + Eros = Agape; Eros + Ludus = Mania; and Ludus + Storge = Pragma. Early research suggests that there are gender differences in instances of these styles: men emphasize the playful, emotional experience of love, whereas women are more concerned with friendship and practical considerations. These findings are consistent with evolutionary explanations of love in mate selection.

LOVE AND SEXUALITY

It may seem ironic that so much research on love does not appear to mention sexual behavior. Is sex not essential to the experience of passionate or romantic love?

Sexual Arousal and Love. Psychoanalytic theory argued that love develops only if sexual desire is thwarted and must be delayed or rechanneled. A more acceptable theory is that sexual arousal is the kind of arousal most commonly mislabeled as love. Even more simply, drawing on reinforcement or reward theories of attraction, insofar as sexual interaction is pleasurable, one will develop strong positive feelings for one's sexual partner.

Sexual Behavior. Prior to the more permissive 1960s and 1970s, sexual contact and intercourse were considered more symbolic of becoming "a couple" than has been true since. Although sexual attitudes in the late twentieth century are more permissive than restrictive, there is evidence since the early 1980s that sexual attitudes and behavior are becoming more conservative. This may be due especially to recognition of the dangers of sexually transmitted diseases like Acquired Immune Deficiency Syndrome (AIDS), genital herpes, gonorrhea, and chlamydia. Researchers speculate that romantic feelings qualified by guilt and fear are somewhat less likely to lead automatically to sexual interaction.

Sexual Preference. Most research on close relationships examines heterosexual relationships, which are more numerous and more conveniently studied. A small but growing number of studies examines homosexual relationships, both gay male and lesbian samples, or includes homosexual individuals and couples in their larger subject populations. Results are few and preliminary but in most important ways findings show no differences from heterosexual patterns of thought, feeling, or behavior. Sexual preference or orientation does not appear to be a significant influence on the experiences of love or the development of intimacy and communication in close relationships. Also, where they have been identified, gender differences appear to be stronger than differences between homosexual and heterosexual orientation. Readers and critical consumers should consider how research biases—studying heterosexual but not homosexual relationships, marital rather than nonmarital partnerships, and so on—affect the meaning and relevance of researchers' findings.

RELATIONSHIP DEVELOPMENT

While many consider love to be the beginning of close relationship development, it is not the mainstay. Theories instead focus on the importance of communication, maintenance strategies, and the management of conflict as critical in determining whether and how relationships will continue.

Theories of Relationship

Two theories of relating that provide an overview of the many processes involved are social penetration theory and relatedness theory.

SOCIAL PENETRATION THEORY

According to theorists Irwin Altman and Dalmas Taylor, close relationships involve a process of social penetration, communication at progressively deeper levels of intimacy. Communication involves self-disclosure, the process of revealing oneself to each other.

Breadth and Depth. Self-disclosed communications involve two dimensions: depth and breadth. Breadth refers to the number of different aspects of oneself that can be revealed in the relationship. For example, being able to talk only about sports would indicate a narrow range, while being able to discuss one's work, family, political opinions, and literary tastes would characterize a broad pattern of self-disclosure.

Depth refers to the level of intimacy attained in self-disclosure. Talking at a safe or superficial level indicates a shallow pattern, while revealing personal hopes and fears is a much deeper level of intimacy.

Stages of Social Penetration. Self-disclosure proceeds in a sequence, as interactions gradually become broader and deeper. Altman and Taylor identify four stages in social penetration:

1. In *orientation,* communication is cautious and superficial.

2. *Exploratory affective exchange* involves friendly but not intimate conversation; most personal relationships proceed no farther.

3. *Affective exchange* characterizes people who see each other frequently and have an extensive shared history.

4. *Stable exchange*, in which feelings are accurately anticipated and interpreted, is achieved by very few relationships.

RELATEDNESS THEORY

George Levinger extended his earlier theory of intimacy development (see chapter 15) to encompass a broad sequence of relationship events, summarized as the ABCDE model. In this model, the stages proceed as follows:

A = *Awareness*: One is acquainted with the other person; this stage may last indefinitely.

B = *Buildup:* Two people become increasingly interdependent, considering how compatible versus incompatible they are.

C = *Continuation*: The relationship becomes committed and solidified.

D = *Deterioration*: In some cases, the connections between partners decline.

E = *Ending*: Partners are divided by separation or death.

Each stage acts as a successive "filter," so that fewer relationships proceed from one stage to the next—most never go beyond Stage A, and those that do usually end in Stage B.

Communication

The most central processes in relationship development involve communication: the sending and receiving of messages. Research on relationship communication has examined the process of self-disclosure, how communicators handle bad news, and the role of communication in relationship success.

SELF-DISCLOSURE

In personal relationships, the essential task of communication is self-disclosure, a term coined by the late therapist Sidney Jourard. Over interactions, partners reveal more and more about themselves to each other. It is important that self-disclosure be appropriate: if a stranger tells you something personal, for example, it will probably offend or repulse you rather than attract you. It is also important that relationship partners respond at the same progressive level, a tendency called *disclosure reciprocity*. For example, if you confide something extremely personal about yourself to a friend, he or she will probably respond by reciprocating, confiding something of similar depth. In contrast, if you reveal something personal only to have your confidant respond superficially, the exchange will be uneven and you may feel rebuffed.

COMMUNICATING BAD NEWS

As people get close to each other, the information they give each other has greater impact. Criticism from a close friend, for example, will be more meaningful and perhaps more painful than criticism from someone who barely knows you. Research indicates that it is difficult for communicators to transmit bad news, since the recipient's reaction will likely be negative. This tendency is called the *mum effect* because possessors of bad news try to "keep mum." The mum effect occurs because the sender wants a positive, not negative, response from the listener. When senders can remain anonymous, they are less likely to keep mum.

COMMUNICATION DEFICIT

Satisfactory relationships involve different kinds of communication from unsatisfactory ones. Researcher John Gottman has found that distressed couples suffer from a *communication deficit,* neither sending nor receiving messages accurately in their interactions.

Negative Affect Reciprocity. During conflict, unhappy couples communicate in a different way—rather than about different issues—from happier couples. Specifically, unhappy couples engage in *negative affect* *reciprocity,* responding to expressions of bad feelings with further bad feelings.

For example, one partner might say, "You made me feel bad when you criticized me in front of your mother." To reciprocate the negative affect, the other might respond, "It's your fault for being too sensitive." Instead of identifying and resolving a problem, their communication has gotten stuck in reciprocating negative feelings. In contrast, happy couples have the ability to separate affect from issues, and to respond to negative affect with an acknowledging or positive response. For example, in response to the complaint above, the partner could say, "I'm sorry you felt bad. Are you worried about my mother's opinion?" This response invites a discussion rather than an argument or fight.

Relationship Awareness. Successful relationship communication also involves an ability to discuss the relationship itself, called *relationship awareness*. This ability makes it possible to identify problems before they escalate. For example, if one partner asks the other, "Is anything wrong?", and a relationship-aware reply would be, "Yes, I'm worried that we don't spend enough time together lately." If instead the reply is, "No, I guess not," the problem will likely only worsen, and the silent partner's worries will grow. Researchers have found gender differences in relationship awareness: in heterosexual relationships, women are more relationship-aware than men; women are also more likely to be the "relationship advocate," considering what is best for the relationship as well as for either partner. These differences seem to be learned; men who develop a good relationship "vocabulary" are better able to communicate effectively.

Maintenance

Research comparing two contrasting clichés—"Absence makes the heart grow fonder" and "Out of sight, out of mind"—concludes that which one is true depends on *commitment*. If partners have made a commitment before being separated by distance, then absence seems to strengthen their resolve to survive the interruption. However, if a relationship is not committed when partners are separated, their divergent paths are likely to take them farther apart. Such research emphasizes the importance of commitment in relationship maintenance. Other research has identified factors affecting relationship satisfaction.

COMMITMENT

Commitment is a pledge to a future course of action. In a relationship, commitment is a person's intention to maintain the relationship. For a commitment to be effective, it should involve stated intentions. These may be ritualized in a public contract, such as a marriage ceremony before friends and relatives. It must also be freely entered; coercion brings compliance, but not commitment.

EXCHANGE THEORY

Researchers John Thibaut, Harold Kelley, and George Homans applied an economic theory of exchange to relationships, and identified three determinants of relationship maintenance: outcomes, comparison level, and alternatives. Your *outcomes* are the rewards minus the costs of being in the relationship. Your *comparison level* is the standard you have set for what you should *expect* from a relationship. Your *alternatives* are other relationships you could have if you were not engaged in this one. These factors combine to determine your satisfaction with the relationship and your likelihood of maintaining it.

Satisfaction. If your outcomes exceed your comparison level, you will generally be satisfied with the relationship. For example, if your past experiences and observations of other couples lead you to conclude that your relationship gives you as much or more than you had expected, you will be satisfied.

Go or Stay? If your outcomes do not live up to your standards (comparison level), however, you will be dissatisfied with the relationship. Will you abandon it? That depends—on what your alternatives are. If there are alternative partners and arrangements you can access, you will probably leave and pursue those. However, if you have no alternatives, you will probably stay. Thus a relationship can be "maintained" simply because, though dissatisfied, partners have no alternatives: they have nowhere else to go, and no one to go to. This is "maintenance" only in a passive sense; partners may only be waiting for something better to come along, without working to communicate or nurture their own relationship.

Conflict

Conflict is inevitable in relationships, since partners are different people and their plans and motives will sometimes clash. But conflict does not have to be terminal. Researchers have identified common sources of interpersonal conflict, and discovered differences between relationships that do and do not survive it.

CAUSES OF INTERPERSONAL CONFLICT

Causes of conflict range from intimacy processes to specific issues like money and family alliances.

Relationship Development. Processes like communication and cohesiveness can be sources of conflict. Couples who communicate poorly or who do not function as a unit are more likely to experience conflict. For example, if partners have separate interests and social lives, they may fail to consider joint goals and make selfish rather than mutual decisions.

Rules and Chores. A major source of conflict is inequity. Inequity results when partners' outcomes are not proportional to their inputs. For example, if a woman does all the household chores and child care work in a relationship, but reaps the same benefits as her husband who appears to be putting in less effort, she will feel cheated and angry. This is why household chores and division of labor are frequent issues in unhappy relationships: partners' relative costs and benefits determine whether the relationship is fair or not.

Gender Differences. Some issues and behaviors upset both genders: unfaithfulness, physical abuse, and verbal abuse. Others are interpreted differently by men and women. In heterosexual relationships, women are more upset when men force sex, ignore their opinions, disguise their own feelings, smoke or drink too much, neglect, tease, or behave rudely. Men are more upset when women are sexually rejecting or unresponsive, moody, or self-absorbed. Some researchers suggest that these "complaint pattern" differences are related to the evolution of gender roles. Others counter that such differences are the result of learned gender roles and heterosexual expectations.

Jealousy. Jealousy is the experience of feeling your relationship is threatened. Jealousy varies across individuals and cultures: it is a learned reaction based on self-esteem, possessiveness, and cultural values. It is most prevalent in cultures that value sexual exclusivity in relationships, and where partners are considered "possessions." People are more likely to feel jealous if they are low in self-esteem or have relatively less power in their relationships.

Researchers have identified some gender differences in jealousy. When threatened, men are more likely to feel angry, blame another person (the partner or the rival), and respond by competing or making their partners jealous. Women are more likely to feel depressed, blame themselves (e.g., for being inadequate), and respond by trying to strengthen the relationship against further threats.

OVERCOMING CONFLICT

Studies of successful and unsuccessful relationships have identified several factors that appear to enhance relationship maintenance.

Friendship. Partners are more likely to stay together if they consider each other close or best friends, like and respect each other.

Commitment. Relationships succeed when both partners value their commitment and want the relationship to last.

Similarity. Partners are more likely to stay together if they agree on values, goals, opinions, and relationship practices like sex and showing affection.

Positive Affect. Relationships last when they are rewarding and involve good feelings, including humor, interest, and pride in each other.

RELATIONSHIP TERMINATION

Why do some relationships fail to survive or last? Researchers have studied breakdown or dissolution—the process of ending—and breakup or termination—the final parting of the ways. In concluding this chapter we review some reasons for breakdown, the processes involved, and how people cope with such loss.

Reasons for Breakdown

While every relationship experiences conflict, not all conflict is terminal. Some conflict is built into the relationship from the start; other difficulties arise in the way partners communicate.

FATAL DIFFERENCES

In a longitudinal study conducted in the 1970s, Charles Hill, Zick Rubin, and L. Anne Peplau examined the fates of 231 dating couples. The 103 couples who had broken up two years later had differed from those who stayed together in important ways. In a couple that eventually broke up, partners were less similar to each other in age, intelligence, educational goals, and physical attractiveness. Moreover, those who eventually broke up were unevenly involved: one partner valued the relationship significantly more than the other.

NEGATIVE EXCHANGE

Couples who break up also appear to handle conflict less effectively than those who stay together. Unhappy couples exchange more negative affect (see negative affect reciprocity, above). They also have more negative interactions and more unpleasant emotions in general than maintaining couples. Finally, unhappy couples are more likely to reveal a negative attributional style: they blame their partners for unpleasant experiences, but do not give them credit for good ones. The more a couple focuses on negative aspects of their relationship, the more likely they are eventually to break up.

RESPONDING TO DISSATISFACTION

Relationship termination—leaving one's partner and ending the relationship—is usually only one option for a dissatisfied partner.

Active versus Passive Responses. Researcher Caryl Rusbult and her colleagues have identified four responses people may make to dissatisfaction in a relationship:

1. *Loyalty:* They may passively hope things will improve.

2. *Neglect:* They may passively allow things to become worse.

3. *Voice:* They may actively express their concerns and make changes to improve the relationship.

4. Exit: They may actively take steps to leave the relationship.

Responding to Inequity. Elaine Hatfield and her colleagues have identified four ways a person can respond to the discovery that a relationship is inequitable:

1. *Changing outcomes:* If your outcomes are low relative to your inputs, you can make greater demands to increase them.

2. *Changing inputs:* Alternatively, you can reduce your investments, so your outcomes are more just.

3. *Changing perceptions:* You may adjust your perceptions and attributions, to convince yourself that your outcomes are actually just.

4. *Exit the relationship:* If outcomes, inputs, and perceptions cannot be changed, you will only relieve inequity by leaving the relationship.

In both Rusbult's and Hatfield's models, leaving is a last-resort response to dissatisfaction with the relationship.

The Dissolution Process

No two experiences of breakdown are the same. Theorists have suggested different models and patterns dissolution may follow.

CHANGES IN INTIMACY

Sociologist Murray Davis likens the end of a relationship to the death of intimacy. Such endings may be either gradual losses or traumatic disruptions.

Passing Away. Over time, intimacy between partners may decline imperceptibly, as a result of three factors: a new intimate who takes priority in one partner's affections; the strain of long-distance separation; or the ageing of each partner over time. Under these influences, partners lessen their interdependence, and eventually part ways. The ending is neither discussed nor mourned.

Sudden Death. Davis says there are three ways a relationship may end suddenly: two-sided ambivalence, both partners alternately clinging and rejecting; one-sided withdrawal, one partner rejecting the other's efforts to maintain; and destruction of the essential connection between partners, when events or behaviors violate the rules of intimacy. "Sudden death" endings involve upheaval and interaction. Partners engage in *termination talk* including a possible *farewell address*. Their post-separation status may be discussed before they part ways.

DUCK'S FOUR-PHASE THEORY

Researcher Steve Duck has proposed a four-phase model of relationship dissolution, identifying the thoughts, feelings, and behaviors that accompany breakdown:

1. In the *intrapsychic phase,* one partner experiences dissatisfaction and contemplates breakup, considering the costs and benefits of leaving.

2. The *dyadic phase* begins when the dissatisfied partner expresses these considerations to the other. They may negotiate, reconcile, or agree to part.

3. In the *social phase,* the partners discuss their impending breakup with members of the social network, and distribute their accounts of events and causes.

4. Finally, in the *grave-dressing phase,* retrospective accounts are reviewed and ex-partners continue separate lives.

Coping with Loss

Whether one leaves a relationship or is left behind, relationship loss can be emotionally devastating. In the wake of relationship breakup, individuals confront several challenges. Other researchers have examined the social consequences of ended and blended relationships.

MARITAL SEPARATION

Sociologist Robert Weiss observes that newly-separated individuals experience several changes in affect, thought, and behavior.

Emotional Consequences. The most common emotional consequence of separation is depression. Individuals become saddened, lethargic, and preoccupied with negative thoughts. Some also experience short-lived euphoria. The newly-separated also experience both social loneliness (e.g., a sense of not belonging in the community anymore) and emotional loneliness (e.g., missing the intimate partner).

Cognitive Responses. The newly-separated may engage in *obsessive review,* a compulsive cognitive search for understanding what happened and why. The individual also develops an *account,* a story explaining the relationship, the partners, and their roles in the breakup.

Behavioral Change. After a relationship has ended, former partners encounter changed circumstances. Men may suffer emotionally because they have no outlets for affective expression without their partners. Women usually suffer financially. The person who initiated the breakup may adjust more quickly than the one who was rejected. Social life, family structure, and socioeconomic status may all change in the wake of termination.

OUTCOMES OF LOSS

Children and Divorce. Despite popular contentions that marriages should be kept intact "for the sake of the children," research suggests that the children of divorce may suffer less than children of intact but unhappy marriages. Children from divorced homes show more disrupted behavior during the first year after the divorce, although these decrease in subsequent years.

Blended Families. Most survivors of breakups seek new relationships. Most divorced persons remarry, and it is likely that most nonmarital breakups do not deter individuals from establishing new partnerships. As survivors of marital breakups remarry, they establish *blended families*, including stepparents and step-siblings. The challenges to blended families include the fact that most members have sustained an important loss (e.g., the death or divorce of parents or spouses), reduced access to non-resident parents, new relationships and new roles. These stresses can create extreme conflict in remarried households.

Studies of successful blended families have identified several factors in family well-being: a good relationship between spouses; equitable contributions to childcare, shared power and decision-making, good relationships with children, and little negative affect about ex-spouses. In such arrangements the benefits outweigh the costs, and all members are motivated to maintain the relationship.

Close relationships involve long-term, affective, interdependent connections between partners. Love is an important part of close relationships. Love may have its evolutionary origins in promoting the survival of pairs and their offspring. The idea of romantic love originated with a medieval blending of Eastern ideas of love with Western mate-selection practices. Love has increased in importance, and most people consider it essential to a commitment.

Different theories of love distinguish it from liking and explain its different forms. In Rubin's theory, love is an attitude involving attachment, intimacy and caring. Berscheid and Hatfield distinguish between passionate and companionate love. Kelley's analysis of Rubin's love scale identified its components as caring, needing, trust, and tolerance. In Davis's model, love is friendship plus a passion cluster and a caring cluster of feelings. Love may be a misattribution of emotional arousal influenced by cultural values. In Sternberg's triarchic theory, different expressions of love are combined from passion, intimacy, and commitment.

Lee's typology identifies six colors of love: eros (romantic love), ludus (game-playing), mania (possessive love), agape (selfless love), storge (friendship), and pragma (practical love). Hendrick and Hendrick have argued that eros, ludus, and storge are primary styles, while agape, mania, pragma are secondary hybrids of them. Love also interacts with sexual arousal, although the experience of love is essentially similar for all sexual orientations.

Social penetration theory depicts intimacy as a process of self-disclosure involving both breadth and depth. Relatedness theory characterizes intimacy as developing in stages, from awareness to buildup and continuation, and sometimes to deterioration and ending. Communication involves self-disclosure, although partners may keep mum about bad news. Unhappy couples suffer from communication deficit, negative affect reciprocity, and inadequate relationship awareness.

Relationship maintenance depends on commitment. Exchange theory defines satisfaction as the result when outcomes exceed partners' comparison levels. Dissatisfied partners will leave if they can identify alternative partners. Maintenance also depends on handling conflict. Most relationships experience some conflict, as a result of relationship development, rules and chores, gender-specific complaints, and jealousy. Couples who overcome conflict and maintain successfully are those strong in friendship, commitment, similarity, and positive affect.

Relationships may break down because of fatal differences between the partners, or negative exchanges of communication. Rusbult's theory states that partners may respond to dissatisfaction with loyalty, neglect, voice, or exit. In Hatfield's theory, responses to inequity include changing outcomes, changing inputs, changing perceptions, or exiting. Leaving is usually the last-resort response to a conflicted relationship.

Dissolution may involve changes in intimacy, either a gradual passing away or a sudden death. In Duck's theory, the four phases of dissolution are intrapsychic, dyadic, social, and grave-dressing. Coping with relationship loss involves emotional change and distress. Newly-separated individuals normally experience depression, euphoria, obsessive review, and loneliness. They develop accounts to explain and make sense of their loss. Children of divorce suffer disruption and difficulty that appears to decrease over time. Most survivors of breakup form new relationships. While blended families face unique challenges and stressors, they can survive if the benefits of their union outweigh the costs.

Selected Readings

Aron, A. and E. Aron, (1986). *Love and the Expansion of Self*. New York: Hemisphere Publishing Corporation.

Bellah, R. N., R. Madsen, W. M. Sullivan, A. Swidler, and S. M. Tipton, (1985). *Habits of the Heart: Individualism and Commitment in American Life*. New York: Harper and Row.

Brehm, S. S. (1991). *Intimate Relationships*, 2nd edition. New York: Random House.

Burnett, R., P. McGhee, and D. D. Clarke, (Eds.). (1987). *Accounting for Relationships*. New York: Methuen.

Davis, M. S. (1973). *Intimate Relations*. New York: The Free Press.

Duck, S. (Ed.). (1982). *Personal Relationships 4: Dissolving Personal Relationships*. London: Academic Press.

Duck, S. (1986). *Human Relationships*. Beverly Hills: Sage.

Duck, S. (1988). *Relating to Others.*. Chicago: Dorsey Press.

Gilmour, R. and S. Duck, (Eds.). (1986). *The Emerging Field of Personal Relationships*. Hillsdale, NJ: Erlbaum.

Harvey, J. H., A. L. Weber, and T. L. Orbuch,(1990). *Interpersonal Accounts: A Social Psychological Perspective*. Cambridge, MA: Basil Blackwell.

Hendrick, C. (Ed.). (1989). *Close Relationships*. Newbury Park, CA: Sage.

Hojat, M. and R. Crandall, (1989). *Loneliness: Theory, Research, and Applications*. Newbury Park, CA: Sage.

Kelley, H. H., E. Berscheid, A. Christensen, J. H. Harvey, T. L. Huston, G. Levinger, E. McClintock, L. A. Peplau, and D. R. Peterson, (1983). *Close Relationships*. New York: W. H. Freeman.

Rando, T. A. (1988). *Grieving: How to Go on Living When Someone You Love Dies*. Lexington, MA: Lexington Books.

Levinger, G. and H. L. Raush, (Eds.). (1977). *Close Relationships: Perspectives on the Meaning of Intimacy*. Amherst: University of Massachusetts Press.

Levinger, G. and O. C. Moles, (Eds.). (1979). *Divorce and Separation*. New York: Basic Books.

Perlman, D. S. and S. Duck, (Eds.). *Intimate Relationships: Development, Dynamics, and Deterioration*. Beverly Hills, CA: Sage.

Schwartz, G. and D. Merten, (1980). *Love and Commitment*. Beverly Hills, CA: Sage.

Sternberg, R. J. (1987). *The Triangle of Love: Intimacy, Passion, Commitment*. New York: Basic Books.

Tennov, D. (1979). *Love and Limerence: The Experience of Being in Love*. New York: Stein and Day.

Wallerstein, J . S. and J. B. Kelly, (1980). *Surviving the Breakup: How Children and Parents Cope with Divorce. New York: Basic Books*.

Weiss, R. S. (1975). *Marital Separation*. New York: Basic Books.

17

Prosocial Behavior

*O*ne thing we expect in personal relationships is help: favors, assistance, compatible goals, and even rescue. Help is not necessarily expected outside of personal relationships. On one hand, strangers are not obligated to assist each other. On the other hand, we are surprised when people who clearly need help do not receive it. Is refusal to help a sensible reaction to a frightening and complex social world? Or does it signify the decline of civilization? Social psychologists have devoted significant effort to understanding—and finding ways to increase—helping behavior.

Helping behavior is sometimes described as altruistic, motivated by selfless concern for others (from the Latin alter, "other"). But it is difficult to determine whether a helpful action is altruistic or more practically motivated. For this reason, social psychologists refer instead to prosocial behavior, any positive action toward others with nonobvious benefits for the helper. Determining whether prosocial behavior is altruistic may be less important than devising strategies for increasing people's helpfulness in general.

This chapter considers prosocial behavior from the point of view of the helper, reviewing patterns in both helping and not helping, and the recipient.

HELPING OTHERS

Studies of prosocial behavior have examined motives for helping others, how helping is learned, whether there is a "helpful type" of person, and how the recipient and the situation influence the helper's actions.

Motives for Helping

Helping behavior may be motivated by inherited predispositions, social norms, and the rules of social exchange.

SOCIOBIOLOGICAL THEORIES

Sociobiologists explain social behavior in terms of inherited biological influences. Since helping behavior is important to species survival, the tendency to help may be genetically programmed into individuals.

Kin Selection. According to sociobiologists, we favor those who have genes in common with us, a tendency called *kin selection*. Thus we should be most willing to help those who are relatives. Research confirms that people are selective in helping victims of disasters, assisting family members first, friends and neighbors second, and strangers last. Even though we do not share genes with non-kin friends, we are similar to them (similarity is an important basis for attraction and intimacy; see chapter 15).

Reciprocal Protection. Another built-in motive for helping is to win helping in return. To help someone is to obligate that person to help you when possible. Thus helping someone else is an investment in your own future.

Critiquing Sociobiology. One problem with sociobiological explanations for helping is the paradox of self-sacrifice. If you were to give your life to another, who would inherit your self-sacrificing tendencies? It would seem that extreme helping actually defeats rather than promotes gene survival. Sociobiologists counter this criticism by pointing out that self-sacrifice does not necessarily obliterate the genes that create it. A parent, for example, is more likely to sacrifice himself or herself for the child than for someone else. This protects the survival of both the child and the helpful genes.

Sociobiology has been influential because it explains helping among unlikely populations, like insects and slime molds. The inclination to help may be so important to a species that the tendency is built into enough individual members to guarantee the survival of the rest.

NORMS

Two social norms motivate helping behavior: reciprocity and social responsibility.

Reciprocity. The norm of reciprocity maintains that we should help those who have helped us. This norm affects us especially in dealing with others of the same status. When we have received assistance that is clearly not motivated by pity, we are more likely to form an intention to return the favor. In fact, if we cannot respond in kind, we may feel slighted, inferior, or angry.

Social Responsibility. If we only helped those who could pay us back, truly needy people would never benefit from our assistance. Instead, the social responsibility norm urges us to help those who *need* help, regardless of how likely they are to reciprocate. In acting on this norm, we are influenced by our attributions about the recipient's deservingness. For example, if you conclude that the problem is the victim's fault, you will be less inclined to help. In other words, if people have chosen their problems, we do not feel obligated to help; but if they are "innocent" victims, we are responsible for offering assistance.

SOCIAL EXCHANGE

Helping another involves obvious costs: time, money, even personal risk. Social exchange theorists argue that helping occurs because it involves benefits to the helper that outweigh the costs.

Nonobvious Benefits. For example, if a volunteer for a charity asks you for a donation, what will you do? The costs include the time you must take to stop and make a donation, as well as the money you donate. But if you decide that the cause is one you support and your donation will make you feel good, the advantages of donating will outweigh its liabilities. In the view of social exchange, no helpful act is truly altruistic, since everyone acts to achieve some goal or reward: boosting self-esteem, assuaging guilt, or being able to "live with oneself." Such rewards may not be obvious but can be strongly motivating.

Concern and Empathy. It is difficult to watch someone suffer, whether a friend or a stranger. The need of a stranger may cause us to experience *distress,* while that of a close friend or partner arouses *empathy.* In response to distress, we may offer help—that will reduce the sufferer's need, and thus our distress—or we may simply walk away; either way we reduce our pain. But empathy is focused on the *other's* pain; the only way to reduce our shared unhappiness is to offer help.

Learning to Help

Helpful behavior is learned in the course of socialization, either through direct reinforcement or observing others.

REINFORCEMENT

The expectation that helping behavior can be reinforced is part of every "please" and "thank you." Words of gratitude indicate social approval and appreciation for favors and assistance. Researchers confirm that positive reinforcement for one helpful act can increase helpers' willingness to help again. Children are encouraged to help in return for praise, thanks, and being appreciated as heroes and good citizens.

MODELING

Helping can be learned by observing competent models. Many research studies confirm that even televised models are effective in increasing children's helpful behavior. Seeing others offer help may also have a *priming effect,* reminding the viewer of the possible benefits of helping.

The Helper

Who is likely to offer help? While research favors the power of situations rather than personality, some aspects of the helper have been identified as influential.

MOODS AND EMOTIONS

Some psychological states can increase a person's helpfulness in different conditions.

Empathy. Observers who feel or develop empathy—a feeling of identifying with another's feelings—for a victim are more likely to offer help. Researchers have found that simply instructing a subject to imagine how a victim must be *feeling*—rather than watching the victim's behavior—can increase watchers' desire to help.

Guilt. Or she may do a "good deed" to restore good feelings or self-esteem. Researchers have found that a subject blamed by a bystander for an accident (breaking a camera) is more likely to offer help to an unrelated bystander needing assistance.

Bad Moods. In a similar strategy to guilt relief, people in a bad mood might undertake to help others in an effort to cancel or elevate their own feelings. Whether a bad mood will increase or decrease helpfulness depends on the difficulty of help required. If the help needed is easy to give and promises to be rewarding, the unhappy person is likely to help. But if the response seems difficult and may not be rewarding, help will not be forthcoming. Attributions about one's mood are also important: a person will help only if he or she feels the mood can be changed, and that helping will help to change it.

Good Moods. Research findings are consistent in confirming that happy people do helpful things. Research studies have found helping increased by a wide variety of experiences that seemed to put potential helpers in a good mood: finding change in a public phone coin slot; receiving a gift of free stationery; and having access to sunshine. Even if the effects are short-lived, they are powerful enough to extend help to someone who needs it.

PERSONALITY

Most people are helpful some of the time; some are consistently more helpful, others consistently less so. It has been difficult to find stable personality traits that predict *consistent* helpfulness. Researchers have found helpfulness to be influenced by some traits, as well as by gender and background.

Helpful Traits. Researchers have identified *empathy* and *self-efficacy* as qualities that are correlated with general helpfulness. Empathetic people are more likely to suffer with the victim, gaining relief only by offering aid. Self-efficacious people are competent people, who may see the world in terms of skills and assistance they *can* offer.

Self-Monitoring. Recall from chapter 4 that self-monitoring is a tendency to monitor one's surroundings to judge how to behave. High self-monitors will also be more helpful if they think that others will approve of such behavior.

Gender Roles. Gender differences in helping appear to be related to gender roles. Men are more likely than women to help in high-risk situations or when technical skills (e.g., auto maintenance) are required. Women are more likely to help in "safe" but time-consuming and less visible capacities, like caring for children. Some researchers suggest that women may be more helpful in close relationships and men more helpful with strangers.

Background. People who grew up in small towns are more likely to help than people from big cities. People who currently live in rural areas are more likely to help than city dwellers. These distinctions are related not to region but to environmental conditions like stress, traffic, noise, and crime rates.

The Recipient

Some victims are more likely to receive help than others. Researchers have identified two important characteristics as gender and race.

GENDER

Women receive help more than men do. Linked with the finding (above) that men often offer more help, this may be a gender-role interaction: men are expected to offer help to women, women to ask it from men. Gender-role may also interact with the type of help required: motorists with car trouble were more likely to be offered assistance if they were women than if they were men (who "ought" to be able to fix their own cars).

RACE

Studies manipulating the race or apparent race of the person needing help show that Caucasians prefer to help Caucasians, but African-Americans are equally likely to help both races. Race and gender may interact, since some studies indicate that while women of both races are helped more than men, African-American men are least likely to be helped.

Reverse Discrimination. Some research has identified a *reverse discrimination effect*. Caucasians who did not wish to appear or think of themselves as prejudiced actually were more helpful to African-Americans than members of their own race. This reverse discrimination effect can be neutralized by giving the would-be helper an easier opportunity to show he or she is not prejudiced.

Situational Influences

Social psychologists have collected ample evidence that characteristics of the situation have an impact on helping. These include the presence of bystanders, modeling, and time.

BYSTANDERS

The presence of others reduces the likelihood that help will be offered. This contradicts a common-sense assumption that the more people who are available, the greater the chances at least one will help. Instead, the presence of others appears to have an inhibiting effect on the processes involved in helping others, especially in an emergency. The reasons for this *bystander effect* are discussed further below.

MODELING

People are more likely to help if they have recently observed someone else offering help. This may be a function of seeing "how it's done" or how easy it is; for example, people are more likely to donate blood after seeing someone else do it. Modeling may also illustrate a local norm for helping; shoppers are more likely to drop coins into a solicitor's container after seeing others do so first.

Disliked models are not emulated. When an unpopular sponsor endorses a cause, others are less likely to support it; if a disliked model refuses to help, observers are *more* likely to help. By doing the opposite of what the model advocates, observers are distancing themselves from him or her.

TIME

In a study by John Darley and C. Daniel Batson, seminary students were asked to plan a sermon on an assigned topic they would then record in another location. There were two independent variables. One was the assigned sermon topic: the Good Samaritan parable (about helping strangers in need) or career planning. The other was time: some subjects were asked to hurry to the recording studio, others were told to take their time. En route to the recording studio, each subject encountered a "man in need," who moaned and coughed. Who helped? Subjects were more likely to offer help if they had time to do so, regardless of whether they had recently contemplated the value of helping others.

Darley and Batson's findings illustrate the power of the situation: when we are caught up in our circumstances (e.g., on our way to an important appointment), we may be more influenced by circumstances than by our private aspirations and values. People who are in a hurry cannot pay attention to interruptions, including people who need their help.

NOT HELPING OTHERS

In the course of studying the factors that affect helping, researchers have discovered the conditions that lead us to be *less* helpful to others. These include decision processes involved in responding to emergencies, diffusion of responsibility, ambiguity, and cost-benefit analyses.

Responding to Emergencies

Emergencies are a special kind of opportunity to help. They are unexpected, we are unprepared for them, and they are more likely to involve strangers. Responding is a complex process of thought, feelings, and action, that is easily disrupted or inhibited.

THE DECISION TREE

Researchers John Darley and Bibb Latané have theorized that emergency intervention is the result of a series of decisions a bystander must make. Only an affirmative choice at each branch of this "decision tree" will result in taking action to intervene:

     1. Is the event noticed?

     2. Is the event interpreted as an emergency?

     3. Does the bystander feel responsible for intervening?

     4. Does the bystander know how to intervene?

     5. Does the bystander take action?

For each decision, if the answer is "no," the decision-making ceases and no help is given. If an answer is "yes," the bystander goes on to the next decision—until either ceasing or finally intervening.

The decision tree takes time to review. Darley and Latané have speculated that those who do not intervene may still be "deciding" whether and how to take action, rather than having determined not to offer help at all. People may be confused rather than intentionally unhelpful.

THE BYSTANDER EFFECT

Darley and Latané developed their model of the intervention decision tree in the course of studying the *bystander effect:* the tendency of individuals to be less responsive in a crisis when other bystanders are present. Darley and Latané and their colleagues have determined that, with others present, each decision in the tree is less likely to be answered affirmatively. The greater the number of other bystanders present, the greater the likelihood that each one will

     (1) fail to notice the event,

     (2) not interpret it as an emergency,

     (3) not feel responsible for intervening,

(4) not determine what to do, and ultimately

(5) not intervene.

One explanation for the bystander effect is social impact. As the number of other bystanders increases, the social impact of the bystanders is more influential in the behavior of any one of them. This social impact exceeds that of the crisis being observed, so that cognitive processes like decision-making are stalled or distracted.

Diffusion of Responsibility

Another explanation for the bystander effect is that responsibility for intervening is diffused or spread out among those present. For example, if you are one of only five people who witness an emergency, you are one-fifth responsible for taking action; but if you are one of 100 witnesses, you are only 1/100th responsible for intervening. This diffusion effect explains why rural settings are more helpful than urban ones: urban environments are more populous, and individuals already feel less responsible for taking any prosocial action.

Ambiguity

Another problem in deciding to intervene in emergencies is their ambiguity, or lack of clear definition.

AMBIGUITY INHIBITS HELPING

If you hear a high-pitched human scream, is it a cry for help? It could be a laugh, or a good-natured protest. What if it is not an emergency—and it is none of your business? The more ambiguous the circumstances, the less likely it is a bystander will interpret the event as an emergency, much less decide to offer help.

PLURALISTIC IGNORANCE

When a situation is ambiguous, bystanders may look to each other for social comparison. The hesitation and confusion of each person is multiplied and seems like a norm. This leads to *pluralistic ignorance,* interpretation of the group's nonaction as a recommendation not to act. For example, if you are in a group and you hear a loud noise, you may reflexively wonder out loud, "What was that?" Remember that the people nearby probably know as little as you do; do not interpret their answers or behaviors as necessarily better informed than yours.

AUDIENCE INHIBITION

If the situation is ambiguous, you cannot be sure how others would respond to your helpfulness. If the crisis is a false alarm, you may feel embarrassed to be "overreacting." You may hesitate to take action because newcomers to the scene might mistake you for an attacker rather than a helper. This fear of negative evaluation causes *audience inhibition.* Such fear of embarrassment or prosecution also inhibits the decision-making necessary to eventually take action.

INCREASING HELP BY REDUCING AMBIGUITY

Researchers recommend that those who really need help be as clear and specific as possible so bystanders will not be confused. Instead of screaming, shout words. Instead of crying "Help!," say "Call the police, I'm being attacked by a stranger!" or "Call the fire department, my house is on fire!" Single out bystanders: instead of saying, "Somebody get help!," point and say, "You in the blue sweater, find a phone and call 911." Such actions reduce the ambiguity of the emergency as well as answering the question of who should help.

Cost/Benefit Analysis

Another interpretation of why people do not help focuses on the costs and benefits for helping versus withholding help.

HELPING VERSUS NOT HELPING

In this model, a bystander conducts a cost/benefit analysis of *both* helping and not helping. He or she assesses the costs and benefits of helping: for example, helping will be risky and expensive, but it might save a life and will make me feel good. The costs and benefits of not helping are also evaluated: not helping will make me look weak and feel bad, but it might save my life. A comparison of the costs involved, and then the benefits, will determine the bystander's decision to help or not.

WHEN BOTH OPTIONS ARE COSTLY

When both helping and not helping promise to be costly, the confused bystander has two options: he or she can take an *indirect* route to intervention (e.g., calling an ambulance); or the situation can be *cognitively reinterpreted* as not critical (e.g., deciding it cannot be an emergency or "someone else" would already have called the police). Thus nonintervention may be a chosen course of action—or nonaction—rather than the result of a failure to make a series of decisions.

RECEIVING HELP

When a bystander has intervened or a Good Samaritan has given aid, has the story ended happily? Until recently little work was done on the experience of receiving help as opposed to offering it. While most people who receive help are probably happy to get it, some people seem determined to reject assistance they seem to need. Researchers offer three explanations for such negative feelings about receiving help: equity theory, reactance theory, and threatened self-esteem.

Equity Theory

People prefer to keep their relationships with each other equitable. This means that relative outcomes should be proportional to relative inputs: neither partner should get more or less than he or she deserves. Receiving help can challenge equity because the helper's inputs are greater than the recipient's, and the recipient's outcomes are (apparently) greater than the helper's. The recipient feels overbenefitted by the helper, and possibly guilty and obligated to an unacceptable degree.

For example, if an acquaintance lends you a large sum of money with no guarantee of repayment, you will feel obligated. You have received much, but invested little (you are not close friends). Unless you are sure you can reciprocate (e.g., pay the money back quickly), you will feel uncomfortable in this relationship. For this reason some may not ask for help or want to accept it from those they are not close to. Within close relationships, partners and friends are more communal in their interactions, and less concerned with equitable exchanges.

Reactance Theory

Reactance is a rebellious, negative reaction against constraints on one's freedom. In some conditions, receiving aid or assistance limits one's choices. For example, hospital patients must remain in the hospital, and have no control over such choices as what to eat, wear, or do. If offers of help have "strings attached," placing limitations on the recipients, the help may be rejected. For example, if a homeless person feels that in order to receive shelter she must comply with rules about where to go and how to groom herself, she may experience reactance and refuse any assistance.

Self-Esteem

If a person's self-esteem (sense of self-worth) is threatened by receiving help, he or she may reject assistance. For example, an unemployed man may feel that accepting money for his family's wellbeing threatens his role as breadwinner and provider in the household. How he feels about accepting short-term assistance depends on whether he thinks his future is controllable or uncontrollable. If he perceives events as controllable, he may accept help while trying to take control once gain; regaining that control will restore his self-esteem. If he thinks events are not controllable, however, he will not try to help himself, but may passively accept more and more help from others. In such cases, help can lead to a form of learned helplessness which incapacitates the recipient.

*B*ecause altruism cannot be observed, social psychologists study prosocial behavior, which takes the form of any help or assistance. Motives for giving help to others include inherited predispositions, social norms, and obligations *of social exchange. According to sociobiological theories, people favor kin selection in offering help. Help may also be given to ensure reciprocation. Sociobiological explanations account for helping in nonhuman species as well.*

Norms for helping include reciprocity and social responsibility. According to the reciprocity norm, we are obliged to help those who have helped us. The social responsibility norm advises us to offer help to those who need it, especially those who deserve it. In the view of social exchange, all helping provides rewards to the helper, although the benefits may be nonobvious. Helping relieves distress and reduces the discomfort of empathizing with the needy individual. People learn prosocial behavior through both direct reinforcement and observation of models.

Personal influences on helping include mood states as well as personality traits. People who feel empathy with the victim are more likely to help. People in a bad mood may offer help to lift their spirits. Being in a good mood for any reason can have powerful if short-lived effects on helpfulness. Personality traits associated with helpfulness include empathy, self-efficacy, and high self-monitoring. Men are more helpful in risky situations and with strangers, women are more helpful in safe situations and close relationships. People from urban backgrounds or in urban settings are less helpful than people in or from small-towns or rural environments. The victim's characteristics also affect helping. People are more likely to be offered help if they are Caucasian and if they are female. Some helpers exhibit a reverse discrimination effect by being more helpful to minority group members.

The presence of bystanders inhibits helping, but observation of models increases helpful imitation. People are more likely to help if they are not in a hurry.

Studies of why people may not offer help have concentrated on emergency intervention. Researchers have identified a decision tree of choices a bystander must make before intervening. The presence of bystanders inhibits helpful decisions, a tendency called the bystander effect. Inhibition of helping may also be caused by diffusion of responsibility over many bystanders. Helping is also reduced by the ambiguity of an event. Ambiguous events are less clearly definable as emergencies. Bystanders fall error to pluralistic ignorance by relying on the nonaction of those surrounding them. A fear of negative evaluation may lead to audience inhibition.

An alternative explanation for not helping is that bystanders conduct a cost/benefit analysis of helping versus not helping. When both responses are seen as costly, help may be offered only indirectly or the event may be cognitively reinterpreted to make help unnecessary.

While most recipients appreciate help, some may resent it. According to equity theory, recipients may feel overbenefitted, and consequently unacceptably obligated to the helper. If help is conditional, the recipient may feel reactance and refuse the limitations on his or her freedom. Finally, help can threaten a recipient's self-esteem if it reduces his or her sense of self-help or self-control. In such cases, accepting help may lead to a dependence on further assistance and a condition of learned helplessness.

Selected Readings

Bar-Tal, D. (1976). *Prosocial Behavior: Theory and Research*. New York: Wiley.

DePaulo, B. M., A. Nadler, and J. D. Fisher. (1983). *New Directions in Helping: Help-Seeking*. New York: Academic Press.

Eisenberg, N. (1985). *Altruistic Emotion, Cognition, and Behavior*. Hillsdale, NJ: Erlbaum.

Latané, B. and J. M. Darley, (1970). *The Unresponsive Bystander: Why Doesn't He Help?* Englewood Cliffs, NJ: Prentice Hall.

Oliner, S. P. and P. M. Oliner, (1988). *The Altruistic Personality: Rescuers of Jews in Nazi Europe*. New York: The Free Press.

Piliavin, J. A., J. F. Dovidio, S. L. Gaertner, and R. D. Clark, III (1981). *Emergency Intervention*. New York: Academic Press.

Rushton, J. P. and R. M. Sorrentino, (Eds.). (1981). *Altruism and Helping Behavior*. Hillsdale, NJ: Erlbaum.

Staub, E., D. Bar-Tal, J. Karylowski, and J. Reykowski, (Eds.). (1984). *Development and Maintenance of Prosocial Behavior*. New York: Plenum.

Wallach, M. A. and L. Wallach, (1983). *Psychology's Sanction for Selfishness: The Error or Egoism in Theory and Therapy*. San Francisco: Freeman.

18

The Environment and Behavior

*T*he environment—physical and social—is part of the situational context of human behavior. We are affected not only by our relationships with others, but by the places and spaces in which we interact. Social psychologists and others have contributed research to the growing field of environmental psychology, *the science of transactions between behavior and the environment.*

Environmental psychology includes many concerns of particular interest to the social psychologist. In this chapter we review general findings in environmental perception and cognition, the social environment, and the impact of human behavior on the environment.

ENVIRONMENTAL PERCEPTION AND COGNITION

The way we interact with and treat our environment begins with the way we perceive and think about it.

Evaluating the Environment

According to many theories of social cognition, we are strongly motivated to make sense out of our environment. We collect information so that we can make predictions and behavioral choices. In particular we are interested in evaluating the physical features and the social climate of the environment.

THE PHYSICAL SETTING

Evaluating an environment involves determining whether it is "good," and whether you "like" it. Evaluative dimensions are affected by culture; for example, a New Yorker might consider the city skyline breathtaking, while a visitor from the Midwest prefers "natural" wonders.

Dimensions of Environmental Preference. Individual preferences vary but can be described by an integrative model developed by Stephen Kaplan and Rachel Kaplan. According to the Kaplans' model, two needs affect viewers' preference for an environmental scene: the need to *make sense* of the environment, and the need to be *involved* with our surroundings. Some settings provide immediate satisfaction of these needs, while others promise future satisfaction.

Combining these two dimensions—needs and time—the Kaplans have identified four environmental qualities that are preferred: coherence, legibility, complexity, and mystery. A *coherent* setting can be made sense of immediately, while a *legible* one promises to make sense eventually. A *complex* scene is immediately involving, while a *mysterious* one—like a path whose end we cannot see—promises future involvement.

EVALUATING THE SOCIAL CLIMATE

A setting involves a social climate as well as natural and built features. The social climate offers three kinds of experiences that can be evaluated: social relationships, personal development, and organizational stability.

We generally prefer environments that foster relationships and interactions with others—when we choose to interact. We also need opportunities for privacy and activity, important aspects of personal development. Finally, the needs of individuals and groups change over time; some settings can be adjusted for these changes, while others resist modification (i.e., they are too stable). For example, an auditorium whose seats are bolted to the floor cannot be rearranged to accommodate small-group discussions or innovative stage productions.

Cognitive Maps

Environmental information may be retained in a map-like memory that is modified by experience. Research on such *cognitive maps* suggests that, when we first experience new environments, we form simple, sketchy memories that are called "strip maps"; for example, when you first move to a new town, you may only feel familiar with the route from your home to your workplace. Other locations and routes are unfamiliar, and not included. As you gain experience, you add detail and alternative routes, and form more complex and comprehensive maps in your memory.

Researcher Kevin Lynch has identified five key features of cognitive maps of cities: paths, nodes, edges, landmarks, and districts. A *path* is a route from one location to another, like a street or highway. A *node* is a point where several paths intersect or meet, like an intersection or mass transit station. An *edge* is a border or boundary, like a shoreline or cliff. *Landmarks* are features of common interest or central function. A *district* is a region of particular character or meaning, like a neighborhood or commercial area.

Cognitive maps help us to remember not only how to get around our environment, but also how to find short cuts, and what resources we can find. Because they are cognitive constructions, they are distorted by biases and preferences. For example, you may remember only the location of a restaurant you like, and not one you seldom visit. Cognitive maps are flexible and can be augmented or modified by experience. As you explore your environment and discover new resources, this information is easily "written into" your ever-changing cognitive map.

ENVIRONMENTAL IMPACT

The environment has a broad and detailed impact on human experience. Most research has examined how physical and social aspects of the environment affect cognition, affect, and performance. In this section we review major findings about the impact of noise, climate, and environmental disasters. In the next section we review the psychological impact of the social environment.

Noise

Noise is unwanted sound; we are most likely to judge sound to be "noisy" if it is *unpredictable* and *uncontrollable*. For example, when you are playing your favorite music at high volume, it is sound, not noise. But if your neighbor plays the same music "too loud" while you are trying to study, it is noise. Loud sounds—whether they are "noise" or "music"—can cause temporary or permanent hearing loss. But even soft sounds—like the mild but erratic snoring of your roommate—are considered to be noise if they interfere with our sleep, concentration, or mood.

Noise is a *stressor*; it disrupts cognition, arouses emotion, and can impair both performance and health. Research has confirmed that children in noisy schools perform more poorly on a variety of tasks than those whose schools are not in noisy neighborhoods. Other studies show that subjects exposed to uncontrollable and unpredictable noise make more errors and experience more frustration than those who have some control over what they will hear and when.

Climate

Like noise, extreme temperatures and hazardous weather conditions are stressors, requiring both physical and psychological adaptation. Environmental psychologists have studied the psychological impact of three climatic stressors: excessive heat; air pollution; and insufficient light.

HEAT

Interest in the behavioral impact of hot weather can be traced to the "long hot summer effect": the correlation of summer heat with the urban and racial unrest of the 1960s. As reviewed in chapter 13, heat is an aversive stimulus associated with heightened arousal and aggressive behavior. In general, as ambient (surrounding) temperature increases, so does the incidence of criminal violence in temperate-zone cities. Heat interacts with other atmospheric conditions like humidity to affect human experience and behavior.

Laboratory studies of the effects of heat on behavior show a curvilinear (curved-line) rather than a linear (straight-line) relationship between heat and aggressive behavior. That is, as a room gets hotter, subjects' behavior gets more aggressive—up to a point; beyond that, aggressiveness *decreases*. This may be because, when a room gets unbearably warm, subjects are more interested in escaping than aggressing.

AIR POLLUTION

Conditions that interfere with comfortable breathing cause stress and irritation. High levels of air pollution have been related to increased numbers of respiratory complaints and psychiatric emergencies. Specific air pollutants like carbon monoxide have been found to interfere with task performance. On a local level, having the air around you polluted with unwanted or uncontrollable smoke or odors can distract you and make you anxious, irritable, and tired. The most common cause of such "personal" pollution is cigarette smoking. The presence of a cigarette-smoking adult will increase both escape behavior and aggressiveness in nonsmokers.

INSUFFICIENT LIGHT

Low lighting indoors has different effects depending on the circumstances. People with romantic partners prefer low light levels, whether they are working or not. People in groups seem to prefer lower light when working on complex tasks—possibly because bright light exaggerates distracting environmental detail. Low levels of artificial light (e.g., in workplaces) has generally been associated with impaired performance and negative mood.

Outdoors, the effects of low light are more consistent. Geographic regions with less sunshine—because of cloud cover or arctic latitudes—have higher suicide rates than sunny climes. An extreme psychological consequence associated with poor light is *seasonal affective disorder*

(SAD), a severe depression worsened by winter darkness. SAD sufferers have been successfully treated with exposure to bright (artificial) light—a result suggesting a biological link between light and mood.

Environmental Dangers

Human occupations and technology have brought people into contact with environmental dangers, both natural (e.g., earthquakes and floods) and manufactured (e.g., radiation and toxic waste).

SELF-JUSTIFICATION

Putting oneself at risk makes no sense; recognizing danger in one's environment creates cognitive dissonance (see chapters 8 and 9). One way to reduce dissonance is to rationalize the dangerous behavior or justify oneself. For example, if you buy a home and later discover that experts fear the ground water is dangerously polluted, what can you do? If you believe your homesite is unsafe, you cannot continue living there. But it is not so easy to sell your house and move. To reduce your dissonance, you may decide that the "experts" must be wrong, you feel fine, and the pollution scare must be a hoax. In this way, many people rationalize placing themselves in continual risk for environmental hazards.

Self-justification is also a motive at work when environmental protection conflicts with local economics. For example, when a local industry (e.g., timber or fishing) is implicated in a conservation issue (e.g., threatening endangered species), those employed by the industry cannot be objective about the issue. They depend on the industry for their jobs. Rather than quit their jobs, they can reduce dissonance by refusing to believe environmentalists' warnings and continuing to work for the industry.

DENIAL

This reluctance to admit or deal with an environmental problem indicates *denial*, a common defense mechanism response to stress or trauma. Denial can prevent residents from recognizing a growing danger, like soil erosion or pollution, until it reaches crisis proportions. When the disaster strikes, people mobilize and work together—until the worst appears to be over. Then denial and destructive habits are resumed once more. This self-defeating pattern of environmental abuse and denial is termed the *crisis effect*.

Denying an environmental problem can make disaster more likely to occur. For example, once a flood has subsided or been dammed, residents may feel a false sense of security that it "will never happen again." Old and new residents settle the area around the dam or levee in greater numbers, straining the ecosystem and increasing the chances and the damage of another catastrophe, a pattern called the *levee effect*.

COMMONS DILEMMAS

Because these hazards afflict entire communities rather than individuals, they involve group conflict and resolutions. For example, reliance on nuclear power produces unmanageable amounts of radioactive nuclear waste. However, the communities that use the power are less eager to store the waste—a social reaction dubbed the *NIMBY* effect for "Not in my back yard!" The problem of radioactive or toxic waste accumulation and disposal is a type of commons dilemma (see Chapter 14). Each individual contributes to the problem, but only cooperative effort by the entire community can lead to a solution.

THE SOCIAL ENVIRONMENT

We share our environment with other people, so much of the environment's impact on us is social. Four social phenomena directly involved with our environment are crowding, privacy, spatial behavior, and territoriality.

Crowding

Crowding is the subjective judgment that one has insufficient space. It is usually caused by density, an objective condition of too many people within an area. High-density conditions may be acceptable, as when you are watching an exciting, well-attended sports event. When high density is *un*acceptable, however, you feel *crowded*.

PHYSICAL VERSUS SOCIAL DENSITY

Crowding is caused by either physical density or social density. *Physical density* involves too little space per person. For example, you feel crowded when you and one other person are riding a tiny, cramped elevator, because of physical density. In contrast, *social density* involves too many people for a given area. You feel crowded in a large room full of people because of social density.

Social density has been found to cause more negative feelings than physical density. The presence of many others involves several potential stressors: insufficient space, social arousal, distraction, and invasion of one's privacy. While people can adapt to crowded conditions, the social and behavioral effects of long-term crowding are usually negative.

Privacy

According to a model developed by Irwin Altman and his colleagues, crowding is experienced when we fail to regulate *privacy* in our social experience. Privacy refers to one's ability to control others' access to him or her. Sometimes you want company or social stimulation, and at other times you do not. When you have more social stimulation than you want, you feel *crowded*; when you have less than you want, you feel *isolated*. Crowding and isolation are problems created when our social environment does not meet our social needs.

PRIVACY REGULATION

To regulate privacy—to get the amount we want, more or less—we try to adapt to our social conditions by using regulation mechanisms, including nonverbal behaviors, movement, and physical props. For example, if you want to be closer to someone who is far away, you can make increased eye contact with him or her, somewhat "closing the gap" between you. In contrast, if people are too close to you and you want more privacy, you can avoid eye contact, move away from them, or use barriers like furniture to separate yourself from them.

WHEN PRIVACY IS LIMITED

Privacy is important to one's sense of well-being, affecting personal control and self-efficacy. Invasions of privacy evoke defensive or escape behaviors. Prolonged intrusions—e.g., denying privacy to patients in hospitals or nursing homes—can create learned helplessness and interfere with recovery from illness. Because a direct way to control others' access to you is to have control over the space you occupy, privacy regulation is intertwined with territoriality (discussed below).

Spatial Behavior

The study of spatial behavior has been dubbed *proxemics*. Two important topics in proxemics are zones of interpersonal distance and the maintenance and defense of personal space.

INTERPERSONAL DISTANCES

Anthropologist Edward T. Hall has identified four zones of interpersonal distance associated with different levels of intimacy and qualities of interaction: intimate, personal, social, and public.

Intimate Distance. Intimate distance extends from zero to 18 inches from one's body. It is the zone for interacting primarily through touch (e.g., with lovers or wrestlers). At this distance, people can see great detail, and speak in low tones and whispers.

Personal Distance. The personal distance zone ranges from 18 inches to four feet from one's body. It is the appropriate distance for friendly conversation, close enough for occasional touch, and voice ranges are normal.

Social Distance. The social zone ranges from four to 12 feet from one's body. Business and formal transactions are most likely to occur within social distance. Props like desks can be used to keep others at social distance; high-status persons keep others farther away, and have more control over whether and when others come closer. Voices may be slightly raised to compensate for distance; little detail is visible.

Public Distance. Interactions across twelve or more feet from one's body are within the public zone. No detail is observable, voices are raised, and nonverbal gestures may be exaggerated. This is the zone for formal addresses and lectures.

PERSONAL SPACE

Environmental psychologist Robert Sommer has theorized that individuals maintain an area around themselves as an extension of their bodies. This *personal space* can be thought of as a portable territory, extended about arm's length in front and to the sides of one's body, somewhat less than that behind him or her. We protect our personal space, control who may enter or approach, and move to adjust to intrusions. For example, if a speaker comes to close to you while you converse, you will automatically back up to restore the personal space separating you.

Variations. Personal space varies with one's age, gender, and culture. Children have smaller personal space than adolescents or adults. Women allow others to come closer and tolerate invasion of their personal space more than men do. Mediterranean cultures have smaller personal space ranges than Americans, while Northern European cultures have larger ranges. These variations suggest that personal space is learned and modified by experience.

Space Invasions. We do not like to have our personal space invaded or encroached upon. For example, if while you are seated on a public bench a stranger takes a seat too close to you, you will move away to restore the buffer zone between you—or escape by leaving. We discourage and control space invasions with a variety of strategies like staring, averting eye contact, shifting, commenting, or using physical barriers (e.g., shopping bags or newspapers).

Territoriality

Territoriality is personal ownership or control of physical space and objects. Ethologists have identified the importance of territoriality to the survival of various nonhuman species. Some have speculated that human aggression is based in territorial instincts (see chapter 13).

TYPES OF TERRITORIES

Human behavior varies for three different kinds of territory: primary, secondary, and public.

Primary Territory. *Primary territory* includes space and objects that are exclusively and permanently controlled by the owner. For example, your home, your bedroom, and your private office are all primary territories.

Primary territory is highly personalized in terms of arrangement and decoration.

Secondary Territory. *Secondary territory* refers to space that one regularly occupies for temporary periods. For example, your usual seat in class is your secondary territory; the classroom is the class's secondary territory—both "belong" to you only for prescribed periods. If you arrive late to class one day to find someone else sitting in "your" seat, you may feel somewhat trespassed upon but probably recognize that it is only "yours" while you occupy it. Secondary territory is not usually personalized since "ownership" is only temporary. When an occupant carves his initials into a desktop, he is both marking territory and vandalizing others' property.

Public Territory. *Public territories* are spaces and facilities that everyone may access. These belong to everyone, and thus to no one person. No individual has right of ownership or control, and public territories are difficult to defend or reserve. For example, on entering a cafeteria you may leave a jacket or books to "save" a table for yourself and your companions—but there is no guarantee that the place will be saved, or that your possessions will still be there when you return. Marks of "ownership" like graffiti are acts of vandalism and not very effective in discouraging use by others.

MARKING TERRITORY

In the last example above, a jacket or book left to "save" a space is an example of a *territorial marker*, a personal possession left to signify occupation and defend against invasion or trespass. Research shows that the more personal the marker, the more effective its defense of the area. As noted above, however, it may be riskier to leave a valued possession itself unprotected (e.g., a jacket or umbrella) than something less valuable (e.g., a newspaper).

HOME TERRITORY

Privacy and Communality. One's home is a special kind of primary territory. It includes space for privacy, such as hygiene and sleeping. But it also includes space for *communality*, interacting with others who are invited into the home. In American homes, living rooms and kitchens are usually communal rather than private spaces. Communal space may feature "shrines" or exhibits of personal information and affiliation, like a desktop or wall display of family photographs and personal trophies.

Home Field Advantage. Another application of "home" is to familiar secondary territory, such as a sports team's base of operations. Researchers have repeatedly confirmed the validity of the *home field* or *home court advantage*: teams playing at home generally do better than when playing away. Explanations include territorial control, self-confidence, familiarity of surroundings, and spectator behavior. In general, playing before home audiences has a social facilitation effect—*except* in the final games of a close contest, when audience-induced arousal can sometimes cause players to "choke" and give poorer performances.

HUMAN IMPACT ON THE ENVIRONMENT

Environmental psychology studies environment-behavior *transactions*, including both environmental impact on humans and human impact on the environment. In this section we review two areas in which behavior consistently affects the shape and function of the environment: environmental design and environmental protection.

Design and Behavior

Humans are the most environmentally flexible species, populating the widest range of world regions and climatic conditions. We confront environmental demands in two ways: by *adaptation*, conforming our behavior to the limits of our spaces; and by *adjustment*, by changing our spaces to fit our needs. Many adjustments are accomplished by designing special spaces and places: public spaces, residential environments, work environments, and special settings for different populations.

PUBLIC SPACES

Public spaces are areas that must accommodate many individuals and different needs. Airport lounges, city plazas, and building lobbies may all be occupied by people who are traveling, talking, eating, waiting, meeting each other, reading, or watching each other engage in these activities.

Some public spaces are more successful than others. Anthropologist William Whyte has identified the following characteristics as important to making public spaces attractive and well-used: access to sunlight; access to water; availability of food; trees (for shade and appearance); attention-focusing events or features (e.g., public sculpture, street entertainers); and most important of all, "sittable" space.

RESIDENCES

Living environments challenge the designer to satisfy different clients: the agencies paying for the design may be different from the individuals who will be occupying the space. Whether a living environment succeeds or fails depends on designing a balance of these different client needs.

Multiple Family Dwellings. Buildings that provide spaces for many families are more affordable than single-family dwellings, but do not offer the same degree of privacy or personalization. Separate units in an apartment building or housing complex are often identical to each other; when territory cannot be personalized, it is harder to defend.

The Pruitt-Igoe housing project, built to house thousands of low-income residents of St. Louis in the early 1950s, was demolished less than 20 years later because it had become dangerous, unhealthy, and crime-ridden. Analysts identified the following sources of its failure: no common spaces for neighbors' socializing; no visual access to children's playgrounds; too much indefensible territory like stairwells and alleys; too vast a scale for personal or community control. The lesson of Pruitt-Igoe was that home environments must allow for both privacy and communality in their designs.

Dormitories. Studies of student residence halls have distinguished between traditional, corridor-style dormitories (with rooms adjacent to long hallways) and suite-style dormitories (separating units with bedrooms and common areas). Open, corridor-style residences allow too much unwanted interaction, limit students' privacy, and suffer from higher crime rates and lower resident satisfaction than suite-style arrangements.

The corridor-style dormitories may be modified by installing unlocked doors that separate the corridor into shorter hallways. Each new section now has the privacy control and social atmosphere of a cluster unit. In such ways designs can be *retrofitted*—corrected to accommodate user needs—rather than demolished and replaced.

WORK ENVIRONMENTS

Traditional work environments assembled people and tasks with little concern for enhancing performance or comfort. Modern designs consider the nature of work to be done and the needs of the individuals likely to be doing it.

Workplace Needs. Workplaces must be designed to accommodate a variety of needs and priorities. These include the following guidelines: secure shelter, social contact, task accomplishment (e.g., having the proper tools handy), personal identification (e.g., symbolizing the worker's status), growing room, and pleasure (e.g., comfort and attractiveness).

Office Designs. Two extremes in office design are the traditional "box" office and the open-space plan. In the traditional arrangement, workers' offices are separate cubicles whose dimensions reflect the status and power of the occupants. In an *open-office plan,* offices are semi-private stations separated by low partitions rather than private rooms.

Although shifting from a closed to an open plan may have a pleasant novelty effect, most workers complain that open-plan arrangements limits privacy and confidentiality, disrupts concentration, constrains social interaction, and reduces their sense of community. Despite employees' dissatisfaction and lowered morale, managers often favor open plans because of their short-term economic gains—e.g., savings on construction and carpet installations. This trend may change when such savings are undercut by long-term declines in productivity.

SPECIAL ENVIRONMENTAL DESIGNS

Studies of human behavior have suggested important guidelines in the design of spaces for special populations.

Schools. Students' performance can be affected by aspects of their setting. Children do better on tests conducted in the same room where they learned the lesson. Larger schools may be *understaffed* (with too few people to occupy important roles) with resulting inefficiency, although large schools offer a wider range of opportunities (if not more time). Students in large schools are more likely to be spectators than participants in learning exercises. Decentralized schools with separate buildings involve more travel time and less social interaction than centralized facilities.

Hospitals. Patients in hospitals are challenged by the need to perform primary-territory functions (e.g., bathing, sleeping) in secondary territory. The lack of privacy and territorial defense they experience can cause distress and may even interfere with recuperation. These problems can be corrected with such devices as lockable cabinets for possessions and nearby bulletin boards for personal markers. Patients can also be given control of where to place specific objects for working and grooming.

Hospital designs must also accommodate the essential needs and personal preferences of professional staff. In some areas staff object to rearrangements than can interfere with their working quickly and thoroughly. Not all hospital wards require the same uniformity and staff control, however. Good hospital designs must strike a balance between patients' needs for privacy and territoriality and staff members' needs for order and consistency.

Prisons. Public discomfort with prison systems is often reflected in designs that merely warehouse people for the term of their sentences. Those who emerge may suffer from pathologies worsened by their dehumanizing environments. The major challenge to prison design is to reduce crowding. More densely populated prisons have higher rates of suicide, violence, death, disease, and rule violation. Research suggests that these dangers can be lessened by reducing social density rather than physical density. Problems rise with the number of inmates per cell. Similarly to office plans, open-plan prisons (with corridor arrangements) are more problem-ridden than those with single-inmate cells and opportunities for privacy. Designers are challenged to balance society's desire to make prisons unappealing with prisoners' psychological needs for privacy and personal security.

Protecting the Environment

Human behavior has great potential to damage our own environment. Some damage is already evident, including pollution of air and water, mismanagement of waste, and the greenhouse effect (imbalance in the biosphere caused by technological pollution and global warming). Two programs for modifying human impact on the environment are energy conservation and controlling population growth.

ENERGY CONSERVATION

Most people know ways to save energy and use alternative, less-polluting forms of energy. People's willingness to conserve energy is less a matter of information (e.g., knowing how to ride a bicycle instead of drive a car) than of attitude (e.g., believing that it is good to save energy, or that one's own efforts will make a difference).

Social psychologists suggest using attitude-change techniques like persuasion in encouraging people to conserve energy in various ways. Research shows that the most effective messages are those that show what people *are* doing rather than what they *should* be doing. Incentive programs can also reinforce individuals for conserving energy, such as offering bonuses for recycling. Methods must still be developed to translate individual efforts into policy changes. For example, legislation can promote more widespread conservation, but legislators and policy-makers are often resistant to reason-based persuasion.

CONTROLLING POPULATION GROWTH

Another way to reduce the damage humans do to our environment is to control or reduce the number of humans drawing on its resources. Population control is a controversial issue involving issues of religion, morality, politics, and nationalism. Is reproduction a personal decision or a matter of public policy? Is it a human right or a social privilege?

Research on controlling population growth has identified the following as the most common reasons people want children: pleasure, religious standards, ingroup expansion, family consolidation, financial value, and security for parents' old age.

Several approaches have been developed to promote family planning. Informational campaigns provide information about how to employ contraception. Service programs provide contraception and sterilization. Incentive programs reward families for limiting their growth; educational opportunities and family care benefits are more effective incentives than cash. According to dissonance theory, incentives should be large enough to induce cooperation but small enough that individuals develop attitudes in favor of their own compliance.

Environmental psychology studies transactions between behavior and the built and natural environment. Environmental perception begins with evaluating the physical setting and social climate. Humans prefer environmental scenes that include coherence, legibility, complexity, and mystery. The social climate is evaluated in terms of whether if offers social contact, personal development, and organizational stability or change. Environmental information is remembered in the form of cognitive maps, featuring important elements of one's experiences in the environment.

The impact of the environment on human experience includes such stressors as noise, climate extremes, and environmental dangers. Noise is most disruptive if it is unpredictable and uncontrollable. Climatic extremes include heat, air pollution, and insufficient light. Heat has been correlated with aggressive behavior. Pollution can damage health and cause irritation. Insufficient light has been linked with seasonal affective disorder. Environmental dangers like disasters and hazards are difficult to deal with because people respond with denial and self-justification. Some dangers can only be solved by community cooperation, efforts that are hampered by the commons dilemma.

The social environment includes environmental behaviors such as crowding, privacy, spatial behavior, and territoriality. Crowding can be caused by either physical density or social density, the latter generally causing more negative effects. Privacy involves controlling one's access by others. Privacy regulation includes nonverbal behaviors and physical barriers. When privacy is limited or invaded we engage in defense or escape to reduce the negative consequences of invasion.

Social contact is usually regulated through maintenance of different interpersonal distance zones: intimate, personal, social, or public interactions. Individuals also maintain a portable zone of territory of personal space in most interactions with others. Personal space varies with gender, age, and culture. Space invasions are defended against or escaped.

Territoriality involves restricting control of space. Primary territory offers the greatest personal control. Secondary territory is occupied temporarily and harder to defend. Public territory is accessible by others and hardest to defend. Territory may be marked to reserve its occupancy; personal possessions are the most effective markers but most at risk for loss. Home territory must offer both privacy and communality. Research has confirmed the home court advantage for sports teams who regularly occupy a playing area.

Human impact on the environment includes design and environmental protection. Public spaces must be designed to invite activity and accommodate different user needs. Residences must provide both communality and privacy, a difficult balance for multiple-family dwellings and dormitories. Work environments must provide for individual workers' needs and task performance, as well as promote healthy social interaction. Open-plan offices offer short-term savings in construction but long-term costs in workers' morale and productivity.

Schools must meet students' needs for attention and interaction as well as teachers' needs for organization. Large schools offer some advantages as well as liabilities. Hospitals must be designed to balance patients' needs for privacy and control with staff needs for order and efficiency. Prisons are plagued by crowding, a problem that can be alleviated by designs that offer inmates moderate privacy and personal control.

Efforts to protect the environment can focus on limiting the damage we do and the number of people who do it. Energy conservation may be increased with persuasive communication. Population growth may be influenced by programs offering information, family planning services, and incentives for limiting family growth.

Selected Readings

Altman, I. (1975). *The Environment and Social Behavior*. Monterey, CA: Brooks/Cole.

Altman, I. and M. Chemers, (1980). *Culture and Environment*. Pacific Grove, CA: Brooks/Cole.

Bell, P., J. Fisher, A. Baum, and T. E. Greene, (1990). *Environmental Psychology*, 3rd edition. New York: Holt, Rinehart and Winston.

Coyne, J. D. and S. C. Hayes, (1980). *Environmental Problems/Behavioral Solutions*. Monterey, CA: Brooks/Cole.

Fischer, C. S. (1984). *The Urban Experience*, 2nd edition. New York: Harcourt Brace Jovanovich.

Freedman, J. L. (1975). *Crowding and Behavior*. San Francisco: W. H. Freeman.

Gifford, R. (1987). *Environmental Psychology: Principles and Practice*. Boston: Allyn and Bacon.

Holahan, C. J. (1982). *Environmental Psychology*. New York: Random House.

Insel, P. M and H. C. Lindgren, (1978). *Too Close for Comfort*. Englewood Cliffs, NJ: Prentice Hall.

Jones, D. M. and A. J. Chapman, (Eds.). (1984). *Noise and Society*. New York: John Wiley.

McKibben, G. (1989). *The End of Nature*. New York: Random House.

Nasar, J. L. (Ed.). (1988). *Environmental Aesthetics: Theory, Research, and Applications*. New York: Cambridge University Press.

Sommer, R. (1969). *Personal Space: The Behavioral Basis of Design*. Englewood Cliffs, NJ: Prentice Hall.

Stokols, D. and I. Altman,(Eds.). (1987). *Handbook of Environmental Psychology*. New York: Wiley.

Taylor, R. B. (1988). *Human Territorial Functioning*. New York: Cambridge University Press.

Wicker, A. (1979). *An Introduction to Ecological Psychology*. Monterey, CA: Brooks/Cole.

Wilson, P. J. (1988). *The Domestication of the Human Species*. New Haven, CT: Yale University Press.

Zube, E. (1980). *Environmental Evolution: Perception and Public Policy*. Pacific Grove, CA: Brooks/Cole.

19

Social Psychology and Health

Health involves adaptive physical, psychological, and behavioral function. Behavioral medicine is a newly-developing field that brings together medicine and behavioral science to understand health and illness. Within behavioral medicine, health psychology considers the ways that experience and behavior influence, and are influenced by, well-being.

In many ways, maintaining health and suffering from illness are social psychological processes: they are affected by our culture, our interaction with health professionals, our beliefs and feelings, and our relationships with others. In this chapter we review the many interconnections between well-being and behavior, and analyze the social psychology of health promotion.

BEHAVIOR, HEALTH, AND ILLNESS

The connections between behavior and well-being include cognitive factors in illness, self-destructive behavior patterns, and the experience of stress.

Cognitive Factors in Illness

Wellness or illness may begin with the way we think. Researchers have found that the incidence and severity of illness can be influenced by attributions and personal control.

ATTRIBUTIONAL STYLE

While attributions for events can vary in many ways, some individuals develop attributional styles, consistently making either internal attributions, for example, or explaining events as due to stable, unchangeable conditions.

Pessimism. A *pessimistic attributional style* is characterized by internal ("It's my fault), stable ("It will never change"), global ("It will affect everything") attributions. Research shows that a pessimistic style of explaining events makes illness more likely.

Optimism. In contrast, people with an *optimistic style* have fewer bouts of illness and are more likely to recover. Optimistic patients tend to see their problems as caused by correctable, external conditions with limited impact.

Unrealistic Optimism. On the other hand, people who are *unrealistically optimistic* have false ideas about their own level of risk for illness. They may see themselves as invulnerable, deny their own susceptibility to illness, and fail to take preventive action in time.

CONTROL

People also vary in their sense of control, over themselves and the events that affect them.

Locus of Control. People who believe they themselves control their experiences and outcomes are said to perceive an *internal locus of control*. Such "internals" believe that their own efforts will make a difference, and work hard to act in their own interests. In contrast, "externals"—those who perceive an *external locus of control*—believe that outside forces influence them in ways they cannot prevent. Consequently, "externals" put little effort into attempting to influence their outcomes.

Learned Helplessness. The work of learning researcher Martin Seligman shows that devlelopment of a pessimistic explanatory style can lead to *learned helplessness,* refusal to engage in coping behavior as a result of experiencing failure. For example, an abused child may believe that she is being punished because she is bad (internal attribution), that neither she nor her punishment will ever change (stable attribution), and that others will treat her the same way (global attributon). As a result she *learns to be helpless,* and does not try to escape the abusive situation or ask for help from outsiders.

Self-Efficacy. Seligman argues that learned helpless is often the cause of depression. If so, treatment of depression and similar disorders must involve attributional retraining, teaching the sufferer that efforts at self-help can succeed. Other research has found that cancer patients who believed they were helpless to combat their illness were less likely to be living ten years later than those who were willing to fight the disease. Successfully coping increases one's feelings of *self-efficacy,* confidence in one's competence and self-control.

Self-Destructive Behaviors

Many diseases and health problems have been traced to unhealthy habits and so-called "lifestyle" factors. Social psychologists have been able to develop some strategies for changing the behaviors associated with addictions and health-threatening habits.

ADDICTIONS

In many ways "addictions" to legal substances—like tobacco, alcohol, and food—are harder to control than the abuse of illicit substances. This is because legal substances are not only available, they are often promoted by advertising and modeling.

Cigarette Smoking. Most people who try smoking more than once become regular smokers, despite the fact that smoking is considered the *major* preventable cause of premature death and disability in the United States. Because smoking is learned while smokers are young, prevention campaigns are aimed at school-age children. Smoking behavior is shaped by personal attitudes, social influence (e.g., persuasion and peer pressure), and self-presentation (e.g., wishing to look attractive to one's reference group).

Theories about attitude formation and social influence have been applied in reducing or preventing smoking by children and adolescents. Successful programs must correct cognitive errors (e.g., believing that "everyone else is smoking"). They can also employ attitude inoculation by encouraging children to develop their own rebuttals of pro-smoking persuasion (see chapter 9). No single technique is universally effective; a combination of strategies works best in preventing smoking. By recognizing both individual rationalizations for smoking and group influences on symbolic habits, health educators may be able to reduce the damage done by cigarette smoking.

Alcohol Abuse. Heavy drinking has been identified as the major health crisis on American college campuses, and linked with problems ranging from family violence, crime, and automobile fatalities to birth defects due to fetal alcohol syndrome. Alcohol-dependent individuals rationalize drinking by claiming it helps them deal with boredom, depression, anxiety, repressed anger, and conflict.

Explanations for alcoholism are important in devising strategies for recovery. The view that alcoholism is a progressive disease may relieve sufferers from taking responsibility for their condition or its correction. In contrast, the view that problem drinking is an unhealthy, elected habit allows alcoholics to make internal, controllable attributions about their problems: "I have a problem because I choose to drink; if I make different choices I can solve the problem."

Overeating. Obese and overweight individuals are ridiculed, socially rejected, and negatively stereotyped. They suffer not only from low self-esteem but increased risk for diabetes and heart disease. The cultural association of food with social approval makes eating habits resistant to self-improvement programs. The most successful weight control programs involve behavioral techniques like monitoring food intake, restricting the locations and times of meals, eating more slowly and attentively, and using non-food rewards as incentives for program adherence. Research also shows that general beliefs ("Most people eat more than they need") are not as influential as personal beliefs ("*I* will lose weight if I stick to this program") in determining behavior.

HIGH-RISK HABITS

Our health can be affected not only by the things we do (e.g., smoking, drinking, overeating) but by the things we *don't* do. In this section we review efforts to overcome people's failure to wear vehicle safety belts and their resistance to practicing "safe sex."

Not Wearing Safety Belts. Seatbelt use works; the risk of fatality is five times greater if you are not wearing your safety belt. Statistics indicate that, even when seatbelt use is required by law, many if not most Americans resist forming the habit of "buckling up."

One explanation for this resistance is false beliefs based on vivid but unrepresentative anecdotes (e.g., that wearing a belt is likely to trap you in burning wreckage). If so, resistance can be overcome with information campaigns that provide accurate accounts of the effects of wearing—and not wearing—seatbelts.

Another explanation is that driving without buckling up is automatic, "mindless" behavior. Automobile manufacturers and consumer protection campaigns have shown that the non-buckling habit can be overcome with reminders like dashboard buzzers and incentives like prizes for "modeling" seatbelt use.

Finally, people may resist wearing safety belts because of reactance formed when legally required to do so. Researchers suggest that, over time and if seatbelt laws are consistently enforced, compliance will reshape drivers' attitudes. Wearing your seatbelt "because it's the law" can eventually lead to the attitude that you are really wearing it "because it's a good idea."

Not Practicing Safe Sex. Since the early 1980s when the dangers of Acquired Immune Deficiency Syndrome (AIDS) were announced, major prevention efforts have focused on persuading intravenous drug users to use clean needles, and urging *all* sexually active individuals to practice "safe sex." Safe sex requires limiting the number of one's sexual partners and using condoms as protection during intercourse.

Unfortunately the spread of AIDS has not been significantly checked, either because people do not know how AIDS is contracted or because they are not complying with recommended behaviors. Researchers have found that the subsequent spread of AIDS is due not to an "information gap" but to a "behavior gap": people know that they *should* practice safe sex, but largely do not *do* so. Why not?

The "reasoned action theory" of behavior says that one's intentions to practice safe sex are a function of three factors: one's attitudes toward safe sex, social norms about safe sex, and one's perceived control over whether one practices safe sex. For example, you are more likely to *intend* to practice safe sex if you have an attitude that favors safe sex, your reference group or peer group encourages it, and you believe you will be able to say or do what is necessary (e.g., using or encouraging use of condoms). In this view, safe sex can be encouraged by promoting good attitudes about it, influencing social norms that encourage it, and teaching individuals how to do what is necessary (e.g., how to buy and use condoms, or overcome awkwardness in asking one's partner to use them).

Stress and Illness

Stress is any event that demands physical or psychological adaptation. Recurrent stresses or inadequate responses lead to the development of illness, weakened resistance, and maladaptive behavior. Here we will review major sources of stress, and consider how responses to stress can be made more effective.

SOURCES OF STRESS

Stressful Experiences. Stressful events are usually the result of environmental demands and changes, predictable or otherwise. Stress can also be the result of interpreting one's experiences as demanding adaptation, whether such interpretations are accurate or not. Three kinds of experiences have been identified as stressors: life changes, traumas, and hassles.

Life changes are positive or negative events that alter one's actions and resources. The top ten stressful life events, in descending order of impact, are death of one's spouse, divorce, marital separation, jail term, death of a close family member, personal injury or illness, getting married, being fired from work, having a marital reconciliation, and retiring. The more such changes—good or bad—you experience, the more you must adapt to new circumstances and use limited resources like personal energy, time, and attention.

Traumas are powerful losses involving great stress and change. In a sense, all of the top ten life changes may be a form of loss: loss of a partner, one's status or well-being, or one's accustomed habits. Researchers confirm that those who have lost a loved one through death have a higher probability of dying within the year, a trend called the *loss effect*. Traumas and losses damage health because they are such supreme stressors: they can overwhelm efforts to cope, and affective states like depression can aggravate physical weaknesses and disease.

Less severe are *hassles*, minor events that cause frustration and demand behavioral adaptation. Hassles include such daily experiences as waiting in line, being stuck in traffic, doing tedious household chores, and making difficult decisions. Hassles are so frequent and numerous that they may be at least as stressful as major life changes.

The Type A Personality. As reviewed in chapter 13, a pattern of behavior termed the Type A personality has been found to be more prone to stress illnesses like heart disease. Type As are more inclined to impatience, perfectionism, time obsession, and anger. They may interpret more situations as stressful or intolerable; once the interpretation is made, the *stress response* is set in motion (see below). Thus Type As are looking at the world through "stress-colored" glasses; they react in a stressed way to more events than non-Type As. Their susceptibility to heart attack and cardiovascular disease is a consequence of their social cognition.

RESPONDING TO STRESS

Different models of stress permit different strategies for managing its effects. One approach to stress management is the General Adaptation Syndrome; it suggests several stategic points for intervention.

Stages of Adaptation. Stress researcher Hans Selye has proposed that recognition of a stressor triggers three physiological stages of the General Adaptation Syndrome (GAS): alarm, resistance, and exhaustion.

In the *alarm* stage, one recognizes and responds to the stressor with increased breathing and blood flow, muscular tension, and attention.

During *resistance*, one takes "fight or flight" action against the stressor, either overcoming it or seeking to escape it. When resistance is successful, adaptation is complete and the stress response ceases. If stress recurs, however, or if resistance efforts are unsuccessful, the response proceeds to the exhaustion stage.

In the *exhaustion* stage, the actions of the alarm stage are repeated, but because the organism is in a weakened state, physiological responses cause normal bodily functions to deteriorate. Over time symptoms may appear of such disorders as ulcers and gastric disorders, heart and circulation problems, headaches, muscle tension, disrupted sleep, emotional distress, and impairment of performance and intellectual function. In extreme cases, exhaustion leads to death.

Defending versus Coping. An important distinction in Selye's GAS model is between *defending* and *coping*. You can defend by hiding from or postponing a recurrent stressor. For example, if you have a headache you can take a pain reliever to reduce the symptoms. In contrast, *coping* involves eliminating the source of the stress, not just its symptoms. For example, if you suspect your headaches are related to hunger, you can eat something before the next headache develops. Coping is the more effective form of resistance. Defenses temporarily relieve symptoms but often permit the stressor to recur in a stronger form.

COPING STRATEGIES

Prevention. One strategy for intervention is *prevention,* reducing the experience of stress before a stressor is interpreted. Since Type As interpret too many events as stressful, a countermeasure involves teaching individuals to interpret *fewer* events as stressful. Teach them effective problem solving strategies and social skills, so that some events can be dealt with as "mere" problems and challenges, not impossible traumas. For example, a student who worries that he cannot pay his rent can learn to keep a balanced budget and set aside money to pay bills. The arrival of the rent bill may never be welcome, but it need not be an occasion for stress.

Improving Resistance. Another strategy is to build up resistance. Physical resistance can be improved with health promotion that includes healthy diet, exercise, sleep and relaxation. Psychological and behavioral resistance can be strengthened with skills education and social support (see below).

HEALTH PROMOTION

Once upon a time the medical model of health care advocated waiting until an illness had developed, and then seeking appropriate treatment. Recently researchers are encouraging a *proactive* approach of identifying the elements of good health and strengthening them. Two aspects of health promotion involve illness prevention and appropriate access to health care services.

Preventing Illness

Illness prevention can be undertaken in two ways: changing cognitions, and developing preventive behaviors.

CHANGING COGNITIONS

As noted earlier, a pessimistic attributional style makes illness more likely and interferes with recuperation. The way we think can make us vulnerable to illness. Three strategies for changing cognitions are learning optimism, attribution therapy, and stress inoculation.

Learned Optimism. People who think positively have fewer problems, develop fewer and less severe symptoms, and experience better recoveries than those who are not optimistic about their health. Characteristics of optimistic thinking include *remaining problem-focused* instead of denying or avoiding the illness, *seeking social support,* and *emphasizing positive aspects* rather than negative aspects of the stressful situation.

Attribution Therapy. People with depressive or pessimistic attributional styles (i.e., blaming negative events on internal, stable, global causes) can be trained to think in alternative ways. Initially patients can be taught to keep a diary of their experiences, accepting credit for their successes and identifying external circumstances that contribute to their failures.

Attributional retraining can also be effective in maintaining behavior-change programs like overcoming addictions and unhealthy habits. Individuals must learn to attribute their successes to their own efforts, not to temporary programs or institutional settings. For example, if a woman believes "I lost weight because the special diet program worked," she may regain the lost weight as soon as the program is over. But if she learns to believe that "I lost the weight because *I* worked hard to do it," she will develop maintenance skills that outlast the program.

Stress Inoculation. Just as forewarning makes a persuasive message less influential, likewise forewarning people about stress enables them to withstand its impact. This procedure is called *stress inoculation.* For example, prior to having surgery, a patient should be told calmly but honestly what will happen and how she will feel at various times when recuperating. Because then she is armed with information, subsequent experiences will not be surprising, her sense of personal control is enhanced, and she will be better able to cope and recover.

PREVENTIVE BEHAVIORS

What do healthy people do that sick people don't? Research has identified two ways that healthy people seem to behave differently from those who are more frequently prone to illness: psychological hardiness, and social support.

Hardiness. *Hardiness* is defined as the ability to stay physically healthy in the face of continued stress. Hardy people can "take" more stress than others without suffering the consequences in weakness or sickness. In particular, hardy people have three kinds of attitudes that sustain them. First, they have a strong sense of *control* over what happens in their lives. Secondly, they have a strong sense of *purpose and involvement* with other people and the world (*commitment*). Finally, they enjoy change, are optimistic about the future, and see problems as *challenges*. Since attitudes are usually learned, it is possible that these "hardiness attitudes" can be acquired by individuals who wish better to manage stress in their lives.

Social Support. *Social support* is the assistance and comfort provided by interactions with others. Sometimes one's friends must be encouraged to offer aid; often, however, the stressed individual need only ask and help will be provided. It is best to be explicit about requesting aid, rather than relying on wishful thinking or mindreading. Being willing to ask for help, in a reasonable and timely way, can be an effective stress management practice.

Social interaction also offers individuals an opportunity to *confide*. Research indicates that talking about your problems with others, either professionals or laypersons, can both relieve stress and assist in finding solutions.

Accessing Health Care

Even among optimistic and hardy people, illness and injury are possible. At that point, it is important that a person be able to recognize symptoms and seek appropriate health care. We conclude this chapter with an examination of illness episodes, difficulties in adhereing to treatment, and problems with health care.

ILLNESS EPISODES

How do you know when you are sick? Recognizing symptoms, seeking help, and applying treatment are the stages in an *illness episode*.

Recognizing Symptoms. When we are involved with people or tasks, we are not aware of bodily signs of health or illness. To recognize symptoms we must overcome *competing cues* or stimuli from our environment that distract our attention and reduce our self-awareness.

Once signals like pain, discomfort, or difficulty are recognized, they must be interpreted as symptoms of a problem. This will only be possible if our culture has provided us with categories for such signals and their causes. For example, if you experience upper-abdominal discomfort, you must be able to associate such sensations with concepts like "indigestion," "heartburn," and "ulcers." This helps you to form a hypothesis or guess about what has caused the problem. Once you decide what the problem might be, you make a decision to take action, like buying non-prescription medication or visiting a physician.

Research shows that most people classify symptoms along four dimensions when making self-diagnoses, considering whether the symptom is

(1) caused by a virus,

(2) in the upper or lower body,

(3) psychological or physiological in origin, and

(4) disruptive to normal activities.

People usually treat viral or nondisruptive problems themselves, while seeking professional help for nonviral physiological problems in the lower body.

Patient-Practitioner Interaction. While most of us are not physicians, we try to judge whether a practitioner seems competent before seeking his or her assistance. Equally important to most patients is whether the practitioner is friendly and easy to communicate with or cool and distant.

Communication is a central task in patient-practitioner interaction and one that is often problematic. Physicians may talk *about* rather than *to* the patient as they work, which can lead patients to feel dehumanized and unimportant. Patients may be distracted and biased in listening to the physician's advice, missing important information or overreacting to his or her language. Finally, it may be difficult to describe your symptoms while you are sick. Problems in communication are serious because they can impede health care and adherence to treatment.

ADHERING TO TREATMENT

Because of fear of the physician, anxiety about the illness, and difficulty communicating, many patients do not adhere as necessary with recommended treatment. Adherence can be improved by improving physician-patient communication and solving other problems of providing health care.

Improving Communication. Physicians can be trained to communicate clearly, limit or explain jargon, and have patients repeat instructions. They can be taught to engage in nonverbal behaviors that signify warmth and acceptance: smiling, learning forward, shaking hands or appropriately touching.

Since physicians are regarded as powerful social figures, they should be trained in appropriate social influence techniques to increase adherence to treatment. In particular, drawing on legitimate power and referent power (see chapter 10) can improve patients' adherence to treatment.

If treatment requires attitude- and behavior-change, physicians should apply persuasive strategies that are especially effective in one-on-one interactions. The physician should invite questions and engage the patient in exchanges to clarify treatment and expectations.

Other Strategies. Since most patients are not familiar with medical practice, they may interpret treatments and procedures as stressors or "threats" in themselves. One solution is for the patient to use an *avoidance strategy,* distracting his or her own attention elsewhere. For example, if you expect to be nervous while seated in the waiting or treatment room, plan to bring a funny or absorbing book to read to take your mind off your self-preoccupation. This can lessen stress once treatment is under way, but should not be used to deny the existence or severity of symptoms before that point.

Since perceived self-control helps promote health and recovery, the patient should seek and be provided with as much information as possible about the problem and its treatment. This erases fear due to ignorance and empowers the patient with a sense of being able to predict what could happen. Contact with a fellow patient or someone who has survived a similar disorder provides a patient with both information and support. Finally, encouraging patients to see their illnesses as changeable, internal experiences over which they have control will help them feel responsible about and involved with their treatment.

*M*aintaining *health or suffering illness begins with cognitive factors like attributions and perceived control. A pessimistic attributional style attributes illness and other negative events to internal, stable, global causes. The pessimistic style is related to illness and poor recovery. Optimistic attributions are associated with health and recovery, although unrealistic optimisim may involve illusions of invulnerability and denial of real symptoms. Whether one's sense of control is internal or external can affect one's sense of well-being. Feeling one's experiences are uncontrollable can lead to learned helplessness. In contrast, a sense of self-efficacy supports healthy habits and adherence to medical treatments.*

Some health problems are the result of self-destructive patterns like addictions and high-risk habits. Addictions like cigarette smoking, alcohol abuse, and overeating can be overcome with the application of persuasion and behavior change techniques. High-risk habits like not wearing automobile safety belts or not engaging in safe sex can be corrected with programs involve social norms, social influence, and persuasion.

Stress and how we respond to it has powerful effects on health. Stress is caused by stressful experiences, like life changes, traumas, and hassles. Stress is also experienced by behavior patterns like the Type A personality. The stress response involves three stages: alarm, resistance, and exhaustion. During resistance, defensive actions reduce symptoms, while coping responses eliminate the sources of stress and are most effective in the long run. Effective coping strategies should be built on preventing stress by reinterpreting events, and improving resistance.

Health promotion relies on both preventing illness and accessing appropriate health care. One way to prevent illness is by changing cognitions about one's health, including learning optimism, retraining attributions, and inoculation against stress. Preventive behaviors include a pattern of hardiness, which involves attitudes favorable to control, challenge, and commitment. Social support is also important in preventing illness, and can provide significant opportunities for confiding.

Accessing health care involves first an illness episode, in which one experiences, attends to, and recognizes symptoms. If health care is sought, the interaction between patient and practitioner can affect the success of adherence to treatment. Adherence can be improved by improving communication in that interaction, and by employing other strategies like avoidance, self-control, contact with other patients, and revising attributions.

Selected Readings

Alloy, L. B. (Ed.). (1988). *Cognitive Processes in Depression.* New York: Guilford.

Burish, T. G. and L. A. Bradley, (Eds.). (1983). *Coping with Chronic Disease: Research and Applications.* New York: Academic Press.

Eiser, J. R. (Ed.). (1982). *Social Psychology and Behavioral Medicine.* London: Wiley.

Freedman, H. S. and M. R. Dimatter, (1982). *Interpersonal Issues in Health Care.* New York: Academic Press.

Gatchel, R. J., A. Baum, and D. S. Krantz, (1988). *An Introduction to Health Psychology.* New York: McGraw-Hill.

Lazarus, R. S. and S. Folkman,(1984). *Stress, Appraisal, and Coping.* New York: Springer-Verlag.

Leary, M. R. and R. S. Miller, (1986). *Social Psychology and Dysfunctional Behavior: Origins, Diagnosis, and Treatment.* New York: Springer-Verlag.

Maddux, J. E., C. D. Stoltenberg, and R. Rosenwein, (Ed.). (1988). *Social Processes in Clinical and Counseling Psychology.* New York: Springer-Verlag.

Sanders, G. S. and J. Suls, (Eds.). (1982). *Social Psychology of Health and Illness.* Hillsdale, NJ: Erlbaum.

Seligman, M. E. P. (1975). *Helplessness.* San Francisco: Freeman.

Seligman, M. E. P. (1990). *Learned Optimism.* New York: Alfred Knopf.

Selye, H. (1976). *The Stress of Life.* New York: McGraw-Hill.

Taylor, S. E. (1991). *Health Psychology,* 2nd edition. New York: Random House.

Temoshok, L. and A. Baum, (Eds.). (1990). *Psychological Aspects of AIDS.* Hillsdale, NJ: Erlbaum.

Weary, G. and H. L. Mirels, (1982). *Integrations of Clinical and Social Psychology.* New York: Oxford University Press.

20

Social Psychology and the Legal System

The relationship between law and social psychology is in some ways a natural convergence of interests. Both traditions are concerned with human social behavior, and with understanding how people can better relate to each other. Social psychologists Lawrence Wrightsman has identified four dilemmas underlying American justice: (1) individual rights versus the common good; (2) equal treatment versus humane judgment; (3) discovering the truth versus resolving conflicts; and (4) using science versus law as the basis for decisions. Each dilemma represents a difficult choice between values that are desirable but often in conflict.

The last dilemma—science versus law—captures the central paradox of using social psychology to understand the creation and application of law. Most legal processes rely on the value of precedent, *the rulings of earlier decision-making bodies. In contrast, as a science, social psychology relies on* empirical evidence *about real influences on human behavior. These two approaches often yield very different views of the world.*

In the last two or three decades, the field of forensic psychology has examined legal assumptions about human behavior. In this chapter we review findings about the legal environment and the roles and social behavior central to questions of the law.

THE LEGAL ENVIRONMENT

The activities central to legal procedure today are based on several assumptions about justice, due process, and public awareness. Social psychologists have examined and questioned many of these assumptions.

Justice and Behavior

A just system is one that is fair. Fairness can be determined in many ways, but a central concept is that of *equity,* the principle that individual outcomes should be related to investments (see chapter 16). Several related concepts affect the practice of law in the United States: distributive justice, perceived injustice, and the just-world bias.

DISTRIBUTIVE JUSTICE

A simple way to determine whether relations among people are equitable is to compare each person's outcomes to his or her investments, and then compare the comparisons. For example, if two people combine their savings to invest $1,000 in a small business, and one year later have multiplied their investment tenfold, how will they now divide up their $10,000? It depends on how much each invested initially. The outcomes are *justly distributed* by considering the partners' original contributions.

If one partner had invested 70% of the start-up money, and the other had contributed 30%, then the profits should be likewise divided, 70-30. In contrast, if they decided to split their profits equally—each receiving 50%—then the 70% investor would be underbenefitted and feel cheated, while the 30% investor would be overbenefitted and might feel guilty.

PERCEIVED INJUSTICE

When a person feels his or her outcomes are not equitable, the result is *perceived injustice.* Because social relationships are usually more complex than the example of the business partnership above, people often feel they have not been dealt with fairly. For example, a woman believes she has worked hard in her life to please her parents, her teachers, her husband and children. If after she is divorced, she finds she is suffering emotionally, socially, and financially, she may feel angry about how unfairly she has been treated—by society and by life. Similarly, a man whose wife has died may feel not only bereaved but bitter, blaming his tragedy on God, or wondering why she was "taken" when others continue to live. In both these cases individuals perceive injustice as a result of complex and difficult experiences.

THE JUST-WORLD BIAS

As reviewed earlier (see chapter 12), part of the rationalism that characterizes Western thought is the expectation that the world is a just place, where people get what they deserve and deserve what they get. Some individuals' thinking is more affected than others' by this *just-world bias*. One consequence of just-world thinking is that victims of crime or injustice are blamed for their suffering. Another consequence is trying to correct "injustices" that are no one's fault by designating someone to make reparations.

Legal Procedure

The two branches of justice in the United States are civil law and criminal law. Civil law deals with disputes between parties, including such procedures are lawsuits, contract disputes, and civil complaints. Criminal law involves breaking the law, a social contract. Thus criminal law deals with conflicts between individual action on the one hand and social norms and group decision on the other. In this sense social psychology has a natural interest in many aspects of criminal law.

Criminal legal procedures begin with arrest, go on to pretrial, plea bargaining and bail-setting, and may culminate in a trial. Because criminal law is enforced on behalf of the community, these procedures are a matter of public record. Thus media interest and communication affect the legal environment as well.

ARREST

Criminal procedures begin with a complaint to police, usually by the victim. Police investigate the seriousness of the offense before arresting the suspect, who is advised of his or her rights and processed. The processing involves recording fingerprints, photographs, and witness identification. In the early 1970s, a prison simulation exercise conducted by social psychologist Philip Zimbardo began with the mock arrest of students assigned the role of prisoners. A central result of their processing was *depersonalization*: each person sacrificed some of his individuality—unique appearance, freedom, social choices—and became eventually more easily victimized by himself and by others.

PLEA BARGAINING

Most criminal complaints do not culminate in a trial, but are disposed through plea bargaining. In a *plea bargain,* the defendant agrees to plead guilty to reduced charges in exchange for requesting a lighter sentence. The defendant's alternative is to plead innocent and go to trial—facing higher charges and heavier sentences, but also the possibility of acquittal. Some researchers have examined the plea bargaining tradition in light of findings about negotiation, conflict resolution, power, and social influence. The defendant's choices are affected by such factors as how the plea is framed, fear of jurors' prejudices, and expectations about the fairness of criminal proceedings. Even innocent people will plead guilty if they fear a trial will result in conviction.

SETTING BAIL

The legal goal of bail is to ensure that a suspect will remain in the community for review or trial. Some suspects are high risk and likely to escape if given the opportunity, while others have community ties like family and work and are low risk for "jumping bail." A judge sets the amount of bail—collateral for the suspect's freedom—after reviewing the prosecutor's recommendation and the defendant's or defense attorney's arguments (e.g., that the defendant is low risk because of ties to the community). Research on bail setting suggests that judges may be more influenced by prosecutors' warnings than other evidence in setting bail.

THE TRIAL

A defendant who pleads not guilty is held for trial. The trial begins with jury selection, a process involving the preferences (and prejudices) of both attorneys. The attorneys' presentations to the jury involves such processes as social influence (with both jurors and witnesses) and persuasive communication. The judge's role involves ruling whether evidence is admissible, instructing jurors' deliberations, and deciding sentence if the jurors convict. Finally, the jury acts as a decision-making group involving many processes of social cognition, social influence, group interaction, and conflict resolution.

The Media

Most members of the community are influenced by media presentations of criminal cases and portrayals of legal proceedings. Television and newspaper coverage of criminal cases is selective; reporters concentrate on sensationalistic crimes like murder rather than commonplace misdeeds like writing bad checks. Because rarer crimes are more newsworthy, increased media coverage leads to illusory correlations and base-rate fallacies. For example, people believe murder rates are higher than they really are because they are given disproportionate media coverage. People also make harsher judgments about crimes that have received higher exposure in news media, since exposure implies seriousness.

LEGAL ROLES AND SOCIAL BEHAVIOR

Social psychological processes help to understand the thinking and behavior of individuals who occupy important roles in criminal procedures: police, attorneys, the defendant, the victim, eyewitnesses, the jury, and the judge.

The Police

Most people's first personal contacts with the law are with police officers, who have been said to make up the "thin blue line" between civilized society and chaos.

LAW ENFORCEMENT ROLES

Law enforcement jobs are often stressful, dangerous, and socially isolating. Trained to see violence others do not notice, police must maintain vigilance and suspiciousness without becoming paranoid or prejudiced. Because their experiences are not representative of other citizens', they can develop attitudes that bias their perceptions of people and justice, their social influence experiences, and their personal relationships.

POLICE INTERROGATION

Besides responding to complaints and maintaining civil order, the police work primarily to collect evidence in criminal cases.

Social Influence. Most evidence is gleaned from interrogating suspects. Police interrogations often apply social influence techniques to extract a confession: winning the suspect's trust, making promises and threats, or encouraging scapegoating (e.g., blaming the victim for "asking for it," or saying an accomplice planned the crime).

Leading Questions. Interrogators may ask *leading questions* like "Where did you conceal the weapon?" instead of "Did you have a weapon?" A leading question "leads" the respondent to make a particular reply. This implies the interrogator already "knows" the truth, like the bogus pipeline technique for attitude measurement (see chapter 8).

Improving Interrogation. Although abusive interrogation is rare, many legal techniques are powerfully manipulative in extracting confessions. Researchers have argued that interrogators trained to ask unbiased (nonleading) questions will yield the most accurate confessions or evidence.

The Attorneys

The attorney's role is the subject of many media portrayals and much public opinion. Attorneys' roles can be demanding and conflictual. Their work requires self-presentation, social influence, and persuasive communication.

THE SITUATIONAL POWER OF ROLES

The attorney's job requires advocacy of a position (plaintiff or defendant in a civil proceeding, state or defendant in a criminal trial). The attorney must also work as an adversary against the position of the other party. Observers may commit the fundamental attribution error when evaluating attorneys' qualities, as in concluding that "Only a heartless scoundrel would defend such an obvious criminal" or wondering "How can she prosecute someone who's obviously a victim of circumstances?" It is hard for observers to distinguish between the situational power of a role like "defender" or "prosecutor" and the personality traits of the actor.

QUESTIONING

Like police interrogators, attorneys can also ask leading questions, during both jury selection and the trial itself. An attorney examining his or her own witness will ask a direct, nonleading question like, "What happened when you arrived home?" But when examining the adversary's witness, he or she may ask, "You did not call police right away, did you?," thus leading the witness or jurors to a particular inference. This can affect jurors' impressions of witnesses, who appear more credible and capable in response to direct (not leading) questions.

PERSUASIVE COMMUNICATION

The major work of an attorney during a trial is persuasive communication. The attorney must influence the jury to pay attention to his or her interpretation of events, comprehend it and yield to it.

Communicator Characteristics. Can a "slick" attorney persuade jurors with weak evidence merely by being attractive and credible? According to the elaboration likelihood model of persuasion (see chapter 9), unbiased jurors will be involved, are more likely to process elaborately, and thus should be unimpressed by peripheral cues like the attorney's attractiveness or presentational style.

The Attorney's Message. Research on what attorneys say during trials has yielded several conclusions about what is and is not persuasive. In opening arguments, an attorney can *inoculate* the jurors against the adversary's arguments. By warning jurors, "My opponent will try to convince you...", the attorney prompts them to form their own counterarguments against that position and in support of his or her own. Since counterargument can be reduced by *distracting* the audience, attorneys may use words, gestures, events, or personal appearance to distract jurors from comprehending arguments or counterarguing. Finally, vivid testimony or depictions can affect jurors' judgments of damage or culpability. For example, showing jurors large, color photographs of accident victims or crash sites can influence their decisions. The jurors rely on the availability heuristic (e.g., choosing the available image or memory as statistically accurate) instead of base-rate information about such events.

The Defendant

The individual on whom most attention in a trial is focused is the defendant. Observers are more likely to commit the fundamental attribution error—to infer that the defendant's behavior, past and present, reflects personal traits and intentions, rather than situational influences. The rationalist bias to blame individuals rather than circumstances can handicap the defendant. Many legal conventions compensate for this danger by giving the defense the benefit of the doubt—assuming innocence until proven guilty, for example. Nonetheless, research has confirmed that perceptions of the defendant can affect the outcomes of a trial.

PHYSICAL ATTRACTIVENESS

Juries and judges are more sympathetic to attractive than unattractive defendants: they are more likely to be acquitted, and get lighter sentences if convicted. Young-looking defendants (e.g., with baby-face features like large eyes) may be judged more naive and less culpable in crimes of intent. Defendants are well-advised (usually by their attorneys) to make the most attractive appearance they can.

SIMILARITY TO THE JURORS

In line with the finding that similarity increases interpersonal attractiveness (see chapter 15), jurors are more sympathetic to defendants similar to themselves. In mock jury studies, such similarity effects have been found for defendants' race, native language, religion, political beliefs, and gender. Such effects are less obvious with real-life juries, especially when jurors have been warned about the dangers of judging by appearances.

The Victim

In civil cases, the victim (plaintiff) pursues a complaint against the defendant. However, in criminal cases the state prosecutes the defendant on behalf of the victim and the entire community. Thus the victim has no individual power or formal role in the proceedings, and is often forgotten.

VICTIM IMPACT

To redress the injustice of "forgetting" victims, some states have passed so-called *victim-impact* laws to permit courts to consider the "value" of people who have been victimized. Should a crime against a "valuable" member of society exact a higher penalty than one against a "worthless" one? For example, does a robber who kills a young mother of two deserve a harsher sentence than one who kills a homeless elderly man? The Supreme Court has ruled against using victim-impact evidence in death-sentence hearings, but other laws and programs are being formulated to put victims' considerations back into the legal process.

ATTRACTIVENESS

One exception is in jurors' perceptions of victims' *attractiveness*. The more attractive the victim, researchers have found, the harsher the sentence the defendant receives.

BLAMING THE VICTIM

Another exception has a reverse effect: jurors with a just-world bias may *blame the victim* as a way of reassuring themselves about their own immunity to the victim's plight. This has been most ommon in rape trials, when inferences are made about whether the victim deserved to be raped or provoked the defendant's attack by dressing or behaving seductively. Such inferences are affected by belief in rape myths (e.g., "Women secretly enjoy being overpowered") and base-rate fallacies (e.g., wrongly believing that most rapes are spontaneous instead of planned by the rapist). To protect the victim and prevent her from being tried instead of the defendant, most states have *rape shield laws* to limit the relevance of the victim's sexual history. Social ambivalence about sexual behavior continues to complicate justice in cases of rape and related crimes.

The Eyewitness

The two forms of evidence introduced into a trial are physical *exhibits* (e.g., weapons, documents) and witnesses' spoken *testimony*. In particular, eyewitness testimony about a crime has powerful effects. Social psychologists have examined the realities of eyewitness memory, accuracy, and confidence, as well as the impact of such testimony on jurors.

EYEWITNESS MEMORY

Eyewitness identifications—of suspects and other details—are often wrong.

Reconst Recall. Research shows that most eyewitness memory is *reconstructive:* what the witness recalls is affected by new knowledge, emotions, needs, and the process of reporting it. For example, asking a witness to estimate the speed of a car "before it smashed into the tree" results in higher estimates than the phrasing "before it bumped into the tree." Because memory is flexible and subject to bias, an eyewitness's recall can be distorted by something she has read or heard, believes, or assumes.

An eyewitness is more likely to be accurate in recall if he or she had good conditions for observing the crime or criminal and if little time elapsed before making the report or identification.

Eyewitness Fact and Fiction. Other factors are often thought to be important (by judges, jurors, and attorneys) but have been found to be unrelated to eyewitness accuracy. These include witnesses' confidence levels, descriptive abilities, and attention to other details of the crime. More confident witnesses have been found to be no more accurate—nor are witnesses who lack confidence necessarily inaccurate. Witnesses who describe suspects (recall memory) are not better at identifying them in lineups (recognition memory). Finally, attention to detail (e.g., remembering what song was playing on the radio during the crime) is not related to overall accuracy of identification. Because witnessing a crime can cause high arousal, accurate encoding may be impossible during such an experience.

Own-Race Bias. Witnesses are more accurate in recognizing and identifying members of their own race. For members of one race, members of another may "all look alike" because of the broad cognitive categories they have formed about variations in appearance. Minority group members like African-Americans seem to be better at cross-racial identification, possibly because minority group members pay more attention to details about the majority than vice versa.

INFLUENCE ON THE JURY

Accurate versus Inaccurate Witnesses. Jurors are convinced by confident eyewitnesses whether or not the witnesses are in fact accurate. Inaccurate witnesses are approximately as willing to testify, as confident, and as persuasive as accurate ones. Jurors are also erroneously impressed that eyewitnesses who recall trivial detail are more accurate overall (when the opposite is true).

Discrediting Eyewitness Testimony. Despite errors in eyewitness memory, jurors may be persuaded to believe it because it is personal, salient, and concrete. The persuasive power of eyewitness testimony can be discredited by providing evidence of impairment (e.g., pointing out a near-sighted witness was not wearing her glasses at the time). The most effective counterargument against one eyewitness is another, contradictory eyewitness.

IMPROVING EYEWITNESS TESTIMONY

Can the role and value of eyewitnesses be improved? Several strategies have been suggested to help eyewitnesses' evidence match juries' high estimations of their accuracy.

Training Interviewers. The police who usually interview witnesses can be trained to ask open-ended questions instead of corroborating suspected details. For example, "Describe what the assailant was wearing" is open-ended and yields more accurate information than "Was he wearing a red shirt?" Interviewers should prime witnesses' memories by having them describe the scene before reporting details, and should avoid using language that hints at assumptions (e.g, "Did you see *the* gun?" instead of "*a* gun?").

Eliminating Lineup Bias. If the suspect is noticeably different from the others in a witness lineup—e.g., much more or less attractive—the contrast can lead to a false identification. Poor witnesses can be identified by having them review "empty" lineups—lineups with no suspects—and eliminating them for making false identifications. Witnesses are also more accurate if they make yes or no responses to a sequence of suspects or photos instead of an entire set simultaneously.

Educating Jurors. Most laypersons are unaware of the inaccuracy of eyewitness testimony. Educating jurors about reconstructive memory and selective perception can reduce false faith in inaccurate eyewitnesses. Expert testimony about the conditions that affect eyewitness memory can help jurors to be more critical in reviewing and evaluating evidence.

The Jury

The jury has been described as the social world in microcosm, because it embodies so many aspects of social cognition, social influence, and social relationships. Important considerations focus on what the jurors bring to the trial as individuals, and how they function as a problem-solving group.

JURORS AS INDIVIDUALS

According to research, jurors generally are more influenced by the weight of evidence than by personal preconceptions or traits. Nonetheless attorneys are concerned with influencing *who* will be on the jury as much as possible in their own favor. There is also evidence that selectively including or excluding jurors for some opinions can affect verdicts.

Jury Selection. Before jurors are impaneled in the jury box, they are selected from a larger pool called a *venire*. Attorneys take turns questioning venire members to decide whether to accept or challenge their service, a process called *voir dire* (from the Old French for "to speak the truth"). During *voir dire*, attorneys may challenge (exclude) a limited number of jurors they fear will find against them, based on how they answer the questions, or even how they look. Can attorneys select jurors to exclude unfavorable prejudices and include favorable ones?

Some social scientists and attorneys believe that *scientific jury selection* can be based on relationships among jurors' demographics and their probably opinions. For example, a defense attorney in a rape trial may assume that a female juror will be too sympathetic to the victim unless she shares some common bond with the defendant. Attorneys may use *voir dire* to select, exclude, and inform jurors before the trial. Because both the defense and prosecution contribute to *voir dire*, however, the result is likely to be balanced.

Death-Qualified Jurors. A "capital" crime is one for which conviction carries a mandatory death sentence. During *voir dire* for a capital case, if a prospective juror claims to be morally opposed to the death penalty, he or she will be excused from service. The result is a jury consisting entirely of "death-qualified" or pro-capital punishment jurors. Are death-qualified jurors any different from other people? Researchers believe so: death-qualified jurors are more likely to be authoritarian, conservative, and prone to convict. A defendant cannot be fairly tried by a jury whose members already favor conviction. The death-qualification process in jury selection has been upheld by the courts despite researchers' evidence that it makes fairness impossible. The courts follow the rule of precedent, not science, and have not applied this research evidence in evaluating death-qualification.

Biases in Decision-Making. Before jurors assemble to deliberate the verdict, they individually draw conclusions about the evidence. Several biases and errors can affect these judgments. If jurors make the fundamental attribution error, they will see the defendant as responsible rather than a victim of circumstances. If they have a just-world bias, they will see the defendant's (or the victim's) plight as being somehow deserved.

Their initial conclusions can also be affected by the hindsight bias: the more severe the outcome (e.g., a victim's death possibly due to defendant's negligence), the more jurors think the defendant "should have known" and is therefore responsible.

JURIES AS GROUPS

Since juries are groups, they can be expected to be affected by social influence, deindividuation, issues of membership and leadership, status, and in-group communication. Moreover, since they are groups charged to make important decisions, they may be influenced by such processes as groupthink, group polarization, and minority influence. Because researchers cannot study actual juries in process, many of the following findings involved the study of mock juries—which may or may not exactly parallel the behavior of real juries.

Leadership Selection. Selection of the foreperson is apparently influenced by seating arrangement: the individual at the head of an oblong table is more likely to be chosen than other positions. The first juror to speak is more likely to be chosen. Males are more likely to be chosen than females, and high-status individuals more than low-status individuals.

Minority Influence. The majority opinion at the start of deliberations usually prevails, but there are exceptions. Research suggests that influential minorities are those which are confident and consistent, and win defections from the majority.

Group Polarization. Jury deliberations usually magnify individual jurors' initial opinions. Authoritarians deliberating in mock juries recommended even harsher sentences than they initially favored, while low-authoritarians are more lenient after deliberation. This shift to an exaggerated norm indicates group polarization.

Group Size and Conformity. Most juries have 12 members, but some venues and cases use six-member juries. Is there any reason to expect different verdicts? Researchers think there is. Because smaller juries admit less diversity, they are less representative of heterogeneous communities. Moreover, a one-sixth minority opinion is a very different social experience in a six-member than a 12-member jury: one lone deviate as opposed to two comrades against a majority. Conformity research suggests that one deviate is less likely to resist majority influence than two. Smaller juries also deliberate for shorter periods of time than larger ones. Many of these arguments have been cited in courts' rulings against five-member juries, but not against six-member juries, which still operate despite research suggesting their inferiority.

The Judge

The judge has vast social influence in a trial: he or she directs *voir dire* and decides on attorney's motions about evidence and witnesses' testimony. Two significant opportunities for social influence are instructing the jury and sentencing.

INSTRUCTING THE JURY

Ruling Testimony Inadmissible. During the trial, the judge instructs a jury whether to disregard evidence or testimony ruled inadmissible. For example, if a witness in a rape trial comments on the victim's sexual history, the state will object and the judge will rule the statement stricken from the court record, advising the jury to "disregard that statement."

Critics compare such after-the-fact correction as trying to "unring a bell." Research confirms that once jurors have heard testimony, they are unlikely to forget it or be uninfluenced by it. Jurors are more likely to forget inadmissible testimony if it favors the prosecution than the defense, and if it came from a confession extracted by threat than one gained by promising leniency. Thus forgetting is selective even when it is possible.

Final Instructions. Before jurors deliberate, the judge instructs them about the law and the task they are to decide. Contrary to television images of five-minute speeches, these instructions can be long and technically complex. Research suggests that jurors may remember the instructions only partially or inaccurately. This problem can be solved by shortening and simplifying the instructions, or giving each juror a copy for reference. Another suggestion would be to deliver the instructions before rather than after the evidence has been presented, before jurors have formed their schemata about the events and decisions involved.

SENTENCING THE DEFENDANT

A sentence can have several different purposes: retribution (enacting public vengeance), deterrence (discouraging other criminals), incapacitation (protecting society from this criminal), and rehabilitation (reforming this criminal). Since these represent different values a judge can have, it is not surprising that judge's sentences vary widely in value-sensitive cases (e.g., sexual abuse, political protest, and drug use). Studies of sentencing patterns have concluded that there is little to no consensus among judges' sentencing practices. However, this diversity may reflect different patterns of cases rather than different values or social norms.

While law is based on precedent and psychology on science, social psychology and the law have many common concerns. Law begins with ideas about justice, including equity or fairness, distributive justice, and perceived injustice. Many people believe in a just world, where people get what they deserve and deserve what they get.

Criminal procedures begin with arrest, usually as a result of a complaint. The arrest process may be depersonalizing to the suspect, affecting the way others see him or her. Plea bargaining involves negotiating certain versus possible outcomes. Setting bail requires the judge to make a prediction of the defendant's behavior. A criminal trial presents defense and prosecution cases in an adversarial format. Media may influence legal proceedings by sensationalizing some crimes and biasing the public and potential jurors.

The police are usually the first social contact in the legal system. Law enforcement roles can powerfully affect individual's behavior and world views. Police who interrogate suspects and witnesses usually employ social influence techniques, including persuasion and leading questions. Interrogation procedures can be improved to minimize manipulative influence and maximize accuracy.

Attorneys are also affected by their roles and situations. Their questioning of witnesses can be either leading or direct. Their presentation of the case to the jurors involves persuasive communication, including communicator characteristics (e.g., attractiveness, credibility) and message factors (e.g., vividness).

The defendant's characteristics can influence jurors' perceptions. Jurors are more sympathetic and lenient to attractive defendants and defendants who seem similar to themselves.

The victim is often the forgotten member of the proceeding. Victim impact laws have sought to redress this imbalance but have been restricted since they presume to calculate victims' worth. Jurors sympathize more with attractive victims. Jurors may also blame the victim in order to reassure themselves that the world is just.

The eyewitness' testimony can be highly influential. Jurors believe eyewitnesses whether they are accurate or not, influenced by apparent self-confidence. Eyewitness memory is often biased because it is reconstructed, distorted by arousal, and biased by better recognition of members of one's own race. Inaccurate eyewitness testimony can be discredited by information about impairment or with a contradictory eyewitness. Eyewitness testimony can be improved by training interviewers to ask unbiased questions, eliminating bias in lineups, and educating jurors about the limits of eyewitness accuracy.

The jury is socially influenced both as individual jurors and as a decision-making group. Individual jurors are influenced in their selection of leaders, in comparing majority to minority opinion, and by group polarization. Although evidence shows that small juries have different deliberations and verdicts from larger ones, the courts have upheld six-member juries as valid.

The judge's influence is greatest in instructing the jury and sentencing the defendant. In ruling certain testimony inadmissible, judges are still unable to keep it from influencing jurors' deliberations. Final instructions to the jury are often too long and complex to be recalled or followed. This can be corrected by shortening and simplifying instructions, or presenting them before the evidence in a trial. Sentencing can serve several purposes, including retribution, deterrence, incapacitation, and rehabilitation. Little consensus has been found among judges' sentencing practices, a problem that could be due to differences in cases as well as differences in judges' values.

Selected Readings

Blau, T. H. (1984). *The Psychologist as Expert Witness*. New York: John Wiley and Sons.

Hans, V. P. and N. Vidmar, (1986). *Judging the Jury*. New York: Plenum.

Kassin, S. M. and L. S. Wrightsman, (1988). *The American Jury on Trial*. New York: Hemisphere.

Rember, C. (1980). *The Law of the Land*. New York: Simon and Schuster.

Saks, M. J. and R. Hastie, (1978). *Social Psychology in Court*. New York: Van Nostrand Reinhold Company.

Wells, G. L. and E. A. Loftus, (1984). *Eyewitness Testimony: Psychological Perspectives*. New York: Cambridge University Press.

Glossary

ABCDE theory	theory that relationships progress in five stages: awareness, buildup, continuation, deterioration, and ending
acceptance	sincere, inward conformity
adaptation-level phenomenon	tendency to become accustomed to elevated levels of comfort or affluence
adaptor	nonverbal cue that reflects one's emotional state
additive task	work requiring group members' cooperation toward a shared goal
affiliation	preference to be with others of one's kind
agape	selfless love
aggregate	nongroup collection of individuals in time and place
aggression	any behavior intending harm to another
alarm stage (of the stress response)	first stage: an event is interpreted as a stressor; includes shock and countershock
altruism	unselfish motivation to help others
anchor	reference point against which choices are compared
androgynous	possessing both feminine and masculine traits
antecedent conditions	causes, stimuli
anti-Semitism	prejudice and discrimination against Jews
anxious-ambivalent	type of insecure attachment characterized attraction to and avoidance of attachment figure
arbitration	third party's assistance in conflict resolution by imposing mutually accepted solution

attachment restriction of social behaviors to significant others; preference for physical contact and social access

attitude evaluative reaction of person, event, or object

attitude inoculation presenting a weak challenge to an attitude in order to strengthen it

attribution process of explaining and understanding behavior

authoritarian behavior pattern characterized by exaggerated respect for authority, rigid thought, and prejudice

autocratic leadership style that is self-directed and dictatorial

autokinetic effect optical illusion that a stationary light in a dark room is moving

availability heuristic assumption that information that is most vivid or available in memory is most representative

avoidant type type of insecure attachment characterized by rejection of or lack of interest in attachment figure

balance theory model of social cognition arguing that cognitive elements are balanced when they agree and imbalanced when they contradict each other

base-rate fallacy erroneously favoring vivid or anecdotal information instead of statistical frequencies

behavioral contagion process in which activities are copied by others who observe them

belief perseverance tendency to perceive events only in ways that confirm one's beliefs

beneffectance self-serving tendency to take personal credit for success and blame failure on external conditions

bogus pipeline technique attitude measurement technique in which subjects are deceived by belief in biofeedback into providing candid attitude reports

brainwashing attitude change accomplished by inducing captives to agree with captors

bystander effect tendency of an individual to be less helpful if other witnesses are present

catharsis release of emotion through direct or vicarious expression

central traits attributes that color interpretation of other attributes in person perception

classical conditioning a basic form of learning in which an originally neutral stimulus, when paired with another stimulus capable of eliciting a reflexive response, comes to elicit that response through association

cluster model Davis's theory that love consists of friendship plus a passion cluster and caring cluster of attitudes

coercive power power based on ability to punish

cognitive attributional therapy treatment that focuses on the client's unrealistic expectations and distorted assumptions, and erroneous patterns of attribution

cognitive dissonance tension produced by incompatibility among one's attitudes and/or behaviors

cognitive map mental representation of an environment

cognitive response theory theory that attitudes are formed after judgment about direction of one's emotional responses

cohesiveness, cohesion tendency of group members to value membership and bond together

collaboration a conflict resolution strategy in which the parties work together on a creative solution to their problem

commons dilemma social trap involving members' use of common resource

communality quality of sharing investments in intimate relationships with no expectation of short-term gain

companionate love / love characterized by affection, respect, and friendship

comparison level relationship outcomes one expects

complementarity degree to which partners' needs and abilities complete each other compatibly

compliance outward and/or insincere conformity

compromise a coping strategy in which each party in a conflict gains something and sacrifices something

conflict conditions created by incompatibility of goals

conflict spiral escalation of conflict as a result of each party's threats and counterthreats

conformity a change in behavior as a result of real or imagined social pressure

conjunctive task work requiring group members cooperation on separate subtasks

consensual validation verification of a subject belief by confirming the support and agreement of one's reference group

consensus agreement among several parties; in attribution, quality of a behavior that others perform similarly

consistency agreement with other attitudes; in attribution, quality of a behavior that is similar on different occasions

consistency theory attitude change model which argues that harmony among cognitive elements must be maintained

contact hypothesis argument that prejudice can be reduced through equal-status interactions among different groups' members

contingency theory theory that leadership depends on interaction of leaders' traits and their situations

control in an experiment, the process of ensuring that the only difference between groups is the experimental treatment

convergent measures research methods whose findings support similar conclusions

coping responses behaviors that restore balance by removing threat

correspondent inference assumption that behavior reflects one's disposition or intentions

covariance, covariation   tendency of two or more variables to change together

crisis effect   tendency to forget disaster as time passes

crowding   feeling of not having enough space

cult   group whose recruitment and maintenance of members relies on group isolation

death qualification   restricting jury membership to individuals who support capital punishment

debate technique   conflict resolution preventing escalation by engaging in active listening

debriefing   after concluding research involving deception, the process of explaining the true purpose to subjects

deindividuation   reduced self-awareness as a result of anonymity and immersion in a group or activity

demand characteristics   clues about an experiment's purpose that influence subjects' behavior

dependent variable   in an experiment, the factor measured by the researcher (in psychology, usually a behavior)

depressive attributional style   pattern of making internal, stable, global self-attributions correlated with depression

differential decay explanation   explanation that sleeper effect (q.v.) is caused by forgetting source sooner than message

diffusion of responsibility   sharing responsibility or guilt equally among group members

discrimination   behavior based on prejudice; treating people differently based on perceived group membership

disjunctive task   work performed by group members who pursue independent subtasks but share in group outcomes

displacement   redirecting emotions and motives from their original targets to substituted objects

dissociation explanation   explanation of sleeper effect (q.v.) as due to loss of connection between message and source

distinctiveness   quality of a behavior that only occurs in specific situations

distraction-conflict hypothesis   explanation of social facilitation due to distraction at others' presence conflicting with attention to task

divergent perspectives hypothesis   explanation that fundamental attribution error is due to different views of actor and observer

divisible task   work performed by individuals whose efforts are independent but related to common goals

door-in-the-face technique   social influence by inducing guilt: a large request that is denied is followed with a smaller request

double-blind experiment   an experiment in which neither the subjects nor the observers know to which experimental condition the subjects are assigned

downward comparison	comparison of oneself with inferior others
dual-concern model	conflict resolution strategy in which each partner sees that mutual attention to needs will result in best outcome
dyadic phase of breakdown	second stage of relationship breakdown, when partners communicate about possible breakup
elaboration-likelihood model	theory that in persuasion, if audience elaborates on message, central factors will affect whether attitude change occurs
emblem	nonverbal gesture that symbolizes specific meaning
emotional loneliness	distress at loss of attachment figure
empathy	sharing another's feelings
environmental psychology	the field of psychology that studies transactions between behavior and the environment
equity	distributive justice; fairness of outcomes in proportion to inputs
eros	romantic, sexual love
ethnocentrism	bias in favor of one's in-group and against out-groups
exchange	relationship based on mutual giving and receiving of resources
excitation-transfer theory	theory that arousal generated by one situation can activate behavior in another
excitation-valence model	explanation that effects of pornography depend on whether pornography was positive or negative
exhaustion stage (of the stress response)	last stage, in which physical alarm resumes in a weakened state
exit	in Rusbult's theory, leaving a relation as an active-negative response to dissatisfaction
expectancy effects	contamination of data due to experimenter's biases about experimental outcomes
expectancy value theory	theory that attitudes form on basis of expected outcomes
experimental realism	ability of an experiment to involve and absorb subjects
experimenter bias	intentional or unintentional bias on the part of a researcher conducting an experiment
expert power	power based on one's superior general knowledge
facework	use of facial expressions for social accounting
false comparison effects	illusions about the normality or abnormality of one's behavior compared to others'
false consensus effect	overestimation of how common one's negative behaviors are

false uniqueness effect	underestimation of how common one's positive behaviors are
field study	research conducted in variables' natural setting
foot-in-the-door effect	tendency to increase willingness to make a large commitment after having made a smaller, related commitment
frame	in decision-making, the context in which the choice is presented
frustration	negative experience of being blocked from attaining a goal
frustration-aggression theory	theory that frustration always results in the impulse to aggress, and aggression can always be traced to frustration
functional propinquity	probability that two people will have random, spontaneous contact
fundamental attribution error	tendency to overestimate dispositional and underestimate situational factors when explaining behavior
gain/loss theory	theory that changes in attraction have more influence than consistent levels of attraction
gender role	set of norms prescribing behavior according to gender
gender typing	categorizing stimuli as feminine or masculine
general adaptation syndrome	a physiological and psychological pattern of symptoms in the wake of a stressor event
generational explanation	hypothesis that age differences in attitudes are due to differences in cohorts' values
Gestalt psychology	the psychological approach which suggests that behavior is motivated by interest in meaning and pattern; from German *Gestalt*, "form" or "pattern"
grave-dressing phase of breakdown	fourth and last stage of relationship breakdown, when partners have separated and reflect on remembered relationship
great person theory	leadership theory that certain traits foster optimal leadership
GRIT	Charles Osgood's conciliation strategy based on mutual demonstration of intention to resolve conflict
group	two or more people who interact and influence each other for a period of time
group polarization	exaggeration of average group member's preliminary opinion after group discussion
groupthink	reduction in quality of task performance as a result of giving group cohesion a higher priority
halo effect	expectation that further information will be evaluated similarly to that already collected
hassles	small-scale annoyances, irritations, and frustrations
hedonic relevance	quality of influence on one's own experience of pain or pleasure
hedonism	principle that behavior is guided by the desire to gain pleasure and avoid pain

heuristic	general guideline or rule-of-thumb
heuristic processing model	theory that persuasion depends on superficial aspects of persuasive message
hindsight bias	erroneous belief, once an outcome is known, that it could have been predicted
homophobia	irrational fear of homosexuals; prejudice against homosexuals
hostile aggression	aggression which intends harm as its sole purpose
identification	acceptance of another party's description as applicable to oneself
illustrator	nonverbal gesture that demonstrates action or physical relationship
impression formation	processes of judging others based on perceptions of them
impression management	process of controlling how one is perceived by others
impressionable-years hypothesis	argument that younger people have less stable attitudes more vulnerable to persuasion
independent variable	in an experiment, the factor manipulated by the researcher
individualism	promotion of self without regard to others
information power	power based on one's specific knowledge
information processing	the sequence of cognitive operations whereby sensory experiences are meaningfully interpreted and acted upon
informational influence	affect on individual behavior resulting from new knowledge or data
ingroup	group of which one is a member
ingroup bias	belief that members of one's own group are superior to nonmembers; also in-group out-group bias
instrumental aggression	aggression applied toward another goal besides harm
integrative relationships	relationships in which each partner is motivated to help the other
interdependence	relationship in which both parties' outcomes are jointly determined
internalization	acceptance of another party's values and standards
intimate distance	zone of physical contact, ranging up to 18 inches from one's body
intrapsychic phase of breakdown	first stage of breakdown, when one partner assesses costs and benefits of leaving
jealousy	experience of perceiving one's relationship to be threatened
jigsaw technique	collaborative learning strategy to reduce prejudice and group conflict
just-world bias	belief that the world is just, therefore people get what they deserve and deserve what they get
kin selection	tendency to favor one's relatives

knowledge bias distortion from reliance on inaccurate information

laissez-faire leadership style that is permissive and nondirective (French, "to permit [them] to do")

law of attraction Donn Byrne's theory that interpersonal attraction increases with expectations of positive reinforcement

learned helplessness nonresponse pattern as a result of failure to control or change events

least-preferred coworker (LPC) the member of a group a leader least enjoys working with

legitimate power power based on one's authority or status

levee effect tendency to overpopulate a risky environment

life cycle explanation argument that attitudes differ by age because of age-related values

Likert scale attitude measurement instrument requiring numerical rating of agreement with each item

locus of control source of influences believed to affect one's life

logical error the assumption that the presence of one characteristic signifies the presence of another

long hot summer effect observation that summer weather is correlated with increased rates of violent crime

longitudinal studies research strategies that study a set of individuals over a period of time

loss effect increased probability of death for survivors within one year after loved one's death

lost-letter technique unobtrusive research method studying subjects' willingness to mail letters with various addresses

low-ball technique foot-in-the-door effect in which second request increases cost of the first request

loyalty in Rusbult's theory, waiting for relationship improvement as a passive-positive response to dissatisfaction

ludus playful love

mania obsessive, possessive love

margin of error range of variability distinguishing sample measure from population

material self one's body and possessions

mediation third party's assistance in conflict resolution by facilitation communication between parties

mindguards in groupthink, self-appointed protectors who prevent group members from hearing or airing disagreement

mixed-motive conflict conflict for which all solutions involve costs to both parties

mum effect tendency not to communicate bad news

mundane realism ability of an experiment to approximate real-world conditions

naive psychology   Fritz Heider's interpretation of social behavior as influenced by identifiable and understandablereasons and motives

naturalistic fallacy   belief that the way things are is the way they ought to be

naturalistic observation   a study that focuses on behavior naturally occurring in its natural setting, rather than manipulated or in a controlled laboratory environment

neglect   in Rusbult's theory, allowing conflict to worsen as the passive- negative response to relationship dissatisfaction

negative affect reciprocity   tendency of couples to exchange bad feelings in communicating during conflict

NIMBY   "not in my back yard," resistance to taking responsibility for community problems

nominal group technique   strategy for improving groupcreativity through postponing discussion and anonyousvoting

norm   in society, a rule for accepted or expected behavior

normative influence   affect on one's behavior resulting from awareness of group norms

obedience   compliance with direct order or command

observational learning   learning by observing the behavior ofothers; vicarious learning or modeling

obsessive review   cognitive search for reasons for relationship breakup

operant conditioning   form of learning in which a response is associated with its consequences; the response becomes more likely in the future if followed by a reinforcer and less likely if followed by a punisher

operational definition   rephrasing of variables under study in terms of how they are measured

outgroup   group of which one is not a member

overconfidence   overestimation of one's accuracy in socialjudgments

overjustification   reduction of intrinsic motivation when an activity is externally rewarded

own-race bias   tendency to have better recognition for membersof one's own race than others

participant observation   method of study in which researcher joins social phenomenon being observed

passionate love   love characterized by intense, labile, emotional experiences and sexual attraction

payoff matrix   arrangement of rewards and penalties for cooperating versus not cooperating in a social dilemma

personal distance   zone of friendly interaction, ranging from 18 inches to four feet from one's body

personal identity   component of social identity based on self-concept

personal space   portable territory or range of space around one's body within which one resist's invasion

persuasion   attitude change

pessimistic attributional style   tendency to explain events in terms of internal, stable, global causes

physical attractiveness stereotype   generalization that physically attractive people have other positive characteristics

physical density   not enough space per person

physical propinquity   physical nearness between people

placebo   a chemically inert material disguised as an active drug; allows testing expectations of subjects who believe they are actually taking a drug

placebo effect   any situation in which subjects believe they are experiencing a manipulation by the experimenter when they are not

pluralistic ignorance   each group member's interpretation of group nonaction as a signal not to act

positive reinforcement   the process by which the presentation of a stimulus increases the frequency of some behavior that it follows

pragma   practical love

prejudice   unjustified negative attitude toward all members of a social group

primacy effect   tendency of first impressions to more strongly influence total impression than later information

primary territory   space and objects one owns or controls

priming   stimulating recall with related perceptual experience

Prisoner's Dilemma   dilemma in which best individual outcome is improbable but preferable to probable joint outcomes

privacy   control over others' access to oneself

prosocial behavior   helping behavior with nonobvious benefits for the behaver

proxemics   study of spatial behavior

proximity effect   influence of physical nearness in increasing interpersonal attraction

psychoanalysis   an approach to therapy, human nature, and personality theory introduced by Freud, emphasizing the role of unconscious motivation in conscious behavior

public distance   formal interaction space, ranging over 12 feet from one's body

public territory   spaces and facilities open to everyone

punishment   any operation which decreases the rate of response

quasi-experimental design   research design applying experimental methods to non-randomly- assigned groups and involving different expectations of outcomes

random assignment   the process of assigning research subjects to different groups on a random basis, so that each subject has an equal chance of receiving any condition

random sampling   in correlational techniques, choosing subjects so each member of a population has an equal chance of being selected for the sample

reactance   reassertion of freedom of choice by violating a rule or proscription

reactive   influencing or influenced by method of research

reasoned action model	theory of attitude-behavior relationship arguing that behavioral intentions are based on attitudes
recency effect	tendency for latest information to more strongly influence total impression
reciprocity norm	social rule requiring responding in kind
reconstructive memory	recall that is inferred from current information or attitudes
reference group	social network one consults for social comparison
referent	attitude object; focus of attention or discussion
referent power	power based on one's similarity to others
reflected appraisal	adopting others' opinions of oneself
regulator	nonverbal gesture that signals adjustment of communication
reinforcement	any operation which increases the rate of a response it follows
related attributes hypothesis	argument that people compare themselves with others who should be similar to themselves
relative deprivation	sense that one's group's outcomes are worse than others'
relationship awareness	ability of partners to discuss their relationship
replication	repetition of findings in similar studies
reporting bias	distortion by withholding information
representativeness heuristic	assumption that someone belongs to a social group based on resemblance to a typical member
repulsion hypothesis	argument that people are negatively affected by those who are dissimilar
resistance stage (of the stress response)	second stage; physical defenses are employed to respond to the threat
retrofit	change an environment's design to accommodate user needs
reward power	power based on one's ability to reward others
risky shift	early label for group polarization in risk-oriented groups
role	set of norms for a specific social position
salient	perceptually distinctive, noticeable
sample	subset of a population chosen for nonexperimental study
scapegoat	alternative target on whom aggression is displaced
schema	cognitive pattern that organizes information and knowledge; plural *schemata*
schematicity	revelance of a quality to one's self-concept
script	cognitive structure or guide for social interaction
seasonal affective disorder (SAD)	depression associated with low levels of light in winter

secondary territory	space one occupies regularly for temporary periods
selective avoidance	tendency to resist attention to contradictory information
selective exposure	preferential attention to stimuli
self-awareness	self-conscious state of focusing attention on oneself
self-censorship	in groupthink, tendency to withhold one's own disagreement with group opinion
self-concept	self-image including assessment of abilities, attributes, and values
self-determination theory	theory that leaders' effectiveness depends on feedback provided to followers
self-disclosure	in communication, revelation of personal information to one's partner
self-discrepancy	quality of information that contradicts one's self-concept
self-disparagement	behavior that appears to injure self-esteem
self-efficacy	feelings of competence and self-control
self-enhancement	protection and maintenance of self-esteem
self-esteem	one's evaluation of oneself
self-fulfilling prophecy	influence that brings about predicted events
self-handicapping	creating an acceptable excuse for failure
self-monitoring	attention to clues about social expectations and modification of behavior accordingly
self-perception	process of inferring meaning or motivation based on observations of one's own behavior
self-presentation	impression management (q.v.)
self-reference	relevance of information to oneself
self-report technique	research method requiring respondents to provide self-descriptions of thoughts and actions
self-schemata	generalizations about oneself
self-serving bias	tendency to perceive and judge one's own actions in ways that preserve self-esteem
semantic differential scale	attitude measurement instrument requiring evaluation of referent along different dimensions
shared infrequency	mutual avoidance of out-group members
situational perspective	view of phenomena in terms of their surrounding conditions and influences
sleeper effect	tendency to accept a persuasive message more after time has passed
social accounting	use of scripts like excuses to smooth interactions with others
social cognition	cognitive processes concerned with social experiences
social comparison	an evaluation of how our own beliefs and behaviors compare to those of others

social comparison theory	theory which proposes that subjective beliefs are verified by consensual validation
social contagion	spreading of behavior by social imitation
social density	too many people occupying a fixed space
social distance	zone of business interactions, ranging from four to 12 feet from one's body
social exchange	theory that relationships are based on reciprocal reward
social facilitation	enhancement of the dominant response through the mere presence of others
social identity	component of one's identity based on group membership
social impact theory	theory that power of social influence is a function of strength, immediacy, and number of sources
social loafing	tendency of group members working on additive tasks to withhold maximum effort
social loneliness	loneliness due to loss of community ties
social penetration	theory that intimacy grows as communication increases in breadth and depth
social responsibility norm	social rule requiring help for those who need or deserve it
social phase of breakdown	third stage of relationship breakdown when partners announce breakup to social network
social trap	dilemma created when individual gains at the cost of his or her community
socialization	transmission of social behavior through childhood learning
sociobiology	study of genetic influences on social behavior
sociogram	a diagram illustrating group structure and group members' preferred associations
source derogation	criticism of message's communicator
spiritual self	one's psychological faculties, including reasoning and feeling
spontaneous self-concept	self-description influenced by immediate circumstances
stigma	social label defining a person as undesirable or deviant
stereotype	generalization about a group of people that distinguishes them from others
storge	companionate love, friendship
stratified sampling	a technique for selecting subjects in such a way that significant subgroups within the population are accurately reflected in the composition of the sample
stress	any demand or set of demands requiring adaptation
stress inoculation	forewarning of stress to increase resistance and coping
subtraction rule	guideline that discounts factors in favor of more sensible alternatives
superordinate goal	mutual goal transcending conflicted parties' separate goals
survey	observational or correlational study that measures reactions of respondents in a random sample; questionnaire
symbolic interaction	association of meaning with social evaluation of event or experience

systematic processing model	elaboration-likelihood model (q.v.)
territorial marker	object or possession left to protect ownership or use of space
territoriality	control of physical space or objects
that's-not-all technique	inducing compliance by adding incentives while the target considers
Theory X	model of management that assumes people dislike work and must be offered coercion and incentive
Theory Y	model of management that assumes people enjoy work that is challenging and allows workers' contributions
Thurstone scale	attitude measurement instrument that lists attitude statements of varying strength
token economy	operant conditioning strategy in which symbolic rewards are used to reinforce desired behaviors
trait	relative stable personality tendency
triarchic theory of love	Sternberg's model of three dimensions of love: passion, intimacy, and commitment
Type A personality	a behavior pattern characterized by impatience, concern with time and punctuality, anger and perfectionism
Type B behavior	a profile that is relaxed, unhurried, and cooperative
ultimate attribution error	blaming out-group members' actions on shared dispositional characteristics
unconditional positive regard	in client-centered therapy, the therapist's acceptance and positive estimation of the client independent of any client behaviors
unrealistic optimism	unfounded belief in one's own probablegood fortune in events to come
venire	pool from which jury is selected
vicarious learning	learning by observing the consequences (e.g., reinforcements or punishments) of others' behavior
victim-impact laws	laws governing testimony about value of victim of crime to community
vividness heuristic	guideline by which one judges the most memorable cases to be typical
voice	in Rusbult's model, demanding for improvement as the active-positive response to relationship dissatisfaction
voir dire	questioning during jury selection
weapons effect	arousal of aggressive motivation by presenceof aggressive cue or weapon
zero-sum conflict	competition in which one party's victory requires the other's loss

Index